MODERN SMALL & COTTAGE SCALE INDUSTRIES

MODERN SMALL & COTTAGE SCALE INDUSTRIES

Written By

EIRI BOARD OF CONSULTANTS & ENGINEERS

ENGINEERS INDIA RESEARCH INSTITUTE

4449, Nai Sarak, Main Road, Delhi - 110 006 (India)

Ph:. 91-11- 23918117, 23916431, 23840361

Fax: 91-11- 2391 6431, 2391 8117

* E-Mail : eirisidi@bol.net.in

* Website: www.eiriindia.org

Sole Distributor :

INDIAN INSTITUTE OF CONSULTANTS, 4/27 ROOP NAGAR, DELHI - 07

PRINTED & PUBLISHED BY

ENGINEERS INDIA RESEARCH INSTITUTE

4449, Nai Sarak, Main Road, Delhi - 110 006 (India)
Ph:. 91-11- 23918117, 23916431, 23840361
* Fax: 91-11- 23916431, 23918117
* E-Mail : eirisidi@bol.net.in
* Website: www.eiriindia.org

DISTRIBUTED BY

SMALL INDUSTRY RESEARCH INSTITUTE (SIRI)
INDIAN INSTITUTE OF CONSULTANTS (IIC)

ISBN : 81-86732-76-4
Printed in New Delhi (INDIA)

Rs. 650

Printed & Published by Sudhir Gupta for "Engineers India Research Institute" 4449 Nai Sarak, Main Road, New Delhi - 110 006

Preface

The book **Modern Small & Cottage Scale Industries** covers almost all the basic and advanced details to setup your own Small & Cottage Scale Industries. The main chapters are Salient Features of Small Scale Industries, Steps in up a Small Scale Industry, Small Industries Development Organisation and its Small Industries Service Institutes, Aerosol Spray, Aromatic Perfumery Compound, Ayurvedic Churns, Automatic Biscuit Making Plant, Automatic Bread & Biscuit Unit, Automatic Plant for Toffee & Candy, Butter Milk, Bread Manufacturing, Bakery Unit, Casein from Milk, Canning of Fruits, Cashew Fruit Juice, Chocolate, Dairy Farm (Buffaloe), Dairy Farm to Produce Milk (Jersey Cow), Dairy Products & Milk Packaging in Pouches, Dehydration of Fruits & Vegetables, Drying of Red Chillies, Flavoured Milk, Frozen Foods, Fruit Juice Making & Packaging in Plastic Containers & Pouches, Fruits & Vegetables Juice with Other Products, Frozen Meat, Ice-Cream & Ice Candy, Jam, Jellies, Pickles & Squashes, Lactose and By-Products Processing from Milk, Lemon Juice Squash, Mango Processing & Canning, Mini Flour Mill, Milk Powder & Ghee, Papad and Bariyan Plant, Perfume for Soap, Detergent and Agarbatties, Potato Chips/Waffers, Pickles, Processed Food, Pouch Filling for Saunf, Supari, Ilaichi etc., Processed Cheese, Rice Puff, Snack Food, Soya Milk & Paneer, Scents and Perfumes, Spray (Perfume), Supari, Tomato Products Manufacturing, Toned Milk, Suppliers of Plant & Machineries and Suppliers of Raw Materials.

The book has been written for the benefit and to prove an asset and a handy reference guide in the hands of new entrepreneurs & well established industrialists.

Director

ENGINEERS INDIA RESEARCH INSTITUTE

Nai Sarak, New Delhi (INDIA)

E-Mail : eirisidi@bol.net.in

CONTENTS AND SUBJECT INDEX

CHAPTERS	PAGE NO.

Chapter 1

SALIENT FEATURES OF SMALL SCALE INDUSTRY

Introduction of Small Scale Industry

In India small scale industries are like small nurseries for budding entrepreneurs. In fact, it has been visualised that no other field of economic activity serves as a stepping stone to those who aspire to climb up the ladder of prosperity than the small scale industry.

Now, the larger scale units can no longer deem themselves as the leading Protagonists in the industrial world like alligators and consider SSI as porpoises. This is attributed to the rapid stride made by the Small Scale Units in a world of competition and specialization.

Small Scale Units are wonderfully coming up in a competitive manner in the market with the Large Scale Units on a commendable stirrup. Their encumbrance in the international market speaks volumes for their, prodigious output to the tune of 40% as their export-potential, 60% being the share of large scale units. This establishes their certified authenticity that their product is gaining so profoundly such an international renown and acclaim.

Besides, some SSI have so much monopolised themselves that they are heavily catering some of the large scale units by simply demonopolising them.

Advantages of Small Scale Industries

1. They play key role in well planned economic development.
2. They are labour intensive and capital saving.
3. They provide high employment potential.
4. Small investment is required.
5. Sophisticated machines and modern technology are of very little use.
6. These are adaptable to semi-urban and urban environment where infrastructure is under-developed.
7. They attract small savings and direct them into productive channels.

8. These are instrumental in removal of regional disparities and economic backwardness in the rural/less developed segments.

Definition of Small Scale Industries

Small Scale Industry has been defined by the Government of India from time to time in terms of the investment proposed to be made in the plant and machinery.

However, "Small Scale Industry" is an establishment having investment in plant and machinery whether held on ownership basis by base or by hire-purchase, not exceeding Rs. 60 Lakhs (extendable to Rs.75 lakhs in certain cases).

Small Scale Industry is categorised in the following heads :

(1) Modern Small Scale Industrial Undertaking

This comprises undertakings in which the investment on plants and machinery does not exceed Rs. 60 lakhs. Small units aiming to export at least 30 per cent of the annual production by the third year are permitted to step up their investment upto Rs. 75 lakhs in plant and machinery.

(2) Ancillary Unit

Ancillary Unit is visualised based on two conditions :

- Investment on plant and machinery not exceeding Rs. 75 lakhs.

- The undertaking should be engaged in the manufacturing activity of parts. components, sub-assemblies, toolings or intermediates, etc. and should cater to at least 30 per cent of its production or subsidiaries to some other units engaged in production.

(3) Service Oriented Small Scale Tiny Industrial Units

These are establishments. encompassing personal or household services located in urban, rural, semi-urban-rural or backward areas having a population not exceeding 50.000 as per 1981 census and having investment in plant and machinery upto Rs. 5 lakhs.

(4) Village or Rural Industrial Unit

This implies any industry located in rural area (population of which does not exceed ten thousand or such other figure) producing any goods or rendering any services with or without use of power and in which the fixed capital investment (in plant and machinery and, land & building) per head of an artisan or a worker does not exceed Rs. 15,000.

(5) Artisan Industrial Unit

It is the unit to which total financial assistance from financial institutions does not exceed Rs. 25,000 and carries on his industrial activity in an area having a population of less than 50,000 as per the 1981 census.

However, special schemes have been framed by most of the commercial banks for this unit wherein composite loans are provided on very liberal terms and conditions.

(6) Cottage or Household Industry

This is the unit which is operated at the cottage level (or entrepreneur's house) by the owner-entrepreneur. For availing facilities/ assistance, different state governments have laid down different parameters and would require to be checked up from the Directorate of Industries /District Industrial Centre.

(7) Small Scale Service Establishment

Service-oriented enterprises having investment in plant and machinery do not exceed Rs. 2 lakhs and are located in rural areas and terms with a maximum population of upto 5 lakhs.

Such establishments are also eligible to avail all facilities, assistance and incentive schemes as are applicable to any SSI.

Further, such service establishments are eligible to all types of facilities and incentives given to SSI including loans from State Financial Corporations (SFC) and banks.

Registration for Small Scale Industries

Under registration for SSI there are :

(a) Provisional (Temporary) Registration

It enables the entrepreneur to initiate necessary steps to bring the unit into existence. It can be done at the distinct headquarters with the DIC or provisional registration is to be obtained from the Directorate of Industries. In case production could not be commenced for reasons outside the entrepreneur's, control, extensions of provisional registration period may be considered.

(b) Permanent (Final) Registration

After the entrepreneur has taken all steps to set up the unit, i.e. (i) constructed /acquired the factory bulding. (ii) installed all requisite machinery. testing equipment and pollution control gadgets (where required) and (iii) obtained power connection, he can apply for permanent registration certificate to the DIC/DI.

After inspection by the GM/Competent Officer nominated by the DIC, and being satisfied of production capability a recommendation for issuance of permanent registration is made.

(c) Registration as Ancillary Unit

The entrepreneur has to fill up the specific application form to get his unit declared as "Small Scale Ancillary Unit". This form is to be submitted to the Directorate of Industries with a copy to the Small Industries Service Instituce (SISI) in the state. The facts stated by the unit are examined by SISI and on being satisfied regarding the eligibility, recommends it to the State Directorate of Industries for registration of such a unit as "ancillary unit". On receipt of such a recommendation, the concerned authority will grant the registration as Small Scale Ancillary Unit.

(d) Benefits of Registration

Provisional registration entitles the new entrepreneur to (1) apply for a shed or plot in an industrial estate or a developed area; (ii) apply to Corporation/Municipality for other licences; (iii) apply for power/water connection; (iv) apply for financial assistance from banks and other institutions; (v) apply to the National Small Industries Corpn. /State Small Scale Industries Corpn. /other institutions for procuring machinery on hire-purchase basis; (vi) obtain sales tax. excise registration, etc. wherever required and (vii) take other steps/approvals that may be necessary for licence of capital goods/ raw materials.

(e) Registration of Existing Units

A unit that is existing now but which has not registered itself earlier can also apply for registration of any stage.

(f) Restrictions on Registration

Undertakings of certain categories cannot get registration as small scale industrial units. Further no SSI registration can be granted to an undertaking which is a subsidiary or owned or controlled by any other undertaking.

(g) Registration/ Cancellation of Registration

It may be de-registered on any one or more of the following grounds:

(a) If the unit remained closed continuously for a period exceeding one year.

(b) If the unit failed / refused or avoided to give full and truthful information as called upon by the registration authority from time to time and in particular the half-yearly report.

(c) If the unit has been proved to have mis-utilised the raw-materials allocated to it.

(d) If the unit is found to be subsidiary of or owned or controlled by medium and large scale undertakings.

(h) Expansion / Diversification

A unit wishing to expand by increasing the production of the item for which it was already licensed, need not obtain any fresh registration or any endorsement on its registration certification unless it involves the addition of new plant and machinery (indigenous or imported) and consumption of additional scarce and imported raw materials. A unit which may like to diversify its production adding one or more items for which it was earlier registered, will have to get its registration duly endorsed for such items after a technical inspection.

(i) Upon Graduating from Small to Medium Scale Unit

When a unit crosses the investment limit prescribed for a small scale/ancillary unit by the process or natural growth, it will need to get approval from SIA, Ministery of Industries, Govt. of India or other technical authorities.

Chapter 2

STEPS IN SETTING UP A SMALL SCALE INDUSTRY

In an industry, as in any work, one has to go through various steps before he reaches the goal. These are elaborated below :

I. Deciding to be an Entrepreneur

To be a strong entrepreneur is the most vital fact behind every successful project. Therefore the imperative need is to know one's qualities, strength and weaknesses as an entrepreneur. One's strength could be his qualifications, training, experience, personality traits and knowledge etc.

Every person, irrespective of his financial status possesses sufficient strength to become an entrepreneur. One may even start with a low investment enterprise and gradually build it up.

After one has resolved himself in regard to the above considerations, the next step would be to gear himself for the endeavour.

II. Training

There are organisations which provide training to potential entrepreneurs which is motivating as well as encouraging.

Training may be technical or managerial. This entrepreneurship development training is conducted by over 700 organisations all over the country by SISIs (Small Industries Service Institutes), District Industries Centres (DICs), Banks, State Financial Corporations, Institutes or Centres of Entrepreneurship Development, Technical Consultancy Organisations, Small Industries of Entrepreneurs Association, Chambers of Commerce & Industries and others, such training is usually given freely and in certain cases one may even get a stipend particularly when EDPs (Entrepreneurs hip Development Programmes) are conducted by the S.I.S.I.

III. Project Identification and Selection

Scrutinization of the selective project of one's choice out of the many existing items, is the discretory prerequisite for starting any industry. First, short listing of ideas generated can be done by considering availability, of technical know-how, investment, health of industry, raw material availability., market demand and supply position etc.

However, the final selection should be done based on all actual market survey. One's personal assessment with regard to his experience, qualification, aptitude. personality characteristics, family background, financial position and the like, serves as a vital fact for project identification.

Further, the project should be profitable enough to meet his financial requirements at present as well as in the years to come.

IV. Location of the Enterprise

Location is of paramount importance for ensuring success of any business including an industrial enterprise. Ali ideal location will be where all raw materials / inputs /feed stocks are available locally, market is in the vicinity. skilled labour is abundant and infrastructural facilities, particularly power, ensured. The site selected should be suitable for construction of industrial structure to house. the plant and machinery. Also, the area should have an industrial culture and market.

Further, an entrepreneur can arrive at a worthwhile decision after taking into account the following aspects:

1. Nearness to market & raw materials.
2. Availability of adequate transport system and facilities for procurement of raw materials, despatching finished goods and speedy delivery.
3. Availability of an industrial area/estate or an industrial zone with essential services viz. power, water, supply and facilities for effluent disposal.
4. Availability of required skilled workers at reasonable wages/ rates.
5. Climatic conditions/ environmental factors which affect the industry.
6. Incentives /concessions applicable for industrially backward areas.

V. Arranging Technical Know-How

Appropriate technical know-how is the key to entrepreneurial success. Quality product are ensured with right technology. However, care should be taken that the technology chosen is conunercially acceptable and is similar to or better than that acquired by present and potential competitions.

One significant consideration to be kept in view is that for any product there may be more than one way of manufacturing. A close study of the advantages and disadvantages of each of the processes should be made prior to choosing the best option.

VI. Constitution of the Firm

Constitution of a firm can be done in variety of forms, proprietorship, partnership, private limited company, public limited company or a co-operative society.

A co-operative society as a form of enterprise is a very convenient form to arrange loans, but extremely difficult to run. A co-operative society is recommended only if members are confident of ensuring smooth operations under all circumstances and for all times. Also, there is a limit on the distribution of dividends in case of a co-operative society. However, certain advantages are offered like getting exclusive facilities under various government schemes.

Whether the firm is sole proprietorship or partnership one's liability is unlimited. The firm's creditors can sue one and recover their debts from one's personal assets. When size of operations are large, a private limited company may be the answer. This way when the firm faces bankruptcy, one's liability is limited to the extent of his shareholding the personal assets are not at stake.

A public limited company shall come in handy when one expands and graduates into a medium or large scale industry.

VII. Registration

After the formation of an enterprise, the entrepreneur while establishing a unit will have to get his firm registered with Registrar of Firms, Income Tax Department and DT/DIC.

If the firm is a partnership firm the partners may get their partnership registered with the Registrar of Firms. For corporate entities, private or public limited company registration with Registrar of Companies is essential.

Registration with Directorate of Industries (DI or DISTRICT INDUSTRIES CENTRE (DIC) is not compulsory but. helpful in obtaining various facilities, such registration is done in two stages: (a) Provisional Registration (b) Permanent Registration.

VIII. Arranging Finance

Finance for the industrial project should be obtained before applying for registration. Finance for business has two components. (a) Fixed Capital and (b) Working Capital.

Fixed capital is the volume of capital required for land, building, plant and machinery, office equipments, furniture, fixtures, fittings, installations and other fixed assets like dies, moulds, jigs, fixtures, types, (in case of printing press), etc.

Working capital is the finance required for day to day operations of the unit for payment of wages, manufacturing/ administrative expenses, purchasing, processing and storing raw materials, goods in process, finished goods, consumable stores/spares, etc. provide credit to trade on sales, meet expenses on workers wages, transport and the like.

Fixed capital can be had in the form of term loan, hire-purchase, or differed payment facilities. Working capital can be arranged from a commercial bank in the form of cash credit, overdraft and bills purchase /discount facility.

Term loans are provided by State Financial Corporations (SFCs) almost every State/Union Territory has one SFC. Where there is no SFC, the State Industrial Development Corporation (SIDC) perform the functions. Apart from these corporations, Banks (Commercial, Co-operative and regional rural banks) also sanction term loans although their main operations are extension of working capital facilities. All SSIs engaged or proposed to be engaged in legally permissible process/service activity are eligible for financial assistance.

Among other sources for raising finance is National Small Industries Corporation (NSIC) which gives machinery, indigenous and imported, on hire-purchase and leasing basis besides extending assistance (including financial) for procurement of raw material, imported and indigenous, and for sale to government agencies.

For margin money which is the amount of money that one has to invest in the project from his own sources, there are a number of schemes through which partially or completely margin money amount required to set up the project is available: There are Special Capital Scheme, Seed Capital Scheme, National Equity Fund and Engmeers Equity Fund.

Chapter 3

SMALL INDUSTRIES DEVELOPMENT ORGANISATION AND ITS SMALL INDUSTRIES SERVICE INSTITUTES

Small industries in their nature bear a relationship to: climatic and geographical conditions: availability of local raw materials and labour forces, proximity of market and an innumerable number of other similar factors. Different parts of our country have varied kinds of small industry concentrations. Thus development of small industry is a state subject. However, unless these developmental activities were co-ordinated, the country's resources could be misdirected.

Hence, the Central Small Industries Organisation (now called as the Small Industries Development Organisation) of the Government of India came into being. This organisation is headed by a Development Commissioner headquartered at Nirman Bhawan, New Delhi, and functions through a network of Small Industries Service Institutes, Branch Institute and Extension Centres. Whereas there are four relatively bigger SISIs located at Mumbai, Kolkata, Chennai and New Delhi, there is an SISI for nearly every state.

Small Industries Development Organisation (SIDO) acts as a policy formulating, co-ordinating and monitoring agency for the development of small industries at national level. It provides a wide range of extension services through its net-work of 26 Small Industries Service Institutes, 32 Branch Small Industries Service Institutes, 40 SISI Extension Centres. 4 Regional Testing Centres, 20 Field Testing Stations, 3 Process-cum-Product Development Centres, 2 Central Footwear Training Centres, 2 Central Tool Rooms, 1 Central Institute of Hand Tools and 2 Production Centres. Each of these institutes is fully equipped with technical officers, workshop and testing facilities to provide technical and other assistance to small scale units in the area of their locations.

There are 76 workshops attached to SISIs/Branch SISIs, Extension Centres and 4 Production Centres including 2 Extension Centres having workshop facilities for technical disciplines like General Engineering, Tool Room, Heat Treatment, Electroplating, Glass and Ceramics, Forging, Chemical labs., etc.

Economic Information

Industry prospect sheets, area survey reports, project profiles, feasibility study reports are brought out by SIDO which provide information on the scope for development of various industries.

Technical Assistance

SIDO provides technical consultancy on the manufacture of technical processes, use of modern machines and equipments, preparation of designs. layout of machinery and assistance on all aspects of production.

Quality Improvement and Testing

With a view to improving the quality of the products being manufactured in the small scale sector, 4 Regional Testing Centres have been set up at New Delhi, Mumbai, Kolkata and Chennai. In addition, there are 20 Field Testing Stations in area of concentration of specific group of industries to provide specialised testing facilities for a particular product or industry group.

Industrial Management and Training

SIDO offers consultancy services in the field of techno managerial, marketing, quality control, production, finance, labour laws, etc. and undertakes special training programmes, in-plant studies, open house discussions and seminars. A panel of consultants consisting of reputed engineers, technologists, scientists etc. on every branch of technology has been drawn up for such jobs or projects where expertise is not available with SIDO. In backward areas, the small scale units can avail of the services of these consultants and the entire expenditure is borne by SIDO. In other areas, the units have to bear 75% of the cost while the rest is borne by Small Industries Development Organisation.

Entrepreneurial Development Programmes

The development of Entrepreneurial Development Programmes and creation of awareness in people towards setting up of small scale industry are two important pre-requisites for industrial development and reduction of unemployment. A number of entrepreneurial development prograrnmes are, therefore, being organised by SIDO through Small Industries Service Institutes and their branches with the help of the State Directorates of Industries, State Financial Corporations, Commercial Banks and other developmental agencies for the benefit of different target groups consisting of both skilled/semi-skilled and educated /uneducated persons. These programmes are also organised for engineering and non-engineering entrepreneurs. Entrepreneurial Development Programmes for non-engineers include women, rural artisans, technicians, weaker sections of the society, educated unemployed and the physically handicapped.

Ancillary Development and Sub-contracting Exchanges

Under the ancillary development programme, individual items are identified for ancillarisation and small scale industries are assisted for securing sub-contract jobs with a view to providing them effective marketing support. As a part of this programme, 16 subcontracting exchanges have been set up in SISIs to promote ancillarisation. These exchanges act as an information-house for matching the requirements of medium/large undertakings looking for sub-contractors with small scale units desirous of securing orders from medium/large undertakings.

Modernisation Programmes

The Modernisation Programme envisages upgradation of obsolete technology of small scale industry through identification of their input needs in rural, urban and backward areas of the country. The main objectives of the programme are :

1. Improvement in production technology.
2. Product Development Design.
3. Testing, Design and Quality Control.
4. Machinery and equipment.
5. Selection of proper raw material.
6. Application of improved management technology.

Under the Modernisation Programme, seminars. industrial clinics, industrial workshops, modernisation courses and study visits are organised. 20 industries have been selected on all India basis and 38 industries on concentration basis in different States.

Government Stores Purchase Programme

The National Small Industries Corporation Ltd. verifies the competence of small scale units for executing Government orders and enlists them for participation in Government Stores Purchase Programme. 409 items are reserved for exclusive purchase, 13 items for purchase upto 75% and 28 items for purchase upto 50% of the requirements from small scale industrial units by the Government purchasing agencies. A price preference extending upto 15% is given to small scale units over medium/ large scale units.

Assistance to Young Engineers

Under the Assistance to Young Engineers Programme, training is provided through specific agencies to units and engineers. The programme envisages financial assistance to trained engineers in the form of subsidy on interest payable on loans taken by them from banks/financial institutions for acquisition of fixed assets. The quantum of subsidy is the difference between the interest at the rate of 7% per annum and the normal rate charged by the financial institutions /banks on the loans so advanced subject to a maximum of Rs. 20,000/- per annum. The scheme has been further liberalised to cover non-trained engineers subject to certain conditions.

Industrial Estates

The facilities being provided by the State Government to entrepreneurs in the Industrial Estates include build-up factory sheds, power and water facilities, roads, godowns, workshops, common facility services etc.

Reservation of Items for Production

With a view to giving protection to small scale units, 873 industries have been reserved for exclusive production in the small scale sector.

Export Promotion

Small Industries Development Organisation provides export marketing information, export consultancy and organises training courses. and seminars for promoting exports from small scale sector.

Trade delegations and study teams are sponsored from the small scale sector to help them develop contacts with foreign buyers. Under this programme 60% of the expenditure incurred by trade delegations and teams on admissible items is met by the Ministry of Commerce under the Marketing Development Assistance Scheme.

Under the advanced licensing scheme, small scale units are able to import raw materials components spares etc. required for export production without payment of customs duty and with/ without having export orders in hand.

Similarly, under the Import Licensing Scheme, small scale units can obtain licence for import outside the duty exemption scheme. Other facilities provided to small scale industries under the Import and Export Policy through Ministry of Commerce are as follows:

(1) Import-Replenishment under the Scheme of Registered Exporters; (2) Cash Compensatory support: (3) 100% export-oriented units; (4) Duty Drawback; (5) For recognition as export houses in small scale sector minimum limit prescribed for select products and non-select products is Rs. 75 lakhs and Rs. 3 crores respectively; and (6) Supply of export credit at concessional rates etc.

Seed/Margin Money Scheme

The objective of the Margin Money Scheme is to assist the State Governments to reduce the incidence of sick units and thereby ensure better utilisation of installed capacities in small scale sector. The quantum of Margin Money ranges between Rs. 1,000/- and Rs. 20,000/- per unit registered in the preceding seven years.

Organisations /Banks Promotes Small Scale Industries

The following orgnisations are helpful to finance, to promote or to develop SSIs in every part of our country

Small Industry Development Bank of India

(SIDBI)

Indian Red Cross Society Building
Red Cross Road, New Delhi-110 001

SIDBI is a banking organisation which is wholly owned subsidiary of DBI. SIBDI finances SSI projects and assists by launching a number of new schemes viz; National Equity Fund Scheme, Single Window Scheme, Scheme for Ex-servicemen etc. It is promoting rural enterperneurship, technology upgradation /modernisation of existing units, strengthening of ancillaries and bringing about qualitative changes in such direction so as to improve the competitive strength of SSI sector.

In its supportive role, SIDBI has also given special attention to tackle the problem fo inadequate marketing infrastructure and delayed payments faced by SSI units.

Khadi & Village Industries Commission

(KVIC)

Gramodaya. 3, Irla Road, Vile parle (W),Mumbai-400056

The KVIC is a statutory body created by an act of parliament (No. 61 of 1956 and as amended by Act No. 12 of 1987). It is charged with planning, promotion, organisation and implementation of the programme for the development of Khadi and other Village industries in the rural areas in Co-ordination with other agencies engaged in rural development wherever necessary. KVIC's functions also comprise building up a reserve of raw materials and implements for supply to producers, creation of common service facilities for processing of raw materials as semi-finished goods and provision of facilities for marketing of KVI products apart from organisation of training of artisans engaged in these industries and encouragement of co-operative efforts amongst them. KVIC is entrusted with the task of providing financial assistance to institutions or persons engaged in the development and operation of Khadi and Village industries and guided them through supply of designs, prototypes and other technical information.

National Bank for Agricultural and Rural Development (NABARD)

10, Bahadur Shah Zafar Marg, New Delhi-110002

NABARD was set up in July, 1982 to provide re-finance assistance to state Co-operative Banks, Regional Rural Banks and other approved institutions for all kinds of production and investment credit to small scale industries, artisans, cottage and village industries, handicrafts and other allied activities. NABARD is also helpful for SSI entrepreneurs to get the loan for setting of Small Scale Industries in any part of our Country.

Risk Capital and Technology Finance Corporation Ltd.

Scope Complex Core-V, 3rd Floor, 7, Lodhi Road,
New Delhi-110003

This is one of the important organisation, which provides loans, equity finance and other helps, in any new technological ventures for such projects, which are latest addition to the industrial streams. It financially supports, for establishing of small, medium and large scale industries.

Chapter 4

AEROSOL SPRAY

"Attar" the indigenous fragrance held away over India till the arrival of the westernised, alcohol-based scents and sprays.

Attar may no longer hold the pride of place in the elite Indian homes now, but it still reigns supreme in traditional households and the countryside. while the speciality of attar is that its ingredients are entirely natural and, therefore, totally harmless. With the advent of extravagantly packaged spray perfumes, attar has lost its competitiveness. This being the case, imaginative packaging could perhaps not only revive attar's old glory but also make it the rage of the west.

The early Egyptian used perfume in their daily lives for cosmetic purposes, burning incense, in their temples and for embalming the bodies of their Pharoahs with aromatic substances. The Greeks and Romans learned the use of perfume from the Eastern races they conquered and it was only in the mid-10th century that France established her supremacy over the perfume trade.

MANUFACTURING PROCESS

Essence and Perfumery

General Procedure :- The essence and perfumery are generally prepared by the following ways.

1. These can be extracted from flowers leaves and woods. After extraction recovered by vacuum distillation water in cool conditions.
2. Essence and perfumery are prepared generally by blending of pure essence with alcohol blending and mixing is the process of easieşts way to be preparation of essence and perfumery.

   For the preparation of essence and perfumery it is required to confirem of the formula of which blending operations can be done to give the exact product.
3. Essence and perfumes can be produced by chemical synthetic way.

Present case I am dealing with the formulation and blending cross for the production of essence and perfumery.

The basic formula of perfumes and essence are given.

Synthetic Rose otto No 1056

Citronellol	200
Phenylethyl Alcohol	100
Geraniol Palmorosa	200
Rhodinol	200
Guaiace wood	50
Eugenol	
Innone Alpha	5
Cinnamic Alcohol	50
Phenyl Acetic Acid	40
Phenyl aectic Aldehyde	3
Trichloro Phenyl Methyl	
Carbinyl Acetate	80
Un decylenic Aldehyde	2

Red Roses, No-1057

		Parts
Phenyl Ethyl Alcohol	-	150
Rhodinol	-	200
Ionone	-	300
Cinnamic Alcohol	-	150
Rhodinyl Acetate	-	100
Trichlor Phenyl Methyl		
Carbinyl Acetate	-	50
Jasmine Compound	-	50

A finished perfume may be prepared as follows :

Violet, no. 1068

Parma violet compound	100
Victoria violet compound	40
Cassie absolute	5
Rose otto	1
Civet absolute	1
Musk ketone	1
Santal	2
Ambergris tincture, 3 per cent	30
Musk tincture, 3 per cent	20
Alcohol	800
	1000

PLANT ECONOMICS

Rated Plant Capacity = 2400.00 Bottles/Day Aerosol Spray

Land & Building (Land 200 Sq.Mts.) Rs. 5,30,000.00

PLANT & MACHINERY

1. Different Storage Tanks
2. Mixing vessel
3. Refrigeration unit
4. Distillation unit.
5. Liquid filling Machine.
6. Labelling Machine.
7. Heater Unit.
8. Miscellaneous.

FIXED CAPITAL

1. Land & Building		Rs.	5,30,000.00
2. Plant & Machinery		Rs.	2,52,000.00
3. Other Fixed Assets		Rs.	50,000.00
	TOTAL	Rs.	8,32,000.00

RAW MATERIALS

1. Essence Compounds
2. Ethyl Alcohol
3. Glass Bottles and Packaging Materials

TOTAL WORKING CAPITAL/MONTH

1. Raw Material		Rs.	7,27,500.00
2. Salary & Wages		Rs.	26,093.00
3. Utilities & Overheads		Rs.	85,500.00
	TOTAL	Rs.	8,39,093.00

TOTAL CAPITAL INVESTMENT

Total Fixed Capital		Rs.	8,32,000.00
Total Working Capital for 3 months		Rs.	25,17,279.00
	TOTAL	Rs.	33,49,279.00

TURN OVER/ANNUM

1. 25 Ml. capacity bottles 360000 Nos.
2. 50 Ml. capacity bottles 240000 Nos.
3. 100 Ml. capacity bottles 120000 Nos

TOTAL	Rs. 1,27,20,000.00

PROFIT SALES RATIO = Profit/Sales x 100 = 14.78 %

RATE OF RETURN = Operating profit / T.C.I x 100 = 56.10 %

BREAK EVEN POINT (B.E.P) = 41.21 %

Chapter 5

AROMATIC PERFUMERY COMPOUND

A perfume can be defined as a blend of odourous materials of natural and synthetic origin which gives a pleasant odour impression.

The art of perfumery is of extreme antiquity. The perfumes have been used from time immemorial and have played an important part in daily life of the people. The idea of perfumes was first conceived and technically employed in the East, especially in India, China, Egypt and persia. The fumes of frankincense and myrrh giving light odours were employed in religion ceremonies and later on balsams, pomades and cosmetics began to serve the needs of mankind.

Progress in the creation of natural perfume industry was made gradually. The first manipulation of perfumes was as therapeutic remedies utilizing immediate resources of nature. Then as time passed on and the experience of mankind accumulated, they became the basis of secular employment of incense. The latter established the art of perfumery.

Unfortunately, the flourishing position which India had attained in Olden times and medieval periods dwindled down due to the lack of scientific knowledge and the inability of Indian manufacturers to adopt themselves to modern scientific advancements. The application of cheap synthetic perfumes in the manufacture of soaps, cosmetics and confectionery, etc. induced Indian perfumes to import and methods of production could not compete with the modern scientific equipments and process. Therefore, improvements in the existing equipments and process are to be introduced early to develop the present state of perfumery industry in the country.

FORMULATION AND RAW MATERIALS

The formulations of aromatic perfumery compounds are given below:-

Fancy Bougnet:-

A.	Vanillin	168 kg.
	95% Alcohol30	4 kg.
	Cinna maldehyde	1 kg.
	Geraniol	1 kg.
	Benzaldehyde	4 kg.
	Amyl butyrate	16 kg.
	Amyl Acetate	16 kg.
	Amyl Valerate	30 kg.
	Amyl formate	36 kg.
	Capronic ether	38 kg.
	Imitation neroli	48 kg.
	Ethyl valerianate	88 kg
	Aldehyde C_{14} (Gamma Unde calactone)	250 kg.
		1000 kg

B)	Lavender Oil, French	40 kg.
	Bergamot Oil	100 kg.
	Geraniol	100 kg.
	Ambrette Oil, 10%	5 kg.
	Ylang-ylang oil	25 kg.
	Clang sage oil	5 kg.
	Rosemary oil	25 kg.
	Jasmine, Synthetic	50 kg.
	Benzoin R.	200 kg.
	Ethyl Phthalate	90 kg.
		1000 kg.

MANUFACTURING PROCESS

Manufacturing process for Fancy and Royale bouquet are given below according to their formulations:

1. Fancy Bouquet:

Formulation:

Vanillin	168 kg.
95% Alcohol	304 kg.
Cinnamaldehyde	1 kg.

Geraniol	1 kg.
Benzaldehyde	4 kg.
Amyl butyrate	16 kg.
Amyl Acetate	16 kg.
Amyl Valerate	30 kg.
Amyl formate	36 kg.
Capronic ether	38 kg.
Imitation neroli	48 kg.
Ethyl valerianate	88 kg
Gamma Undecalctone (peach Aldehyde)	250 kg.
	1000 kg

Process

The ingredients according to the above formulations are taken in a mixer cum blender with 150 kg capacity. Alcohol five times the weight of ingredient is mixed in the mixer. The mixer is equipped with stirrer and M.S. Jacket in which cold water is circulated. After proper blending the whole mixture is left for a suitable time to produce the required perfume in the mixture. The inside temperature of blender is kept low with help of cold water circulation. When the required perfume is generated the mixture is packed in small quantities with the help of a packing machine. The packed product is taken to storage, which is now ready for sale.

2. Royale Bouquet:

Formulation:

Diphenyl methane	5 kg.
Vetivert Oil	5 kg.
Clary sage oil	5 kg.
Jasmine absolute	10 kg.
Violet, synthetic	25 kg.
Santal wood oil, English	25 kg.
Coumarin	25 kg.
Musk Ketone	50 kg.
Heliotropin	50 kg.
Hydroxy-Citronellol	50 kg.
Iso-butyl phenyl acetate	50 kg.
Rose oil, Bulgarian	50 kg.
Amber, Synthetic	50 kg.

AROMATIC PERFUMERY COMPOUND

Musk Extract, 3%	50 kg.
Benzoin R.	50 kg.
Benzyl benzoate	250 kg.
Ambergris extract; 3%	250 kg.
	1000 kg.

Process:

The ingredients, according to the above formulations are taken in a mixer cum blender with 150 kg. Capacity. Alcohol five times the weight of ingredients is mixed in the mixer. The mixer is equipped with stirrer and M.S. Jacket in which cold water is circulated. After proper blending the whole mixture is left for a suitable time to produce the required perfume in the mixture. The inside temperature of blender in kept low with the help of cold water circulation. When the required perfume is generated the mixture is packed in small quantities with the help of a packing machine. The packed product is taken to storage which is now ready for sale.

PLANT ECONOMICS

Rated Plant Capacity = 10.00 Kg./Day Perfumery Compound

Land & Building (Land 1200 Sq.Mts.) Rs. 21,05,000.00

PLANT & MACHINERY

1. Blender
2. Refrigeration system
3. Packaging machine
4. Miscellaneous equipments like storage for raw materials, pumps etc.
5. Lab equipments

FIXED CAPITAL

1. Land & Building	Rs.	21,05,000.00
2. Plant & Machinery	Rs.	7,15,000.00
3. Other Fixed Assets	Rs.	2,00,000.00
TOTAL	Rs.	30,20,000.00

RAW MATERIALS

1. Vanillin
2. 95% Alcohol
3. Cinnamaldehyde
4. Geraniol
5. Benzaldehyde
6. Amyl butyrate
7. Amyl acetate
8. Amyl valerate
9. Amyl formate
10. Capronic Ether
11. Imitation Neroli
12. Ethyl valerianate
13. Gamma. Undecealactone
14. Diphenyl methane
15. Vetivert oil
16. Clary sage oil
17. Jasmine Absolute
18. Violet synthetic
19. Sandal wood oil

20. Coumarin
21. Musk Ketone
22. Heliotropin
23. Hydroxy Citronellol
24. Iso-butyl phenylacetate
25. Rose oil, Bulgarian
26. Amber synthetic
27. Musk Extract
28. Benzoin
29. Benzyl benzoate
30. Ambergris extract
31. Ethyl alcohol
32. Packaging Materials as Aluminiumcans/bottles etc.

TOTAL WORKING CAPITAL/ANNUM

1. Raw Material	Rs.	5,01,500.00
2. Salary & Wages	Rs.	7,26,000.00
3. Utilities & Overheads	Rs.	3,71,750.00
TOTAL	Rs.	15,99,250.00

TOTAL CAPITAL INVESTMENT

Total Fixed Capital	Rs.	30,20,000.00
Total Working Capital For 2 Months	Rs.	2,66,541.00
TOTAL	Rs.	32,86,541.00

TURN OVER/ANNUM

Receipt by sales of 3,000 kg of Fancy and Royale perfume	Rs.	33,00,000.00

PROFIT SALES RATIO = Profit / Sales x 100 = 21.18 %

RATE OF RETURN = Operating profit / T.C.I x 100 = 21.27 %

BREAK EVEN POINT (B.E.P) = 67.34 %

Chapter 6

AYURVEDIC CHURNS

MANUFACTURING PROCESS

Ayurvedic churns manufacturing comes in tiny scale. As this industry requires very few investments and all the machinery and equipments are fluently available in India.

Formulation of Ayurvedic Churn

Sito paladi Curna :-

Saranagharsamhita madyamkhanda, adhyaya 6, 134-135 and 1/2.

Sitopala (FL)	192 gm
Vamsarocana	96 gm.
Pippali (Fr)	48 gm.
Ela (sthula) (sd)	24 gm.
Trak (st.Bt)	12 gm.

Dosage 1 to 3 gm.
Anupana
Ghee, Honey

Important Therapeutic use

Arocaka, agnimandiga, Pittaja avara, Jvara, hasta pada daha, parsvasula, kraya.

Hinqwatraka churns:-

(Bhairalyaratnavali, Agnimandyadiogadhikara 37)

Sunlhi	(RJ)	39
Marica	(FV)	39
Pappali	(FV)	39
Ajmoda	(FV)	39
Saindhava		
Sveta Jiraks	(FV)	39
Krana Jivaka	(FV)	39
Hingu	(FV)	39

Anupana
Ghee
Important therapeutic uses
agnimandy, sula, bulma.

PLANT ECONOMICS

Rated Plant Capacity	=	120.00 Kgs./Day
Land & Building **Land Area 104 sq. mt.**	=	Rs. 9,40,000.00

PLANT & MACHINERY

1. Chakki
2. Immamdasta
3. Tasle
4. Packing machine
5. Chalani
6. Tarazu baat
7. Daba teen
8. Jar fibre
9. Bhabka
10. Sagwan Drum

FIXED CAPITAL

1. Land & Building		Rs.	9,40,000.00
2. Plant & Machinery		Rs.	1,12,300.00
3. Other Fixed Assets		Rs.	2,23,000.00
	TOTAL	Rs.	12,75,300.00

RAW MATERIALS

1. Safed Moosli, Salam Pumja, Akiq, Chop Chinni, Sanai, A harad, Misri, honey, Gilo Bhasm etc.
3. PACKING EXP:(Polythene wrappings & PVC small bottles

TOTAL WORKING CAPITAL/MONTH

1. Raw Material		Rs.	6,27,500.00
2. Salary & Wages		Rs.	41,400.00
3. Utilities & Overheads		Rs.	7,400.00
	TOTAL	Rs.	6,76,300.00

TOTAL CAPITAL INVESTMENT

Total Fixed Capital	Rs. 12,75,300.00
Total Working Capital for 1 Month	Rs. 6,76,300.00
TOTAL	Rs. 19,51,600.00

TURN OVER/ANNUM

By Sale of 36000 Kg. Ayurvedic Medicines (Churn & Asav)	Rs. 99,00,000.00

PROFIT SALES RATIO = 14.76 %

RATE OF RETURN = 74.48 %

BREAK EVEN POINT (B.E.P) = 28.12 %

Chapter 7

AUTOMATIC BISCUIT MAKING PLANT

Biscuits are one of the important bakery items and can be used whole day irrespective of time. It is very common for morning breakfast and also used as a snacks.

Biscuits are generally classified into soft biscuits, hard biscuits and crackers.

Biscuit doughs are made mainly from flour, fat, sugar and water, with minor amounts of flavor, colours, and aerating agents and possibly eggs and fruits.

Obtained from the milling of wheat by the gradual reduction system. The object of milling process is to separate as cleanly as possible, the endosperm of the grain from the enveloping skins and embryo. The flour for biscuit, should be weak and low in protein content, the protein content may be 8.5 per cent of less.

Fat is used in biscuit to remove hardness and to improve the shortness of the biscuits - that is to lower the Millard reaction and polymerization particularly in alkaline conditions, and invert sugar is effective in diminishing checking in biscuits. Sugars also affect the heat denaturation of flour protein. Aerating agents commonly used are ammonium bicarbonate by itself and sodium bicarbonate with either sodium pyrophosphate or calcium hydrogen phosphate. Ammonium bicarbonate has the advantage that it leaves no residue and evolves a greater volume of gas per unit weight than any of the others but, in the absence of phosphate and sodium ions, it leaves a raw taste in the biscuits. Sodium pyrophosphate residues give a burning taste and excess sodium bicarbonate give a fine granular texture to the biscuit (which is desired) but only at the expense of a burning taste.

RECIPES FOR VARIOUS TYPES OF BISCUITS

1. Arraroot Biscuit:

Flour	2.5 Kgs.
Shortening	250 gms.
Sugar	175 gms.

Arrowroot	175 gms.
Eggs (optional)	3 Nos.
Water/milk	750 ml.

2. Digestive Biscuits:

Wheat Meal	2.0 Kgs.
Shortening (vanaspati)	500 gms.
Sugar	100 gms.
Eggs	4 Nos.
Sodium bicarbonate	7 gms.
Milk	1.25 Litre

3. Honey Comb Biscuits:

Flour	2.0 Kg.
Sugar	1.0 Kg.
Shortening	500 gms
Egg	1 Nos.
Vegetable Oil	15 gms.

4. Almond Fruit Biscuits:

Almonds	500 gms
Powdered Sugar	500 gms.
Eggs	3 Nos.
Flour	60 gms.
Raspberry Jam	As Requisite

5. Soda Biscuit:

Flour	6 Kgs.
Salt	30 gms.
Vanaspati	200 gms.
Cream of Tar Tar	30 gms.
Soda Bi-Carbonate	50 gms.
Water	2.5 Litre

6. Coconut Biscuit:

Maida	450 gms.
Sugar	200 gms.
Shortening	250 gms.
Eggs.	4 Nos.

Chopped Coconut	200 gms.
Water	As required.

MANUFACTURING PROCESS

Most type of biscuits use weak flours of low protein content. Good biscuit flours can be obtained if the weak varieties one chosen and they are melted in a sound condition.

The gluten of distensible natures rather them elastic protects doughs against creep.

Flour, sugar, fat, water or milk are the main ingredients whose relative proportions differ according to the variety of biscuit being made. Baking powder ponder aeration. A uniform & stiff dough is prepared by batch mixing of dough ingredients.

The dough parses through rolls where it acquires a uniform texture & thickness final contrast of thickness are achieved by passing through other rolls.

Thus, a dough sheet of uniform thickness is prepared which is passed under cutter for stamping out the biscuit shapes. these are called biscuit blank,

Biscuits are baked in a traveling oven where moisture content in the biscuit is reduced to about 3%.

The variation in proportioning ingredients is so wide spread that no limit can,really, be put. Analytical data can be referred for guidelines to some extent one type of biscuitmay contain 45 to 50% of sugar while another (water biscuits & cream crackers) contain lecithin 1% sugar. However the whole activities of biscuit manufacture can be divided in the following categories:-

1. Procurement of raw materials of required properties & their tests (if needed).
2. Mixing & Blending in a double action horizontal mixing machine (batch -by-batch).
3. Flour shifter is used for transferring flour to mixers.
4. Mixed batch of main ingredients go to automatic continuous heavy duty rotary moulding machine Here, doughs one prepared and divided before transferring to the sheeter rolls.

5. Dough sheets of inform thickness are none made form the divided dough and cut to the required sized shape of the biscuits in a Rotary cutting machine.

6. The biscuit blank are collected in boxes or conveyed on a continuous conveyer for further treatments and the cutting wastages are automatically returned to the mixer for reprocessing into dough sheet.

7. Oil spraying machine converts the plain of light sweet biscuit in salted ones by infusing saline, contents uniformly all over the biscuit surface which in due coarse of time penetrates deeper & gets absorbed by biscuit material

8. While mixing ingredients in the mixing machine, the care is taken that finely ground/ pulverized sugar powder only is mixed. mixing is required to be fully uniform.

   A sugar grinding machine is used for this purpose.

9. As a final step, in biscuit manufacture, the biscuit blanks are placed in baking trays. The trays are either freely placed or fabricated with the wire belt continuous conveyer. The biscuits in trap one spread in such a way that one side of each biscuit is in direct contact with the baking pan.

10. After loading biscuits in the baking trap, as the loading and the conveyer is allowed to travel for ward into the baking oven chambers. The trap carrying biscuits cross oven chambers one after the other till they reach the other and of the oven where baked biscuit one unloaded automatically & collected in boxes.

11 As the biscuit travels the entire length of the baking oven (from loading end to unloading end) the biscuit gets properly baked at 270°C working temperature of the oven. After this baking only 3%of moisture is left in the biscuit.

12. The biscuit is still hot when collected from the unloading end of the oven. It is there fore, cooled on a cooling conveyer. The water jacketing system is fed with chilled water in this unit for the quick cooling of biscuit to flowing chilled water through the jacket.

13. At the end of all these biscuit mfg. processes the samples are tested in accordance with the relevant B/S - Standard of specifications.

PLANT ECONOMICS OF AUTOMATIC BISCUIT MAKING PLANT

Rated Plant Capacity =		5.00 MT/Day
LAND & BUILDING (Land Area 800 sq.mt.) =	Rs.	16,95,000.00

PLANT & MACHINERY

1. Automatic/continuous rotary moulding & cutting machine
2. Three roll shutter
3. Oil spraying Machine
4. Mixing Machine
5. Planetary mixing Machine
6. Cooling conveyor
7. Flour shifter
8. Sugar grinding
9. Electric oven
10. Plus S.T. Packing & forwarding
11. D.G. Set
12. Distribution transformer
13. Multi-colour Flexo-printing Machine
14. Automatic Biscuit packaging Machine
15. Testing laboratory equipments
16. Delivery van & Misc. equipments e.g. tubewell weighing & measuring equipments.

FIXED CAPITAL

1. LAND & BUILDING	Rs.	16,95,000.00
2. PLANT & MACHINERY	Rs.	44,07,200.00
3. OTHER FIXED ASSETS	Rs.	4,80,000.00
TOTAL	Rs.	65,82,200.00

RAW MATERIALS

1. Wheat Flour
2. Vanaspati
3. Sugar
4. Baking Powder
5. Fats
6. Milk
7. Salt
8. Yeast
9. Miscellaneous e.g. Honey, Flavours, Colours & Fruits and Packing Materials.

TOTAL WORKING CAPITAL/MONTH

1. RAW MATERIAL	Rs.	22,10,727.00
2. SALARY & WAGES	Rs.	1,09,250.00
3. UTILITIES & OVERHEADS	Rs.	1,57,000.00
TOTAL	Rs.	24,76,977.00

TOTAL CAPITAL INVESTMENT

TOTAL FIXED CAPITAL	Rs.	65,82,200.00
TOTAL WORKING CAPITAL FOR 3 MONTHS	Rs.	74,30,932.00
TOTAL	Rs.	1,40,13,132.00

TURN OVER/ANNUM

By sales of 1500 MT. of various types of biscuits (Sweet, Salty & cream sandwiched)	Rs.	4,50,00,000.00

PROFIT SALES RATIO = Profit / Sales x 100 = 24.40 %

RATE OF RETURN = Operating profit / T.C.I x 100 = 78.36 %

BREAK EVEN POINT (B.E.P) = 33.67 %

Chapter 8

AUTOMATIC BREAD & BISCUIT UNIT

The project proposes to procure fully indigenous plant for manufacturing various types of biscuits, the varieties include NICE, BOURBORNE and other cream Glucose, Mini Glucose, High Count, Star etc. (both Sweet & salty).

The plant & machinery, proposed to be purchased for the manufacture of various types of biscuits for the purpose of pulverizing, mixing, rotary moulding, rotary cutting, continuous biscuit baking oven, dough brake, cooling cover, automatic biscuit packing machine & wrapper printing etc.

The total connected load required will be 180 KVA at 430V/ 3 phase/ 50 cycle of AC supply A 300 KVA transformer will be installed to disturb power.

The plant capacity of biscuit making is 2 TPD on single shifts basis. This same automatic biscuit making unit falls under small scale sector and the arrangements are adequate for B.I.S. - approval of the products. The plant requires around 500 Sq.Mts of covered area for various activities including main work shop.

PLANT ECONOMICS OF BREAD AND BISCUITS PLANT

Rated Plant Capacity = Bread = 4000 Loaves/Day
Biscuits = 750 kgs/Day

LAND & BUILDING

Land Area 500 sq.m = Rs. 13,25,000.00

PLANT & MACHINERY

1. Bread Making Unit:Flour sifter
2. Dough Kneader
3. Divider
4. Moulding machine
5. Heating Oven
6. Bread slicing & sealing machine
7. Misc. equipment e.g. vessels, trays pans, work tables, cooling rack
13. Packing equipment
14. Biscuit Making Unit: Sugar Grinder
15. Planetary type mixer
16. Automatic biscuit cutting and punching machine fitted with rotary moulder
17. Electric baking oven with conveyor
18. Tanks (PVC)

8. Bucket evevater & conveyers hoists with motors platform weighing scale.
9. Pumps motors and blowers
10. Counter scales
11. Instrumentation & accessories
12. Laboratory testing equipment (L.S.)
19. Cooling conveyor
20. Oil Sprayunit
21. Packing equipment
22. Trays trolleys & other accessories
23. Laboratory equipment
24. Instrumentation and accessories
25. Conveyers, bucket elevators tools, jigs, hoist etc. Tanks

FIXED CAPITAL

1.	Land & Building	Rs.	13,25,000.00
2.	Plant & Machinery	Rs.	15,50,001.00
3.	Other Fixed Assets	Rs.	2,90,000.00
	TOTAL	Rs.	31,65,001.00

RAW MATERIALS

1. Bread:Flour
2. Fat
3. Salt
4. Dry yeast
5. Vegetable oil
6. Miscellaneous (Mis. and bread improvement)
7. Biscuit:Flour
8. Fat
9. Sugar
10. Milk Powder
11. Yeast
12. Salt
13. Ammonium carbonate
14. Miscellaneous & Packaging Expenditure

TOTAL WORKING CAPITAL/MONTH

1.	Raw Material	Rs.	4,86,545.00
2.	Salary & Wages	Rs.	61,625.00
3.	Utilities & Overheads	Rs.	75,000.00
	TOTAL	Rs.	6,23,170.00

TOTAL CAPITAL INVESTMENT

Total Fixed Capital	Rs.	31,65,001.00
Total Working Capital for 3 Months	Rs.	18,69,510.00
TOTAL	Rs.	50,34,511.00

TURN OVER/ANNUM

1. Bread loaves 1200000
2. Biscuit 300 Tons

Rs. 1,47,00,000.00

PROFIT SALES RATIO = Profit / Sales x 100 = 37.99 %

RATE OF RETURN = Operating profit / T.C.I x 100 = 112.39 %

BREAK EVEN POINT (B.E.P) = 28.13 %

Chapter 9

AUTOMATIC PLANT FOR TOFFEE & CANDY

The common Confectionery are:-

1. Hard Candy or Hard Sugar Boiling, e.g. Acid drops, pear drops, bulls eyes etc.,
2. Hard and pulled goods.
3. Caramel and Toffee.
4. Coated confections like pan coated confections comfits or dryers.
5. Lozenges.
6. Jelly crystal.

Manufacture of Hand Candy:-

A solution of can sugar to which is versugar of glucose or a chemical reagent to bring about particle inversion is added, is cooked , is cooked in a steam jacketed kettle, and transferred under suction to a vacuum cooker and concentrated vacuum boiling gives a light coloured product. A supersaturated sugar solution with a glass-like consistency is obtained. The product is quickly cooled by spreading on an oiled, water cooled table or plate.

Flavouring and coloring material are added the product thoroughly mixed. It is cut into shapes by frame cutters.

A particular variety of hard sugar boiling is the so-called pulled or stain goods or satinettes. In their preparation, the cooled sugar boiling is kneaded. Pulled an lapped a number of times during which treatment tiny air bubbles are incorporated into the mass. The appearance of the product depends on the duration of pulling. Short pulling gives a ration, silk-like finish prolonged pulling and lapping imparts a chalky appearance.

The cooking temperature for hard boiled products is 300-310°F while 280°-290°F for pulled or sation goods. The maximum temperature employed in vacuum boiling for hard boiled products is 260-270°F.

Hard & Pulled Goods

Hard and pulled goods may be employed in the production of filled goods. Pulled candy of different colours are arranged on a table to give the required design or rolling , the batch is rolled in an automatic batch feeder by tapered rollers into a rope which is passed through sizing rolls, cut and moulded into different shapes, in automatic machines, the good are dried by and twist -wrapped.

Caramel & Toffee

Caramel and toffee contain milk and butter in addition to the usual ingredients, the former being softer. Butter is however, partly or wholly replaced by coconut or coco butter.

In the manufacturer of caramels, butter and milk are emulsified in a homogenizer to a creamy product and added along with other ingredients icing sugar, corn syrup corn flour, or cashew powder to the boiling fitted with mechanical with stirrers. The mixture is cooked (260-280) rapidly. the material is poured on oiled slabs, flavoured and moulded by castings.

Toffee is cooked to a higher temperature 290-300° that ceramelisation occurs and the resulting product is cut. The temperature employed in vacuum boilers is 230-240 ^{O}F. The product from the boiling pan is fed into an automatic bathe feeder formed into a rope by size rollers, and fed to an automatic plastic cut and wrap machines.

Plain toffee is prepared from sugar and corn syrup only while mild and fats are added to the better varieties to impart -flavour and to develop a softer and more pliable texture.

Coated Confections

These are also known as pan coated confections, comfits, or dragees consists of nuts or seeds, or boiled goods or chewing gums, coated with a hard glossy sugar covering. The nuts of other center are placed in a rotating coating pan and giving and under coated of gum arabic or gelatin (10%) and sugar syrup (30°F) and a final coating of sugar.

Composition of fondants

Sugar	60 parts
Water	20 "
Corn Syrup	20 "
Cooking Temp.	234-240°F.

Lozenges:-

Lozenges are prepared by cold mixing of sugar, gum arabic, gelatin or stearine, and flavouring materials. Two types of lozenges are produced plain lozenges are made by cutting pieces from a sheet of dough and drying in air. Out lozenges, and made from mixtures of icing sugar and flavour with gum as binding materials.

Jelly Crystals:-

Jelly crystal is made by mixing refined sugar with gelatin solution, flavour, and colour no cooking is needed.

Confection are wrapped in glassine, cellophane, or waxed paper , and packed in tin containers. Boiled good are packed in 400 gm, 800 gm , 1kg, 5 kg. containers, and toffee in 400 gm, 800 gm 1 kg. containers.

FORMULATIONS

Toffee Formulation :-

Sugar	12 Kgs
Glucose	3 Kgs
Water	5 Litres
Salt Butter	1 Kg
Edible starch	Sufficient
Colour	q.s.
Flavour	q.s.
Milk (S.M.P)	1 Kg.
Ghee	1 Kg.

Candy (Hard-boiled)

Sugar	25 Kgs
Water	25 Kgs
Citric acid	100 gms
Colour	q.s.
Flavour	q.s.

Ayurvedic Products :-

Spices	q.s.
Salts	q.s
Sugar	q.s
Other ingredients	q.s.

FLOW DIAGRAM FOR THE MANUFACTURE OF TOFFEE

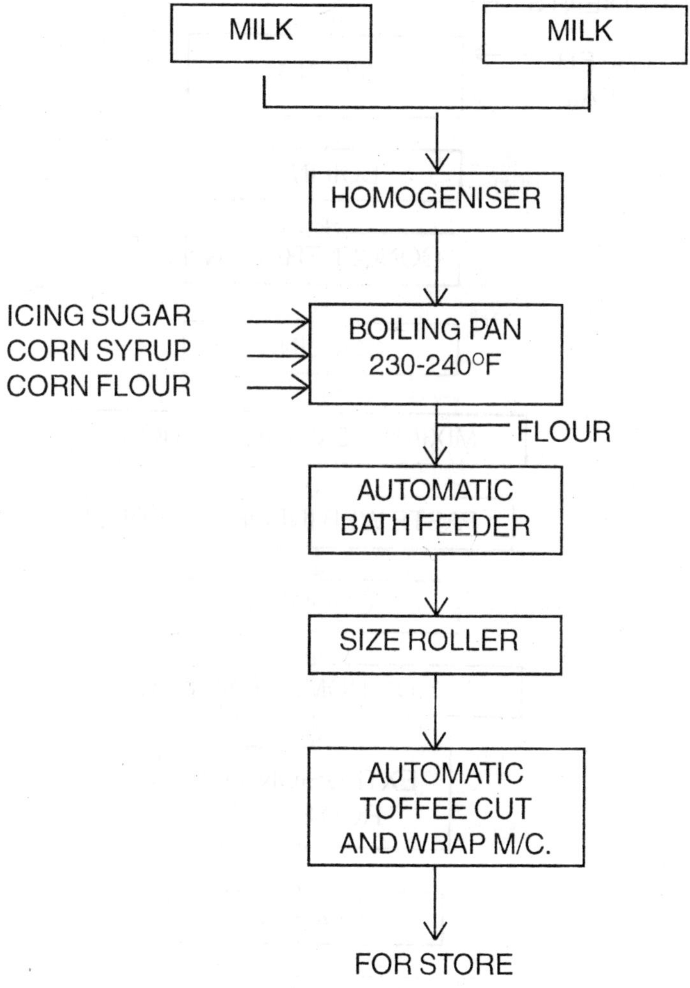

FLOW DIAGRAM FOR CANDY MANUFACTURING

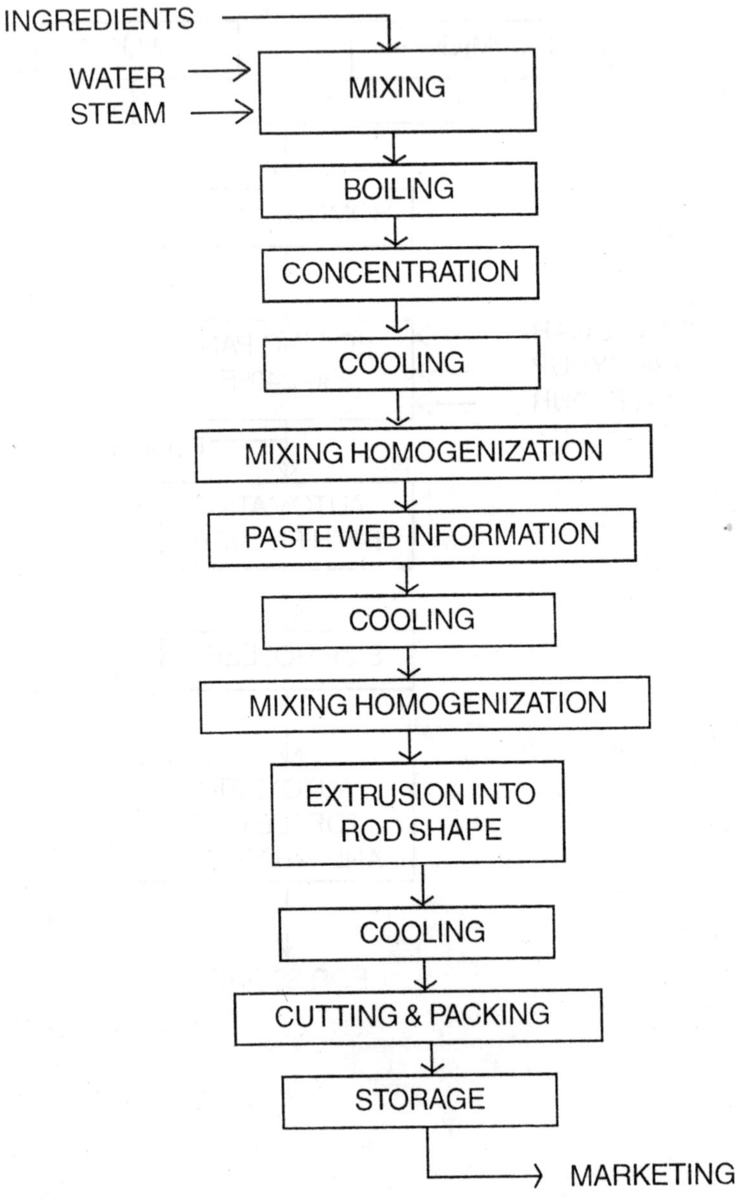

PROCESS FLOW SHEET FOR AYURVEDIC PRODUCTS

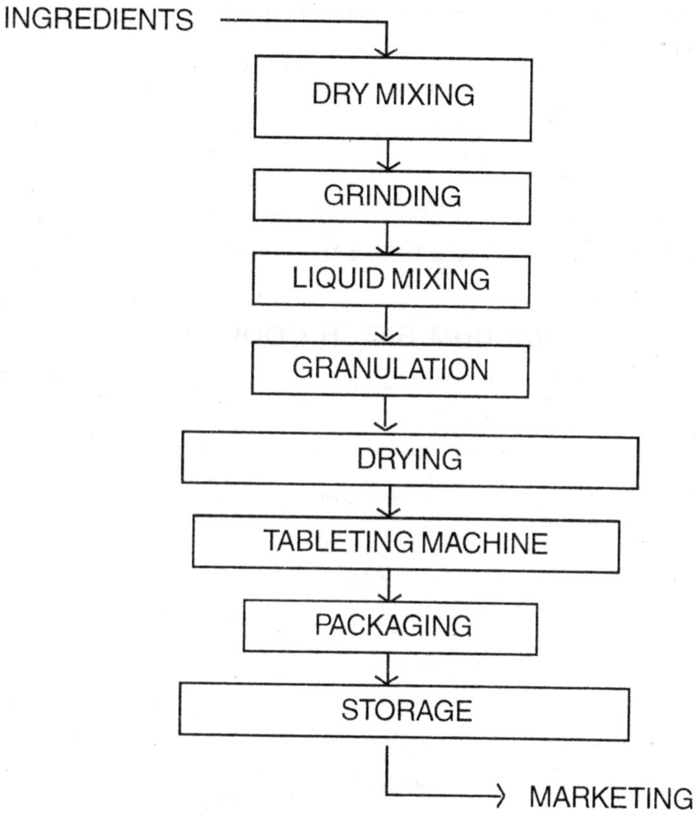

DETAILS OF CONFECTIONERY MACHINERIES
CONTINUOUS VACUUM BATCH COOKER

Continuous Cooking & Vacuumising in batches, ensures high transparency & low moisture in candy batch.

Output	:	Upto 800 Kgs./Hr.
Application	:	Hard Boiled Candies
Power Load	:	7.5 H.P.
Nett Weight	:	2000 Kgs.
Dimensions (LxWxH)	:	2700 x 1000 x 1800 (mm)

VACUUM BATCH COOKER

Easy to operate, require minimum space economical with all contact parts of stainless steel or food grade metals.

Output	:	45/90 Kgs./batch
Application	:	Hard Boiled Sweets, Milk Toffees, Jam etc.
Power Load	:	7.5 H.P./11.5 H.P.
Nett Weight	:	900/1100 Kgs.
Dimensions	;	For 45 Kgs. 1450x1500x2200 (mm)
(LxWxH)	;	For 90 Kgs. 1450x1500x2200 (mm) 1000x500x600 (mm)

ROTARY KNEADING MACHINE

Very easy to operate, continuous motion with oil water cooled contact parts takes less two minutes to mix a batch

Output	:	45 Kgs./batch
Power Load	:	3 H.P.
Nett Weight	:	1000 Kgs.
Dimensions	:	2000x1800x1600 (mm) (LxWxH)

Rotary Kneading Machine is used for the uniform mixing & kneading of cooked mas without any manual effort. The cooked mass after discharging from the cooker or boiling pan is left to cool a little on the cooling table. Then after adding all the ingredients such as Citric Acid/Spices, digestive drop, Men-

Then after adding all the ingredients such as Citric Acid/Spices, digestive drop, Menthol crystals or scrap, it it transferred to the Rotary Kneading machine, which automatically mix all the ingredients in the batch & also cool down it.

SALIENT FEATURES

1. It is automatic, no need to mix the batch with rods.
2. It is hygienic, as there is no need to touch the batch, as in general practice.
3. All the contact parts are of stainless steel.
4. Fast operation, mixing of one batch in less than two minutes & it helps in cooling the batch also as all the contact parts water cooled.
5. Better use of scrap upto 20% scrap can be mixed.
6. It ensures uniform mixing of all the ingredients throughout the batch.
7. Simple operation, all the functions are simple without any hydraulic or cam mechanism.
8. Batches mixed on this machine have better shining as compared to manual kneading.

PULLING MACHINE

Pulling Machine for Hard Boiled Sweets & Toffees batches.

Capacity	:	25 Kgs./35 Kgs.
Power Load	:	2H.P./5 H.P.
Nett Weight	:	200/275 Kgs.
Dimensions (LxWxH)	:	850x600x1225 (mm)

BATCH FORMER

Universal Batch Former for different type of Toffee, Candy or Buttle Gums making machines with Electronic Reserve & forward system & motorised lifting.

Capacity	:	49/90 Kgs.
Power Load	:	1.25 KW
Nett Weight	:	600/750 Kgs.
Dimensions (LxWxH)	:	2300x700x1450 (mm)

ROPE SIZER

Universal Rope Sizer for Toffee, Candy or Bubble Gums with all food grade contact parts. Can be used with various type of machines.

Power Load : 1.0 H.P. III Phase

Nett Weight : 350/450 Kgs.

Dimensions (LxWxH) : 900x550x1125 (mm)

CENTRE FILLER

Continuous operation centre filler for jams, honey or other type of syrups can be used with various type of machine.

Power Load : 1 H.P.

Nett Weight : 150 Kgs.

Dimensions (LxWxH) : 1000x500x300 (mm)

PLAST-O-PLAST SWEET FORMING MACHINE

New version of Plast-O-Plast machine with spring loaded, Round, Sturdy Punches. Very long life Die require minimum maintenance

Capacity ; Upto 2500 Kgs./Shift

Power Load : 2 H.P.

Nett Weight ; 650 Kgs.

Dimensions (LxWxH) ; 850x910x1200 (mm)

UNIPLAST SWEET FORMING MACHINE

Universal Sweet Forming Machine Suitable for Toffee, Candy or Bubble Gum from solid to upto 65% liquid filling. Generates very low scrap.

Capacity : Upto 800 Kgs./Hr.

Nett. Weight ; 950 Kgs.

Dimensions (LxWxH) : 1000x1300x1600 (mm)

AUTOMATIC PLANT FOR TOFFEE & CANDY

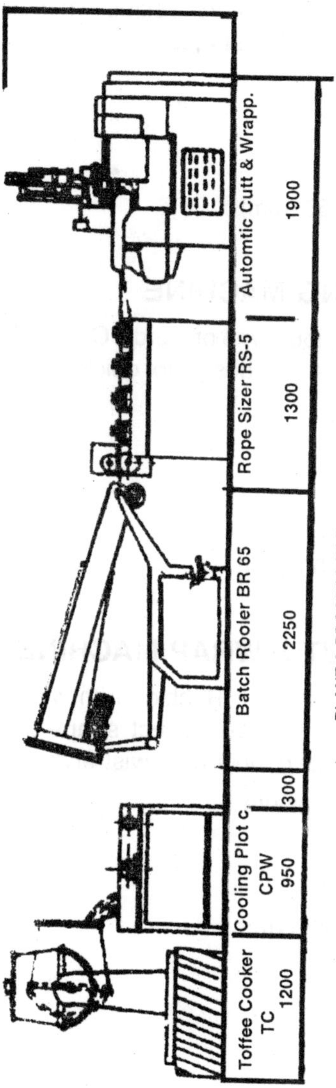

PLANT & PROCESS FOR MAKING TOFFEES

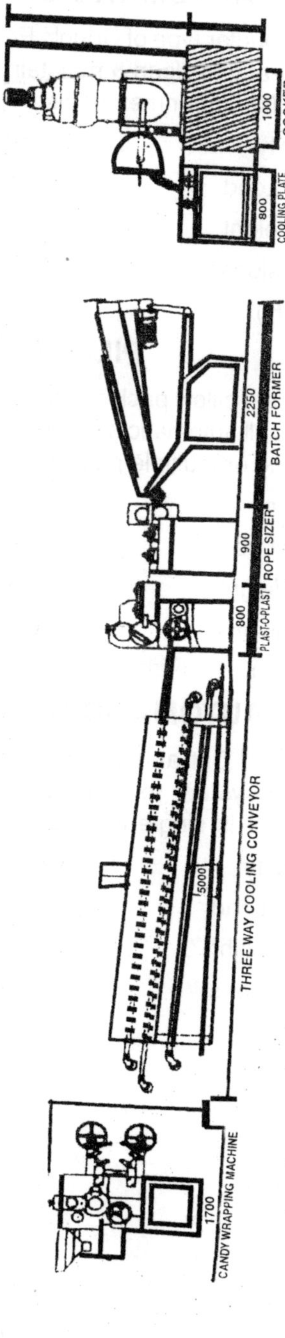

PLANT & PROCESS FOR CANDY PLANT

AUTOMATIC CANDY WRAPPING MACHINE

Most Popular type of Double End Twist Wrapping in the world. Simple operation & easy to clean & maintain, can be set to different sizes in minutes. No Sweet No Paper merchanism to avoid paper wastages.

Capacity	:	Upto 350 Pcs./Min.
Power Load	:	1.5 KW
Nett Weight	:	1000 Kgs.
Dimensions (LxWxH)	:	1600x1450x1650 (mm)

PILLOW PACKING MACHINE

Universal pillow packing machine for various type of candy, Caramel or Ball gum. Gull automatic & easy operation. Flexible design for quick change over of single or multiple packing in a pouch.

Capacity	:	800 Pcs./min.
Power Load	:	3 KW
Nett Weight	:	900 Kgs.
Dimensions (LxWxH)	:	2000x1800x1500 (mm)

AUTOMATIC TOFFEE CUT & WRAP MACHINE

Universal Cut and Wrap machine for Toffee or Bubble Gum with scissor cutting system to minimum Scrap and ensure correct shape of piece. Available in single twist (Basket Type) or double end twist style.

Capacity	:	Upto 350 pcs./minute
Power Load	:	1.5 K.W.
Nett Weight	:	940 Kgs.
Dimensions (LxWxH)	:	1750x9150x1930 (mm)

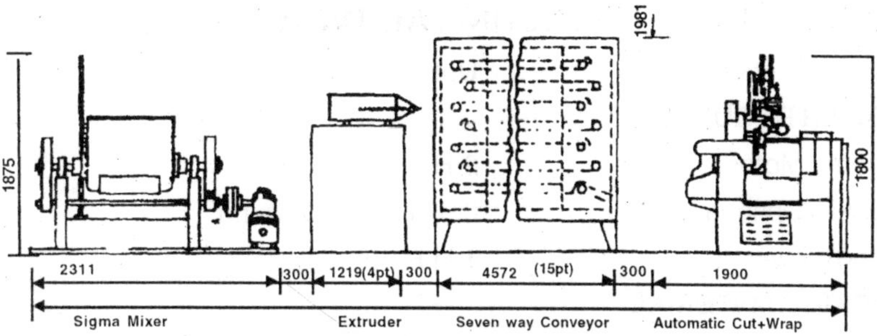

Plant & Process for Making Bubble Gum

AUTOMATIC CUT & WRAP MACHINE

Automatic cut & wrap machine suitable for Toffee, Candy or Bubble Gum available in three type of wrapping. Oil bath lubrication, Continuous Motion Cam Mechanism ensure low vibration & smooth operation.

Capacity	:	Upto 700 Pcs./Min.
Power Load	:	2.5 KW
Nett Weight	:	1250 Kgs.
Dimensions (LxWxH)	:	1600x1250x1950 (mm)

DOUBLE TWIST LOLLIPOP WRAPPING MACHINE

Lollipop Wrapping Machine is very suitable for double end twist Lollipops. This is an Automatic Machine and only unwrapped Lollipops has to be put into the machine & the wrapping film roll is fitted manually and machine does the rest work automatically.

When the Lollipops are put into the hopper, these are passed through a frequency controlled vibratory track which transfers the Lollipops to feeding plate & also separate the scrap which comes along with the lollipops. The Lollipops then pour into the cavities of feeder plate and is transferred to the front of paper feeding device where these are picked up into the rotating chamber, which takes it in front of twisting fingers and after twisting these are delivered through the delivery chute. Those wrappers which do not unwound can be wrapped on the standard Machine. However on hot Air Blower (Optional) can be supplied for BOPP, CPP, HM, Wrappers, to retain the twist with thermostatically controlled Hot Air Blower.

TECHNICAL DATA

Wrapping Speed	:	Upto 200 Pcs./min.

POWER REQUIRED

Electric Motor	:	2 H.P.
Hot Air (Optional)		0.67 H.P. (500 watts)
Turbo Blower	:	1 H.P.

PACKING MATERIAL

Continuous printed Cellophene, Wax Paper, PVC (Non magnetic) CPP, HM, Cellophene & BOPP with hot Air.

DIMENSIONS

Max. Paper Roll Diameter	:	300 mm
Case Dimensions	:	1550 x 1600 x 1750 mm (LxWxH)
Machine Gross Weight	;	1150 Kg.

PLANT ECONOMICS

Rated Plant capacity = 4.00 TON./day

LAND & BUILDING

Land Area 500 sq.mts. = Rs. 15,00,000.00

PLANT & MACHINERY

1. Toffee cut & wrap machine.
2. Cooker (S.S),
3. Boiler
4. Candy forming machine
5. Candy wrapping Machine
6. Pouch making machine.
7. Tableting Machine
8. Powder mixer.
9. Granulator
10. Grinding machine.
11. Genset

FIXED CAPITAL

1. Land & Building		Rs.	15,00,000.00
2. Plant & Machinery		Rs.	20,35,000.00
3. Other Fixed Assets		Rs.	4,85,000.00
	TOTAL	Rs.	40,20,000.00

RAW MATERIALS

1. Sugar
2. Glucose
3. Butter
4. Colour.
5. Flavours.
6. Ingredients for ayurvedic products (salt,spices,sugar & others)
7. Packaging materials

TOTAL WORKING CAPITAL/MONTH

1. Raw Material		Rs.	20,04,570.00
2. Salary & Wages		Rs.	1,05,750.00
3. Utilities & Overheads		Rs.	1,86,500.00
	TOTAL	Rs.	22,96,820.00

TOTAL CAPITAL INVESTMENT

Total Fixed Capital	Rs.	40,20,000.00
Total Working Capital for 3 Months	Rs.	68,90,460.00
TOTAL	Rs.	1,09,10,460.00

TURN OVER/ANNUM

1. By selling 300 tons of toffee
2. By selling 600 tons of hard candy,
3. By sale of 300 MT products

TOTAL Rs. 3,48,00,000.00

PROFIT SALES RATIO = Profit / Sales x 100 = 13.17 %

RATE OF RETURN = Operating profit / T.C.I x 100 = 42.02 %

BREAK EVEN POINT (B.E.P) = 46.95 %

Chapter 10

BUTTER MILK

Fermented milks refer to those milks which have been made by employing selected micro-organization to develop the characteristics flavour and/or body and texture.

Fermentation has been defined as the metabolic process in which chemical charges are brought about on an organic substratum, whether protein, carbohydrate, or fat through the action of enzymes whether protein carbohydrate or fat through the action of enzymes, liberated by specific living micro-organism.

The fermented milks are natural Butter milk, cultured butter milk, Acidophilus milk, Bulgarian butter milk, kumiss, kefer, yoghurt and Dahi.

The by-product obtained from the churning of sweet cream is essentially the same in composition as skim milk. As a beverage, buttermilk owes its flavour to the lactic acid and other substances present in small amount which differ in excellence according to the nature of the organism.

Much of the so called buttermilk at the present times consist of skim milk artificially soured by the addition of a suitable culture, which may be of the ordinary lactic acid bacillus or the similar B. bulgaricus whole milk, as skim milk, is thus treated so called acidobhilus milk is a produce prepared by careful sterlization and inoculation with a pure culture.

In certain countries, fermented milk food, are favoured over fresh, fluid milk for reasons safety better flavour and texture, and possible beneficial therapeutic effect where inadequate transport pasteurization, and refrigeration facilities exist inparticularly in hot climates, many authorities prefer to sour the milk first; in this manner the presence of enormous number's of harmless lactic acid bacteria and their metabolic and products discourage and growth of food poisoning and disease producing bacteria. The traditional flavour and texture quality are not necessarily retained, but economically and from a lowered calorie point of view low fat, cultured butter milk made with starters has more allure.

PROPERTIES & CHARACTERISTICS OF BUTTER MILK

1. Much more palatable than milk.
2. Nutritine value usually increased.
3. It is more easily assimilated by the human system than milk.

4. It contain beneficial antibiotics.

5. It possess therapeutic properties.

6. The regular consumption of butter milk claimed to increase longevity of human beings.

MANUFACTURING PROCESS OF BUTTER MILK

Natural Butter Milk : This is a by-product of churning cream for butter making. Ripened cream which has undergone a clean, lactic fermentation is usually preferred. Also included, under Indian condition, is country butter milk obtained as a by product of churning whole milk curd for production of country butter.

Cultured Butter Milk : This is obtained by inoculation and incubation of Pasteurized skim milk with lactic starter.

Details of manufacture :

Preparation : For the manufacture of cultured butter milk, fresh skimmed milk is preferable. The solids content should range from 9 to 10 percent. The skimmed milk should bo free from antibiotics and inhibitory substances. If milk containing an appreciable amount of fat is used. It should be homogenized. If cream or butter fat is desired in the product, it may be added to the cold, butter milk when the curd is broken up. Manufacturing milk is heated in a holder pasteurizer vat to 82-88°C (180°-190°F) for thirty minutes with frequent stirring and then cooled to 22°C (72°F) one percent bulk lactic starter is added and mixed thoroughly in the milk and then allowed to incubate at 21-22°C (70-72°F) without further agitation until coagulation occurs and an acidity between 0.80 and 0.85 percent is reached. The curd is broken up by slow agitation to give a smooth consistency and cooled to 5-10°C. It is then packed and stored at 5-10°C until distribution.

Creaming : Creaming imparts a rich flavour to the butter milk and has the effect of decreasing the viscosity (viscosity can also be decreased by adding 20 to 25 percent of pasteurized sweet whole milk during break up of the curd).

Salting : Salt at 0-1 percent may be added to the finished product to increase its flavour.

Adding Butter Granules : Butter granules or flakes are sometimes added to cultured butter milkmade from skimmed milk to simulate an old fashioned churned butter milk appearance.

Wheying-off or Whey Separation :

The water content of normal milk is about 87 percent; that of skim milk is about 91 percent. When the milk forms a curd in the manufacture of cultured butter milk, this water remains but it is loosely held by the protein as a sponge holds moisture. Part of it may be expelled from the protein and appears as a watery layer or in pockets. This condition is called "wheying-off" or "whey separation". The free liquid is actually whey, not water, and it contains soluble minerals, proteins, lactose, and vitamins.

Too Much Viscosity :

Many cultured butter milks are so thick that they appear more like custards than fluids, and in this condition it becomes difficult to empty the container. The lack of fluidity, ideal for yogurt but not butter milk, also decreases its refreshing qualities. The most important cause is excess acidity. As the acidity increases, the butter milk body thickens.

PLANT ECONOMICS

Rated Plant Capacity	=	200.00 Kg./Day
LAND & BUILDING (Area reqd. 1500 sq.mt)		Rs. 48,00,000.00

PLANT & MACHINERY

1. Homogenizer
2. Filteration unit
3. Pasteurization unit
4. Incubator
5. Refrigeration unit
6. Storage tank for skimmed milk made of stainless steel
7. D.G.Set
8. Material Handling equipments Viz; Conveyor belt, Bucket elevator etc.
9. Pouch filling & Sealing Machine
10. Laboratory & Milk Testing Equipments
11. Boiler
12. Misc. pipe fitting, pumps,motor, Valve viz; fixture,tools etc.

FIXED CAPITAL

1.	Land & Machinery	Rs.	48,00,000.00
2.	Plant & Machinery	Rs.	32,00,000.00
3.	Other Fixed Assets	Rs.	4,00,000.00
	TOTAL	Rs.	84,00,000.00

RAW MATERIALS

1. Skimmed milk
2. Lactic starter
3. Misc. Cream, Salt, Butter granules etc.
4. Flexible Pouches

TOTAL WORKING CAPITAL/MONTH

1.	Raw Material	Rs.	5,76,500.00
2.	Salary & Wages	Rs.	1,18,375.00
3.	Utilities & Wages	Rs.	1,11,200.00
	TOTAL	Rs.	8,06,075.00

TOTAL CAPITAL INVESTMENT

Total Fixed Capital	Rs.	84,00,000.00
Total Working Capital for 2 Months	Rs.	16,12,150.00
TOTAL	Rs.	1,00,12,150.00

TURN OVER/ANNUM

Received By sale of Butter milk
(600000 kgs) in pouch of 200 ml (3000000) Rs. 1,50,00,000.00

PROFIT SALES RATIO = Profit / Sales x 100 = 18.16 %

RATE OF RETURN = Operating profit / T.C.I x 100 = 27.20 %

BREAK EVEN POINT (B.E.P) = 57.64 %

Chapter 11

BREAD MANUFACTURING

In the manufacture of bread the yeast is essential agent. It ferments the dough produced carbondioxide and alcohol yeast breaks the sugar into simple sugar by the Siamese and raises the dough. Mostly in bakeries compressed or active dry yeast used.

The quality of bread depends upon the activeness of yeast. As yeast in more active than less sugar remain in flour mill produce poor crust colour and less active yeast means more sugar in flour and dark colour of bread will produce so in the bread a amount of sugar and yeast is needed.

PROCESS OF MANUFACTURE

The process of manufacture of bread starts with mixing and formation. mixing and fermentation of dought is carried out by two methods (i) straight dought method and (ii) sponge dough methods.

FORMULAE :

(I) BREAD WITH OR WITHOUT ASCORBIC ACID :

Ingredients	*% of Flour (Wt.Basis)*
Flour	100
Water	66
Sugar	8.00
Yeast	3.00
Shortening	3.25
Salt	2.01
Milk (Dry)	1.00 +
Yeast food	0.525
Monocalcium Phosphate	0.145
Sodium Propionate	0.10
Oxidizing agents	-
(Potassium bromate & Potassium iodate)	0.009

Variable.

(II) STANDARD BREAD

Flour	5000
Water	150
Milk solid	100
Acidulant	6
Yeast	100
Salt	75
Sugar	400
Monoglycerides	1.25
Water	3.450
Potassium bromate (based upon Flour wt.)	60
Potassium iodate (based uponflour wt.)	15
PPM (Part per million)	25

PLANT AND MACHINERY

1. Flour Shifter: Heavy duty fitted with automatic feeding elevator of automatic feeding elevator of sieving capacity on bag of flour (90) kg in 10 minuted fitted with 2 motors of 1 HP. Each and adjustable Aluminium hopper.

2. Water Measuring Tanks:

   Stainless Steel construction calibrated water measuring tank with visual level gauge, thermometer and two outlets valves fitted on stand. Capacity 150 litres.

3. Dough Kneading Machine:

   Heavy Duty (RVK) type with one mixing pan capacity 150 kg. flour in 15/20 minutes fitted with 5 HP electric motor (2 Nos.)

4. Extra Pans for RVK Kneader (2Nos.)

5. Single Pocket Dough Divider:

   Capacity 30 pieces/minutes app. fitted with NGEF or equivalent make 2 H.P. motor.

6. Rounder:- One bowl type dough piece rounder driven by 1 H.P. electric motor through reduction geares, having a revolving cast iron cone with stationery matching internal cast-aluminium spiral track with capacity to round upto 3500 pieces per hour and with heavy duty gear box and 1 HP motor HFEF or equivalent makes.

7. Straight through Moulder :-

   Capacity 2000-3000 leaves per hour and can also be used for twist bread purposed, fitted with 2 HP Motor (NGEF or equivalent) and driven through gear box)

8. Intermediate Providing Table:-

   Round table for first providing 8 ft. diameter with sunmica top fitted with 1 HP. NGEF or equivalent make motor

9. Travelling Oven: Capacity app. 1200 leaves per charge with an Indirect Heating system through recirculation of flues, fitted with 2 H.P. Main Motor, 3 H.P. recirculating Pan Motor, 2 HP. driven exhaust fan, Oven 2 HP. driven exhaust fan, Oven imparting top and bottom heat to baking pans in the entire cycle with capacity to bake 30000 leaves of 400 gms size per day complete with medium pressure burner. All motors of NGEF or equivalent make.

10. Tunnel-Type Final Proofer:-

    A Bread Tunnel-Type insulated final proofer, with recirculation duct on top with inline 1 HP motor driven fan/steam heater/ steam humidifier, having 1 HP. motor driven automatic rack-pusher, capable of accomodating upto 8 nos. Proofing racks for manufacturing 1,250 x 400 gm. leaves an hour.

11. Final Proof Trolleys: A set of heavy duty 12 Nos. trolleys for final proof made out of B-class GI pipe, 4 Heavy duty casters GI wheels meant for use in final proof tunnel each trolley having 8 tiers.

12. Baking Pans & Lids: A set of 1000 Moulds having 3 pans each and 400, 18 gauge MS Lids made out of 24 gauge tinplate for production of upto 1250 leaves of 400 gms size per hour.

13. Hot Leaves Collection Table: One 6 ft. Heavy Duty Structural Frame Diameter Turnatable having sunmica top driven by 1 HP. Motor, 900 RPM NGEF or Equivalent make, and fitted with reduction gear, for hot leaves collection having knockout plate form for manual depending.

14. Bread Cooling Tunnel with Pusher: A Bread cooling facility comprising of approx. 22 ft. long tunnel to accomodate 10 Nos. cooling racks, with 2 Nos. 36" size blower and exhaust

fans run by 2 H.P. motors each, having an air-washer located on top of tunnel with recirculating pump headers/nozzles/ base tank and cowl for blowing air through tunnel, complete with electrical controls, and suitable for cooling upto 1,250 x 400 gm. loaves per hours.

15. Bread Cooling Trolleys: 12 Nos.

    Bread cooling Trolleys having 8 racks made of B-class GI Pipe, Heavy Duty duly Galvanised

16. Salt Conveyor: A length of salt conveyor with 1 HP, Motor drive for moulds from oven to Moulder.

17. Slicer and Sealer:- Heavy duty 4 Nos. Bread slicing machine and 4 Nos. Sealing Machine Capacity upto 600 loaves per hour, Gravity Food.

18. Boiler: Coal Fired Baby Boiler or 250 kg. Steam per hour capacity complete with all fittings.

19. Refrigerated Chest for Yeast: Refrigerated Cabinet for storing compressed yeast capacity 200 kg. with 1 HP. Motor.

20. Bread Baskets: 600 Nos. made of MS plant.

21. Installation Charges

22. Laboratory with apart uses

PLANT ECONOMICS OF BREAD PLANT

Rated Plant Capacity = 10000 Loaves/Day
LAND & BUILDING (Land Area 668 sq.mt) = Rs. 16,56,200.00

FIXED CAPITAL

1.	Land & Building	Rs.	16,56,200.00
2.	Plant & Machinery	Rs.	14,00,000.00
3.	Other Fixed Assets	Rs.	5,00,000.00
	TOTAL	Rs.	35,56,200.00

RAW MATERIALS

1. Wheat Flour
2. Salt
3. Sugar
4. Milk Powder
5. Edible oil
6. Shortening
7. Yeast
8. Wrappers & Other Misc.

TOTAL WORKING CAPITAL/MONTH

1.	Raw Material	Rs.	23,43,125.00
2.	Salary & Wages	Rs.	1,10,400.00
3.	Utilities & Overheads	Rs.	2,34,400.00
	TOTAL	Rs.	26,87,925.00

TOTAL CAPITAL INVESTMENT

Total Fixed Assets	Rs.	35,56,200.00
Total Working Capital for 1 Month	Rs.	26,87,925.00
TOTAL	Rs.	62,44,125.00

TURN OVER/ANNUM

1. Receipt from sales of 10,000x300 loaves of 800 gms.
2. By sale of 10000X300 loaves of 400 gm.

Rs. 3,60,00,000.00

PROFIT SALES RATIO = Profit / Sales x 100 = 6.44 %

RATE OF RETURN = Operating profit / T.C.I x 100 = 37.14 %

BREAK EVEN POINT (B.E.P) = 57.05 %

Chapter 12

BAKERY UNIT

(Pastries, Bread, Buns, Cake, Toffee etc.)

Pastries, Bread, Cakes, Toffies etc. comes under the bakery product. Now the advancement of age age food habits of the ready-made food. Most of all the bakery items are under the category of ready-made food. Now school going children are like to have the items like parties cakes, breads etc. for their tiffin use office going peoples like to take breads and parties products, in our daily break fast table also take. The share of bakery products even daily wages laborers also habiterated to spend their lunch by taking bread or like that baking product. By the large utilities of baking products in our life takes part the program of progress of bakery unit itself.

PROCESS MANUFACTURING OF BUNS

Theory and procedure of buns are similar to the breads only ingredients composition are different, even some excess ingredients required.

Formulations of different types of buns are given below:

NORMAL BUNS (SWEET BUNS)

Name of the Ingredients	Percentage of Ingredients
On the Basis of	
Maida	
Milk	10-12%
Shortening	8%
Sugar	10-15%
Whole eggs	5%
Yeast	8.5%
Salt	1.0%

HAMBURGER BUNS

Name of the Ingredients	Percentage of Ingredients
Maida	
Cream of Tartar	3%
Sodium Carbonate	1-15%
Shortening	15%
Sugar	40%
Egg	15-20%
Milksufficient to make dough	
Tuti Fruity	2%

GENERAL PROCESS

Sugar dissolves in part of the water, in sugar solution added all the yeast to make a yeast sugar homogeneous solution. Sodium carbonate, salt are dissolved in other part of water. Now melt the shortening if it is solid form.

Take flour in kneading mixer added yeast sugar solution, mix homogeneously, after complete mixing added salt's solution then added shortening to the whole mixture to form a soft dough. When proper homogeneous dough has been prepared, keep the dough for one hour to make a fermented dough of well in seated volume at temperature 30°C-35°C. Then the knock back operation will start. After knock back it is pass through the divider and rounder. After warded all the rounded dough put in the mould and keep it for 40 minutes 60 minutes for final proofing. Then the dough is put in the bakery oven at the temperature of 200-300°C.

After complete baking it is takes out and keep it for looking about 2 hours. Now pack it and market the product.

PLANT ECONOMICS OF BAKERY UNIT,BUNS,CARE,TOFFEE ETC.

Rated Plant Capacity = 1243.70 Kgs/Day
LAND & BUILDING (Land Area 500 sq. mt.) = Rs. 7,00,000.00

PLANT & MACHINERY

1. Auto Sifter
2. Dough Kneader
3. Dough Grinder
4. State Convet
5. Dough Rounder
6. Dough Moulder

7. Diesel Rotary Rock
8. Cooling rack
9. Trolley
10. Automatic Slicer
11. Cream Milk
12. Dies and Mold
13. Electrically Heating Kettle
14. Cooling Chamber
15. Packing, and sealing Machine
16. Miscellaneous Machine

FIXED CAPITAL

1.	Land & Building	Rs.	7,00,000.00
2.	Plant & Machinery	Rs.	8,29,500.00
3.	Other Fixed Assets	Rs.	2,75,000.00
	TOTAL	Rs.	18,04,500.00

RAW MATERIALS

1. Flour
2. Shortening
3. Salt
4. Sugar
5. Egg
6. Milk Solid
7. Yeast
8. Butter
9. Glucose solid

TOTAL WORKING CAPITAL/MONTH

1.	Raw Material	Rs.	2,48,058.00
2.	Salary & Wages	Rs.	22,920.00
3.	Utilities & Overheads	Rs.	26,100.00
	TOTAL	Rs.	2,97,078.00

TOTAL CAPITAL INVESTMENT

Total Fixed Capital	Rs.	18,04,500.00
Total Working Capital for 3 Months	Rs.	8,91,234.00
TOTAL	Rs.	26,95,734.00

TURN OVER/ANNUM

1. Pastry Products: 120000 Kgs.
2. Paste 30000 Kgs.
3. Bread/Bun 99540 kgs
4. Toffee 123570 Kgs

Rs. 52,01,250.00

PROFIT SALES RATIO = Profit / Sales x 100 = 18.31 %
RATE OF RETURN = Operating profit / T.C.I x 100 = 35.32 %
BREAK EVEN POINT (B.E.P) = 49.13 %

Chapter 13

CASEIN FROM MILK

Casein is an important bye-product of milk, that can be manufactured very easily. After the extraction of butter, the residue is usually thrown off. This can be utilised in making casein.

Casein made from butter separated milk "Skim Milk". In order to obtain the protein from the milk rapidly, a little quantity of acid is added. By doing so, the milk will coagulate and water will be separated.

Casein is sold in granular or powder form. It is an essential raw material by which a number of items are produced. In the past few years, the plastic was prepared from casein which was known as casein plastic. In recent years there have, however, been absolute by other durable cheap and better plastics made from synthetic material.

MANUFACTURE OF CASEIN

If we want to make better quality of casein the fat content of the skim milk, from which it is made, should be minimum. Therefore it is necessary, the cream may be again separated from skim milk so that its fat content is minimum.

After separating the last trace of cream from the skim milk it is heated 350°C and filled in the wooden tank equipped with a hand agitator or mechanical agitator. For co-agulation of casein 150 ml of dilute hydrochloric acid (1 part of acid into 1 parts water) and is added by spray pump slowly and stirring is continued. Milk starts coagulating as the acid is added and coagulated man settles down at bottom. When complete coagulation has taken place, the mass is allowed to settle for half an hour. Now the stop coke is opened and the whey is drained over a draining cock made of wire cloth fixed in wooden frame, so that the coagulated mas is retained over it. The coagulated mass is again dropped into the tank for washing.

Now-a-days a different types of filter is using to separate whey.

Washing is done in the tank by adding dilute acid water (8 C.C. acid in 50 ltr. of water). The acid is added sufficient quantity so that coagulation is completely under water. After ten minutes, the water is drained out. Two such type of required more. It should be remembered that washing should be such type that there should be leaving no whey.

The coagulation is hanged in a cloth so that water tickles down.

Even after this process there is sufficient water present necessity squeezing and processing. For this the cloth fieled with coagulation is put under two wooden frames and pressed by putting some weight.

A screw press may be used for the same purpose as it makes the pressing very easy. The casein is now form of a cake.

Now the cake should be cut in the pieces. Then the pieces are rubbed on over a 10 mesh more cloth fixed in a wooden frame. Granules of casein are obtained below the sieve.

The next step is to dry the granules. If the production is 5-10 kg. casein per day and it is shiring run that the charging can be done in open by spreading the granules over white sheets on a coat, but if larger production is required a tray dryer will be needed.

Tray dryer is a almirah which is heated inside with electric elements. Granule is placed in trays which are put in place over the sacks provided in the almirah. The heating can also be done with coal.

The granules are next ground lo powder. Different types of grinding machines are available including driven. If powder is available that it is casein to run the grinder in the keep of 1/2 H.P. motor. The powder is packed in polythene bags which are placed in card board boxes. Indian standard institution has prescribed the requirement for edible quality casein code No. IS : 1167-1965.

NOTE

1. Skim milk should not have any cream.
2. Spray should be slower.
3. Complete coagulation of whey should be.
4. Moisture contents should be minimum.
5. For grinding purpose, a pulveriser should be used.
6. Drier temperature should not be more than 100°C.
7. Moisture content should be minimum.

The process can be completed in the following steps.

1. Cream separation.
2. Coagulation of whey.
3. Washing with water acid solution.
4. Removal of water from casein.
5. Pressing.
6. Granulation or powder.
7. Drying.
8. Grinding.
9. Testing.
10. Packing.

PLANT ECONOMICS

Rated Plant Capacity = 160.00 KGS/Day
LAND & BUILDING = Rs. 1,68,500.00
(Land 100 sq.mt.)

PLANT & MACHINERY

1. Cream Separator
2. Wooden tank
3. Spray press
4. Screw Press
5. Oscillating granulator
6. Tray dryer
7. Grinding Machine
8. Misc. Accessories

FIXED CAPITAL

1.	Land & Building	Rs.	1,68,500.00
2.	Plant & Machinery	Rs.	51,300.00
3.	Other Fixed Assets	Rs.	31,000.00
	TOTAL	Rs.	2,50,800.00

RAW MATERIALS

1. Skim Milk
2. Hydrochloric Acid

TOTAL WORKING CAPITAL/MONTH

1.	Raw Material	Rs.	4,00,700.00
2.	Salary & Wages	Rs.	35,160.00
3.	Utilities & Overheads	Rs.	10,000.00
	TOTAL	Rs.	4,45,860.00

TOTAL CAPITAL INVESTMENT

Total Fixed Capital	Rs.	2,50,800.00
Total Working Capital for 2 Months	Rs.	8,91,720.00
TOTAL	Rs.	11,42,520.00

TURN OVER/ANNUM

By selling 48000 Kg. of Casein	Rs.	67,20,000.00

PROFIT SALES RATIO = Profit / Sales x 100 = 16.30 %
RATE OF RETURN = Operating profit / T.C.I x 100 = 95.88 %
BREAK EVEN POINT (B.E.P) = 30.95 %

Chapter 14

CANNING OF FRUITS (PINE APPLES SLICES, LITCHI, CHERRIES, STRAWBERRIES IN SYRUPS)

PROCESS OUTLINES OF CANNING OF FRUITS

The canning of fruit involves several distinct operations which are more or less common to all kinds. The first of these is that of preparation; thus gooseberries have to be snibbed, strawberries plugged, blackcurrants strigged, and so on. For the snibbing of gooseberries and the strigging of currants machines are used, but strawberries have to be plugged by hand. After being prepared, the fruit is graded either by hand or machinery; it is then washed, if necessary, and filled into the cans.

The latter pass to a syruping machine and then to an exhaust box, where the temperature of the contents is raised, and air adhering to the fruits or gases held internally are released. This reduces the oxygen content of the gases in the cans and also ensures a good vacuum when the cans are cooled. As the cans leave the exhaust box they pass on singly to the closing machine, where the lids are spun on. The head-space at this stage should not be too large or vitamin C will be destroyed during processing; on the other hand, it should not be too small or hydrogen swells may form too easily. A good depth of head-space is about 3/16 inch when the lids are spun on.

The remaining processes are sterilising and cooling. Continuous cookers and coolers are largely employed for these processes. The finished article is then stacked to await labelling and casing.

MANUFACTURING PROCESS

CANNING:-

Apples, Bananas, Grapes, Guavas, Litchi, Mangoes, Oranges Papaya, Pears & Pineapples among fruits are chosen for the canning process. The details of the process is given below.

The whole process can be divided into following step.

1. **SORTING AND GRADING:-**

After preliminary sorting, the fruits are graded. This is necessary to obtain a pack of uniform quality as regards size, colour, and is done be hand or with the help of grading machines.

2. **WASHING:-**

The graded fruits are washed with water in different ways, such as soaking or agitating in water, washing with cold or hot water sprays, etc.

3. **PEELING, CORING AND PITTING:-**

The washed fruits are prepared for canning by peeling, coring, pitting by machines. Some cases it is done by hand, by heat treatment and by lye solution.

4. **CAN FILLING:-**

The cans are washed with water to remove any adhering dust or foreign matter. In large canneries, the cans are washed with jets of compressed air, water.

The cans are filled with fruits by a automatic cans filling machine. The cons are filled with hot sugar syrup for fruits and with hot brine is to improve the taste of the canned product, to fill up the inter-space between the fruits in the can, and to facilitate further processing. The syrup should be filled at a temperature of 175°-180°F and suitable head space should be left in the can so that when the closing end is fitted the space left inside ranges from 1/8" to 3/16".

After this lid is partially seamed to the can by a single first roller action of a double seamer. Before sealing the cans finally, it is necessary to remove all air from the contents. This is done by heating the cans for 5 to 25 minutes, depending on the nature of the product, at the end of the exhaust, the temperature at the centre of the can should be about 175°F. After exhausting, the cans sealed by special closing machines known as double seamers.

5. **PROCESSING :-**

After the above process heating of canned foods is done to inactivate bacteria. Fruits can be processed satisfactorily at a temp. 212°F in boiling water. The temp. and time of processing, therefore, vary with the size of the can. The larger the can, the greater the processing time and vice versa.

6. **COOLING:-**

After processing the cans are cooled rapidly to stop the cooling process and to prevent stack-burning especially in cans at the centre of large stacks, where they may remain hot for several hours, cooling is done by immersing or passing the hot cans in tanks containing cold water.

7. **LABELLING, STORING & PACKING:-**

After cooling, the cans are labelled by machine, and packed in strong wooden cases. They are stored in a cool and dry place.

SYRUP FOR CANNING

For canning fruits sugar syrup covering liquids are employed. Syrup of sugar, glucose, or corn is used for fruits. The process of preparing these for different requirement, on commercial as well as domestic scale, are dealt with below.

PREPARATION:-

Syrups can be made either by the 'cold process' or by the 'hot process'. IN the cold process, sugar is placed in a tank and cold ware poured over it and stirred. The solution is then filtered through a thick flannel bag, muslin cloth, or fine brass wire gauze to remove insoluble impurities. sometimes, warm water may also be added to facilitate the dissolving of sugar. In the hot process, sugar and water are placed in a steam-jacketed kettle ad boiled and the scum removed. The syrup is clarified further by filtration. Steam helps to sterilize the syrup and to prolong its preservability. The quantities of sugar and water required to prepare syrups of a given Brix are given in Table.

TABLE
RELATIONSHIP BETWEEN BRIX READING AND COMPOSITION OF SYRUP

DEGREES BRIX 68oF.	WEIGHT OF SUGAR TO BE ADDED TO EACH GALLON OF WATER 1 B.	VOLUME OF SYRUP FROM ONE GALLON OF WATER GAL.	WEIGHT OF SUGAR CO-TAINED IN ONE GALLON OF SYRUP 1 B.
10	1.11	1.067	1.04
11	1.23	1.076	1.14
12	1.36	1.085	1.25
13	1.49	1.093	1.36
14	1.62	1.101	1.47
15	1.76	1.111	1.58
16	1.90	1.119	1.70
17	2.04	1.127	1.81
18	2.19	1.137	1.93
19	2.34	1.146	2.04
20	2.50	1.157	2.16
21	2.66	1.167	2.28
22	2.82	1.176	2.40
23	3.00	1.187	2.52
24	3.17	1.198	2.64
25	3.34	1.208	2.76
26	3.52	1.220	3.01
27	3.70	1.231	3.01
28	3.89	1.243	3.13
29	4.09	1.256	3.26
30	4.30	1.269	3.38
31	4.50	1.281	3.51
32	4.72	1.294	3.64
33	4.92	1.309	3.77
34	5.17	1.323	3.90
35	5.40	1.338	4.03
36	5.64	1.353	4.17
37	5.89	1.369	4.30
38	6.14	1.384	4.44
39	6.41	1.401	4.58
40	6.69	1.419	4.71
41	6.97	1.437	4.85

42	7.26	1.454	4.99
43	7.56	1.474	5.13
44	7.88	1.494	5.27
45	8.20	1.514	5.42
46	8.55	1.536	5.57
47	8.90	1.558	5.71
48	9.26	1.580	5.86
49	9.64	1.604	6.01
50	10.03	1.628	6.16
51	10.44	1.654	6.31
52	10.86	1.681	6.45
53	11.31	1.710	6.61
54	11.77	1.739	6.77
55	12.26	1.770	6.93
56	12.77	1.803	7.08
57	13.29	1.837	7.23
58	13.85	1.871	7.40
59	14.43	1.907	7.57
60	15.05	1.948	7.73
61	15.69	1.988	7.89
62	16.37	2.032	8.05
63	17.08	2.077	8.21
64	17.84	2.124	8.39
65	18.62	2.174	8.57
66	19.47	2.229	8.75
67	20.39	2.287	8.92
68	21.32	2.344	9.10
69	22.23	2.411	9.27
70	23.40	2.480	9.44

In commercial practice, syrups of desired Brix are prepared either according to a formula by which a known weight of sugar is added to a given volume of water, or by adding sufficient water to a known weight of sugared to get the desired volume of syrup. for example, addition of 5 gallons of water to 50-35 1b. of sugar will produce 8.14 gallons of syrup of 50 degrees Brix. Similarly, to get 5 gallons of syrup of 50 degrees Brix, using 30-80 1 b. sugar, sufficient water is added to obtain the required quantity. Generally, to avoid unnecessary weighing a 2 cwt, (224 1b). bag is taken as the measure and a known volume of water added to the sugar.

Table - 2
Canning & Preservation of Fruits & Vegetables

Fruit	lb. of sugar/gallon of Water	Degree Brix
Blackberry	10 to 12	50 to 55.0
Black currant	15 to 17	60 to 64.0
Damson	15 to 17	60 to 64.0
Plums	8 to 9	44.4 to 47.7
Gooseberies	8 to 9	44.4 to 47.7
Raspberries	10 to 12	50 to 55.0
Loganberries	17 to 20	64 to 66.0
Sour Cherries	9 to 11	47.7 to 52.7
Red currant	17 to 20	63 to 66.0
Rhubarb	10 to 12	50 to 55.0
Strawberries	13 to 15	57 to 60.0
Sweet cherries	6 to 8	37 to 44.5

Canning of Pineapple:-

Ripe and juicy fruit with characteristic colour and aroma should be selected and washed in cold water.

Removed the crown, peel and cut the fruit into transverse slices of 1.25 cms. thickness with a stainless steel knife. Prepare the sugar syrup by mixing 1 cup of sugar with one cup of water and bring them to boil. Place the pineapple rings (5-6) in butter size can (plain). Fill the interspace with syrup 1.25 cms. head space. Exhaust, seal pasteurize and cool in dry place.

Canning of Litchi:-

A large number of litchi varieties are grown in different parts of India, most of them are not well established. The same variety may be known under different names in different places and these tend to be deceptive. In Bihar, which has largest area under litchi cultivation in India, the important varieties are China, Deshi, Dehra Rose, Purbi, Bedana, Mclean and Muzzaffarpur. The important varieties grown in Western Uttar Pradesh including Dehra Dun, Punjab and Haryana are Seedless Early, Seedless Late, Early Large Red, Late Large Red, Kolkatta, Rose Scented, Khatti and Gulabi. The varieties recommended for growing in Punjab and Haryana are Saharanpur, Dehra Dun, Kolkatta, Muzaffarpur, Seedless Late and

Rose Scented. Among the eight varieties, Muzaffarpur, China, Deshi, Purbi, Elachi early, Elachi Late and Bombai, ave been growing in West Bengal. Bombai, Elachi Early, Elachi Late and China are considered important both for quality and yield.

Cherries Canning:-

Two fairly distinct classes of cherry are canned: the sub-acid red or purple fruit (Morello, May Duke), and the sweet white fruit (Napoleon Bigarreau, Amber Heart). The former are packed in lacquered cans and in a plain syrup of 40° Brix. White cherries are packed in plain cans in syrup containing erythrosine to colour them red. After filling and covering with hot syrup, the cans are exhausted for four to six minutes at 185°F, the lids are spun on, and the cans cooked for 16 to 20 minutes at 210°F, and cooled.

Cherries packed in lacquered cans are prone to rapid hydrogen swell formation (q.v.). It is therefore essential to ensure that they are given a heat process sufficient to inactivate the enzymes in the stones of the fruit. In plain cans, corrosion is not usual and no special precautions need be taken.

Cherries are abnormal in their susceptibility to form hydrogen swells (q.v.), and cool storage of the cans is therefore essential.

Glace, Maraschino, or cocktail cherries are sweet white cherries, with the pits removed, which have been impregnated with sugar syrup to give a total solids content of about 74 percent and coloured with a red or green dye.

Black Currants:-

The chief merits of canned blackcurrants are their high content of vitamin C and their strong and characteristic flavour. Canned blackcurrants generally contain about 100 mg. of vitamin C per 100 g. of canned material. An A. 2 can will thus provide the full daily requirement (30 mg.) of vitamin C for about twenty people.

The fruit should be ripe, and should be prepared by removing the stalks. This is known as strigging, and on a commercial scale is carried out by a machine which consists of an inclined reciprocating screen through the interstices of which mechanical fingers rotate at a very rapid rate. The currants are fed on to the higher end of the screen, and are freed from the stalks by the gentle tapping of the rotary fingers. The stalks, freed from the fruit, are drawn through the screen by the rotating fingers into a receptacle below, while the fruit rolls down the inclined screen into another vessel at the bottom of the machine. Before being filled into cans, the fruit should be carefully picked over to remove small strigs not detached by the machine. The following times and temperatures are recommended:

Can.	Exhaust at 180°-190°F	Cook in Stationary Cookers at 212°F	Cook in Automatic Cookers at 212°F
A.2.	6 minutes	15 minutes	7 minutes
E. 1.	5 minutes	12 minutes	6 minutes

Canning of Straw Berries:-

Strawberries for canning purposes should be firm in texture of good color and flavour, and of large size. The most important requirement is firm texture.

The principal difficulty in the coming of strawberries is the softening of the fruit during sterlization, which result in the Can containing only from one-third to one half its volume of berries.

Strawberries shrival if canned in too heavy a sirup, although a fairly heavy Sirup is necessary to develop and retain the berry flavour.

A sirup of 50° balling is satisfactory.

Strawberries are washed and placed with sugar and little matter in a steam Jacketed pressure Kettle and boiled very rapidly. The partially collapsed berries are then filled into Cans, the syrup is partially evaporated before it is added to the cans. The cans are closed and processed for 1.0 months (No 2 and 21/2 Cans) in boiling matter and cooled quickly. The cans used are Acid Resistant lacquered Cans.

Processing Details (Canning):-

Mashing :- Washing of strawberries can be made more effective by causing the product to soil during washing with high pressure water sprays.

Filling :- Before filling the Cans are subjected to steam jet remove any adhering dust and subsequently washed with water. Now the strawberries are filled in the cans with hot sugar syrup.

Exhausting :- Exhausting is a process in which air and other intrapped gases are removed from the Cans after filling and before the cans one sealed. In filling, the syrup is normally filled hot as (above 80° or above) to allow air in the head space to expand and get partially displaced by steam from the hot liquid.

Sealing :- Cans are sealed by special can sealing machine known as double seamer.

Processing :-It consist of exposing the under pressure to sterilize the content.

Cooling :- After processing the cans are cooled rapidly to stop the cooking process and to prevent stock burning especially in cans at the Centre of large stacks, where the remain hot for several hours.

Labelling and Storning :- Labelling serves to indentify the poducts by kind and make and also protect the cans from rusting.

DATA OF CANNING STRAWBERRIES

Fruit	Types of Can	Strength of of Syrup °Brix	Processing time in minute at 100°C and at 1 atm pressure		
			N0.2	No.21/2	No.of Cans
Strawberries	Lacqured	50	10	15	20

Canning of Gooseberries:-

Gooseberries are best picked underripe, but the berries must not be too immature or they will have little flavour. For canning, green varieties of medium size are preferable, and the following varieties are generally satisfactory: Careless, Keepsa, and Lancashire Lad. Gooseberries which are to be canned must first of all be washed and the stalks and blossom ends removed. On a commercial scale this is done by a machine known as a gooseberry snibber. The interior of this machine is roughened by means of carborundum, and is fitted so that water may be sprayed on to the fruit. The berries are tipped into the machine, the water is turned on, and the belt is moved on to the fast pulley. This causes the base to move at a high speed, the berries are thrown against the roughened surface and the tops and tails are thus rubbed off. The outer skin of the berries is also removed to a certain extent during the operation, and this is an advantage, as it allows the sugar syrup to get into the fruit after canning without the berries wrinkling.

The following times and temperatures are recommended:

Can.	Exhaust at 180°-190°F	Cook in Stationary Cookers at 212°F	Cook in Automatic Cookers at 212°F
A. 2.	6 minutes	10-15 minutes	5-7 minutes
½	6 minutes	2-8 minutes	6-8 minutes
E. 1	5 minutes	10-12 minutes	5-6 minutes

Cans : Types and Sizes:-

The older class of can with the soldered top has now been replaced almost entirely by the sanitary can in which the lid is spun on mechanically. The side of the can is generally lock-seamed, although in certain cases a lap seam is still used.

The method of stating the dimensions of a can, which is used in America and in Great Britain, is to express the dimension of diameter and height each by means of three figures, the first figure representing inches and the next two the number of sixteenths of an inch. Thus a can measuring 3 7/16 by 4½ inches would be given as 307 x 408.

Standard types and sizes of can are now commonly used throughout the fruit and vegetable canning industry and considerable progress has been made towards the agreement of International Standards.

Some Standard Size of Cans

Cans.	Overall Size		Conventional Dimensions	Capacity
	Inches.	Inches.	(1/16 in.)	
5-oz	$2\frac{11}{16}$	$2\frac{1}{8}$	211 x 202	5.5
8-oz.Bean	3	$2\frac{1}{2}$	300 x 208	8.2
Picnic	$2\frac{11}{16}$	$3\frac{1}{16}$	211 x 301	8.3
A. I	$2\frac{11}{16}$	4	211 x 400	11.1

Cans.	Overall Size Inches.	Inches.	Conventional Dimensions (1/16 in.)	Capacity
E. I	$3\frac{1}{16}$	4	301 x 400	14.2
16-oz	3	$4\frac{5}{8}$	300 x 410	16.1
No.1 Tall	$3\frac{1}{16}$	$4\frac{9}{16}$	301 x 409	16.4

PROCESS FLOW DIAGRAM FOR CANNING

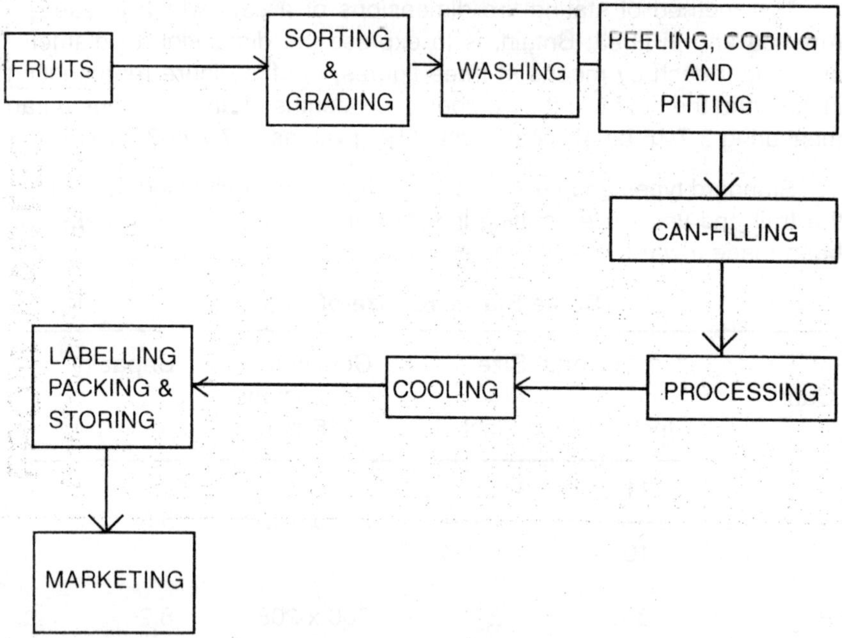

PLANT ECONOMICS

Rated Plant Capacity = 5000.00 Cans/day

LAND & BUILDING

Land Area 2000 sq.mt. = Rs. 44,00,000.00

PLANT & MACHINERY

1. Rotary Fruits washing machine,
2. Sugar Syrup Making unit
3. Fruits Grader,Rotary type,
4. Aluminium and rest unit
5. Peeler
6. Carborandum
7. Fruits Slicer
8. Fruits Slicer, electrically
9. Rotary Dicing & Cubing machine
10. Reforming unit
11. Double Seaming machine
12. Seam checking Gauge
13. Hand Can Tester
14. Vacuum Tester
15. Flange Rectifiers
16. Empty can washer & steriliser
17. Working table stainless steel
18. Aluminium Trays
19. Storage and Fixing Tanks
20. Syrup filling machine
21. Laboratory Equipments
22. Steam Boiler oil fired

FIXED CAPITAL

1.	Land & Building	Rs.	44,00,000.00
2.	Plant & Machinery	Rs.	31,36,000.00
3.	Other Fixed Assets	Rs.	13,80,000.00
	Total	Rs.	89,16,000.00

RAW MATERIALS

1. Fresh Fruits Viz. Pine apples, cherries, plums, litchis, raspberries,
2. Sugar
3. Packaging materials
4. Misc. Labels cartons

TOTAL WORKING CAPITAL/MONTH

1.	Raw Material	Rs.	19,90,000.00
2.	Salary & Wages	Rs.	2,07,000.00
3.	Utilities & Overheads	Rs.	3,91,000.00
	Total	Rs.	25,88,000.00

TOTAL CAPITAL INVESTMENT

Total Fixed Capital	Rs.	89,16,000.00
Total Working Capital for 3 Months	Rs.	77,64,000.00
Total	Rs.	1,66,80,000.00

TURN OVER/ANNUM

By sale of Canned Fruits
(15,00,000 Cans of 500 gm) Rs. 4,35,00,000.00

PROFIT SALES RATIO = Profit/Sales x 100 = 19.92%
RATE OF RETURN = Operating profit/T.C.I x 100 = 51.96%
BREAK EVEN POINT (B.E.P) = 43.41%

Chapter 15

CASHEW FRUIT JUICE

USES AND APPLICATION

Cashew apple juice is used as a beverage for drinking purposes.

It is also used for wine manufacturing and cashew-feni manufacturing.

It is consumed by all categories of people.

It is consumed in hotels, restaurants, juices, corners, etc.

It is consumed in picnic parties, excursions, birthday parties, marriage parties and kitty parties etc.

MANUFACTURING PROCESS

The cashew apple is soft and juicy. When tender, it is acidic and highly astringent, but when fully ripe, it is sweet and only slightly astringent. The fruit is edible and yields a delicious beverage.

Each cashew apple yields 20-25 cc, juice.

The cashew apple juice beverage is prepared by following operational steps.

1. Ripe tendered cashew apples are purchased from market.
2. The fruits are inspected to remove insect or bacterial infestation fruits.
3. Then it is weighed in the weighing scale for required quantity.
4. The fruits are washed with clean water several times to remove dusts, soils, pesticides etc.
5. The fruits are now passed through juice extractor to remove out all juices from cashew apples.
6. The juice is collected in the stainless steel tank.
7. The collected juice is filtered, standardized by addition of sugar, citric acid and edible colour (like beta carotene) etc.
8. The standardized juice is now deaerated by passing through deaeration tank (made of stainless) to remove out all the soluble

gas or oxygen to protect the juice from enzymatic changes by aerial oxidation.

9. The juice is now pasteurized by passing through plate heat exchanger to kill all the pathogens present in it.
10. The pasteurized juice is now packed in the clean glass bottle and crown cork is fitted on the same.
11. The bottled juice is now sterilized in an autoclave for 15-30 seconds at 121°C temperature.
12. The sterilized bottles are bring out from the autoclave and left for cooling. The bottles are labelled with requisite information.
13. These juice bottles are now packed in corrugated cardboard boxes, stored and sent for marketing.

PROCESS FLOW SHEET FOR CASHEW APPLE FRUIT JUICE

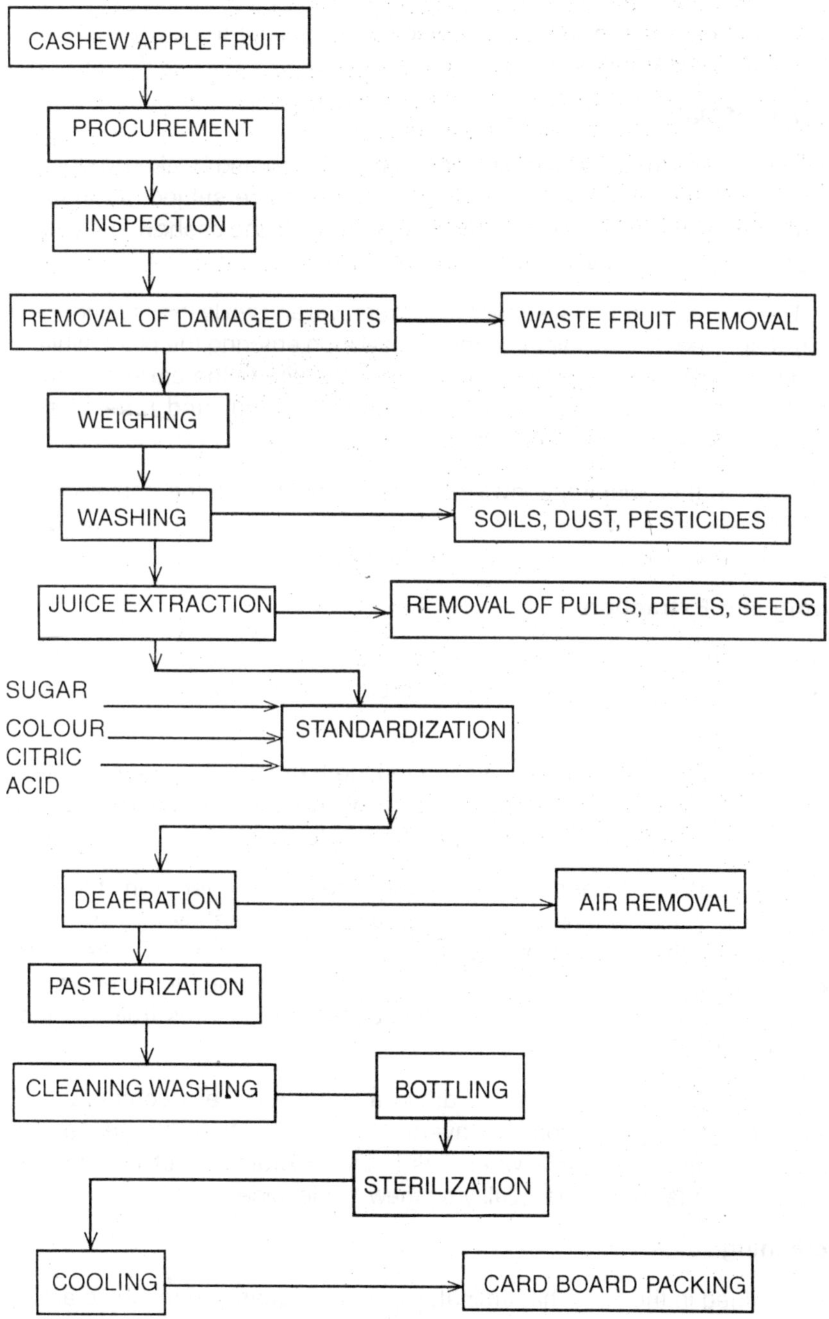

PROCESS OF MANUFACTURING

The processing operations are taken into consideration, while cashew apple juice preparations.

Storage of Material & Cleaning :

While the cashew apple raw material can be stored and stocked in storage bins, it is necessary to give due consideration to the subject so that no changes in form and shape as well as no damage to the cashew apples will occur during storage by loads.

The raw material is first subject to dirt removal and while this is performed it is transported by conveyor into the plant. Upon entering the plant, while it is led to the cleaning conveyor, it is at this place where the earth and sand attached to the raw material, together with the soot, and remnants of agricultural chemicals, among others, must be removed.

While in the cleaning conveyor, a brush attached to the conveyor roll rotates and the raw material, while being transported, is thoroughly cleansed using edible detergents and fresh clean water.

Sizing and Extraction :

While many and various methods exist in regard to juice extraction, the method being widely utilized at the present time is the In-Line Extractor System.

In this system which employs the In-Line Extractor, in juice extraction is effected by a cup matching the size of the cashew apple, the raw material is separated, in advance, according to size.

The separated cashew apples the Feeder Hopper from the belt conveyor in a row where they are, one by one, accurately thrown into a lower cup by the feeder flipper when next an upper cup is lowered with extraction taking place in the lower sector's strainer tube. In other words, in this process, the juice and the solid substances such as fruit rind etc. are separated.

Due to the fact that cashew apple among fruits, are comparatively easier to extract juice, from the average juice extraction ratio, is said to range between 25% - 35% when this In-Line Extractor is utilized for the purpose of obtaining good quality cashew apple juice.

Screening :

Included in the juice that eminates from the squashing machine are to to be found fragments and segments or film of rind together with coarse pulp. For the purpose of removing these substances, they are first screened and separated by a 0.5 mm punching screen in a finisher.

Next, coping with requests, the pulp is separated by decanter and disk centrifuge. Should the pulp not be thoroughly removed, the juices are viscous and in the concentration process get scorched leading to a decline in flavor. Also in the event that the pulp is extremely small in quantity, the coloring of the juice deteriorates and the taste also becomes light and watery.

While it is stated that the most appropriate pulp volume is in the range of 3% to 5%, it is nevertheless possible to adjust this pulp volume by controlling the centrifuges.

Pre-heating & Cooling :

The extracted juice is then heated to temp. 90°C for inactivation of enzyme, after which it is cooled to 40°C.

Sugar Syrup Preparation :

In this stage, sugar, citric acid and water as shown in the formulation are mixed homogeneously with warning to form sugar syrup. This sugar syrup is filtered and mixed with cashew apple juice to make homogeneous product.

To this homogeneous product the rest ingredients like colour, essences are added. Then the whole product is mixed homogeneously for 30 minutes. In this stage the RTS-orange juice beverage is ready for bottling.

The beverage (RTS) is now filled in the cleaned glass bottle. Then crown cap is fixed and sealed on the bottle. The packed cashew apple juice bottle is now pasteurized/sterilized in the continuous bottle sterilizing machine.

As soon as the cashew apple juice bottles are coming out of the sterilizing machine, it is cooled and placed in the crates and despatched for marketing to the consumer.

FLOW DIAGRAM OF READY TO SERVE BEVERAGES

Cashew Apple Beverage

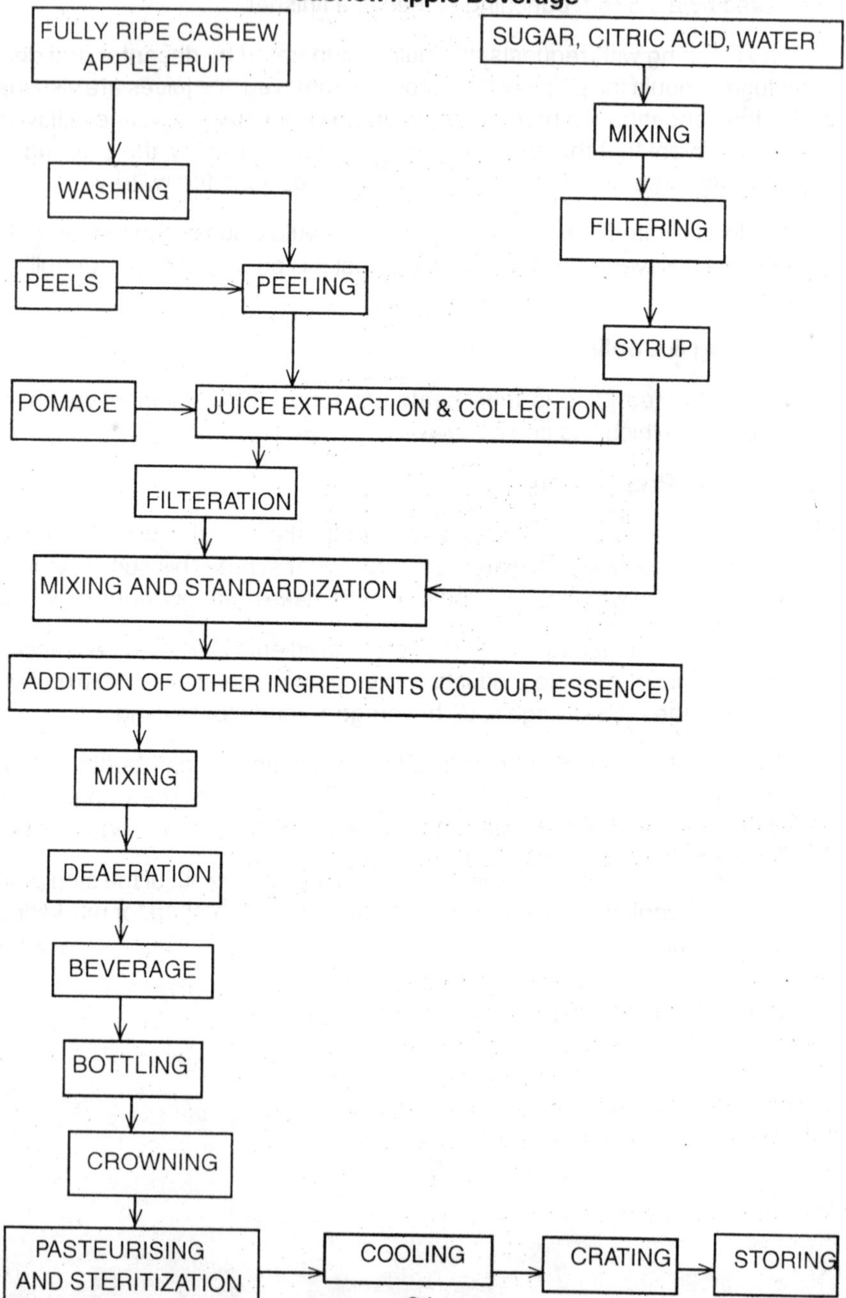

PLANT ECONOMICS

Rated Plant Capacity = 5.00 MT/Day

LAND & BUILDING

Land Area 1 acre = Rs. 30,30,000.00

PLANT & MACHINERY

1. Conveyor belt
2. Goose neck elevator
3. Fruit washing Unit
4. Automatic peeling machine
5. Pulping juice extraction unit
6. Filtration unit
7. Final Beverage blending tank,
8. Plate exchanger (S.S. plates)
9. Boiler (Oil fired)
10. PVC Sintex tank (for water)
11. Card board boxes sealing machine
12. Pipes, pumps, valves

FIXED CAPITAL

1.	Land & Building	Rs.	30,30,000.00
2.	Plant & Machinery	Rs.	43,65,000.00
3.	Other Fixed Assets	Rs.	18,50,000.00
	Total	Rs.	92,45,000.00

RAW MATERIALS

1. Cashew apple fruit,
2. Sugar,
3. Citric acid,
4. Colour (sun set yellow),
5. Essence,
6. Laboratory chemicals
7. Crown
8. Glass bottle (250 ml),

TOTAL WORKING CAPITAL/MONTH

1.	Raw Material	Rs.	11,86,250.00
2.	Salary & Wages	Rs.	3,97,537.00
3.	Utilities & Overheads	Rs.	3,77,000.00
	Total	Rs.	19,60,787.00

TOTAL CAPITAL INVESTMENT

Total Fixed Capital	Rs.	92,45,000.00
Total Working Capital for 3 Months	Rs.	58,82,361.00
Total	Rs.	1,51,27,361.00

TURN OVER/ANNUM

By sale of Cashew apple juice (RTS) beverage, 250 ml size bottle	Rs. 3,60,00,000.00

PROFIT SALES RATIO = Profit/Sales x 100 = 24.55%

RATE OF RETURN = Operating profit/T.C.I x 100 = 58.42%

BREAK EVEN POINT (B.E.P) = 45.41%

Chapter 16

CHOCOLATE

CHOCOLATE MANUFACTURING

Chocolate has two major distinguishing characteristics ,its flavor and its texture. Although many different flavors of chocolate exist, all must be free from objectionable tests and yet incorporate at least some of the pleasant ones, which the consumer will associate with the product. A primary feature of the texture is that it must be solid at room temperature of 20-25 deg. C(70-75 deg.F) and yet a liquid which appears smooth to the tongue. The processing of chocolate is related to obtaining these two criteria , and is therefore devoted either to developing the flavor of product using a raw bean would produce a very unpleasant taste or treating it so that it will flow properly and be free from large gritty material.

Although many different methods of chocolate making exist most traditional ones are based on process outlined in fig. and briefly described below.

Preparation of Cocoa nib -flavor development

The cocoa tree produces pods containing pulp and the raw beans. The outer pod is removed together with some of pulp and the beans are fermented . This enables chemical compounds to develop inside the beans which are the precursors of the flavor in the final chocolate. Failure to carry out this stage properly cannot be rectified by the processing at a later date. This is also true of the subsequent stage when the fermented beans are dried . Poor control at this stage can give rise to moulds, which give a very unpleasant flavored product even if the fermentation has been correct. In addition, correct transport conditions are required when the beans are moved from the country of growing to that of chocolate manufacture.

On arrival it is then necessary to clean the beans to remove metal and stones and other extraneous material which might contarminate the product. Further flavor development is subsequently obtained by roasting the beans . This also loosens the shell round the outside of the bean, and enables them to break more easily. The beans are then broken and relatively lighter shell particles removed by a winnowing action. The presence of shell in final chocolate is undesirable as it will impair the flavor as well as causing excessive wear to the subsequent grinding machine . It should also be noted that the shell content of chocolate is legally restricted in some markets.

The majority of chocolate preparations contain sugar. Some preparations, used for special purposes, are unsweetened or contain saccharin as sweetening agent. Chocolate consumed as beverage often contains up to 20 % arrowroot starch or some otherfarinaceous substance. Chocolate contains more fat than beverage cocoa, and in its manufacture block cocoa is employed as such. In the preparation of products of high quality, cacao butter, obtained as a by-product in cocoa manufacture, is added and the fat content augmented. Due to the high price of coco butter, however, cheaper non-greasy digestible fats, having the hard and brittle, or snap properties of cacao butter, and a low m. (not exceeding 37-38°), are sometimes used to replace cacao butter either wholly or in part. Important among such substitutes is Borneo tallow and refined and deodorized styrenes from coconut and palm kernel oils. More recently hydrogenated coconut and palm kernel oil are being employed.

Plain chocolate is prepared by incorporating sugar, cacao butter, and flavoring materials with cocoa mass, and grinding the mixture in a mill or malinger, to a fine particle size. Eating chocolate contains about 50% sugar. Sucrose should be finely ground before incorporation. Vanilla is the principal flavoring agent, though other essential oils, e.g., cinnamon, clove, mace and nutmeg are sometimes used. The ground mass is then refined by passing it repeatedly through water-cooled massive steel rollers to give a smooth velvety mass without grit. More coco butter is added and the mixture is conched or subjected to rolling pressure in a granite rectangular box fitted with granite rollers having a to-and fro motion. Conching, which is continued for 12-96 hrs., has the effect of removing moisture, mellowing, and eliminating harshness and acidity. It also helps in securing a homogeneous velvety mixture in which every particle of sugar is uniformly coated with cacao butter and improves the keeping properties (Corsbie-Walsh, 220). The conched mass is transferred to tanks and stirred at 120-130°. This treatment liquefies the fat and ensures it s uniform distribution throughout the material thus minimizing the tendency for fat bloom.

The tempered chocolate is cooled, and molded into blocks, bars, cakes, and fancy shapes. Refrigerated moulds are used for removing the liberated latent heat, the rate of heat removal being so controlled that the fat sets in a finely crystalline form.

Milk chocolate contains in addition dried milk powder. The proportion of ingredients used by different makers Vary. Chocolates containing block milk are said to have better texture and better keeping quality than those made with dried milk. Freshly prepared condensed milk may also be incorporated. The product obtained is reported to have the characteristic fresh milk flavor.

GRINDING - PARTICLE SIZE REDUCTION

Up to this stage the cocoa is in discrete pieces, several millimeters in diameter. Subsequent processing may take several forms, but all require the solid cocoa particles , sugar and any milk solids to be broken so that they are small enough not to be detected on the tongue. The actual size depends upon the type of chocolate and the market in which it is sold but in general the vast majority of particles must be smaller than 40 μm ($1.5 * 10^{-2}$ inch).

The most common method of achieving this by the use of five -roll refiner . In order to enable the chocolate ingredients to pass through refinery, however it is necessary to get them into a paste from . This may be done in a variety of ways one of the most common is to grind the nib to form cocoa mass which is liquid at temperatures above the melting point of coco butter. This usually involves hammer mills, discs, mills ball mills, three roll refines or a combination of four. The sugar can than be added in a granulated or milled from and the two mixed with extra fat (and milk powder if milk chocolate is being manufactured). The mixing may include some grinding and traditionally a malinger pan was employed for the purpose. This machine has a rotating pan, often with a granite bed, on which two granite rollers rotate, scrapers ensure mixing by directing the material under the rollers. The modern requirement for a continuous higher through put method has lead to development of devices like the two roll refiner. Which perform an equivalent amount of crushing . An alternative approach, which avoids producing mass is to use the malinger type process to grind the nib, together with other ingredients. This method of making chocolate has tended to lose favour since the demise of the malinger pan.

As described previously , the cocoa mass can also be incorporated into chocolate crumb. This also must be crushed and mixed with fat in order to provide a suitable paste for processing in a refiner.

Couching - Flavor and texture development

Although the fermentation, drying and roasting are able to develop the precursors of chocolate flavor. There are also many undesirable chemical compounds present. There give rise to acidic and astringent tastes in the mouth. The object of couching is to remove the undesirable flavors while developing the pleasant ones. In addition to previous grinding process will have created many new surfaces particularly of sugar which are not coated with fat. There prevent the chocolate flowing properly when the fat is in a liquid state. Because of this chocolate can not yet be used to make sweets and does not have the normal chocolate textures in the mouth. The couching process,therefore, coats these new surfaces with fat and develops the flow chocolate over an extended period in a large tank. Some manufacturers prefer to limit the conching time by restricting the couching process to primarily one of liquefying the chocolate. This is made possible by treating the cocoa mass at an earlier stage in order to remove some of the less desirable volatile chemicals.

CONCHING

ROLLER CANCHES

The origin of the name of this machine is supposed to be from latin meaning "Shell", and traditional canche bears some resemblance in shape to a shell. This is longitudinal canche which consists of a flat granite bed upon which heavy granite rollers attached to robust steel arms more backwards and forwards. The shape of the ends & cause it to splash but are the rollers into the main body of the chocolate.

To assist mechanical arrangement the rolls are usually made to reciprocate from a crank on a drinking rod so that several tanks can be operated from the drive.

Although this seems a very inefficient piece of machinery at less the effect of producing the desired final flavor in the chocolate free from all "Larshness", which is very apparted in non called chocolate. The full effect of this process does not occur until the chocolate is fluid . The chocolate from the refiners is in the form of "Flakes" and to transform thin to a fluid paste or liquid requires mechanical mixing and the addition of cocoa butter. It is necessary to conserve cocoa butter as much as possible for economy reasons. Therefore, the fluidity must be obtained as much as possible by mechanical means. All emulsifier in the form of lecithin is also added to increase fluidity.

To assist the efficiency of there canches, mechanical devices for transforming the refined flake into a more fluid paste have been used before transferring to the conch. Kneaders similar to those described under "Mixing" have been described used successfully. In the newer earthiness conching processes the reduction of the refiner flake to a more fluid paste which can be conched either take place rapidly in the canche itself or in an independent seclras of the machine before the canche proper.

Roller canches are all very similar in design but very enormously in size. In one large manufacturers factory whole batteries of small single roller canche tanks have been seen the rollers reciprocating fairly rapidly and the tank capacity only 300 lb.

At the end of the scale another smaller manufacturer uses a double roller canche working more slowly with a capacity of 10 tons.

There facts illustrate the necessity for continued fundamental research into this processes. The newer Conching methods which have been developed mostly try to initiate the slow mixing process of the roller canche exposing renewed surfaces of the liquid chocolate to the air, and their value has been assessed almost entirely by organoleptic test using trained testing panels.

The roller canche process ~~uses~~ temperature which are within fairly defined limits, which are for milk chocolate 46 deg.-52 deg. C.(115 -125 deg.C) and for dark chocolate 60 -70 deg.C (140 deg.c - 160 deg.F) High temperature (upto 140 deg.F) may be used for milk.

Chocolate to give carnmelized flavors, and up to 180 deg.F or above for dark chocolate to give a slightly burnt or high roast flavor. With dark chocolate the higher temperature can be applied to this films a heated rollers and here by reduce the total canching time.

The canching times used are usually to 24 his for milk chocolate or 20 -90 his for dark chocolate. It dark chocolate is used for covering purposes , stray added flavors are sometime used and in case canching periods can be reduced each considerably to as like as four hours.

Viscosity of chocolate -use of emulsifiers

With the development of highly automatic chocolate moulding and enrobing machinery, the accurate control of fluidity a viscosity has become very important further name, it has become necessary to conserve the expensive weather ingredients by the use of emulsifiers and mechanical methods to get increased fluidity to lower fat content chocolates. The fluidity or viscosity of chocolate cannot be defined by a single figure as, because of the presence of many solids (sugar, weoa material, crumb)- It behaves as a has-newtom,ain liquid and its actual viscosity depends on the speed at which it is mixed i.e. rate of shear.

The solid can be further increased by the presence of local butter crystals which must, of necessity , be present in tempered chocolate,a nd since this can be available facts depending on the method of tempering and the amount of the seed a true viscosity of chocolate use in a process is difficult to obtain. In practice it is usually sufficient to control the viscosity of the untempered chocolate, and simple factory instruments based in the redwood viscometer for this, and the falling Ball for thick chocolates, have been employed successfully. There are used in the factory department and are calibrates against laboratory instruments of the rotating cylinder type and compared with chocolate fat contents obtained by analyhi with the increased automatics and the use of automatic appearing devices, viscosity control is now more easily achieved provided there is not great variations ingredients.

Traces of free moisture will increase viscosity neatly and moisture determination as the chocolate will non necessarily give any useful information. It is more appropriate to inspect plant for minute water or steam leaks a to examine the ingredients being used sugar a crumb may contain local partless of damp material but this to less likely in bulk suppliers. It may occur occasionally in bulk storage bins due to a faulty or prised seam. "Rework" can cause trouble, particularly it invest sugar is present and very occasionally ,under conditives of extreme atmospheric humidity, moisture can be absorbed on the this layers of chocolate as the refining rolls.

FORMULATIONS

Milk Chocolates

	Milk High	chocolate Average	Low	Typical milk crumb	Enzyme Treated milk chocolate
	%	%	%	%	%
Cocoa mass	14	11.78	10	12.00	12.00
Whole milk powder	23.6	19.08	18		10.92
Whole milk (roller)					
Whole Milk (Spray)					
Enzyme heated (WMP)					3.00
Sugar	46	48.73	55		52.23
Added cocoa butter	16	19.98	16.5	18.0	21.35
Lecithin	0.4	0.35	0.38		0.3
Salt				70.0	
Vanillin		.08	.06	.06	
Total	100	100	100	100	100
Total fat	80.00	31.5	27.00	31.32	32.0

Milk Chocolate

	Dutch milk chocolate	British milk chocolate
	%	%
Cocoa mass	15.7	15.84
Milk powder	16.22	13.28
Whole milk (roller)		
Whole milk (spray)		
Enzyme treated (WMP)	Skinned milk powder	
	7.57	
Sugar	30.83	45.20
Added cocoa butter	29.20	25.36
Lecithin	Cinnamon	
0.16		
Salt	0.16	
Vanillin	Vanilla pods	
	0.16	.04
Total	100	100
Total fat	42.06	37.50

Coating chocolate

i) Typical CBE coating

	Park		Milk	White		
	A	B	A	B	A	B
Cocoa Mass	40	20	10	10	-	-
Cocoa powder		10	-	-	-	-
F.C. Milk powder	-	-	20	-	20	-
Skimmed milk powder	-	-	-	15	5	20
CBE	10	20	22	27	27	32
Sugar	50	50	48	48	48	48
Total	100	100	100	100	100	100
Total fat	32	32.5	32.5	32	32	32

ii) Typical lauric fat coating (For covering centers, cookies panned goods)

	Park		Milk		White	
			A	B	A	B
Cocoa powder(10-12%)	14		5	5	-	-
F.C.M powder	-		10	020	-	
S.M. Powder	7		10	17.5 5	20	
Lauric CBR	31		29	31.527	32	
Sugar	48		46	46	48	48
Total	100	100	100	100	100	
Total fat	32	32	32	32	32	

iii) Typical non-lauric fat coating (for cakes, water and crispy centers)

	Park		Milk	White		
	A	B	A	B	A	B
Cocoa mass	10	-	10	-	-	-
Cocoa powder	15	20	-	5	-	-
F. C Milk powder	-	-	6	-	20	-
S. M powder	-	-	12	17	5	20
Non-lauric CBR	28	33	28	34	30	35
Sugar	47	47	44	44	44	45
Total	100	100	100	100	100	100
Total fat	35	35	35	34.5	35	35

Couverture chocolate

Cocoa nib	Sugar	Added Fat	Total fat	Protein index	Nib/sugar
41	46	13	36	5.5	0.89
38	46.5	16	35.5	5.35	0.02
37	51	11.5	32	5.18	0.72
37	45.5	17.8	37	5.25	0.81
34.5	48	18	36.5	5.0	0.72
32	46.5	21	38	4.44	0.69

Dark Chocolates

Ingredient	Bitter sweet			Dark		
	High %	Av. %	Low %	High %	Av. %	Low %
Blended beans /cocoa mass	70	60.65	55	43	39.62	35
Sugar	29.8	36.25	42.04	48	48.08	50.37
Added cocoa butter		2.6	1.70	7.83	11.75	14.15
Lecithin	0.3	0.3	0.3	0.3	0.35	0.30
Salt				.06	.06	.06
Vanillin		0.2		.04	0.14	0.12
Vanillin beans						
Total	100	100	100	100	100	100
Total fat	37.10	35.35	31.4	31.2	33.1	33.1

Dark Chocolate

Ingredients	Dark Chocolate
Blended beans/cocoa mass	43.18
Sugar	43.40
Added Cocoa butter	13.04
Lecithin	0.30
Salt	
Vanillin	
Vanilla beans	
Total	100
Total fat	36.35

Milk Chocolate:

Fat - free cocoa mass	- 15%
Cacao Butter	- 25%
Sugar	- 40%
Milk Powder	- 20%

English Milk Chocolate:

Protein	- 7.4%
Milk Fat	- 5.5%
Cacao Butter	- 26.3%
Lactose	- 8%
Sucrose	- 43.2%

Chocolate Toffee:

Sugar	- 10 lb.
Corn Syrup	- 10 lb.
Coconut Butter	- 8 oz.
Salt	- 1 table spoonful
Fresh Cream	- 2 mt.
Evaporated milk	- 2 lb.
Butter	- 21 lb.
Butter Chocolate	- 2.5 lb.
Vanilla flavor	- 3 teaspoon fulls

Chocolate Annex Caramels

Sugar	- 11 lb.
Corn Syrup	- 15 lb.
coconut	- 1 lb.
Salt	- 1 Teaspoon full
Fresh 18% light cream	- 4 qt.
Evaporated milk	- 8 lb.
Caramel	- 5 lb.
Bitter chocolate cut up)	- 4 lb.
Vanilla flavor	- 3 teaspoon fulls
Dipping Marshmallos	- 3 lb.

The sugar, corn syrup, salt, coconut butter and cream are placed in a large copper pan on the stove and stirred until dissolved. When the batch stirred until dissolved. When the batch begins to boil, the evaporated milk is stirred in gradually stirring is continued while the patch is cooking. The caromed plastic is added and the batch is cooked until it forms a medium balls when tested in cold water. The batch is removed to a stand and the chocolate and flavor are added and stirred until completely melted. After adding the marshmallows and mixing well the batch is poured out on a greased slab between iron bars and spread out evenly with a pellet knife. It is allowed to cool until it is hard enough to hand. Then it is passed through a sizing machine, cut into square caramels and wrapped as usual. This batch yield 48 pounds product.

PROGRESS FLOW CHART

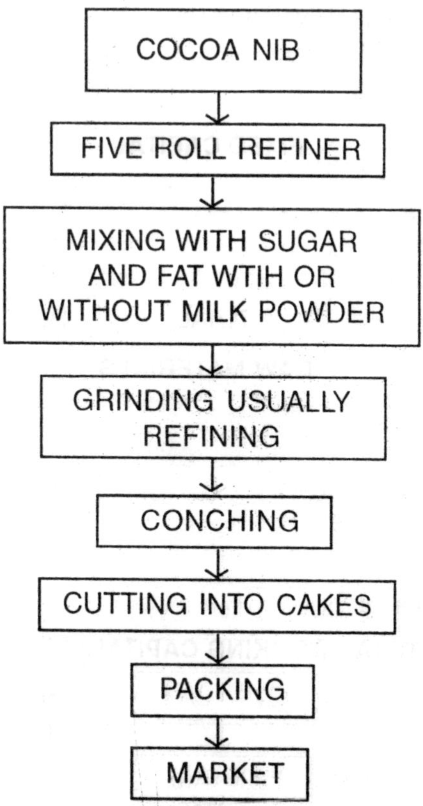

PLANT ECONOMICS

Rated Plant Capacity = 500.00 Kg./Day

LAND & BUILDING

Land Area 500 Sq.mts. = Rs. 12,63,000.00

PLANT & MACHINERY

1. Pulveriser for Sugar
2. Mixer
3. Refiner
4. Conching Machine
5. Tank (ss)
6. Moulding Tray
7. Pumps, Pipe fittings valves and Miscellaneous machinery
8. Printing & Wrapping

FIXED CAPITAL

1.	Land & Building	Rs.	12,63,000.00
2.	Plant & Machinery	Rs.	4,85,000.00
3.	Other Fixed Assets	Rs.	2,83,000.00
	TOTAL	Rs.	20,31,000.00

RAW MATERIALS

1. Milk Powder
2. Sugar
3. Flavours,Essences etc.
4. Cocoa Butter
5. Cocoa Mass
6. Packaging material

TOTAL WORKING CAPITAL/MONTH

1.	Raw Material	Rs.	5,48,300.00
2.	Salary & Wages	Rs.	88,530.00
3.	Utilities & Overheads	Rs.	84,000.00
	TOTAL	Rs.	7,20,830.00

TOTAL CAPITAL INVESTMENT

Total Fixed Capital	Rs.	20,31,000.00
Total Working Capital for 2 Months	Rs.	14,41,660.00
TOTAL	Rs.	34,72,660.00

TURN OVER/ANNUM

1. By Sale of 3000000 Pcs. Chocolate of 50 gms. Weight	Rs.	1,12,50,000.00

PROFIT SALES RATIO = Profit / Sales x 100 = 17.26 %

RATE OF RETURN = Operating profit / T.C.I x 100 = 55.92 %

BREAK EVEN POINT (B.E.P) = 43.35 %

Chapter 17

DAIRY FARM (BUFFALOE)

The domesticated water buffallo is one of the gentiest of all farm animals. Despite an intimidating appearance it is more like a house hold pat-sociable, gentle, and serve. In rural Asia the care of buffalloes is after turned over to small boys & girls aged about 4 to 9.

Another belief is that the buffallo is exclusively a tropical animal. River type buffalloes, However, have been used to pull snow plows during Bulgarian winter.

Buffallo milk has a higher content of both butter fat and non fat-solids than cows milk does. Throughout much India it is in such demand that Cow's milk is sometimes hard to sell.

Breeds: The major genetic division of the buffallo are the swamp Buffallo of the eastern half of the Asia, which has swept back horns and the river buffalo of the western half of Asia which usually has the curled horns. There is also the mediterranean buffalo, which is of the river type but has been isolated for so long that it has developed some unique characteristics.

Although there is only one breed of swamp buffallo, certain sub-groups seem to have specific inherited characteristics. Swamp buffalloes range from 250 kg for some small animals in China, 200-300 kg in Berma and 500-600 kgs in Laos. Only in India and Pakistan are there well defined breeds with standard qualities. There are eighteen (18) river buffallo breeds in south asia which are further classified as the Murrah, Gujrat, Uttar Pradesh, Central Indian & South Indian breeds.

COMPOSITION OF CATTLE FEED

There is no definite composition to Buffalo feed compound but in general practice the following composition is followed :-

Ground nut Cake	25%
Wheat bran	27%
Grain Husk	15%
Maize	30%
Mineral	1%
Salt	2%

MANUFACTURING PROCESS

The manufacturing process for Dairy milk is started with the milking buffaloes by hand (at small scale) & milking buffaloes by machine (at large scale).

The detailed process is given here with :-

MILKING BUFFALOES BY HAND

The profitable operation of a dairy herd depends in a large part upon how well you milk your buffaloes. You can do everything else carefully and well, but if you do not milk your buffaloes properly, you can never be successful in dairying. Poor milking habits cause low production, mastitis, & poor quality milk. An important part of milking buffaloes is to produce the cleanest possible milk. Milk must be low in sediment.

Although machine milking is rapidly replacing hand milking, many dairymen still use the latter. In milking by hand, buffaloes must be carefully prepared to produce high quality milk.

COOLING & STORING MILK

The careless handling of milk between milking & delivering to the plant can cause high bacteria counts to develop in the milk thus a mechanical cooler is employed for the purpose. Whole of the milk should be stored at 50^{0}F to prevent spoilage. Storage Tanks made of stainless steel are employed for storing the raw milk.

FILTERATION :

The cold raw milk is filtered, however, it can be filtered before cooling & storing in tank, but the precaution is to be taken at this stage so that no foreign matters or undesired materials may be carried on.

HOMOGENIZATION:

Filtered milk is fed into homogeniser. Homogenization is the process by which the milk is emulsified and are further divided to produce a more stable emulsion that will not separate on standing. The fat is emulsified with liquid part of milk that are water mostly. Hence, to prevent sedimentation or fat in milk. This homogenization process is done. By this way high quality homogenized milk is produced.

After feeding the milk into homogenizer, the pressure of the homogenizer is increased about 2500 psi. However, if this pressure does not produce milk that meets the standard, it may be necessary to use a pressure as high as 3000 to 3500 Lb.

CLASSIFICATION:

The milk is passed through a clarifier as it leaves the homogenizer. Cold milk clarification is preferred to hot milk. This clarification operation can be performed before homogenization. But the complete clarification can be achieved at this stage.

Clarifier can be replaced by cream separator but since the separator bowl is not designed to hold a large amount of sediment and consequently is not efficient for clarifying a large volume of milk. However, This operation can be omitted to get high quality milk.

PASTEURIZATION:-

In this process, the clarified milk is fed to pasteurizer and heated to the required temperature & held there during the holding period (usually at 145°F & for at least 30 minutes). Vat pasteurizer with jackets & agitators is employed for the pasteurization.

The milk is heated by hot water or steam passing into the space between the two tanks. In this process, excessive heating of any part of the milk & a consequent "cooked" flavour is prevented.

At the end of the holding period, the cold water is circulated through the jacket or coil of the pasteurizer, Temperature of the milk may be quickly lowered 10° to 15°, & at this point the heated flavour will not continue to develop. This is done to destroy all pathogenic bacteria.

REFRIGERATION OR FREEZING SYSTEM

After the complete processing of milk it is to be stored in a cold upto chilling condition so that no unwanted micro-organisms/pathogenic organism can be developed in the processed milk. It is stored until delivered for distribution i.e. for packing in Cans or pouches.

PLANT ECONOMICS

Rated Plant Capacity	=	DAIRY FARM (1200 LTR./DAY)
LAND & BUILDING (Land required 2000 sq.mt.)	=	Rs. 21,80,000.00

PLANT & MACHINERY

1. Steam boiler
2. Homogenizer complete with accessory
3. Refrigeration system consists of air compressor, refrigerants & cerenlating tube tank
4. Pasteurizer with cooling arrangement
5. Filter (ordinary)
6. Pouch making, filling & sealing Machine complete automatic with printing arrangement
7. Milk reception tank
8. Milk Cans (Aluminium)
9. Dies different capacity
10. Buffalloes Kundi 100 Nos.
11. Misc. other equipments such as Laboratory & testing equipments

FIXED CAPITAL

1.	Land & Building	Rs.	21,80,000.00
2.	Plant & Machinery	Rs.	17,17,000.00
3.	Other Fixed Assets	Rs.	4,20,000.00
	TOTAL	Rs.	43,17,000.00

RAW MATERIALS

1. Raw Material for Buffaloes feed green fodder/Cattle feed
2. Health expenses (medicines) etc.
3. Raw material i.e. pouch, Polythene sheet etc.
4. Misc. other items such as printing ink etc.

TOTAL WORKING CAPITAL/MONTH

1. Raw Material	Rs.	59,500.00
2. Salary & Wages	Rs.	38,750.00
3. Utilities & Overheads	Rs.	15,200.00
TOTAL	Rs.	1,13,450.00

TOTAL CAPITAL INVESTMENT

Total Fixed Capital	Rs.	43,17,000.00
Total Working Capital for 3 Months	Rs.	3,40,350.00
TOTAL	Rs.	46,57,350.00

TURN OVER/ANNUM

By sale of 1200 x 365 litres of Milk	Rs.	52,56,000.00

PROFIT SALES RATIO = Profit / Sales x 100 = 45.14 %

RATE OF RETURN = Operating profit / T.C.I x 100 = 50.94 %

BREAK EVEN POINT (B.E.P) = 42.88 %

Chapter 18

DAIRY FARM TO PRODUCE MILK (JERSEY COW)

There are different kinds of milk obtained from different animals, like cows, buffalow, goat, camel and many others. But generally we use goat milk, cow milk, and buffalow milk. The following gives analysis of milk from goat and cow.

INGREDIENTS	COW MILK	GOAT MILK
Water	87.40	87.54
Solids	0.75	0.85
Casein	3.00	3.00
Albumen	0.40	1.00
Fats	3.75	4.50
Sugar	4.70	4.50

People with very low vitality have to live on milk products for some times, with fruit to supplement, it. In some foreign countries, milk obtained from animals like vama selue Hippopotamies, Gluens, pig and Blue whole etc. is used.

CATTLE FEED

The success of the development project depends largely on the availability of well - balanced feed in respect of carbohydrates, proteins vitamins & minerals. Therefore the need for balanced cattle feed as an addition to the green fodder & hay for the general improvement of the cattle health forms an essential part of the intensive cattle development programme.

In general practice the following composition is followed for cattle feed.

Groundnut Cake	25%
Wheat bran	27%
Grain Husk	15%
Maize	30%
Mineral	1%
salt	2%

Some more formulations are as folows: -

A.	Wheat or rice bran	55%
	Soya Bean or Groundnut cake	35%
	Molasses	8%
	Mineral Supplement	2%
B.	Wheat or rice bran	26%
	Coconut	65%
	Molasses	8%
	Mineral Supplement	2%
C.	Citrus Pulp	27%
	Coconut Cake	63%
	Molasses	8%
	Mineral Supple	2%

MANUFACTURING PROCESS

The manufacturing process for Dairy milk is started with the milking cows by hand (at small scale) & milking cows by machine (at large scale).

The detailed process is given here with :-

MILKING COWS BY HAND

The profitable operation of a dairy herd depends in a large part upon how well you milk your cows. You can do everything else carefully and well, but if you do not milk your cows properly, you can never be successful in dairying. Poor milking habits cause low production, mastitis, & poor quality milk. An important part of milking cows is to produce the cleanest possible milk. Milk must be low in sediment.

Although machine milking is rapidly replacing hand milking, many dairymen still use the latter. In milking by hand, cows must be carefully prepared to produce high quality milk.

COOLING & STORING MILK

The careless handling of milk between milking & delivering to the plant can cause high bacteria counts to develop in the milk thus a mechanical cooler is employed for the purpose. Whole of the milk should be stored at 50°F to prevent spoilage. Storage Tanks made of stainless steel are employed for storing the raw milk.

FILTERATION :

The cold raw milk is filtered, however, it can be filtered before cooling & storing in tank, but the precaution is to be taken at this stage so that no foreign matters or undesired materials may be carried on.

HOMOGENIZATION:

Filtered milk is fed into homogeniser. Homogenization is the process by which the milk is emulsified and are further divided to produce a more stable emulsion that will not separate on standing. The fat is emulsified with liquid part of milk that are water mostly. Hence, to prevent sedimentation of fat in milk. This homogenization process is done. By this way high quality homogenized milk is produced.

After feeding the milk into homogenizer, the pressure of the homogenizer is increased about 2500 psi. However, if this pressure does not produce milk that meets the standard, it may be necessary to use a pressure as high as 3000 to 3500 Lb.

CLARIFICATION:

The milk is passed through a clarifier as it leaves the homogenizer. Cold milk clarification is preferred to hot milk. This clarification operation can be perform before homogenization. But the complete clarification can be achieved at this stage.

Clarifier can be replaced by cream separator but since the separator bowl is not designed to hold a large amount of sediment and consequently is not efficient for clarifying a large volume of milk. However, This operation can be omitted to get high quality milk.

PASTEURIZATION:-

In this process, the clarified milk is fed to pasteurizer and heated to the required temperature and held there during the holding period (usually at 145°F & for at least 30 minutes). Vat pasteurizer with jackets & agitators is employed for the pasteurization.

The milk is heated by hot water or steam passing into the space between the two tanks. In this process, excessive heating of any part of the milk and a consequent "cooked" flavour is prevented.

At the end of the holding period, the cold water is circulated through the jacket or coil of the pasteurizer, Temperature of the milk may be quickly lowered 10° to 15°, & at this point the heated flavour will not continue to develop. This is done to destroy all pathogenic bacteria.

REFRIGERATION OR FREEZING SYSTEM

After the complete processing of milk it is to be stored in a cold upto chilling condition so that no unwanted micro-organisms/pathogenic organism can be developed in the processed milk. It is stored until delivered for distribution i.e. for packing in cans or pouches.

TESTING:-

The testing of milk is an essential for the quality control purposes. However, testing may be done prior to storage under freezing condition. But it is better to test the final product before packing. When product is cleared from testing or quality control section then it is ready for packing & distribution and sent to packing section.

PACKING:-

There are two methods adopted from packing milk. Firstly packed or stored in aluminium milk cans for distribution. Secondly, milk packed in plastic pouches of capacity 1/2 kg, 1 kg, & 2 kgs packs.

Milk is stored in milk cans. There will no difficulty. It is traditional. But, in pouches filling of milk is to be performed with a great care and skilled operator is to be employed for this purpose. Automatic pouch making, milk filling & pouch sealing machine is available with printing provision.

Milk filled & sealed in pouches is now ready for despatch and distribution for marketing.

PLANT ECONOMICS

Rated Plant Capacity	=	700.00 LTS/Day
LAND & BUILDING (Land 1 Acre)	=	Rs. 27,87,500.00

PLANT & MACHINERY

1. Steam Boiler
2. Homogenizer
3. Refrigeration
4. Pasteurizer with cooling arrangement
5. Filter (ordinary)
6. Pouch making, filling and sealing Machine complete automatic with printing
7. Milk reception tank (stainless steel make)
8. Milk can (aluminium)
9. Dies

FIXED CAPITAL

1.	Land & Building	Rs.	27,87,500.00
2.	Plant & Machinery	Rs.	5,12,500.00
3.	Other Fixed Assets (Including Jersey Cows)	Rs.	10,60,000.00
	TOTAL	Rs.	43,60,000.00

RAW MATERIALS

1. Raw material for cattle feed.
   Green Fodder/cattle feed
2. Health expenses
3. Raw material for pouch polythene sheet

TOTAL WORKING CAPITAL/MONTH

1.	Raw Materials	Rs.	57,187.00
2.	Salary & Wages	Rs.	28,560.00
3.	Utilities & Overheads	Rs.	32,000.00
	TOTAL	Rs.	1,17,747.00

TOTAL CAPITAL INVESTMENT

Total Fixed Capital	Rs.	43,60,000.00
Total Working Capital for 2 Months	Rs.	2,35,495.00
TOTAL	Rs.	45,95,495.00

TURN OVER/ANNUM

By sale of 252000 litres milk (Homogenized and pasteurized)	Rs.	37,80,000.00

PROFIT SALES RATIO = Profit / Sales x 100 = 40.10 %

RATE OF RETURN = Operating profit / T.C.I x 100 = 32.98 %

BREAK EVEN POINT (B.E.P) = 42.97 %

Chapter 19

DAIRY PRODUCTS & MILK PACKAGING IN POUCHES GHEE, BUTTER, PANEER AND CASEIN, FLAVOURED MILK, CHEESE, YOGHURT AND ICE CREAM

Milk is an Important human food. It is palatable, easy to digest and highly nutritives. It contains proteins, fat, sugar, minerals and a liberal quantity of different kinds of vitamins.

In World milk production, India ranks next only to the United States of America and the U.S.S.R. But the milk produced in India is far from adequate for its vast population as the daily average consumption per head comes to even less than half of the optimum requirement of about 310 grams.

Unlike rich countries like the U.K. and the U.S. dairying in India is a subsidiary occupation of almost all the farmers. More than 60 per cent of the families involved in dairying belong to the small or marginal farmers or even agricultural labourers.

In the first half of the 1900 dairying in the country was largely unorganised, except for military farm which were established and largely stocked with the european breeds. In the plantation areas, pure breed exotic bulls were randomly crossbred with local cows. Apart from the "pockets" of improved animals thus created, dairying was largely left in the hands of traditional producers, middle man, product makers and vendors.

MANUFACTURING PROCESS

COOLING AND STORING MILK:

The careless handling of milk between milking and delivering to the place can cause high bacteria counts to develop in the milk, a mechanical cooler is employed for the purpose. Whole of the milk should be started at 50°F to prevent spoilage. Storage tanks made of stainless steel are employed for storing the raw milk.

FILTERATION:

The cold raw milk is filtered, however, it can be filtered before cooling and storing in tank, but the precaution is to be taken at this stage so that no foreign matters or understand materials may be carried on.

STANDARDISATION:

Milk is standardised according to ISI specification or according to requirements by wholesaler.

HOMOGENISATION:

Filtered milk is fed into homogenizer. Homogenization is the process by which the milk is emulsified and are further divided to produce a more stable emulsion that will not separate on standing. The fat is emulsified with liquid part of milk that are at water mostly. Hence to prevent sedimentation of fat in milk that homogenization process is done. But this way high quality homogenized milk is produced.

After feeding the milk into homogenizer, the pressure of the homogenizer is increased about 2500 psi. However, of this pressure does not produce milk that meets the standard, it may be necessary to use a pressure high as 3000 to 3500 LB.

A uniform, steady pressure is necessary to secure satisfactory homogenization. The milk should have a slight, positive pressure. Otherwise air may be drawn into the pistons which causes the needles of the pressure gauge to vibrate. Such a result indicates irregular presssure.

Sediment may appear in the operation which is undesirable. To reduce sediment, clarification is done.

CLARIFICATION :

The milk is passed through a clarifier is it leaves the homogenizer. Cold milk clarification is preferred to hot milk. This clarification operation can be perform before homogenization but the complete clarification can be achieved at this stage clarifier can be replaced by cream separator but since the separator bowl is not designed to hold a large amount of sediment and consequently is not efficient for clarifying a large volume of milk. However, this operation can be omitted to get high quality milk.

PASTEURISATION :

The milk after clarification is passed through a plate heat exchanger for pasteurisation. In plate heat exchanger (P.H.E.) the milk is pasteurized by UHT method. It is modern method of pastedurisation of milk and used where large volumes of milk are handled. The UHT pasteuriser gives a continuous flow of milk which is fully pasteurised and free from pathogens.

After complete processing milk is stored in cold upto chilling conditions so that unwanted micro organisms/pathogenic micro Organism can not be developed in the processed milk. It is sacred until delivered for distribution to wholesalers.

Testing:-

The testing of milk is an essential for the quality control purposes however may be done prior to storage under freezing condition.

Distribution:-

After Complete processing, the processed milk is checked for proper pasteurisation by quality controller. Then the milk at 1 or 2°C is supplied to the wholesalers present at distant places by the tanker or by filling in the big stainless steel cans. Under chilling conditions Temp may rise to 7 to 8°C during transportation.

MANUFACTURE OF CASEIN

If we want to make better quality of casein the fat content of the skimed milk, from which it is made, should be minimum. Therefore it is necessary, the cream may be again separated from skimed milk so that its fat content is minimum.

After separating the last trace of cream from the skim milk it is heated 350°C and filled in the wooden tank equipped with a hand agitator for mechanical agitator. For coagulation of casein 150 ml of dilute hydrochloric acid (1 part of acid into 1 parts water) and is added by spray pump slowly and stearing is continued. Milk starts coagulating as the acid is added and coagulated mas settles down at bottom. When complete coagulation has taken place, the mass is allowed to settle for half an hour. Now the stop coke is opened and the whey is drained over a draining cock made of wire cloth fixed in wooden frame, so that the coagulated mas is retained over it. The coagulated mass is again dropped into the tank for washing.

Now-a-days a different types of filter is using to separate whey.

Washing is done in the tank by adding dilute acid water (8 C.C. acid is 50 list of water). The acid is added sufficient quantity so that coagulation is completely under water. After ten minutes, the water is drained out. Two such type of required more. It should be remembered that washing should be such type that there should be leaving no whey.

The coagulation is hanged is a cloth so that water tickles down. Even after this process there is sufficient water present necessiry squeezing and processing. For this the cloth filled with coagulation is put under two wooden frames and pressed by putting some weight.

A screw press may be used for the same purpose as it makes the pressing very easy. The casein is now from of a cake.

Now the cake should be cut into pieces. Then the pieces are rubbed on over a 10 mesh more cloth fixed in a wooden frame. Granules of casein are obtained below the sieve.

The next step is to dry the granules. If the production is 5-10 kg. casein per day and it is stirringly run that the charging can be done in open by spreading the granules over white sheets on a coat, but if larger production is required a tray dryer will be needed.

Tray dryer is a almirah which is heated inside with electric elements. Granul is placed in trays which are put in place over the sacks provided in the almirah. the heating can also be done with coal.

The granules are next ground to powder. Different types of grinding machines are available including driven. If powder is available that it is casein to run the grinder in the keep of 1/2 H.P. motor. The powder is packed in polythene bags which are placed in card board boxes. Indian standard institution has precized the requirement for edible quality casein code No. IS: 1167-1965.

YOGHURT FROM MILK

It is an indisputable fact that the enormously increasing popularity of yoghurt, now becoming available throughout the world, is primarily based on the cultural and biochemical performance of lactic cultures, namely, Streptococcus thermophilus and Lactobacillus bulgaricus. These are the corner stones upon which the success or failure of yoghurt processing hinges.

Although our knowledge regarding the growth and biochemical performance of yoghurt lactic cultures in cow milk has been well established, there is paucity of informtion on this aspect in milk of other species like buffalo. Attempts have been made to obtain information on the ability of lactic cultures in the preparation on three types of yoghurt; namely, plain yoghurt, fruits yoghurt and sweetend yoghurt by the procedure indicated in the flow sheet.

Processing:-

Cow and buffalo milk samples are individually steamed for 30 min., cooled to a temperature of 43°C then inoculated at 3% level with Str. thermophilus and Lb. bulgaricus in equal proportions (1:1). The contents are mixed thoroughly and filled in glass bottles covred with lids or aluminium foil caps, transferred to water bath maintained at 42°C±0.5°C. After incubation for 3.0-3.5 hrs. when the coagulum is formed, the bottles are removed from waterbath, cooled at 30oC for 1/2 hr. and transferred to refrigerator for overnight storage.

PLANT ECONOMICS

Rated Plant Capacity = 3390.00 Kgs./Day
(Milk Processing = 10000 litres/day)

LAND & BUILDING (Land 8553.mts.) Rs. 1,16,51,500.00

PLANT & MACHINERY

1. Centrifuge or Cream separator
2. Pasteuriser with cooling arrangements and accessories
3. Refrigeration system consists of air Compressor, refrigerator and brine circulating tank
4. Filter ordinary
5. Milk reception tank (stainless steel)
6. Water softener unit
7. Steam boiler
8. Miscellaneous equipments as laboratory testing equipments
9. Automatic Pouch filling & sealing machine.
10. Vacuum Pan Evaporator
11. Vertical Storage Tank with stirrer
12. Vertical storage tanks
13. Neutralisation tank
14. Pasteurisation Unit
15. Fermenting tank
16. Churner
17. Ghee receiving kettle
18. Pipe fitting, pumps, motor, valve and other miscellaneous machinery
19. Screw Press
20. Oscillating Granulator
21. Tray Dryer
22. Grinding Machine
23. Wash Water Storage tank,

FIXED CAPITAL

1.	Land & Building	Rs.	1,16,51,500.00
2.	Plant & Machinery	Rs.	98,30,000.00
3.	Other Fixed Assets	Rs.	33,00,000.00
	TOTAL	Rs.	2,47,81,500.00

RAW MATERIALS

1. Milk
2. Chemicals for butter paneer, cheese flavoured milk etc.
3. Hydrochloric Acid
4. Cans, Polyethene, packets, Corrugated boxes etc.
5. Culture or Innoculum

TOTAL WORKING CAPITAL/MONTH

1.	Raw Material	Rs.	45,05,800.00
2.	Salary & Wages	Rs.	2,75,310.00
3.	Utilities & Overheads	Rs.	6,32,500.00
	TOTAL	Rs.	54,13,610.00

TOTAL CAPITAL INVESTMENTS

Total Fixed Capital	Rs.	2,47,81,500.00
Total Working Capital for 2 Months	Rs.	1,08,27,220.00
TOTAL	Rs.	3,56,08,720.00

TURN OVER/ANNUM

1. Paneer 60,000 Kgs.
2. Butter 300000 Kgs.
3. Ghee 372000 Kgs.
4. Casein 42,000 kgs.
5. Milk 600000 litres in pouches
6. Cheese 60000 kgs.
7. Ice cream 210000 Kgs.
8. Yoghurt 180000 kgs.

TOTAL Rs. 10,26,60,000.00

PROFIT SALES RATIO = Profit / Sales x 100 = 28.64 %

RATE OF RETURN = Operating profit / T.C.I x 100 = 82.56 %

BREAK EVEN POINT (B.E.P) = 30.09 %

Chapter 20

DEHYDRATION OF FRUITS & VEGETABLES (FREEZE DRYING METHOD)

Dehydrated vegetables, however, lost some of their popularity owing to some undesirable changes in colour, taste and flavour during storage and distribution. Dehydration techniques have since been greatly improved to get over most of these defects so that the modern dehydrated food is really a first class product in every way. It is sometimes said that the dehydration industry will one day be the most important one among the food preservation industries employing various other well-known methods of preservation such as canning, freezing, addition of chemical preservatives, etc. There is scope for advanced scientific as well as development work in the field of food dehydration, especially of fruits and vegetables.

RAW MATERIALS

VEGETABLES:- Beans, Carrot, Cabbage, Cauliflower, Capsicum, Mushrooms, Peas, Coriander, Potatoes, Onions etc.

FRUITS:- Bananas, Papayas, Apples, fruit Juices, Guavas etc.

FREEZE DRYING IS ADVANTAGEOUS IN THE FOLLOWING WAYS :

(1) Retention of original shape, Colour, aroma and texture.
(2) Retention of freshness and nutritive value.
(3) Quick and complete reconstitution.
(4) Light weight and long shelf life
(5) No need of refrigeration during transport and storage.

MANUFACTURING PROCESS

1. Fruits and vegetables are sorted and graded.
2. Then these are washed with clean water by automatic washing machine to remove soil and attached pesticides.
3. The washed fruits and vegetables are peeled to remove outer skin.
4. These are then sliced or diced into thickness of 2mm - 4mm.
5. The diced fruits & Vegetables are steam blanched for 5 minutes.
6. The vegetables are dipped in potassium Metabisulfite solution for

3-5 minutes and fruits are dissolves in water containing L-Ascorbic Acid (Vitamin C).

7. These fruits & vegetable treated products are now freeze dryed by automatic freeze-drying by automatic freeze-drying.
8. These dryed products are now packed in pouches by automatic vacuum packaging form-fill-seal machine. These pouches are now packed in cartons or cardboards, stored and market.

PROCESS FLOW SHEET FOR VACUUM FREEZE DRYING OF FRUITS & VEGETABLES

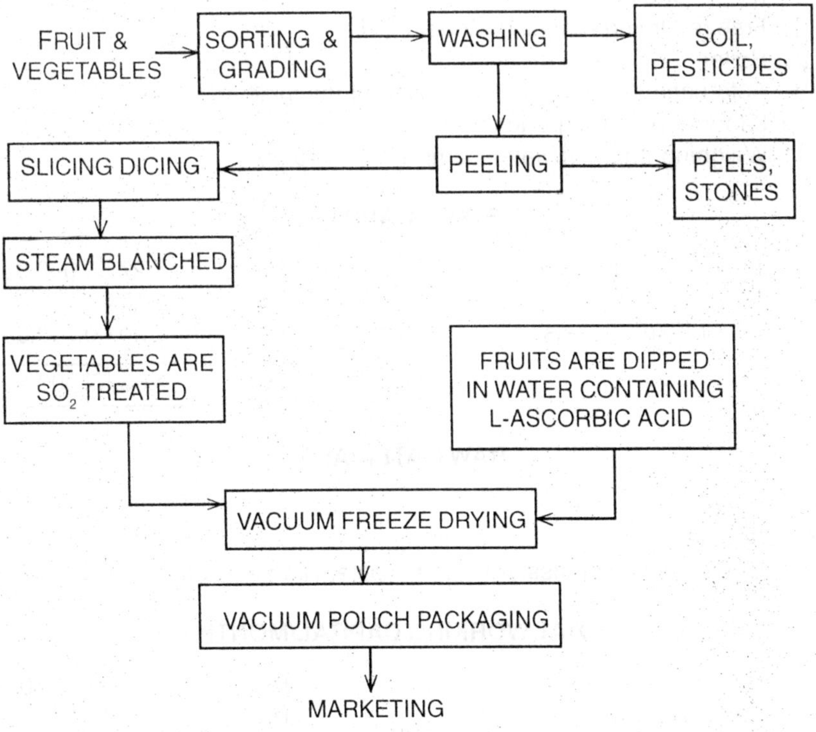

PLANT ECONOMICS

Rated Plant Capacity = 500.00 Kgs./Day

LAND & BUILDING

Total Land Area 2 Acres = Rs. 27,50,000.00

PLANT & MACHINERY

1. Automatic Washing machine
2. Automatic peeling machine
3. Blanching machine
4. Dicing or cubing machine
5. S.S. Tank
6. (S.S.) Strainer
7. Freeze Drying machine Model FDIT
8. Boiler
9. Automatic Vacuum pouch packaging machine
10. Laboratory testing equipment.
11. Weighing balance water pump valves motors

FIXED CAPITAL

1.	Land & Building	Rs.	27,50,000.00
2.	Plant & Machinery	Rs.	1,16,07,000.00
3.	Other Fixed Assets	Rs.	20,00,000.00
	Total	Rs.	1,63,57,000.00

RAW MATERIALS

1. Fruits
2. Vegetables
3. Chemicals as potassium metabisulfite, vitamin C etc.

TOTAL WORKING CAPITAL/MONTH

1.	Raw Material	Rs.	2,89,000.00
2.	Salary & Wages	Rs.	42,120.00
3.	Utilities & Overheads	Rs.	1,13,400.00
	Total	Rs.	4,44,520.00

TOTAL CAPITAL INVESTMENT

Total Fixed Capital	Rs.	1,63,57,000.00
Total Working Capital for 3 Months	Rs.	13,33,560.00
Total	Rs.	1,76,90,560.00

TURN OVER/ANNUM

By sale of 75000 kgs of Dehydrated Fruits/Veg.	Rs.	1,57,50,000.00

PROFIT SALES RATIO = Profit/Sales x 100 = 26.56%

RATE OF RETURN = Operating profit/T.C.I x 100 = 23.65%

BREAK EVEN POINT (B.E.P) = 62.53%

Chapter 21

DRYING OF RED CHILLIES, HALDI, DHANIA, PEA AND GREEN PEAS

Uses & Application

The uses of the product is generally in food making i.e. in vegetable making and other uses of the product are categorized as follows :-

Red Chilli

Dry chilli is extensively used as a spices in India. Curry powder is made by grinding roasted dry chilli with other condiments such as coriander, cumin and tumeric-Capsicum Preparation are used as counter-irritants in lumbago, neuralgia and rheumatic disorders. Taken internally capsicum has a tonic , and carminative action and is specially useful in atonic dyspepsia.

Pharmaceutical requirements are chiefly met by the highly pungent varieties of capsicum grown in sierra Leone Nyasaland and Zanribar. Indian capsicum known in trade as Mumbai Capsicum in used as substitute.

Haldi (Turmeric)

It is an auspicious article in all religious observances in Hindu households. It is a normal constituent of condiments, curry powders and prepared mustards. It is also used for dyeing wool, silk and unmordanted to which it imports a yellow shade in an acid bath. Inspite of its poor light fastness it is still used for dyeing cotton, sometimes in combination with other natural dyes like indigo and satllower to impart different shades. It is used in colouring matter in pharmacy, confectionery and food industry.

In Indian systems of medicine, turmeric is used to some extent as a stomechic, tonic and blood purifier.

Dhania

The fruits are considered carminative, diuretic, tonic, stomachic antibilious, refrigerant and aphrodisiac. they are used chiefly to conceal the odour of other medicines and to correct the qualities of shubarb and senna (U.S.D, 329). they are considered also to lessen the intoxicating effects of spirituous liquors.

Peas

Pea is esteemed primarily for the nutritional value of its seeds. Peas are consumed both in the fresh form as vegetable and in the dried form as pulse, while in America and Europe considerable quantities are used for such processing the dried seeds of the field peas constitute the chief article of commerce. In India, it is often split, like other pulses into dal or in some places used for making roasted or parched pea.

Green Peas

It is used as vegetable, the green plant as well as the pods and grains and the hay are valued as folder. As a green folder, in mixture with oates, pea is said to be very favorable for milk production, having a high nutritive value.

MANUFACTURING PROCESS

Here manufacturing process is given below to the drying and powdering of Red Chilli, Haldi, Dhania, Peas and green Peas :-

1. Selection and grading

The best quality of the product are selected and graded from the raw. The worst quality are abstracted and the best quality has send to the further processing.

2. Washing

The materials should be thoroughly washed with water and in some cases thoroughly scrubbed while washing so remove soil and other extraneous matter.

3. Peeling

It is necessary to peel some of the matter before further processing. So peeling is done by peeling machine or manually.

4. Drying

It is done to get the dry product. It is done either by sun drying or by Mechanical equipments. e.g. Tray drier, belt drier etc.

5. Grinding

Grinding is done by grinding machine for the different meshes as required for the individual product.

6. Packing and storage

Packing is the most vital step for the success of the dehydration Industries. The dried and powdered product be quite dry and should be packed in moisture proof contains.

Tin containers are most suitable for it. But new a days it is replacing by plastic packing.

Dehydration of the Product

The drying of individual product are given as follow :-

Lal Mirch (Chilli) Only the ripe chillies are used for processing. In India, they are mostly sun dried. Sometimes chillies are given steam treatment for 5 minutes before spreading for drying. This helps retention of calyx and gives fast colour to the finished product. The retention of caly prevents the seeds from falling out, chilli are although usually sun dried, tray dries may also be used, temperature should not exceed 50-60°C. Dried chilli have 8 to 10% moisture, and keep well. Tray 0 loading of 5 kg raw chillies/m^2 of tray area is considered good. Dry chillies are packed in jute bags.

Turmeric (Haldi) The turmeric rhizomes are removed from soil and washed thoroughly. There are then boiled in big iron vats using the available fuel at the place, till soft. The pieces are dried in sun till they give metallic sound when broken. Then they are given polish and coloured with turmeric solution. Mother shizomes and fingers are cured separately. They are stored in jute bags or ground in hammer mill and then packed as usual.

Coriander The plants are pulled out by the roots and after drying, the fruits are threshed out. They are further dried in sun, winnowed and stored in bags.

Peas Only tender peas are dehydrated. They are blanched for 1-2 minutes in boiling water and dried at a temperature not exceeding 145°F.

Green Peas Peas for dehydration should be even less mature than for canning. The temdeometer reading may range from 85 to 95. Green pods are brought to the plant. The peas are then removed from pods. It may be noted that peas deteriorate rapidly after removal from the pod, primarily because of unavoidable mechanical housing, these are then graded.

The peas are thoroughly washed with water, sorted to eliminate pod pieces, stem and dehydrated peas. Blanching may be accomplished minute the blanched peas are then slit the Machine which make a 1/8" slit in each pea.

Slitted peas are then dehydrated in tray-tunnel dryers, cabinet dryers continuous belt dryer or belt trough dryer. In a two stage tunnel dryer temperature of about 80-85°C for the initial stage and 70°C for the second stage are recommended. In high circulation continuous belt dryers temperatures from 90-95°C may be used during the early part of the drying cycle. When 8% moisture level is achieved peas are removed from the dries. The centers of the peas dry slowly, hence they should be dried.

Until crisp to moisture content below 5% in bin dryer using dry air at about 50°C. The Product is then packed in moisture proof pouches and bags.

PLANT ECONOMICS

Rated Plant Capacity = 1157.00 Kgs./Day

LAND & BUILDING

Land Area 800 Sq. Mt. = Rs.8,40,000.00

PLANT & MACHINERY

1. Tunnel dryers with fan & Trays.
2. Peeling Machine
3. Screen grading machine
4. Washing Machine
5. Blanching Machine
6. Grinding Machine
7. Trollies, Trays etc.
8. Preparation table
9. Weighing Machine
10. Laboratories equipment
11. Packing filling machine automatic
12. Miscellaneous

FIXED CAPITAL

1.	Land & Building	Rs.	8,40,000.00
2.	Plant & Machinery	Rs.	10,10,000.00
3.	Other Fixed Assets	Rs.	1,90,000.00
	Total	Rs.	20,40,000.00

RAW MATERIALS

1. Red Chilli
2. Haldi (Turmeric)
3. Dhania (Coriander)
4. Peas
5. Green Peas

TOTAL WORKING CAPITAL/ANNUM

1.	Raw Materials	Rs.	18,50,000.00
2.	Salary & Wages	Rs.	5,14,500.00
3.	Utilities & Overheads	Rs.	3,55,000.00
	Total	Rs.	27,19,500.00

TOTAL CAPITAL INVESTMENT

Total Fixed Capital	Rs.	20,40,000.00
Total Working Capital for 3 Months	Rs.	6,79,875.00
Total	Rs.	27,19,875.00

TURN OVER/ANNUM

By Selling of 60 MT of Dried Chilli
62 M.T. of Dried Turmeric (Haldi)
75 MT. of Dried Coriander (Dhania)
75 MT. of Dried Peas
75 MT. of Dried Green Peas

Total Rs. 48,34,500.00

PROFIT SALES RATIO = Profit/Sales x 100 = 25.20%

RATE OF RETURN = Operating profit/T.C.I x 100 = 44.79%

BREAK EVEN POINT (B.E.P) = 50.54%

Chapter 22

FLAVOURED MILK

The freezing of fluid milk and concentrated milk is not being practical on any large commercial scale, but since there is a growing demand for this product, the industry should develop into a sizeable one. At the present time, frozen milk is of value only in those places where fresh milk is scarce, expensive or not available. There has long been a demand for milk that would retain its natural flavour on shipboard during long voyages; like wise in the tropical countries where cows are few and good milk is very scarce.

B. I. S. SPECIFICATIONS

1. SCOPE:-

1.1 This code prescribes the techniques used in the manufacture and the methods of sampling and test for pasteurized milk.

2. Terminology:-

2.0 For the purpose of this code, the following definitions shall apply.

2.1 Milk-milk shall include cow's or buffalo's, whole or skimmed, standardized, toned, double toned and recombined milk or other kind of milk as defined under the prevention of food adulteration Rules, 1955 as amended from time to time.

2.2 Milk plant or Dairy-it shall be taken to include the building, machinery, equipment and appliances necessary for the collection, pasteurization, cooling bottling or filling in other containers and storage of milk.

2.3 Pasteurization - It shall refer to:-

a) The process of heating every particle of milk at a specified temperature;

b) Holding the milk at such temperature continuously for a specified period in a standard and properly;

c) Immediate cooling after heating.

2.3.1 The milk shall be heated to at least 63°C and held at 63°C continuously for at least 30 minutes, or it shall be heated to at least 71.5°C and held at 71.5°C continuously for at least

15 seconds. Other temperature and time combinations that enable the pasteurized milk to meet the requirements.

2.3.2 The holding the milk, it should be cooled immediately in the standard and properly operated equipment to a temperature not exceeding 5°C.

2.3.3 The pasteurized milk should be maintained at a temperature not exceeding 10°C until it leaves the milk plant for distribution.

3. General Requirements:-

3.1 Milk plant- The building where the milk is received, processed, bottled and stored and the equipment and containers are cleaned and sterilized, shall be constructed according to approved design (see IS:2491-1972). The floors, walls and ceilings, doors and windows, arrangement for lighting and ventilation, toilet and hand washing facilities for protection of milk and cleaned equipment from contamination in the building shall conform to the requirements specified in IS: 2491-1972.

3.2 Water supply:- The water supply shall conform to the tolerances specified for water for dairies (see IS: 4251-1967) and shall be easily accessible and adequate.

3.3 Sanitary piping:- All piping used to conduct milk shall be sanitary milk piping of a type which can be easily cleaned and sanitized (See IS:3382-1965).

3.4 Equipment and Containers:- Milk receiving equipment, storage tanks pasteurizing and cooling equipment, cans, bottles, aluminium foils and other packing materials with which milk comes into contact shall be of smooth impervious, non-corodiable, non-toxic material and so constructed as to be easily cleaned and sanitized. Milk bottles, cans, tanks and other items of equipment shall conform to relevant Indian standards prescribed for this purpose.

3.5 Cleaning and Sanitisation of Plant Equipment and Containers:- The pasteurization plant and other equipment used for receiving, processing storage and bottling, and milk cans and bottles used for filling milk, shall be cleaned and sanitized according to the method prescribed in IS: 5253-1969.

3.5.1 After sanitization and during usage or storage, the equipment and containers shall be protected from contamination.

3.6 Surroundings and Waste Dispoal:- The immediate surroundings shall be kept in a neat and clean condition and proper arrangements made for the disposal of waste.

3.7 Personnel, Health and Cleanliness:- All employees and other persons handling milk or equipment in the plant shall be examined periodically by a competent authority and certified to be physically be competent fit and free from infections with the organisms of typhoid, paractyphoid fever or other communicable diseases. All persons working in the milk plant shall wear clean garments preferably white suits and caps, and strictly adhere to rule of personal hygiene.

4. Raw Milk

4.1 Chemical Requirements for milk-milk shall satisfy the standards prescribed for the corresponding raw milk under the prevention of Food Adulteration Rules, 1955.

4.2 Bacteriological Requirements:- As far as possible raw milk with methylene blue reduction time of not less than one hour in summer and not less than two hours in winter should be accepted for pasteurization.

5. Pasteurization

5.1 The pasteurization of milk shall be performed according to the procedure specified under 2.3. The pasteurizing vat or pasteurizer shall be equipped with accurate temperature indicating and recording devices. High temperature short time plants shall should be provided with automatic flow diversion valve.

6. Hygienic Requirements:-

6.1 The pasteurized milk in dairy plant shall conform to the requirements.

7. Bottling and packing:-

7.1 Bottling, capping of bottles and packaging of pasteurized milk shall be done in standard equipment. The caps shall be made of aluminium foil.

7.2 Bottles shall be of standard quality (See IS:1392-1971) and shall be cleaned and sterilized in standard equipment using standard procedure.

8. Marking

8.1 The following information (full or abbreviated) shall be marked legibly on the container;

a) Pasteurized milk,

b) Cow/buffalo/standardized/skimmed/tonned/double toned milk,

c) Name and address of the plant,

d) Date of manufacture, and

e) Net content.

9. Sampling

9.1 Representive samples of pasteurized milk for testing conformity to this code shall be drawn as described in Appendix F of IS: 4238-1967.

10. Tests

10.1 The tests shall be carried out as prescribed in appropriate clauses of Indian Standards.

10.2 Quality of Reagents:- Unless specified otherwise, pure chemicals and distilled water (See IS:1070-1977 shall be used).

Flavouring Essence

Strawberry Essence:-

Straw berries, fresh	-	16 ounces,
Angelica (california)	-	6 fluid ounces
Brandy (california)	-	6 ounces
Alcohol	-	8 ounces
Water	-	Q.S.

Mash the berries to a pulp in a mortar or bowl, and transfer to a flask, along with the Angelica, brandy, alcohol and about 8 ounces of water, let macerate over night then distil off until 32 ounces have passed over. Colour strawberry red. The addition of a little essence of vanilla and a pint of lemon improves this essence.

Vanilla Essence

Vanilla beans chopped fine	-	30 parts
Potassium Carbonate	-	1 parts
Boiling water	-	1,450 parts
Alcohol	-	450 parts
Essence of musk	-	1 part

Dissolve the potassium carbonate in the boiling water, add the vanilla, cover the vessel, and let stand in a moderately warn place until cold. Transfer to a wide mouthed Jar, add the Alcohol, Cork, and let macerate for 15 days; than decant the clear essence and filter the remainder. Mix the two liquid and add the essence of musk.

PROCESS OF MANUFACTURE

Treatment Before pasteurization:-

Adequate storage capacity for raw milk is necessary for efficient operation of a plant. Many plants hold the current days receipts in storage tank at 40°F or below, so that once the next days operation has been started no shot downs will be necessary. Delays during the pasteurization process result in bum on of milk in contact with heating surfaces, as well as waste of labour, heat-and refrigeration.

The process steps usually taken before pasteurization are:-

1. Filtering or clarifying,
2. Separating,
3. Standarizing,
4. Vitaminizing,
5. Homogenizing.

PLANT ECONOMICS

LAND & BUILDING (Land area 500 sq. mts.) = Rs. 6,25,000.00

PLANT & MACHINERY

1. Milk processing unit complete with cream extraction machines, pasturization unit, cooling unit etc.
2. Packing unit, complete with filling machine, sealing machine etc.
3. Milk storage tank
4. Other miscellaneous

FIXED CAPITAL

1.	Land & Building	Rs.	6,25,000.00
2.	Plant & Machinery	Rs.	13,12,000.00
3.	Other Fixed Assets	Rs.	83,000.00
	TOTAL	Rs.	20,20,000.00

RAW MATERIALS

1. Raw Milk
2. Flavouring saffron, cashewnut (four pieces), pista, Almonds, Elachi etc.
3. Empty Bottles
4. Miscellaneous

TOTAL WORKING CAPITAL/MONTH

1.	Raw Material	Rs.	46,11,000.00
2.	Salary & Wages	Rs.	52,750.00
3.	Utilities & Overheads	Rs.	41,000.00
	TOTAL	Rs.	47,04,750.00

TOTAL CAPITAL INVESTMENT

Total Fixed Capital	Rs.	20,20,000.00
Total Working Capital for 2 Months	Rs.	94,09,500.00
TOTAL	Rs.	1,14,29,500.00

TURN OVER/ANNUM

1. By sale of flavoured milk, 1500 Ton (75,00,000 Bottles of 200 ml each)
2. By sale of 80,000 kgs. of Ghee

TOTAL Rs. 6,21,00,000.00

PROFIT SALES RATIO = Profit / Sales x 100 = 4.43 %

RATE OF RETURN = Operating profit / T.C.I x 100 = 24.07 %

BREAK EVEN POINT (B.E.P) = 54.84 %

Chapter 23

FROZEN FOODS

USES

Frozen foods is used to preserve fruits and vegetables and non vegetables.

Once they are kept in the cold storage, they do not get spoiled even after many months.

Some times, in production reason of certain vegetable or non vegetable, the demand for that thing decreases, which in Turn decreases the consumption the surplus amount of that particular item is kept in cold storage.

So this item, when needed, can be taken from the cold storage & can be made available to consumers very easily.

MANUFACTURING PROCESS

The rapidity with which fish decomposes has resulted in various process of prescription and curing which aim at preserving the fish from the attacks of putrefactive organisms. The method for this purpose are freezing drying, salting pickling and smoking.

Refrigeration fishes are kept in small refrigerators or ice boxes, which cool the air this preventing to a certain extent the growth of microorganisms. But the freezing of fish does more than this. They are often reduced to a temperature below zero, faha, and in this condition may be kept for long periods and transported considerable distances

As soon as the catch reaches the refrigeration plant, the fish are washed in cold running water to cleanse them from scime & dirt and fish that are heavy feeders or are of any oily nature are eviscerated coilest small fish, such as mackerel, whiting etc. are frozen in their natural slate in pans, in which they are placed head to tail. The pan when full is set upon the shelf of what is known as the quicker this is done the better favoured are the fish after thawing.

Large, fish like halibut, salmon cool, etc. are frozen separately until they are of the consistency of a coke of ice. It usually takes ten or twelve hours to freeze through a thick fish the next step is to give the fish an icy coat or greaze, and the manner in which this is carried out is most important, for unless properly geazed, the skins of frozen fin may twin white or get tractured whilst the bodies shrink owing to evaporation of moisture, from the flesh. Glazing is carried out for the purpose of giving each fish an airtight envelope of ice, which prevents the evaporation of moisture, deterioration of oils in the fush of salmen and other oily fish, and protects the fish from mechanical injuries. The method of doing it is as follows. The frozen fish enter the glazing room where the temp. is about 25°F and are quickly put through a trough of clean water, kept near to freezing point. This water forms a thin film over the surface of the fish, which solidifies almost instantly in the cold air of the room. The fish are passed through the trough two or three times, until the film is thick enough to protect the entire surface. In some refrigerating plants, brine is used for ice coating the fish then pass to cold storage, when they remain until required.

Harrings, in particular, are subjected to quick freezing at about -40°F followed by cold storage they are said to keep palatable for nine months.

Salman, after thawing, is sometimes found to be discoloured yellow near to the skin to possess a particular rank taste. This is due to disruption of the fat cells, caused by insufficient glazing of the surface of the fish thawing then sets the oil of the disrupted cells free which is subject to oxidation and rancidity and the taint spreads to surrounding flesh number of anti-oxidants, including vitamin (ascorbic acid) have been used from time to time on fish and fillet before freezing to retard this process.

Frozen fish, after thawing, can generally be distinguished from fresh fish by reason of its dull appearance and absence of sheen its softer and flabby condition, and also by small particles of ice which may often be seen on the fish.

CHEESE

Cheese varies considerably in its composition, depending upon whether it is made from or skimmer milk. The cheeses, (e.g. dutch cheeses) ore characterized by their hold and dry consistence, whilst those made from whole milk are softer and richer in flavour. These again are divided into pressed cheeses, Eleu-veined cheeses, and soft cheeses. Cheddas, caerpilly, and double and dingh gloucester are examples of the pressed cheeses, stilton blue dorest of the blue-veined variety and the French and Swiss cheeses are of soft variety.

American and Canadian cheeses are example of the whole-milk variety. Some falty and richly flavoured cheeses, such as Stilton, have cream added to the milk before making. The natural colour of cheese is pale yellow or straw coloured: the pink or orange hues of certain kinds are produced by the addition of annetto cream cheeses contain about 40% of butter fat, whole-milk cheese 34%, and those made from skimmed mill 10-22 percent.

Moisture content 23-25% for cream cheese 30-40% in whole-milk cheese is formed by the action on milk of rennet, a product of the fourth stomach of the calf, which, in combining with the phosphates produces precipitation and coagulation of the cascirion and varying proportions of fats and salts. When kept at a suitable temp. this undergoes a process known as 'ripening' changes in the casein and lactose, as well as the formation of certain salts and acids are the results of this ripening process.

The process of making is as follows milk, on reception at the factory, is strained into large vats which are jacketed for cooling or heating purposes, if the milk requires to the cooled (and this depends on time of the year) cold water is circulated through the jacket the milk constantly being stirred to prevent rising of the cream and ensure even cooling a quantity of 'starter' is added and evenly distributed through the milk, which is now by passing steam through the jacket and the temp. raised to 80-90 colouring matter is added, if the cheese required is the coloured variety, and the milk tested for acidity; if this a the correct percentage the rennet is added, the amount added and the temp. at which it is done varying with the class of cheese being produced. This effects coagulation are noticed. The card is then left until signs of wagulation are noticed. The card is ben left until it is ready for cutting. An operation performed with american knives, first with the vertical knife and then the horizontal knife until it is cut. Evenly into small cubes, after which it is again tested for acidity the curd is gain stirred to get it enter a loose condition and subsequent treatment depend upon the class of cheese being made. Cheddas cheese are scalded at this stage by passing steam through the jacket of the cheese vat, after which the card is pilled into a mass and the whydrown. If it is next cut into blocks and placed clothes on a rak and left for several hours, and tested for acidity before the ext. process, i.e. grinding after being ground and haging salt added the end is ready for processing. The moulds are lined with cheese clothes and weighed quantities of curd placed in them. Pressure is applied either by mechanical means or by chains or serious in the case of cheddards they are passed for 3 days being removed for turning etc. each day after which the cheese are removed from the moulds and placed in the repening room which is kept at a temp. of 56-65°F. The cheeses are turned daily for the first month and attain a good flavour in about 3 to 4 months cheese is not allowed to ripen to the same extent as was the practice years ago, a milder flavour being more popular now with the public repening is a bacterial process and it is interesting to note the cows given penicillin as treatment for mastitis or other conditions, excretes enough of the antibiotic in their milk to kill the bacterial essential for normal cheese making.

The repening of cheese, which is really a process of decomposition render it liable to the attacks of moulds and aminol parasites, including acari and the "cheerfly", the soft, greasy kin ds are more often attacked than the hard and dryskimmed milk cheeses Blue, black and red moulds are common on source check whilest the cheese acarus and the larvae of the cheese fly are common animal parasites. To prevent attacks of parasites, the rinds of cheese, which consist of the cloth passed into the exterior of the cheese, are flouring matters or antiseptic solutions. The curing and again of cheese needs special core to prevent surface defects appearing special valve ventilated cases for holding cheese have been introduced in recent years, lacquered internally to avoid surface sicoloration. Abhnorneal tastes, tall owiners being the most common, and internal discolorations are also found in cheese. Numerous taints have been observed and may be due to the presence of yeasts in the milk, faulty feeding of the cow, the use of dirty utensils, or some defet of temp., starter, renat etc., in the actual cheese making among the discolorations may be mentioned the brown patches existing in the interior of stilton cheese and some what prevalent a few years ago. There is nothing on the exterior of the cheese to indicate that it is so affected the cause is dere to the presence of discolouring organisms in the milk.

PREPARATION FOR FREEZING

Meat :

The preparation of meat for freezing is essentially the same as cutting for retail sales loin, ribs or round sections beef, pork loins or bomb racks, loins or legs are cut into steaks, chops, roasts or legs and other portions for cooling. These portions are placed in cartons or overwrapped hand in preparation for freezing.

Vegetables continued

Vegetables are brought to the processing plant in the whole or cut or vined state. Some products such as peas or beans may be size graded prior to further treatment corn may be judged for maturity orgenoleptically, on the basis of moisture content, or the refractive index of the kernel "milk" may be used as a criterion of maturity. Some vegetables are selected to includes a general maturity range butars not graded specifically.

Some vegetables are dryclined prior to washing peas and lina beans are passed through a fanning mill Broccoli is sorted and trimmed by hand or the batt end may be removed with a rotating knife, then the speers may be spilt with a hand knife to portions of suitable size. The bare of the brusels sprout is trimmed off by machine. Corn must be husked before it can be washed. This is done in machine which cuts off the stalk attachment and removes the husk as the ear posses over rubber rollers. Spinach is dry cleaned by passing it through rotating rels; dirt, stones, and other detritos passing through the spaces in the reel to the outside.

Prior to washing cauliflower, the base of the cluster and the leaves are trimmed off with a hand knife, the core is cut out and the individual floweretts are broken off. The flowerettes are then passed through a cylindrical rod cleaner to remoke detritus. Peas and lima beans are washed in feotation-type, water-filled machines which pass them over stone traps in such a manner that dense materials sink to the bottom and are removed. The products pars over the top and are separated from water by means of a reel. Special washers may be used for bear in which case the product is passed through a mineral-oil detergent-water emulsion when tracated in this manner and passed into water, sound peas sink and are separated, thistle buls, nightshade berries, skin and other foreign material float and are then used to clean the sound peas.

Real-type washers with forced sprays may be used to wash some products prior to blanching soaker-types washers with agitating sprays may be used for brocoli, brussel sprouts and cauliflower flowerettes Carrots usually receive both spray/and soaker-type washings. Green beans are not washed before blanching spinach is washed in moving water in tanks fitted with a drum which immerses the product as it moves along. It is then passed through a wet reel where it is further washed with water sprays, then passed over a wire-mesh belt for drainage, inspection and removal of foreign material.

Other operations which must be carried out before the products are blanched include shape beans. Shipping by machine, cross-cutting or Frenching, also by machine, carots-steam peeling spray waghing, trimming and slicing: cut corn-cutting the kernels from the cob by machine if the product is to be beanched in this form.

All vegetables, except onion, must be blenched prior to freezing, to inactive enzymes, which would otherwise cause the development of offtlavours during frozen storage Blauching is carried out in hot water or in sterm. In water blenching the product is conducted through water at 190 to 210°F.

In steam blanching the product is carried on a belt through a hooded section into which live steam is injected.

The time and temp are regulated in such a manner that the enzymes which could case off-flavour development are inactivated. Tests for calalase or peroxides are used to determine the adequacy of blanching. It is considered that a negative peroxidan test is better indication of the adequacy of blanching than a negative catalase test. After blanching, vegetables are quickly cold at least 70°F. This may do done by emptying the product from the blander into a fluve of running water which serves to cool the products and convey to the next operation. In some cases blanched products re emtied into a perforated or rod-type cylindrical reel fitted with forced water sprays or into a finnel-shaped tank, with a stream of cold coates.

Corn is blanched on the for or as cut kernels as it passes along on a hooded, wire-mesh belt. The cut product must be cooled on the belt with atomiged water sprays but corn on the cob may be cooled in a tank of slowly moving water.

After blanching and cooling, lima bear as passed through a quality grades or separator containing nearly saturated Irine (Nace John). The less mature beans float and can be removed from the surface while the corinkled, over-mature lbeans sink and are removed from an outlet near the bottom of the separation tank. Over-mature beans are discarded. Beans which float will become the frozen product and these must be washed to remove salt this done by flaming in water or by passing through a rod reel fitted with water sprays whole kernel (cut) corn is cleaned before packaging to remove silk and husk particules. This may be done in a quality separator containing water instead of brine. In this case corn kernels are removed at the bottom outlet, silk and foreign material floating off at the top. Peas are passed through a quality separator or grades as are lima bears.

However, the density of brine solution used to separate over-mature peas in lower than that used for lima beans. The more desirable (loss mature pear float and are removed at the top the more mature peas sink and are removed at the bottom outlet. Separated peas are washed to remove brine.

All vegetables are passed over inspection belts prior to packaging here small pieces of product, weeds and other unwented materials are removed by hand. Asparagns, French at green beans, broccali, brussels spronts and cauliflower may also be size granded at this time.

After blanching and cooling and prior to packaging spinach must be pressed and drained to remove water picked up during processing. This is done by passing the product over a wire mesh belt fitted with a weighted roller which rides on the spinach as it passes by, Packages are filled by hand.

Lima beans, cross cut string beans, cut corn and peas are filled into packages by automatic volumetric follers. A certain proportion of the filled packages are check weighed.

Carrots are often loose frozen as individual cubes prior to packaging this permits use in mixtures with peas after freezing they are packed "in bulk" in polyethylene bags and metal containers and stored at temp. near O°F until mixed with other vegetables and packaged in retail or institutional size containers volumetric fillers my be used for placing the mixed, frozen products in packages.

Fruits

Frozen apple slices or sections are used for bakery products. Apples are peeled and cred by machine, then passed over a belt where trimming is done by hand. They are then sliced by machine passed over a vibrating screen to remove small pieces and then over an inspection belt prior to freezing, apples are treated to prevent browning due to enzyme action during freezing and storage. The apples are allowed to stand for at least 8 hours in a refrigerated room prior to breezing to allow the SO_2 to penetrate, otherwise browning will in the interior.

Blanching and cooling or soaking in solutions containing salt, sugar and/or ascorbic acid are also used to retord browning in frozen apples soaking may be combined with vacuum treatment.

Apple slices, to be frozen are usually packed in enamelled, slip-cover cans holding 30 to 50 lbs of product. The filled containers are placed in cold rooms or tunnels at temp blow O°F for freezing.

The warehousing of Frozen foods Prefer Freezing alone will not is sure the successful distribution of frozen foods-successful storage is at least as important as freezing itself. Unless frozen foods are warehoused under proper conditions of storage and temperature, all of the careful production and quality control methods that a packer may have used could easily be lost control methods that a packer may have used could easily be lost before the product is delivered to the final consumer. To avoid endangering the quality and/or nutritive value of frozen foods, consideration must be give to numerous factors that are involved in the proper warehousing of frozen foods are temperature humidity methods of storing, and methods of handling.

Temperature: The proper storage temperature is a vital point in the storing of frozen foods. In the beginning of the industry, it was assumed by many that as long as the product was properly quick frozen it would remain unchanged indefinitely during long. During long-contained storage also, at that time there was considerable question investigators as to what was the proper storage temperature.

Today, no one questions the fact that frozen foods should be stones at O°F or below. Many recognized authorities in the industry recommend temp. as low as-20°F. For the long time storage of certain products. It is the Universal opinion that most frozen products may be held in a satisfactory manner at a storage temp of O°F. A few products, such as asparagus, corn on the cob, mushrooms, snap beans, apples, pickles, poultry and fatty fish, such as mackered and salmon should be stored at -50 F or lower

All frozen foods should be reduced to a temperature of O°F In the centre of the product before being placed in a refrigerated room to be used for storage. Packers should make contain that their products are thoroughly frozen before moving then to storage in other words, a refrigerated room
used for the storage food should be near used for frozing separations. In cold storage room freezing such as may be used by the cold pack fruit industry, or by some pacleers of loose frozen vegetables, it is recommended that freezing from those in which frozen foods are being stored.

Unless that recommendation is followed, it will be impossible to maintain constant, oniform temperature in any storage room. Every effort should be made to avoid fluctuations in temperature in cold storage room. Several a Uniform temperature.

The refrigeration system should have ample capacity and sufficient coil area or plate area in the cold storage room a vestibule or outer room should be constructed, preferably on the in side of the room it a vestibules or outer room is not feasible, a tarpaulin or piece of heavy canvas should be hung on the inside of the storage room door.

The effect of fluctuating storage temperatures on the quality of frozen foods has been studied by numerous Investigators Hustratid and Winter stored snap beans, Corn, plas straw berries, raspberries and muskmelon for six months at a constant temperature of 5°F, and at temperatures fluctuating from O°F to -20°F in comparing the two different storage conditions.

METHODS OF STORAGE AND HANDLING PRODUCTS

From a theoretical stand point, frozen foods should be stacked in solid piles in such a way as to reduce to a minimum air circulation around the products. Such system is practical only when the storage has a cold floor and the products are not piled against warm walls, and when all of the foods moved into the storage are as cold or colder then the storage itself. Under such conditions-desiccation and oxidation will be less than when considerable air circulation is permitted.

In actual practice, frozen foods are foten unloaded from trucks or refrigerated cars in which the products have warmed above the storage temperature in this case, it is important that the food temperature be quickly reduced to that of the storage.

Frozen foods are warehoused in a number of different types of containers. Permanent floor racks may be made by placing 2 * 45 on edge and mailing 1 * 45 at right angles to the length of the celling coils in order not to interfere with the nature of air circulation with in the cold storage room. The cases may be piled on fork type pallets or on floor rocks, so that the first layer of containers is at least two, and preferably four inches above the floor.

Permanent floor racks may be made by placing 2 x 25 of edge and mailing 1 x 45 or 1 x 65 at right angles and on top of the 2 x 45 at right angles to the length of the ceiling coils in order not to interfere with the natuin of air circulation with in the cold storage room. Strip of woods (dannage should be used to separate about every 2 or 3 ft. of layers of containers of frozen foods dannage streps should be not less than 3/4 in thick and not more than 4 in wide in this way, horizontal, air circulation is themselves, serve as damage strip can must be taken when using pallets, or floor racks and damage to avoid having the containers overlap the edges. If this precaution is not taken, part of the bottom layer of cases will crash down over the ends. In addition to damage to the containers, the crushed part may hinder air circulation.

One of the problems encountered in ware housing frozen foods is the poor stacking strength of some containers, annually referred to as shipping cartons frozen foods should not staclacl within fine feet of any non-refrigerated spaces, such as opening to stairs or elevator wells. When defrosting coils by scrapping, a tarpaulin must be placed over the stacks of frozen products and directly under the coils to prevent frost and ice from fulling on the cases.

In the handling of frozen foods today must ware houses use pellets and forklift tracks.

Beside from the basic consideration of temperature, humidity, and methods of storking and handling, other precautions should be observed in the storage of froze every care should be taken to prevent and delay what so ever the moving frozen foods from freezers to storage rooms and from storage rooms to refrigerator care and trucks. The length of that frozen foods are not in refrigerated space at 0°F. should be held to an absolute minimum.

PLANT ECONOMICS

Rated Plant Capacity	=		15.75 MT/Day

LAND & BUILDING

Land (Area 800 sq. mt.)	=	Rs.	27,38,520.00

PLANT & MACHINERY

FOR FROZEN FOODS AND VEGETABLES :

1. Ammonia refrigerating cabinet
2. Washing machine motor
3. Peeling machine
4. Water reservoir tank
5. Cutting machine
6. Automatic sorting machine
7. Automatic chopping machine
8. Freezing tank
9. Automatic packing machine
10. Depolluting equipments
11. Piping, valves and other fittings
12. Lab. testing equipments

FOR TOMATO PASTE (CONCENTRATE) :

13. Pulper supreme equipped
14. Hydraulic juice press
15. Automatic weighing, filling and packing machine
16. Rotary fruits and vegetable washing machine equipped
17. Conveyor
18. Vacuum pan evaporator.

19. Double seaming machine
20. Reforming unit
21. Open pans for heating crushed tomatoes
22. Assorted vessels of aluminium stainless steel trays basin tanks
23. Testing equipment and instruments
24. Steam jacketed kettle

FOR DEHYDRATED ONION & ONION POWDER

25. Dryer
26. Direct oil fired burner
27. Conditioning bins
28. Stainless steel tables
29. Benches
30. Stainless steel trays
31. Automatic weighing, sealing and packing machine
32. Galvanised iron tanks
33. Water blancher
34. Peeler
35. Grinding mill
36. Cutting equipment

FOR POTATO AND POTATO POWDER :

37. Peelers
38. Slicers
39. Blancher trays
40. Electrically heated dryer
41. Wooden preparation tables
42. Micro-pulverizer
43. Heat sealing machine
44. Boiler
45. Piping & pipe fittings, electrical
46. D.G. Set

FIXED CAPITAL

1.	Land & Building		Rs.	27,38,520.00
2.	Plant & Machinery		Rs.	87,35,004.00
3.	Other Fixed Assets		Rs.	17,60,000.00
		Total	Rs.	1,32,33,524.00

RAW MATERIALS

FOR FROZEN FOODS AND VEGETABLES:

1. Liquid ammonia
2. Vegetarian foods, fruits and vegetables
3. Non-vegetarian foods
4. Chemicals, preservatives

FOR TOMATO PASTE (CONCENTRATE) :

5. Tomatoes
6. Chemicals/salts/basil leaf
7. O.T.S. Flattened
8. Labels
9. Cardboard boxes

FOR DEHYDRATED ONION & ONION POWDER

10. Raw wet onions

FOR POTATO AND POTATO POWDER :

11. Fresh potatoes
12. Sodium metabisulphite
13. Anti - Cooking material (Silicate, aluminium, calcium, magnesium etc.)
14. Packaging materials

TOTAL WORKING CAPITAL/MONTH

1.	Raw Material	Rs.	74,77,400.00
2.	Salary & Wages	Rs.	2,55,238.00
3.	Utilities & Overheads	Rs.	2,00,800.00
	Total	Rs.	79,33,438.00

TOTAL CAPITAL INVESTMENT

Total Fixed Capital	Rs.	1,32,33,524.00
Total Working Capital for 3 Months	Rs.	2,38,00,314.00
Total	Rs.	3,70,33,838.00

TURN OVER/ANNUM

By sale of Vegetarian Frozen Foods & Vegetables
By sale of Non-Vegetarian Frozen Foods (Miscellaneous foods) 500 tons
By sale of 24,00,000 cans of Tomato Concentrate of 500 gms each
By sale of 13,50,000 kgs of Dehydrated Onions
By sale of 4,50,000 kgs of Onion Powder
By sale of 225 tonnes of Dehydrated Potato
By sale of 225 tonnes of Potato Powder

Total Rs. 13,37,75,000.00

PROFIT SALES RATIO = Profit/Sales x 100 = 20.73%

RATE OF RETURN = Operating profit/T.C.I x 100 = 75.28%

BREAK EVEN POINT (B.E.P) = 31.12%

Chapter 24

FRUIT JUICES MAKING & PACKAGING IN PLASTIC CONTAINERS & POUCHES (FRUIT-JUICES : MANGO, PINEAPPLE, APPLE, LITCHI)

MANUFACTURING PROCESS

Juices of Mango, Pine Apple, Apple, Guàva, Litchi, etc. on deliver to the plant, the fruit is passed over a roller conveyor or between revolving brushes to remove leaves or other debvis before entering a tank containing a chlorine rotations or detergent. Strong currents of wash solutions direct the flating fruit toward a roller elevator over which sprays of fresh water remove the wash solution. It is important that chlorine to removed from fruit containing polyphenols since they may react with chlorinc to form chlorophinols which give a medicinal flavours to the Juice. In addition to removal of debvis or dirt, washing reduces the number of micro organisms on the fruit; thereby making subsequent Juice sterilization process move effective. Reduction in microbial content by washing as difficult where the interior of the fruit is open to the atmosphere apples. A second brushing is sometimes combined with fresh water sprays. The spud of brush rotation, alignment and stiffness of the livistles are varied with the rigidity of the fruit surface and the intent of the operation, as for example the removal of bruised tissues.

Sorting

The fruit receiver final inspection on ruler conveyors to ensure freedom from imperfection before it is regulated into different size grades. Spots of rot on a few apples can cause an adverse flavour in a large inspection samples are frequently analyzed.

Mechanically harvested grapes are dumped from collection bins into a hopper pan which individual barries and partial elusters are elevated to a stemmer - crusher on a woven wire belt. Foreign materials such as baves, cluster steams, etc. are removed manually, Juice drauning to the base of the hopper is combined with that from the crushed pulp.

Several types of sizing equipment have been used, e.g. inclined diverging belts or rolls, roller conveyors with varying space between the rolls or revolving drums located at different heights above a fud conveyor. The fruit of each size category is collected on a cross - conveyor and delivered to a temporary storage bin or directly to the extraction units. Stationary surfaces on the grader are usually converted with foam rubber to minimise brashing.

Communition

A variety of methods are used to break the fruit for Juices rebase depending as the struders of raw materials, the clarity desired in the final Juice, and enzymatic discolauation and destruction of pectin.

The most common disintegrator is the hammer mill or a variations of it where fixed or free - swinging hammer force the fruit particles through a screen.

In Europe the fruit is fed into the centre of a cylinder and propelled by lears past stationary knives. Graded fruit contains less fines and permits the formation of a more porous press cake.

For the production of tomato puree or concentrate the chopped material is dripped into a tank of stivved pulp where pectic enzymes are immediately inadivated. The bottom of tank provides agitation and maintains a pulp temperature of 93°C.

Many fruit pulps have a mucilaginous character that make Juice extractions difficult specially with continuous presses. The nature of this stifferiness of the pulp can be overcome somewhat by the addition of press aid. In Europe grand apple have been treated with commercial pectic enzymes following aeration of the pulp to facilitate Juice extraction on a belt press. As Press aids, fibrous materials, coarse wood flour, rice hulls and beached or unbleached wood pulp are used.

Owing to composition and structural differences in fruits a variety of procedures are used to extract - Juice. They are divide into two classes

1. Citrus &
2. Deciduous

The citrus juices from oranges, lemons or grape fruit are automatically conveyed to one of several types of intractors and processed.

Until a decade ago deciduous Juices were extracted with draped pressed, Loosely forms were filled with comminuted fruit and the edges folded over to form cheeses that were separated by racks having square lattice openings. These racks permitted Juice drainage & provided stability to a stack of cheeses when it was moved into position between press platens. Juice started to flow during cheese formations and reached a maximum flow rate with a pressures of 25 lb p.s.i. on the cheese. The flow declined until the end of cake compression at 100 - 150 lbs p.s.i.

The Juice are classified & pasteurized before storage & packaging. Fruit Juices generally have a P.H of 4 or less and spoilage is usually limited to yeast and mold growth. Under such an acid condition, commercial sterility is achieved by filling the containers at 88°C followed by inversion for one minutes or slow cooling under water sprays. Chemical preservatives like potassium and sodium salts of sorbic Benjoic and sulfurous acids are also allowed up to 0.1% by weight.

Fruit Juices can also be preserved by freezing. Fruit Juices are concentrated by evaporation and ceromatic flavouring is collected from distillate for readying to concentrate.

All the steps such as cleaning, sorting, blanching, extractions, classification, & pasteurization etc. are similar except some differences in the peeling and pulping machines.

The Juices are packed in plastic containers, or bottles, tetrapacks containers or pouches L.D.P.E by automatic machines as required.

Bottling

The bottling machine must be capable of being steamed for 20 minutes but it must be sterilised effectively, as the design of many internal parts makes it a happy hunting ground for years and other organisation.

Bottling Room It is quite possible to bottle in thoroughly adequate manner. The bottles should not be open to the air on their journey from the bottle steriliser to the filler a simple cover in all that is needed and glass sides enable the operator to follow the course of bottles within.

From the filler to the crowner the bottles must again be protected, but once the crown is fixed, after it has been sterilized by heat, So_2 or other means, they are safe from outside infection.

Elaborate precaution are taken to bottle, The bottling room is completely separated for the purpose and has are door, the only other exit being a narrow slit through which the conveyor belt takes the filled bottles out of the room. A cylinder of compressed air within the room maintain an internal pressure of about one atmosphere above normal so that a (instant leakages) of air takes place from the room for the outer air and not vice versa.

The Juice is sterilised in the usual type of filter and is led to the filter by a sterile house, the great point to remember is that in some products one single yeast cell can destroy Juice in bottle cleaning in most important efficiency can be combined with simplicity workmen in the room should be provided with rubber boots and gloves etc.

PLANT ECONOMICS

Rated Plant Capacity = 12000.00 Lts./Day

LAND & BUILDING

Total Land Area 2 acres = Rs. 42,80,000.00

PLANT & MACHINERY

1. Fruit Storage Tanks
2. Washing/Steaming/lye treatment vessel
3. Automatic pineapple processing machine
4. Comminutor
5. Blancher
6. Shredding Machine
7. Juice Extractor (Vertical press master).
8. Filter press
9. Juice processing vessels
10. Intermediate Juice storage tanks
11. Deaeration Unit, with vacuum pump
12. Filling & Packing Machine (Automatic)
13. Chilling Units
14. Weighing Machine
15. Boiler
16. Laboratory Equipments
17. Pipe fittings, Pumps & valves etc.
18. Miscellaneous Expenses

FIXED CAPITAL

1.	Land & Building	Rs.	42,80,000.00
2.	Plant & Machinery	Rs.	56,00,000.00
3.	Other Fixed Assets	Rs.	14,45,000.00
	Total	Rs.	1,13,25,000.00

RAW MATERIALS

1. Mango Fresh Fruit
2. Apple Fresh Fruit
3. Pineapple/Orange
4. Litchi
5. Preservatives (like citric acid, sodium, benzoate etc.), sugar, salt barley water essences etc.
6. Plastic Pouches (laminated) labels

TOTAL WORKING CAPITAL/MONTH

1.	Raw Material	Rs.	75,71,000.00
2.	Salary & Wages	Rs.	2,09,375.00
3.	Utilities & Overheads	Rs.	5,48,300.00
	Total	Rs.	83,28,675.00

TOTAL CAPITAL INVESTMENT

Total Fixed Capital	Rs.	1,13,25,000.00
Total Working Capital for 3 Months	Rs.	2,49,86,025.00
Total	Rs.	3,63,11,025.00

TURN OVER/ANNUM

By sale of 9,00,000 litres of Mango Juice
By sale of 9,00,000 litres of Apple juice.
By sale of 9,00,000 litres Pine apple.
By sale of 9,00,000 litres Litchi Juice

Total Rs. 12,42,00,000.00

PROFIT SALES RATIO = Profit/Sales x 100 = 12.96%

RATE OF RETURN = Operating profit/T.C.I x 100 = 44.33%

BREAK EVEN POINT (B.E.P) = 42.29%

Chapter 25

FRUITS & VEGETABLES JUICE WITH OTHER PRODUCTS

Procurement of Raw materials

Fruit and vegetables produce as raw materials both primary and secondary are available in abundants in vast surrounding area where the Project is located. With the best means of transport agro based raw materials availability to the Project will not be a problem, rather the abundants raw materials availability is enchancing to the Project.

Fruits

1. Guava
2. Banana
3. Plum/peach/Pears
4. Mango
5. Pineapple
6. Orange
7. Litchi

LIMITS FOR PERMITTED PRESERVATIVES IN FRUIT PRODUCTS

Permitted preservatives are

(a). Benzoic acid including salts thereof, and
(b). Sulphurous acid including salts thereof

The quantities of individual preservatives used in various fruit products shall be as mentioned in the table given below :

Fruit product	Preservative	Parts per million
1. Fruit and fruit pulp or juice (not dried) for conversion into jam or crystallized, glazed or cured fruit or other products		
(a) Cherries	Sulphur dioxide	3,000
(b) Strawberries and Raspberries	do	2,000
(c) Other fruits	do	1,000
2. Fruit juice concentrate	do	1,500
3. Dried fruits		
(a) apricots, peaches, apples, pears and others	do	2,000
(b) raisins or sultanas	do	750
4. Squashes, crushes, fruit syrups, cordials, fruit juice and barley waters	Sulphur dioxide	350
	or	
	Benzoic acid	600
5. Jam, marmalade, preserve and fruit jelly	Sulphur dioxide	40
	or	
	Benzoic acid	200
6. Crystallized, glazed cured fruit (including candied peel)	or	
	-	
	Sulphur dioxide	150
7. Fruit and fruit pulp not otherwise specified in the schedule	Sulphur dioxide	350
8. Sweetened ready-to-serve beverages	Sulphur dioxide	70
	or	
	Benzoic acid	120
9. Syrups and sherbets	Sulphur dioxide	350
	or	
	Benzoic acid	600

MANUFACTURING PROCESS

Mango Juice Manufacturing Process

The operation describes in this report are, where possible, performed by mechanical equipment, however, substitution of hand operations is not precluded if the same principles are followed.

WASHING

Washing fresh Mangoes accomplished one or more of the following purposes

a) Remove soil or earthy substances.
b) Remove mold, yeast, bacteria and/or spores of these micro organism.
c) Remove insects, insect eggs, larve of fragments.
d) Remove downy or spinery portions of skin.
e) Remove toxic and flavour or odour bearing residues of sprays and dusts.

To a soak tank into which raw Mangoes are discharged. Tank may contain cold or warm water (to 120°F) with or without addition of a harmless detergent. The time in soak tank to soak, is 2-3 minutes. Mangoes are elevated to brush washer with transverse revolving fibre or nylon brushes which fumable the product under sprays or water or high pressure. Washed fruit is now ready for final inspection and/or trimming.

SORTING AND TRIMMING

The sorting and trimming operations remove whole units by sorting, or portions of units by trimming with knives.

EXTRACTION OF JUICE

Washed, sorted and trimmed fruit drops into a juice extractor where paddles or brushes revolving inside a circular, perforated screen separate juices and pull (which flows through the screen) from the seeds, skin and tough tissues. The waste material is discharged from the end of the juice extractor.

Many other methods are also available for extraction of fruit juices and anyone of them can be adopted.

BLENDING OF JUICES

Juices are frequently packed with added sugar, salt, spices, harmless food colours, vitamins and citric or other fruit acids. It is also desirable at times to blend juices from several varieties of fruits to produce pleasant flavours or colours. The blending is normally accomplished in open kettles. The kettles may contains steam coils or be steam jacketed. Generally, they are equipped with mechanical agitators which thoroughly mix the contents without incorporating air into the product. All types of juices which requires this treatment are handled in exactly the same while the other is used for filling, after which the juice continues through the regular processing steps.

DE-AERATION

Where pre-heating is employed, de-aeration should follow immediately. This step is preferred by pumping the preheated juice into a closed container and drawing a vacuum of 10-15 inches on the vessel. This makes free the juice of any entrapped air. Removal of air which contains oxygen, aids in retention of colour and flavour and vitamin content. It prevents the oxidation of fruit juice and there by prolong the shelf life of product.

PASTEURIZING, FILLING. STERILIZING COOLING

These operations are considered because the acidity range of fruit dictates the types of operations and their order.

The PH is generally 4 and the spoilage is usually limited to yeast and mold growth. Under such acid condition, commercial sterility is achieved by filling the containers at 190°F, followed by inversion, for one minute or slow cooling under water sprays. In addition this heat treatment is usually sufficient to inactivate pectolytic and oxidative enzymes. The spores of some molds such as Byssochlamys and certain pencillium commonly found on fruit surfaces are more heat tolerate. This mold contamination can be greatly reduced by rejection of fruit-bearing rots, brushing the fruit surface with water sprays, or immersion in chlorine water followed by a fresh water rinses.

Preheated and de-aerated juice is filled into cans or bottles at temperature of near 160°F and caps or lids are applied. Containers are placed in crates and into boiling water. The cook time is measured from the time the water in the retort comes to a second boil. Cooking continues for the specified time, depending upon type and size of the container. Temperature of 195-200°F at centres of bottles is usually sufficient for a period of 6-8 minutes. The containers are then removed from boiling water and placed in cold running water until the contents of the containers, initial cooling water must be warm (130°-140°F) to temper the glass and prevent breakage from shock.

In some areas of the world the cost of cans and glass containers is prohibitive. For this reason other types of container must be considered. Juices can be packaged in plastic containers, tetrapacks container or pouches LDPE by automatic machine as desirable or heat sealed polyethylene bags if harmless preservatives are added. In the event this type of packaging is employed, the following procedure could be followed:-

(a) Extracted juice is pumped to blending kettles and all the ingredients added (sugar, acid, etc.) and the juices heated to 180oF to inactivate the enzymes.

(b) The juice is cooled to approximately 140°F and filled into polyethylene or other suitable plastic containers and sealed.

(c) Containers can be air or water cooled.

Extreme caution must be exercised in the filling, sealing, cooling and distribution of products packed in plastic containers to avoid rupturing them.

CHEMICAL PRESERVATIVES

The most common preservatives used in fruit juices are the potassium and sodium salts of sorbic, benzoic and sulfurous acids. The amount of sodium benzoate should not be greater then 0.1 wt% in any case and a common rate of addition of 0.08% may impart an objectionable odour. Potassium metabisulfite, and potassium Sorbate can also be used as preservatives. Instead of a sulfite salt, SO_2 can also be added as a gas (350-600 ppm) but So_2 must be removed before canning as it can be reduced by tin creating an H_2S odour and darkening the interior of the container.

The preservative used should be dissolved in a minimum amount of water before addition to juice to prevent the immediate precipitation resulting from its direct addition to juice it should be added after pasteurization.

LABELLING & CASING

Where production is small, labels are ordinarily applied to containers manually. Where labour costs are high, or where volume is large, the use of automatic labelling machine is necessary.

The containers are usually cased manually after labelling, the exception being in operations which produces large volume of a single container sizes. Automatic casers are not adjustable and therefore, usually confined to large volume operations.

Glass containers are hard cased normally to prevent breakages.

STORAGE

All caned and glass packed mango juice are subject to a loss of flavour, colour and vitamins during storage.

The most acceptable storage is that in which the temperature remains nearly constant at about 70°F. These conditions should be maintained within commercial practibility.

Consumption as an beverage as processed.

PLANT ECONOMICS

Rated Plant Capacity = 2.00 Tons/Day

LAND & BUILDING

Total Land Area 1600 sq.mt. = Rs. 48,28,000.00

PLANT & MACHINERY

FRUIT PROCESSING SECTION :

1. Working Tables
2. Aluminum Trays heavy duty,
3. Rotary fruits & vegetable washing machine
4. Water heating tank
5. Pulper Super Deluxe made of S. S.
6. Fruit Mill, all contact parts
7. Hydraulic juice press
8. Storage & mixing tank
9. Rosing machine
10. Water storage tank

BOTTLING SECTION :

11. Tubular pasteuriser
11. 4-Head Bottle washer
12. Rotary Bottle washing machine
13. Semi automatic Bottle filling machine
14. Semi automatic Crown corking machine
15. Super Refractometer
16. Pocket Refracto meter
17. ABBE Refractometer Table model
18. Laboratory Equipments
19. Boiler
20. Water Demineralizer
21. Pipes, pumps fittings, tanks, trolleys
22. Miscellaneous tools, jigs, fixtures

FIXED CAPITAL

1.	Land & Building	Rs.	48,28,000.00
2.	Plant & Machinery	Rs.	51,44,740.00
3.	Other Fixed Assets	Rs.	21,00,000.00
	Total	Rs.	1,20,72,740.00

RAW MATERIALS

1. Ripe Mango
2. Ripe Litchi
3. Orange and other fruits
4. Tomato
5. Coconut (green)
6. Sugar
7. Citric Acid
8. Colour (beta-carotene)
9. Essence
10. Salt
11. Spices
12. Potassium Meta bisulphite
13. Acetic Acid
14. Benzoic Acid
15. Laboratory chemicals
16. Glass bottle, crown
17. Glass Bottles for pulp and ketchup 500 ml size, with sticker, tapes, caps, cartons

TOTAL WORKING CAPITAL/ANNUM

1.	Raw Material	Rs.	1,15,47,800.00
2.	Salary & Wages	Rs.	21,18,000.00
3.	Utilities & Overheads	Rs.	18,70,000.00
	Total	Rs.	1,55,35,800.00

TOTAL CAPITAL INVESTMENT

Total Fixed Capital	Rs.	1,20,72,740.00
Total Working Capital for 3 Months	Rs.	38,83,950.00
Total	Rs.	1,59,56,690.00

TURN OVER/ANNUM

By sale of Mango juice in (200 ml Bottle),
(5,00,000 Nos.)
By sale of Litchi juice in 200 ml Bottle,
By sale of Orange and other fruit juice (200 ml size)
By sale of Tomato juice (200 ml)
By sale of Tomato Pulp (500ml)
By sale of Tomato Ketchup (500 ml)
By sale of Coconut water in bottle
(200 ml size) (15,00,000 Nos)

Total Rs. 3,06,00,000.00

PROFIT SALES RATIO = Profit/Sales x 100 = 32.82%

RATE OF RETURN = Operating profit/T.C.I x 100 = 62.93%

BREAK EVEN POINT (B.E.P) = 39.72%

Chapter 26

FROZEN MEAT

PROCESS OF MANUFACTURE

All the sheeps are subjected to medical check up to be sure that they are free from any disease before they are slaughtered. The sheep is slaughtered by a sharp knife by removing half neck to cut the all the blood circulating nerves and vein and it is bled to death. Then the hides are removed. Before the viscera is removed they are again subjected to inspection by vetinary staff. Then the interior of the animal is thoroughly cleaned.

The quantity of field of dressed meat obtained per animal depends largely on its live weight, size and breed ,and also on topographical and climatic conditions. The average dressing yield in terms of the original live weight for indian sheep and goats calculated about 40% .

After the carcass of the sheep is divided into sides and quarters, it is further subdivided into recognised portions known as cuts. The bigger cuts, generally made at the points of articulation are known as joints. The value of meat depends to a great extent on the appearance and shape of these cuts. Mutton and goat meat cuts are the legs, loins, racks, breasts shank and shoulders. Besides the dressed meat certain parts of the carcass and their organs called offals are also sold as meat. Edible offals include tongue, sweet bread (pancreas) kidneys, heart, liver, tripe (the first and second stomach of cattle i.e. the rumen and reticulum), and tails.

In edible offals includes the hides, hair, bones, horns and hoofs. Blood and miscellaneous scraps of meat and fat may be used for both edible and inedible purpose.

Percent. For storing mear for long periods, frozen storage is used and the temperatures recommended are -23 deg to 18 deg. Meat may be frozen in whole carcasses, in large cuts or as consumer cuts. It is usually wrapped and packed in fibre board or wooden bases before freezing. The two methods of freezing and commercially adopted nowadays are blast freezing and plate freezing, the former being used for irregularly shaped items like material fast and are preferable to slow freezing of chilled meat in still air at -10 deg to 15 deg, since the drip on thawing and consequently the loss in soluble nutrients and consumer appeal, are much less in fast-frozen meat. Storage life of frozen meat and meat production kept at -18 deg is as follows: lamb, 6-16; liver, 2-4 months.

In India, raw meat is mostly sold fresh and is not ordinarily stored in any appreciable quantity while extensive cold storage facilities are available in western countries for the storage of meat and its products for long periods. Meat is sometimes stored for long periods. Meat is sometimes stored for 12-36 hr in ice during warm weather; mechanical refrigeration is resorted to only in major cities. Refrigeration results in the quick removal of body heat from the carcass and thus helps in slowing down rigor mortis and in achieving optimum preservative qualities .

Storage of meat at chilling temperature above the freezing point of meat (-2.2deg) is known as refrigerated storage and that below the freezing point as frozen storage is used and the temperatures recommended are -23 deg to -18 deg. Meat may be frozen in whole carcasses, in large cuts or as consumer cuts. It is usually wrapped and packed in fibre board or wooden boxes before freezing. The two methods of freezing and plate freezing, the former being used for irregularly shaped items like beef quarters and small carcasses and the latter for items of regular shape. Both these methods freeze the material fast and are preferable to slow freezing of chilled meat in still air at -10 deg to -15 deg, since the drip on thawing and consequently the loss in soluble nutrients and consumer appeal, are much less in fast-frozen meat. Storage life of frozen meat and meat products kept at -18 deg is as follows :lamb,6-16; liver,2-4 months.

Curing

Four methods are generally followed for curing meat, viz,

1) Sweet Pickle Curing
2) Dry Salt
3) Curing, dry curing
4) Injection curing.

Meat curing agents includes sodium chloride, nitrite, Ascorbate or erythorbate and possibly sodium phosphate, sucrose, dextrose, or corn syrup, and seasoning the salts content of processed meats varies 1-12 %, according to the type of product, salt is used for flavour,preservation and extraction of myofibriller protein, whereas nitrite per mole colour development, flavour and preservation by unhabiting the growth of microorganisms and fat oxidations. Erythorbate acts as color stabilizer, reduces fat oxidation, and inhabits undesirable.

Canning

Canned meat may be processed to be commercially sterile or semi-preserved. The objective of commercial sterilization is to destroy all harmful bacteria or bacteria that may cause spoilage of the products under normal unrefrigerated storage. However, the process does not kill the spores of all heat-resistant bacteria. Therefore, it is essential to cool the cans rapidly after processing and avoid storage above 33 deg C. The most persistant type of bacteria are performing organisms. The common vegetative and non performing pathogenic bacteria are killed with adequate processing and are of little or no importance in spoilage.

The amount of heat, time, and temperature required for a given degree of sterility depends upon the nature of the product, the pH. curing salts, shape and size of the can, and the type of heat-processing retort used. Some products are packed into the can hot and others cold. Hot filling eliminates the need to apply a vacuum during can closure. The vacuum is necessary to avoid excessive strain on the can and its seems during processing and to minimize oxidative spoilage of the product.

Semi-preserved or pasteurized products depend on during on curing and chilled storage for their preservation.

Irradiations

Preservations of meat by irradiation methods is of recent introduction. The types of irradiations are known, viz, non-ionizing (making use of microwaves, inferred and ultra-violet rays),and ionizing (utilizing cathode and gamma rays). The former type has poor penetration characteristics, catalyses oxidative ranacity of the fat and causes discolouration of the meat pigments: bactericidal effect is obtained only with radiations near 2600 A. The use of the latter type of radiations otherwise known as cold sterlization, kills micro-organisms without producing heat but may cause some adverse effects like fat deterioration and unpalatable irradiation odours.

Irradiation doses lower than the sterilizing dosages are reported to be more practicable when used in conjunction with refrigeration, antibiotics and chemicals.

Nitrite reactions Phosphate facilitate myofibriller protein extraction, inhibit fat oxidation and improve colour development. Sugar and seasonings are used principally for flavour.

CONCLUSION

Large cut muttons are stored in freezer within the short period of time to change due to microorganism and enzymes. If the meat is to be kept for longer period, it should be frozen when the meat is thoroughly chilled it is then cut into suitable small pieces for packing into can. The prepared (cut dressed and trimed) meat is balanced if it is to be canned in brine to reduce or to kill the micro-organism. It is then filled into can and hot-brine is filled upto the brim of the can. It is exhausted and sealed. The sealed cans are processed at 12lb pressure for a definite period of time depending upon the size of the cans.

PROCESS FLOW CHART FOR MUTTON PROCESSING

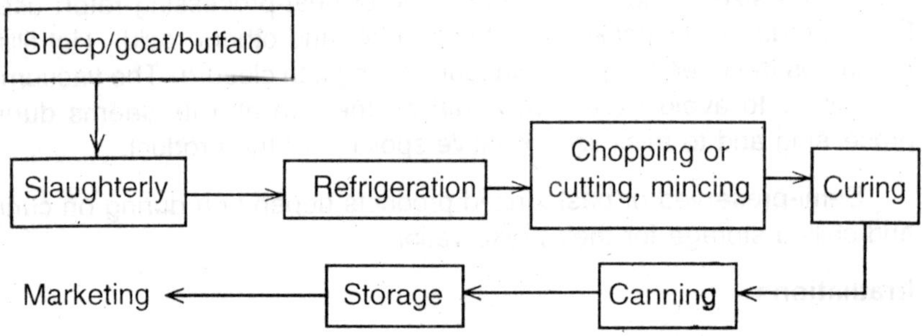

PLANT ECONOMICS

Rated Plant Capacity = 10.00 Tons/Day

LAND & BUILDING

Total Land Area 2 acres = Rs. 51,10,000.00

PLANT & MACHINERY

1. Slaughtering equipments
2. Jet spray washing unit
3. Hangar made of Stainless steel
4. Electric rotating circular knife
5. Meat cutting and chopping machine
6. Jacketed Vessel (Stainless Steel)
7. Meat mincer
8. Bone separation Unit
9. Autoclave
10. Automatic weighing can filling and sealing unit
11. Weighing bridge
12. Exhaust Box
14. Preparation table stainless steel
15. Boiler
17. Conveyor Belt
18. Waste treatment Unit

FIXED CAPITAL

1.	Land & Building	Rs.	51,10,000.00
2.	Plant & Machinery	Rs.	33,01,000.00
3.	Other Fixed Assets	Rs.	18,30,000.00
	Total	Rs.	1,02,41,000.00

RAW MATERIALS

1. Buffaloes
2. Goats
3. Sheep
4. Packaging Materials
5. Chemicals, Preservative and salts, oils etc.

TOTAL WORKING CAPITAL/MONTH

1.	Raw Material	Rs.	27,95,000.00
2.	Salary & Wages	Rs.	1,93,375.00
3.	Utilities & Overheads	Rs.	1,70,750.00
	Total	Rs.	31,59,125.00

TOTAL CAPITAL INVESTMENT

Total Fixed Capital	Rs.	1,02,41,000.00
Total Working Capital for 3 Months	Rs.	94,77,375.00
Total	Rs.	1,97,18,375.00

TURN OVER/ANNUM

By Sale of 3000 Tons of Processed Canned Meat	Rs.	6,00,00,000.00

PROFIT SALES RATIO = Profit/Sales x 100 = 29.05%

RATE OF RETURN = Operating profit/T.C.I x 100 = 88.39%

BREAK EVEN POINT (B.E.P) = 26.88%

Chapter 27

GUAVA JAM AND JELLY

SPECIFICATIONS OF JAM & JELLIES

Specification for Jams :-

Product	Kind & Variety of fruit	Minimum % of fruit in the final product on fresh fruit basis w/w	Minimum % of soluble solids in the final product w/w	Special Characteristics	General Characteristics
Jams	Any fruit of suitable variety	45	68	The finished product shall have a heavy consistency	It may be a single or mixed fruit jam. The fruit used shall be mature, fresh, sound, clean & free from fermentation and mould. Dry or canned fruit, preserved pulp or juice may be used. Pectin derived from any fruit may be added, when necessary. The only substances that may be added are sugar, dextrose invert sugar or liquid glucose, flavouring matter, ascorbic acid, citric acid, permitted colours & preservatives. It shall have the flavour of the original fruit & shall be free from burnt or other objectionable

					flavours, crystallization, mould growth & shall show of no sign of fermentation. If packed in cans, it shall not show any positive pressure at sea level. No artificial sweetening matter shall be added.
Fruit	Any	45	65	Fruit jellies shall be made from clear strained fruit extract prepared by boiling the fruit with water.	The fruit shall be clean and free from fermentation and mould. The finished product shall be reasonably uniform & shall be of good keeping-quality & attract colour. The only substance that may be added are sugar dextrose, invert sugar or liquid glucose, ascorbic acid, citric acid, permitted colours & preservatives. fruit jelly shall be a product of gelationous consistency prepared by boiling by boiling strained fruit extract with sugar. It shall be clear sparkling, transparent and of an attractive colour. It should not be syrupy, sticky or gummy and should retain the flavour & aroma of the original fruit. No artificial sweetening matter shall be added. It shall show no sign of fermentation.

MANUFACTURING PROCESS

Ripe guavas, preferably with plenty of pulp and less seeds, are used for the preparation of jelly. The fruit is washed well and cut into thin slices. They are covered with an equal weight of water containing 2 grams of citric acid for every kg of guava taken. The mixture is heated gently for about 30 minutes to extract pectin from the slices. The extract is drained, and to the residue, water equal to 1/4th of the weight of slices is added, and a second extract is taken. The two extracts are combined and strained through a piece of thick cloth to remove the coarse particles. The strained extract is allowed to settle overnight in a tall vessel. Next day, the clear supernatant liquid is syphoned off without disturbing the sediment at the bottom of the vessel. The extract which is clear, is tested for its pectin content by the alcohol precipitation method or by the jelmeter. The required quantity of sugar (generally on equal quantity) is added to the extract and the mixture boiled down to the desired consistency. The finished jelly is packed in glass jars or in cans. Guava jelly with its attractive purplish red colour and pleasant taste and aroma, is a fairly popular product in this country and also in some other countries.

PROCESS FLOW SHEET

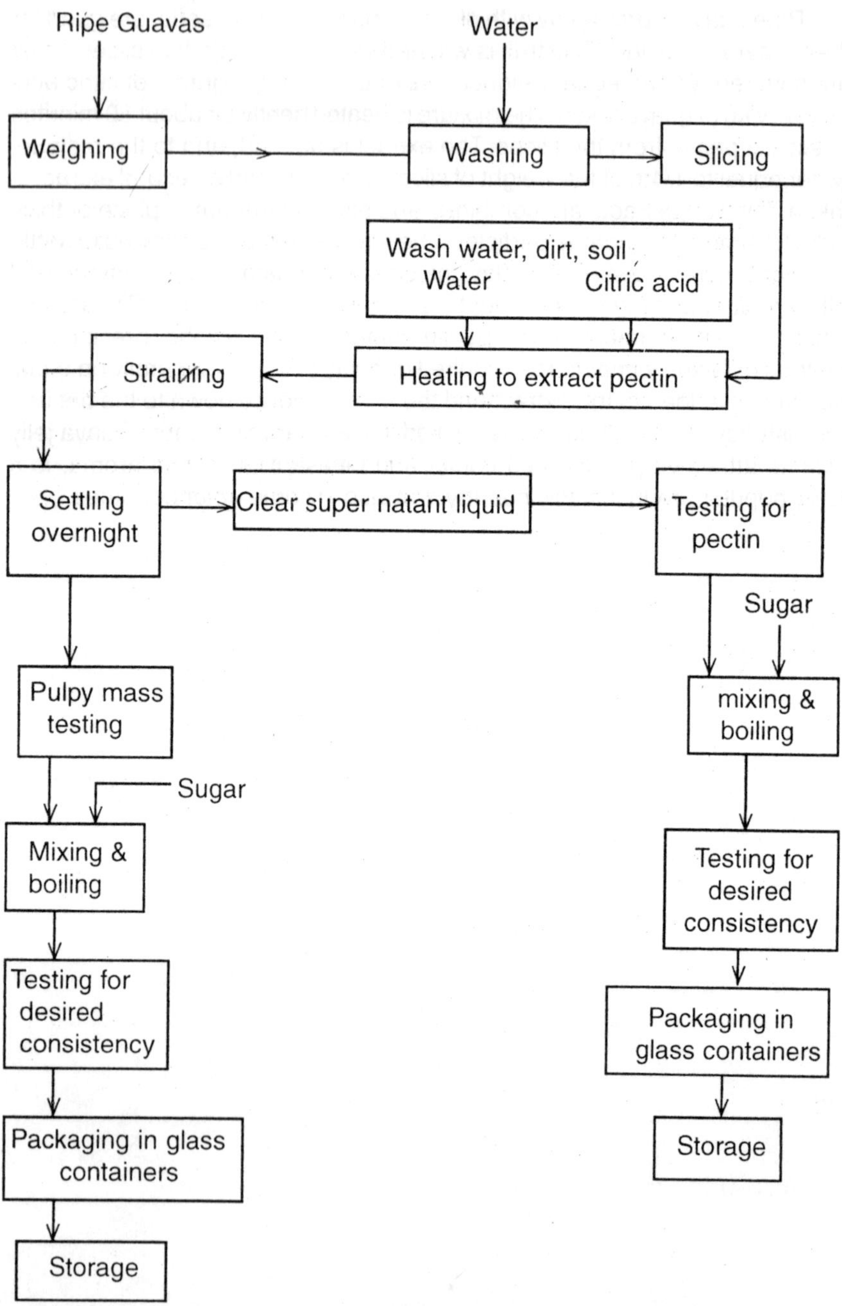

PLANT ECONOMICS

ated Plant Capacity = 400.00 Kgs./Day

LAND & BUILDING

otal Land Area 250 Sq. Mt. = Rs. 4,55,000.00

PLANT & MACHINERY

1. Stainless steel tank
2. PVC-Sintex tank
3. Water pump
4. Fruit slicer
5. Stainless steel semi circular tank
6. Heating furnace or chullah.
7. Stainless steel straining
8. Stainless steel water storage tank
9. S.S. filling tank
10. Bottle/jar sealing machine
11. Laboratory equipment

FIXED CAPITAL

1.	Land & Building	Rs.	4,55,000.00
2.	Plant & Machinery	Rs.	3,34,000.00
3.	Other Fixed Assets	Rs.	2,30,000.00
	Total	Rs.	10,19,000.00

RAW MATERIALS

1. Guava
2. Sugar
3. Citric acid
4. Glass bottles
5. Corrugated paper cartons
6. Adhesive tapes

TOTAL WORKING CAPITAL/MONTH

1.	Raw Material	Rs.	2,24,100.00
2.	Salary & Wages	Rs.	45,500.00
3.	Utilities & Overheads	Rs.	49,500.00
	Total	Rs.	3,19,100.00

TOTAL CAPITAL INVESTMENT

Total Fixed Capital	Rs.	10,19,000.00
Total Working Capital for 3 Months	Rs.	9,57,300.00
Total	Rs.	19,76,300.00

TURN OVER/ANNUM

By sale of 60000 Kgs of guava jelly
By sale of 60000 Kgs of guava jam

Total	Rs.	51,60,000.00

PROFIT SALES RATIO = Profit/Sales x 100 = 16.40%

RATE OF RETURN = Operating profit/T.C.I x 100 = 42.83%

BREAK EVEN POINT (B.E.P) – 52.63%

Chapter 28

ICE-CREAM & ICE CANDY

Ice - Cream is a frozen dairy product food product made by freezing a pasteurized mix with agitation to incorporate air and insure uniformity of consistency. The mix is composed of a combination of milk products, sugar, dextrose corn syrup in dry or liquid form, water or other optional ingredients, with or without eggs or eggs products with harmless flavoring and with or without added stabilizer or emulsifier and all of wholesome edible material.

Ice - candy is the hardened ice cream without emulsifier. In ancient times, sugar must have been a highly valued consumption item. Therefore, there was no candy that used sugar as liberally as we do in the present age. But a complete change occurred in the picture. Anyone can now enjoy the sweet state of candy. Today, there is a great varieties of candies, which meet the desires of children.

Ice - cream must have evolved from Ice beverages and water ices that were popular in the early medical period. Wires & fruits juices were cooled with ice and show brought from mountains by runners to the court of New, Emperor of Rome in the first century. Early plants were established in western countries in cities like New York, Chicago.

FORMULATIONS

CANDY PRODUCTS AND CONFECTIONERY CHOCOLATE

PEANUT BARS

Sugar	3 Lb.
Corn Syrup	3 Lb.
Water	1 Pt.

Cook to 240°F. Then cold and pours of washed peanuts and cook for 10 minutes. Remake from fire and in chocolate.

Fruit Jelly Candies

Fruit Juice	2 qt.
Sugar	3 Lb.
Corn Syrup of Invert Syrup	3 Lb.
Commercial Pectin Syrup	1 qt.

Mix fruit juice and pectin syrup. Add the sugar and corn, or invert, syrup. Boil to 222-223°F Remove from fire. Put into starch molds or oiled pans, about 1/2 inch deep. Allow to burden 24 hours. Remove from molds and dust with powdered sugar or dip in chocolate.

Sugar Coating for Candy

Cocoa Butter Substitute	35 lb.
Powdered Skin milk	15 lb.
Powdered Sugar	50 lb.
Salt	2 oz.
Vanillin	1/2 oz.

This may be coloured and flavored with oil soluble colors.. After melting the cocoa butter substitute, add the other materials gradually in a dough mixer and finally run over finishing rolls at a temperature of 110°F. In using, run an enrober at 104°F.

French Chewing Candy

Mixture No. I

Corn Syrup	25 lb.
Albumen - Dissolved in	3 lb.
Nulomoline	25 lb.
Water	6 lb.

Boil the corn syrup to 245°F. Add the Nulomoline and stir until it is melted. Place the batch into a heater. Start the beater. Then gradually add the aqueous albumen solution and heat until light.

Mixture No. 2

Sugar	30 lb.
Cream (20% butter fat)	10 lb.
Numbomoline	5 lb.
Coconut Oil (76°F m.p.)	7 lb.
Corn Syrup	25 lb.

Ice-Cream Preparation

Albumen	10 oz.
Sugar	80 oz.
Whole dried milk	10 oz.
Indian Gum	5 oz.
Vanillin	1.5 oz.

Or

Dried Milk	50 oz.
Sugar	50 oz.
Cream of Tartar	4.4 oz.
Sodium	2 oz.
Vanillin	0.06 oz.

Chocola` Cream

Milk	32 oz.
Sugar	16 oz.
Flour	2 oz.
Salt	1/8 oz.
Eggs	4 oz.
Cream	32 oz.
Vanillin	1/4 oz.
Unsweatened	5 oz.

MANUFACTURING PROCESS

PREPARATION OF THE MIX

A very important process involved in the manufacture of ice cream is preparing the mix. Preparing the mix involves, assembling the ingredients from storage area to the preparation zone, weighing or metering and mixing ingredients and the pasteurization, homogenization, cooling and storage of the mix.

According to the recent studies on ice cream manufacturing plant methods, equipment, and layout it is found that four methods are in for processing mix.

1) The bulk ingredients and continuous high temperature short time pasteurization.

2) Ingredients in cans and high temperature short time pasteurization

3) Bulk in gradients and batch pasteurization.

4) Ingredients in cans and batch pasteurization

The lowest cost method for preparing mix is the can and batch pasteurization method due to the low cost of requirement involved.

ORDER OF ADDING INGREDIENTS

All liquid ingredients (cream, milk, condensed milk, syrup etc.) are placed in the vat and the agitation and heating shorted at once. the dry ingredients including MSNF, dried eggs, cocoa, sugar, and stabilizer are added while the liquid material is agitated and before the temp. reaches 120°F. It gelatin is the stabilizer used, it is best to and it after it is thoroughly mixed with an equal volume of sugar and before the liquid reaches 120oF. When butter plastic cream, frozen cream are added they should be cut into fairly small pieces and added in time to allow complete melting before the pasteurizing temp. is reached.

PASTEURIZATION OF MIX

Pasteurization of all mixes is compulsory because this process destroys all pathogenic or decease producing bacteria, thereby safe guarding the health of the consumer. Pasteurization requires only slight additional expense, since the mix is usually heated to facilitate solution, and since the homogenization process can be accomplished best at the pasteurization temperature level.

Proper pasteurization consists in rapidly heating to a definite temperature, holding at that temp. for a definite minimum of time, and then rapidly cooling to below 40°F.

Reasons for high temperature pasteurization result in (1) Greater bacterial kill resulting in lower bacterial count in ice cream (2) Suitable temperature and time of pasteurization result in (a) Better body and texture

(b) Better flavour.
(c) Protection against
(d) Saving of stabilizer
(e) Increased capacity

For maximum benefits the mix probably should be processed at 210° - 220°F.

HOMOGENIZING OF THE MIX

Homogenization is usually accomplished by forcing the mix thro's small crifice under suitable conditions of temperature and pressure, using a positive displacement plunger pump to furnish the pressure. The orifice consists of a value and seat in which the two adacent surfaces are parallel and lapped smooth and is surrounded by an impact ring against which the mix impringes as it leaves the valve. The break up of fat particles is caused by the shear forces set up in a thin stream of mix traveling at high velocity between the closely adjacent surfaces of the value and seat and then by a sheltering effect as it impragas on the impact ring upon leaving the valve.

COOLING THE MIX

Cooling the mix immediately after homogenization to 32° - 40°F is essential after which it should be held in aging tanks until used, unless the mix is cooled to a temperature of 40°F or lower it will become very viscous and the ice cream will not melt down smoothly. Also temp. below 40°F retard the growth of bacteria coolers of the surface or cabinet types are generally used for ice cream mix.

AGING THE MIX

Experimental work shows that appreciable benefits result from an aging period although little is gained by aging longer than 4 hr.

Aging mix before freezing has been practical since the in addition of the ice cream industry. The changes which undoubtly occur during aging are (1) The fat is solidified (2) If gelatin has been used as a stabilizer it swells and combines with Water (3) The proteins of the mix may change slightly.

(4) The viscosity is increased, largely due to the previously mentioned changes. The aging temp. should not exceed 40°F. When the mix has been properly aged, it is ready for the freezing process which generally follows immediately.

THE FREEZING PROCESS

Freezing the mix is one of the most important operations in the making of ice-cream for upon it depends the quality, palatability and yield of the final product.

ICE CREAM PREPARATION (FREEZE IT)

Albumen	10 oz.
Sugar	80 oz.
Whole Dried Milk	10 oz.
Indian Gum	5 oz.
Vanillin	1.5 oz.
Dried Milk	50 oz.
Sugar	50 oz.
Cream of Tartar	4.4 oz.
Sodium	2 oz.
Vanillin	0.06 oz.

Package 4.5 ounces = 127.5 grams.

Stir contents of the package into 1/2 pint. (one cup) cold milk. Stir until dissolved. Whip 1/2 pint (one cup) chilled whipping cream. Add the dissolved freeze. It to the whipped cream and mix freeze.

Chocolate Ice Cream

Milk	32 oz.
Sugar	16 oz.
Flour	2 oz.
Salt	1/8 oz.
Eggs	4 oz.
Cream	32 oz.
Vanillin	1/4 oz.
Unsweatened	4 oz.

CHOCOLATE

Eat milk and add flour, salt the sugar. Stir thoroughly in double boiler for 20 minutes after batches brought to a boil. After the mass thickness add the beaten eggs and cook for 5 minutes longer with content stirring. Cool, add cream which has been whipped into a stiff paste and then add the flavouring add the melted chocolate which was previously mixed with a little sugar and warm milk to form a paste. Put in a refrigerator or pack in ice and salt until frozen.

PROCESS DESCRIPTION

The process here describes is roughly divided into two units, namely are to concentrate the material and the other to form hard candies. The former consists of an automatic dissolving machine, receiving tank, automatic vacuum concentrator, cooling table, kneeling machine and hot table, while the latter requires machines described in the latter half beginning from the batch roller, of the plant layout.

The process of the vacuum concentrator unit is to evaporate material under low temperature with reduced pressure. How to carry this process and what machines should be used for this process are very important factors because they decide the taste and colouring of the final product.

Vacuum concentrators widely employed now in Japan are highly automated to make the processing time as short as possible. The candy materials taken out of the concentrators are then mixed with various additives, spius or unique flavours according to the desires of candy makers. The mixing process requires sufficient kneading to obtain excellent products.

After kneading is sufficiently carried out, the candy is drawn in rope shape of determined newsier by the batch roller (set with sizing roller). The machine employed in this plant is designed to make a drawing of 50 m of rope per minute.

The drawn candy is then put into the hard candy forming unit. Where candies are made, formed by the plastic forming machine.

The forming machine will not a only perform at high speed but also, provided with a number of die permit various kinds of forming.

The formed candies are finally cooled down to normal temperatures and charged to the packaging machine. The process for cooling down is carried out by a cooling conveyer, where it is also possible to check and adjust ill formed candies.

PLANT ECONOMICS

Rated Plant capacity	=	500.00 Lit./Day
LAND & BUILDING (Land 400 sq.mt.)	Rs.	3,30,000.00

PLANT & MACHINERY

1. Milk Storage S.S. Tank
2. Freon compressor
3. Brine tanks
4. Homogenizer (Churner)
5. Blending tank
6. Lab. Equipment
7. Baby Boiler
8. Mis. Equipments & Accessories

FIXED CAPITAL

1.	Land & Building	Rs.	3,30,000.00
2.	Plant & Machinery	Rs.	2,24,500.00
	TOTAL	Rs.	5,54,500.00

RAW MATERIALS

1. Fresh Milk
2. Fat Cream
3. Sugar
4. Stabilizer, colour essences, Chemicals dry fruits
5. Containers Big Cup
6. Small Cup
7. Stocks for bar
8. Ice blocks for trolleys

TOTAL WORKING CAPITAL/MONTH

1.	Raw Material	Rs.	3,05,625.00
2.	Salary & Wages	Rs.	26,040.00
3.	Utilities & Overheads	Rs.	45,000.00
	TOTAL	Rs.	3,76,665.00

TOTAL CAPITAL INVESTMENT

Total Fixed Capital	Rs.	5,54,500.00
Total Working Capital for 2 Months	Rs.	7,53,330.00
TOTAL	Rs.	13,07,830.00

TURN OVER/ANNUM

1. By sale of Big cup 6,00,000
2. Small Cup 9,00,000
3. Ice Cream bars 4,50,000
4. Ice Candy bar 4,50,000

TOTAL Rs. 74,25,000.00

PROFIT SALES RATIO = Profit / Sales x 100 = 35.24 %

RATE OF RETURN = Operating profit / T.C.I x 100 = 200.09 %

BREAK EVEN POINT (B.E.P) = 19.38 %

Chapter 29

JAM, JELLIES, PICKLES & SQUASHES

MANUFACTURING PROCESS FOR SQUASHES

1. ORANGE SQUASH :

First of all oranges are peeled and rags sticking to the segments is removed. Now the juice from segments is extract by using screw type s juice extractor and juice is collected and sieved to remove coarse seeds etc. and if necessary heated and packed in bottles.

The formulation is given below:-

Orange juice 10° Brix	45 Kgs.
0.8% acidity	45 Kgs.
Sugar	74 Kgs.
Citric Acid	2.33 Kgs.
Essence of orange	1.125 Kgs.
Water	57 Litres.
Orange Colour	qs
Potassium meta bisulphite	110 gms.

From the above formula, the squash obtained will have the following specification :

Juice	25%
Brix	45°
Acidity	1.5%

2. FORMULATION FOR OTHER SQUASHES :

In all types of squashes the method is same that is extraction of juice and addition of ingredients. Therefore, it is needless to repeat the process but to be familiar with formulations is essential.

(a) MANGO SQUASH

Mango Pulp 18°	45 Kgs.
Brix 0.5% acidity sugar	62.6 Kgs.
Citric acid	1.2 Kgs.
Water	71.8 lit.
Preservative	110 gms.

SPECIFICATIONS :

Juice	25%
Brix	45°
Acidity	0.8%

(b) PINEAPPLE SQUASH

Pineapple juices 80° Brix 0.5 acidity	45 kgs.
Sugar	74.8 Kgs.
Citric Acid	2.475 kgs.
Pineapple flavour	1.125 Kgs.
Water	56.5 Kgs.
Yellow colour	qs
Preservative	110 gms.

SPECIFICATIONS :

Juice	25%
Brix	45°
Acidity	1.5%

(c) LEMON SQUASH:

Juice 10° 5% acidity	45 Kgs.
Sugar	76 Kgs.
Citric Acid	460 gms.
Water	57.5 lit.
Essence of lemon	1.125 Kgs.
Preservative	110 gms.

SPECIFICATIONS

Juice	25%
Brix	45°
Acidity	1.5%

The equipments required for squashes are as under :-

1. Conveyor type juice extractor	1 No.
2. Mixer with heating arrangement	1 No.
3. Sealing Machine	1 No.
4. Buckets etc.	

MANUFACTURING PROCESS FOR SAUCES & KETCHUP

Sauce of any fruit can be prepared but the most popular sauce. It is also used as chutney. Manufacturing process of all varieties of fruits sauces is almost similar.

First, the fruits are peeled, sliced, and ground. The spices, and other additives are added. Thickening agents also are added to prevent or retard sedimentation of the solid particles in suspension. In India, apple pulp is often used for this purpose. Sometimes, the fruit, which is used for making sauce, is boiled pulped as a filler. The starches of maize potato, arrowroot, sago and rye also are used as thickening agents. The use of Indian gum locust, kernel gum tragacanth, karaya gum, glatin, irish moss, pectin and other similar substances is also advised. These are however, as good as the starches.

Formula for tomato Sauce

Tomato pulp (6% soluble solids)	29.250 Kgs.
Cardamom, pepper and cumin in equal quantities	8.5 gms.
Cinnamon, broken	10 gms.
Cloves, headless	8.5 gms.
Mace	5.7 gms.
Salt	5.7 gms.
Onions, chopped	154 gms.
Garlic ground	18 gms.
Sugar	2.140 Kgs.
White vinegar 100 grain	580 c.c.
Red Chilli powder	15 gms.

It is cooked to about half its volume i.e. about 28% solids, Eng point is determined by refractometer. It is filled into plain cans and processed for 45 min in boiling water.

CHILLI SAUCE

To 22.4 kgs. of peeled tomatoes, add 1 kg. of sugar 10 gm. of red chillies 0.9 Kg. of washed, peeled finely chopped onions, and the following spices tied loosely in a cloth bag.

Mace	7 gms.
Cinnamon broken	18 gms.
Cumin cardamom and black paper in equal quantities	22.5 gms.

Ground white paper	10 gms.
Ground ginger	10 gms.

Cook the whole mass in steam :- jacketed kettle to about 25.2 Kgs. crushing tomatoes with a ladle, if necessary. Add 2.14 Kgs. of kgs. of sugar and 0.675 Kg of salt and 1.57 Kgs (100 grain) vinegar. Continue the cooking of the mass further for about 5-10 minutes after which pack immediately in plain a cans seal and sterilize for half an hour in boiling water.

JAMS AND JELLIES

Jam is a product prepared from fruits. Jams should have 45% minimum of fruit in final product based on fresh fruit but in case of raspberry and strawberry, minimum percentage of fruit is be 25% minimum percentage of soluble solids in the final product is 68% and the finished product shall have a heavy consistency.

MANUFACTURE OF JAMS

They are generally prepared from almost all the fruits and from some vegetables. First, fruits are boiled in small quantity of water and thus pulp is made. Now the sugar is added to the pulp. The proportion of sugar to fruit varies with the variety of the fruit its ripeness, and the effect desired, although usually the amount of sugar used in equal to the amount of fruit in case of berries, plums, apricots, pineapple and other fruits. Sweet prunes require lesser sugar and in some cases even one fourth the amount of fruit is sufficient.

In manufacturing jams, boiling is essential so that fruit pulp and sugar are mixed intimately. Jams are concentrated to a boiling point of 102-105°C, and point varying with fruit variety, proportion of sugar and other factors. A jelly thermometer may be used with advantages to determine the end point of the boiling processes. The usual finishing point is 65 to 68% soluble solids as determined by abbe refrectometer.

At this stage jams are packed in cans or tins but sometimes, glass bottles of wide mouth may also be used. If the product contains a very high concentration of sugar (70% or above), it will not spoil in most climates. Most commercially prepared jams are not concentrated to this high density, however, and should be pasteurized at 80°C for 30 mins. or packed at 90 to 95°c in preheated glass containers, in order to prevent moulding or fermentation.

JELLY

In manufacturing unit, the essential substances are pectin, acid and sugar, of these pectin is most important. To obtain good quality jelly, proper proportions of substances may be used. Pectin and acid are added to those fruit juices which are deficient in these substances. Citric, tartaric or suitable acid are added to make up the deficiency of acidity in fruit juice.

MANUFACTURING PROCESS

Jellies are prepared from acqueous fruit extracts fruits are cut into slices so that pectin and acid may be extracted easily. Only a minimum quantity of water would be added to the fruit for a simple extraction of pectin. If necessary, a second or even a their extraction may also be taken and mixed with the first extract. If large quantities of water are used, jelly will be weak, and if too little water is used, the extract will be difficult to clarify. The length of boiling will vary according to the variety of and texture of the fruit. Apples normally require only 20 minutes or less and oranges from 30 to 60 min. The fruit should be heated only long enough to soften it sufficiently to permit through extraction of the juice by pressing and long enough to render it mushy.

In jelling making process, boiling is most important step because it dissolves the sugar and cause union of the sugar, acid and pectin to form jelly. Its principal purpose is to increase the concentration of the sugar too the point where jelling will occur. Prolonged boiling results in loss of flavour, injury to colour, and hydrolysis of the pectin consequently it is a frequent cause of jelly failure. The boiling is continued until on cooling the product will form a jelly of the desired consistency. The concentration of the mixture, when this point is reached will depend upon several factors viz the concentration of pectin concentration of acid, ratio of sugar to pectin and acid and texture desired.

Finally jelly is packed in cans or bottles near boiling point or nearly 95°C and sealed hot. Such procedure sterilizes the jelly glass and lid, and as the package is hermetically sealed, the product does not mould or foerment. It has been noted that at 0.05% acidity (as citric) 75 gms. of sugar per 100 gms of jelly was necessary to form jelly, while at 1.05% acidity jelly formed when the finished product contained only 53.5 gms of sugar per 100 gms of jelly.

PROCESS CONDITIONS OF MANUFACTURING JAMS & JELLIES

While manufacturing jams the most important observation is the PH of the material. Since the pH is the controlling factor is the setting of jams, it is sometimes necessary to adjust it the optimum. This is done by adding acid salts of citric or tartaric acids or alkalines like sodium bicarbonate or calcium carbonate. Teh addition of about 31 gms of the buffer salt to 50 kgs. of gam will generally change the pH about 0.1 of a unit.

The pH of the material has great influences on the inversion of sugar and the setting of jam of marmalade. The pH required to produce a good firm set in pectin jelly is 3.30 but in jams it varies with the kind of fruit used.

pH RANGE FOR DIFFERENT KINDS OF JAMS

TYPE OF JAM	PH RANGE	OPTIMUM pH
Apricot, Greengage, plum	3.2 - 3.5	3.35
Apple and Damson, Apple and plum	3.2 - 3.5	3.35
Apple and Raspberry	3.4 - 3.5	3.40
Orange marmalada	3.4 - 3.5	3.40
Gooseberry	3.4 - 3.5	3.40
Raspberry	3.5 - 3.7	3.60
Raspberry and Red Currents	3.5 - 3.7	3.60
Strawberry	3.7	3.7
Mango	3.3 - 3.6	3.4

MANUFACTURING PROCESS OF CHUTNEY

Apple Chutney

RECIPE - I

Apple	18.1 kg
Sultanans	9.0 kg
Onion powder	226.7 g
Sugar	13.6 kg
Slat	28.3 g
Cassia, ground	28.3 g
Pimento, ground	28.3 g
Nutmeg, ground	14.1 g
Caramel	283.4 g
Acetic acid	0.9 kg
Malt vinegar	13.6 litres

RECIPE - II

Apple	2.7 kg
Onions	to taste
Brown sugar	2.27 litres
Preservative sugar	2 heads
Cayenne (red chilli powder)	1/4 tea spoonful
Garlic	1/2 tea spoonful
Salt	3 tea spoonful
Vinegar	2 tea spoonful

Sweet Mango chutney

RECIPE

Peeled mango slices	0.9 kg
Sugar	0.9 kg
Slat	56.6 g
Mixed spices (cardamon, cinnamon, cumin etc. in equal quantities)	28.3 g
Garlic, chopped	6.0 g
Red chilli powder, finely ground	14.0 g
Vinegar	113.4 g
Onions, chopped	28.3 g
Ginger, green	113.4 g

Peach Chutney

RECIPE

Dried peaches	0.9 kg (equal to 4.5 kg of peeled peaches)
Onion	0.45 kg
Raisin	0.45 kg
Sultanas	0.22 kg
Cinnamon, powder	14 kg
Ginger, ground	14 g
Vinegar	1.1 litre

Plum Chutney

RECIPE

Plums, fully ripe	1.8 kg
Sugar	1.8 kg
Vinegar	0.45 kg
Mace (Jalvari) not ground	1 blade
Cloves (headless)	6 in number
Pepper, black, ground	10 in number
Chilli, Kashmiri, finely ground	7.0 g
Salt, finely powdered	14.1 g

Tomato Chutney

RECIPE

Tomato	13.6 kg
Onions, chopped	9.5 kg
Sugar	18.1 kg
Salt	0.9 kg
Ginger	56.0 g
Chillies	14.1 g
Vinegar	20.4 litres
Garlic vinegar	9.0 litres

The chutneys are prepared from fruits, vegetables. The fruits or vegetables are cut into slices or pieces of suitable size and softened by boiling in water. Slow cooking at a temperature below the boiling point yields a better product than brisk heating at a comparatively higher temperature. Onion and garlic are added at the start to melow their strong flavours. Spices are coarsely powdered before they are added to the product. Sometimes a vinegar extract of spices is used instead of whole spices.

Sweet chutneys such as mango and apricot chutneys are generally cooked to consistency of Jam to avoid fermentation of product during storage. Where vinegar is used in large quantities, the amount of sugar reduce correspondingly because vinegar itself serves partly as a preservative.

Bottling

Only clean and dry bottles and jars earlier sterilized in boiling water should be used and they should be warm at the time of filling. If the bottles are jars are not properly clean, fermentation organisms adhering to the walls of the containers. It is safer to pasteurize the filled bottles after sealing them at 82°C for about 30 minutes in 0.45 or 0.5 kg size jars

PLANT ECONOMICS

Rated Plant Capacity = 416.66 Bottles/Day

LAND & BUILDING

Total land area 1000 sq.mt = Rs. 9,50,000.00

PLANT & MACHINERY

1. Screw type juice extractor made of aluminium & one sieve
2. Vacuum filling machine
3. Pulveriser/Grinder Machine
4. Pulper Super Deluxe
5. Steam Jacketed Kettle
6. Fruit Mill
7. Storage tank and mixing tanks
8. Drying/Heating/Dehydrator, Sturdily built fitted
9. Vacuum Tester
10. Working table stainless steel top
11. Boiler
12. Aluminium trays & trollies
13. Crown corking heavy duty
14. Bottle washing M/c.
15. Peeling knives made of stainless steel.
16. Fruit cutting knives
17. Fruit Cutting knives
18. Stainless steel knives, extra large
19. Sterlization tank with steam heating coil

FIXED CAPITAL

1.	Land & Building		Rs.	9,50,000.00
2.	Plant & Machinery		Rs.	4,01,760.00
3.	Other Fixed Assets		Rs.	1,25,000.00
		Total	Rs.	14,76,760.00

RAW MATERIALS

1. Pine Apple ripe
2. Mango Season
3. Bamboo Shoot
4. Citric Acid
5. Lemon fully pipe
6. Sugar
7. Pectin
8. Common salt
9. Spices complete range
10. Chemical preservatives potassium metabisulfite sodium Benzoate etc.
11. Packaging materials
12. Glass Bottles

TOTAL WORKING CAPITAL/MONTH

1.	Raw Material	Rs.	1,24,353.00
2.	Salary & Wages	Rs.	49,750.00
3.	Utilities & Overheads	Rs.	25,500.00
	Total	Rs.	1,99,603.00

TOTAL CAPITAL INVESTMENT

Total Fixed Capital	Rs.	14,76,760.00
Total Working Capital for 3 Months	Rs.	5,98,811.00
Total	Rs.	20,75,571.00

TURN OVER/ANNUM

By sale of 10,500 Bottle of 450 gm. Mixed Jam & Jellies
By sale of 21000 (250 gm) Bottle of Mixed Jam & Jellies
By sale of 10,500 (500 gm) Bottles mango pickles
By sale 21000 Bottles 250 gm) of mango pickles
By sale of 9000 Bottles (500 gm) of Mixed pickles
By sales of 18000 Bottles (250 gm) of Mixed pickles.
By sales of 9000 Bottles (500 gm) Bomboo shoot pickles
By sales of Tomato Products
(Ketchup, Sauces Etc.) 9000 Bottles
By sale of Squashes (Full range)
17077 Bottles of 650 ml each.

Total Rs. 34,28,195.00

PROFIT SALES RATIO = Profit/Sales x 100 = 14.46%

RATE OF RETURN = Operating profit/T.C.I x 100 = 23.88%

BREAK EVEN POINT (B.E.P) = 64.45%

Chapter 30

LACTOSE AND BY-PRODUCTS PROCESSING FROM MILK

Properties of Lactose

MOLECULAR FORMULA = $C_{12}H_{22}O_{11}H_2O$

It is white, hard, crystalline mass or white powder. It is sweetness, odorless. It is stable in air. Soluble in water, insoluble in ether and chloroform; very slightly soluble in alcohol. It's specific gravity 1.525. It decomposes at 203.5°C mp. It is nontoxic.

Grades :- Crude, Fermentation, spray dried, edible, U.S.P.

Lactose is the only sugar available commercially that is derived from animal rather than plant sources. It is available in the varying degrees. The fermentation grade is 98 wt.% pure, whereas USP lactose is refined to 99.8 wt.% purity. This not very soluble in water (20 gms/100 gms water at 25°C), nor is it varysweet (less than one third the sweetening power of sucrose). Typically, lactose, which is a reducing sugar, reacts with amines and amino compounds with resultant browning.

The concentration of lactose in milk products ranges from 4.8 wt.% in whole milk to 73.5% in sweet driedwhey.

Lactose (milk sugar) is the only sugar available commercially that is derived from animal rather than plant sources. The concentration of lactose in milk products ranges from 4.8 wt% in whole milk to 73.5 wt% in sweet dried whey, a by products from the manufacture of cheese. Lactose is prepared commercially from whey as the crystalline monohydrate. It is available in varying degrees of purity. The fermentation grade is 98 wt 5 pure, whereas VSP lactose is refined to 99.8 wt% purity. Although the monohydrate is the commercially available form of lactose, the sugar can be crystallised at high temperature to give the B - anhydride.

PROCESS OF MANUFACTURE

First, milk is taken and filtered to remove suspended impurities like straw or anything. Then it is slightly warmed. The milk is then passed through a cream separator cream separated milk is then passed through a plate heat exchanger where the skim milk is pasteurised at 70.6°C in 15 seconds. The present pathogen will be killed at that temperature in plate heat exchanger.

The milk coming out from plate heat exchanger is heated in a vacuum pan evaporator. Where it concentrates. The concentrated milk is now passed through a spray dryer where the removal of moisture takes place leaving behind 3% moisture in the milk powder. The milk powder so manufactured is packed automatically by automatic filling sealing and packaging machine in the can. The product so filled in the can is in nitrogen atmosphere, so that it will remain as usual in the can for longer period.

LACTOSE MANUFACTURING

Production

Generally cheese sweet_ whey or casein (acid) whey(Cheese, Processed Cheese and Whey is used as raw material for production of lactose. Today, permeates from the ultrafiltration of milk or sweet whey are also coming into consideration. With all types of raw materials precaution have to be taken regarding the minerals prest; calcium salts may give rise to deposition in evaporators.

The liquid whey (ca.6.5% dry matter content) is clarified (a) and concentrated in falling film evaporators (b) to 55-65% total solids. Upon cooling (c), the greater part in the lactose crystallizes as lactose monohydrate. The crystal slurry is transferred to a line of decanters and centrifuges and washed several times. Thus, after drying, milling and fractionation, yellowish lactose (edible grade) of different pamele size is obtained.

After the washing stage the raw product can be redissolved(i), treated with activatedcarbon(j) and recrystallized to refiner or pharmaceutical grades of lactose. From 1000 kg liquid whey 32.5 kg lactose and 32.5 kg delactosed wheypowder are obtained.

Environmental Protection : To avoid pollution the dryer should be provided with a cyclone to remove the powder from the exhaust air. Fluid cleaning streams must be purified by simple aerobic or anaerobic digestion before entering a public sewage treatment.

PLANT ECONOMICS

Rated Plant Capacity	=	22.62 MT./day
LACTOSE	=	*1638 MT/ANNUM.*
CASEIN	=	*1638 MT/ANNUM.*
WHEY POWDER	=	*1638 MT/ANNUM.*
GHEE	=	*1872 MT/ANNUM.*
LAND & BUILDING (Land Area 20 Acre)	Rs.	1,50,70,000.00

PLANT & MACHINERY

1. Milk Storage Tank
2. Ordinary Filter
3. Milk Pasteuriser
4. Milk Cream Seperator
5. Cream Storage Tank
6. Refrigeration Systems for Milk Chilling
7. **For Casein** : Acid treatment Tank (S.S)
8. Washing Tank
9. Oscillating Granulator
10. Fluidised bed dryer
11. Micropulveriser
12. Automatic Casein Powder in Pouches
13. Whey Storage Tank
14. Candle filter
15. Falling film Evaporator
16. Crystallisation Tank
17. Dryer
18. Micro-pulveriser
19. Redissolving tank
20. Filter
21. Automatic Sieving machine
22. Automatic Pouch filling Weighing, Sealing machine.
23. Centrifuge
24. Ghee receiving kettle
25. Automatic Pouch Weighing, filling, sealing for Ghee.
26. Water Softener
27. Boiler
28. Pipes, Pumps, Valves, Fittings and Other accessories.
29. Laboratory equipment
30. Miscellaneos

FIXED CAPITAL

1.	Land & Building	Rs.	1,50,70,000.00
2.	Plant & Machinery	Rs.	2,72,60,000.00
3.	Other Fixed Assets	Rs.	1,06,00,000.00
	TOTAL	Rs.	5,29,30,000.00

RAW MATERIALS

1. Milk
2. Chemical Preservative etc.
3. Hydrochloric Acid
4. Pouches, Tins, Cartons, Labels and other packaging materials.

TOTAL WORKING CAPITAL/MONTH

1.	Raw Material	Rs.	2,78,72,000.00
2.	Salary & Wages	Rs.	3,03,840.00
3.	Utilities & Overheads	Rs.	5,03,000.00
	TOTAL	Rs.	2,86,78,840.00

TOTAL CAPITAL INVESTMENT

Total Fixed Capital	Rs.	5,29,30,000.00
Total Working Capital	Rs.	5,73,57,680.00
TOTAL	Rs.	11,02,87,680.00

TURN OVER/ANNUM

1. By Sale Casein 1638 MT
2. By sale of Lactose 1638 MT
3. By Sale of Whey Powder 1638 MT
4. By Sale of Ghee 1872 MT

TOTAL Rs. 59,20,20,000.00

PROFIT SALES RATIO = Profit / Sales x 100 = 36.49 %

BREAK EVEN POINT (B.E.P) = 14.19 %

Chapter 31

LEMON JUICE SQUASH (Lime Squash, Cordials)

LEMON SQUASHES

Formulation - 1

(25 % Juice, 45° Brix, 1.5 % acidity)

Ingredients	(Kgs)
Lemon juice, 10° Brix 5 % acidity	45.4
Sugar	76.5
Citric acid	0.5
Water	57.5
Essence of lemon	1.300
Potassium metabisulphite	0.113

Formulation -2

(25 % juice, 65° Brix, 2 % acidity)

Ingredients	Kgs
Lemon juice (10° Brix, 5 % acidity)	45.4
Sugar	115.5
Citric acid	1.30
Water	26.50
Essence of lemon	1.30
Potassium metabisulphite	0.113

LIME SQUASHES

Formulation - 1

(25 % juice, 45° brix, 1.5 % acidity)

Ingredients	Kgs.
Lime juice 10° Brix, 6 % acidity	45.4
Sugar	76.5

Water	59
Potassium metabisulphite	0.113

Formulation - 2

(25 %, 65o Brix, 1.5 % acidity)

Ingredients	%
Lime juice	45.4
Sugar	113.5
Water	23
Potassium metabisulphite	0.113

LIME JUICE CORDIAL

Formulation - 1

(25 % juice, 35° Brix, 1.5 % acidity)

Ingredients	Kgs.
Clarified lime juice,10°Brix,6% acidity	45.4
Sugar	58.5
Water	77.1
Colour	q.s.
Potassium metabisulphite	0.113

Formulation - 2

(25 % juice, 50° Brix, 1.5 % acidity)

Ingredient	Kgs.
Clarified lime juice, 10o Brix, 6% acidity	45.4
Sugar	86.5
Water	50.0
Colour	q.s.
Potassium metabisulphite	0.113

PROCESS OF MANUFACTURING

Lemon Squash

European lemon, eureka lemon, and galgal are generally used for the preparation of lemon squash. Lemon squash requires addition of flavour to improve its taste.

Extraction of Juice

The tight skinned lemons are cut into halves with a halving machine having circular knife. The halves are pressed by rose fitted to a rosing machine.

These machines are of various sizes and capacities. The reamed juice is collected in a vessel. It contains plenty of coarse tissues, seeds etc. To remove these, it is filtered through a net cloth or passed through a sieving machine known as pulper, in which the juice gets brushed. The sieved juice is utilized for making squash.

Preparation of Squash

The above juice is taken in a stainless steel tank fitted with S.S. agitator/stirrer. Sugar, citric acid, flavouring materials, colour & preservative (potassium metabisulphite) are added to the juice in correct proportions.

Initially sugar, citric acid and water are mixed and heated. Any dirt is skimmed off. The syrup is cooled slightly and filtered through cloth. The clean syrup is blended with the juice. The edible colour, flavour also are added.

After mixing all the ingredients, the preservative, potassium metabisulphite predissolved in the little quantity of the juice or water, is added to squash.

The product is homogenized and packed in the sterile glass bottle with 1.2-2.5 cm head space. The bottles are then closed with crown corks or pilfer proof clousers, which have been dipped in 1 % potassium metabisulphite solution to sterilize them. The bottles are washed dried and labelled. Then packed in cartons and stored in a cool and dry place.

Lime Squash

Lime or kagzi nimboo is widely used for making lime squash. These limes are available in large quantities in Gujarat, Maharashtra, Andhra Pradesh, Karnataka, Tamil Nadu etc.

The fruit is cut into halves by means of halving machine. Then juice is pressed out by means of stone roller-type presses. Seeds are removed by sieving through cloth.

Sugar is first made into a syrup, which is filtered and added to the juice. The preserved squash is bottled as usual.

Lime Juice Cordial

Lime juice is extracted as above. It is stored in a large carboys or upright wooden barrels lined with microcrystalline wax. Fifty-six g of potassium metabisulphite is added to every 45 Kg of the juice to preserve it during storage. The juice settles gradually, and the sediment forms a compact layer at the bottom, leaving a clear juice at the top. This process takes 2 to 3 months. The clear juice is syphoned off. This method is rather slow and time-consuming. Clarification of the juice can also be achieved quickly by adding gelatin and tannin in proper proportion, based on preliminary laboratory trials. Sugar, water, colour, if necessary, and preservative are added to the clear juice, and the mixture is then filtered by means of a filter press. Filter aids are added in this process to facilitate filtration. The clear cordial is bottled as usual.

PROCESS FLOW SHEET

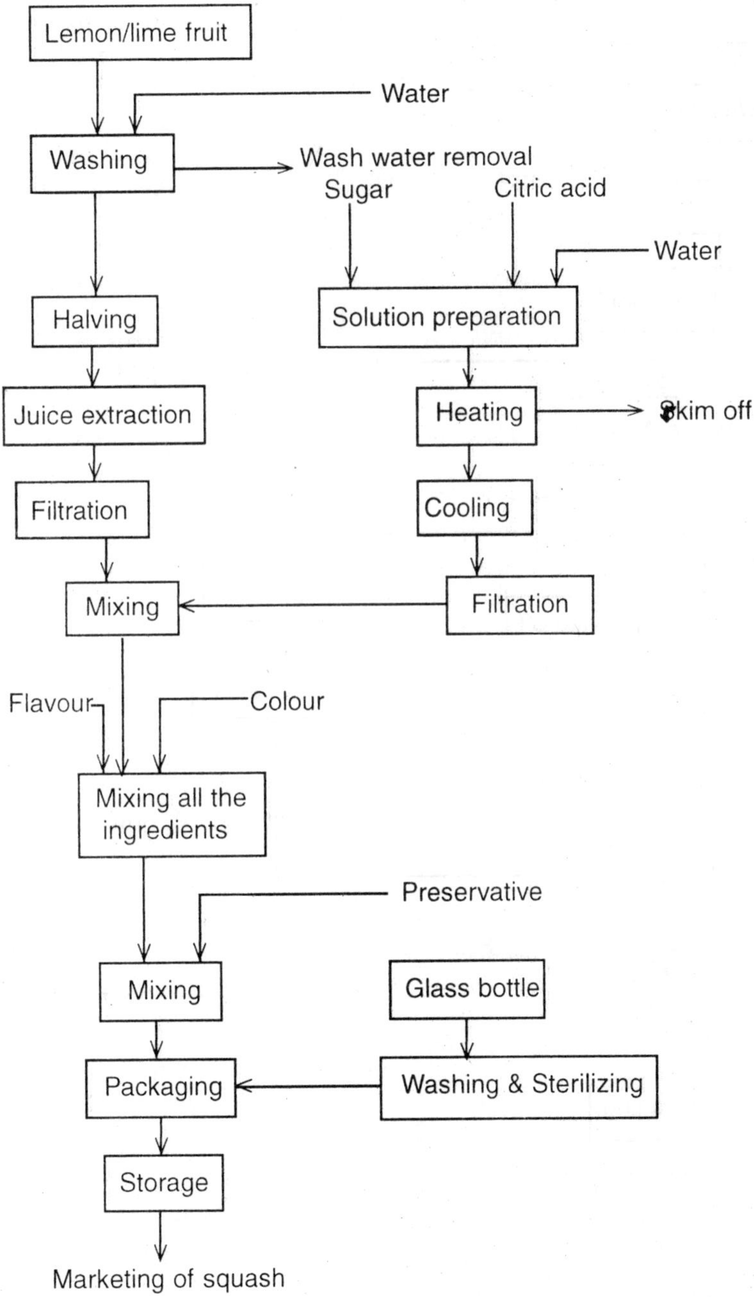

LIME JUICE CORDIAL

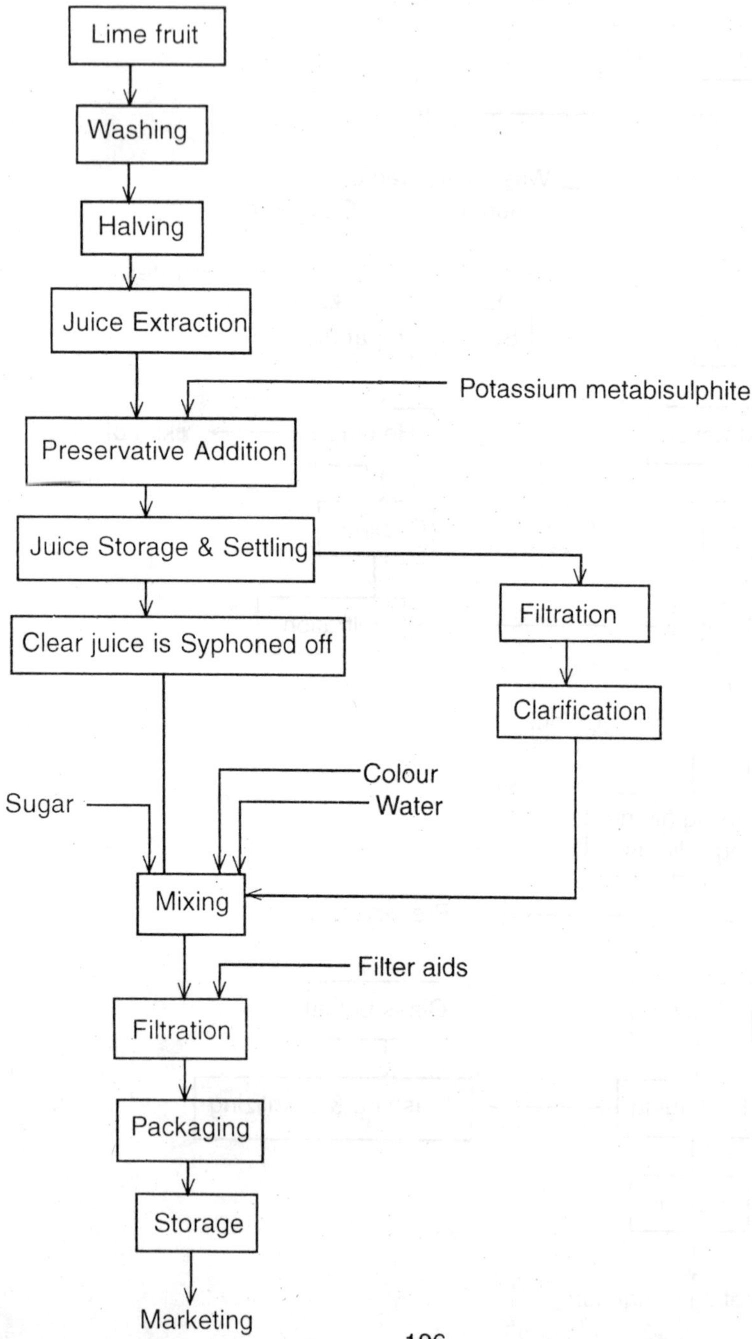

PLANT ECONOMICS

Rated Plant Capacity = 1000.00 Kgs./Day

LAND & BUILDING

Total Land Area 500 Sq. Mt. = Rs. 10,75,000.00

PLANT & MACHINERY

1. S.S. Washing tank,
2. Halving machine
3. Ream type juice extractor
4. Plate & frame filter press (polypropylene plate)
5. Stainless steel tank
6. Stainless steel tank with stirrer, motor etc.,
7. Semi-automatic bottle filling & sealing machine
8. Laboratory equipment.
9. Pipes, pumps & fitting valves

FIXED CAPITAL

1.	Land & Building	Rs.	10,75,000.00
2.	Plant & Machinery	Rs.	12,10,000.00
3.	Other Fixed Assets	Rs.	8,00,000.00
	Total	Rs.	30,85,000.00

RAW MATERIALS

1. Lemon/lime fruit
2. Sugar
3. Citric acid
4. Potassium metabisulphite
5. Colour, essence
6. Glass bottle, & aluminium caps
7. Cartons, stickers
8. Adhesive taps.

TOTAL WORKING CAPITAL/MONTH

1.	Raw Material	Rs.	4,36,920.00
2.	Salary & Wages	Rs.	93,750.00
3.	Utilities & Overheads	Rs.	54,000.00
	Total	Rs.	5,84,670.00

TOTAL CAPITAL INVESTMENT

Total Fixed Capital	Rs.	30,85,000.00
Total Working Capital for 3 Months	Rs.	17,54,010.00
Total	Rs.	48,39,010.00

TURN OVER/ANNUM

By sale of lemon squash, lime squash
lemon juice cordials etc.
429000 bottle (700 ml), Rs. 1,15,83,000.00

PROFIT SALES RATIO = Profit/Sales x 100 = 28.33%

RATE OF RETURN = Operating profit/T.C.I x 100 = 67.81%

BREAK EVEN POINT (B.E.P) = 37.81%

Chapter 32

MANGO PROCESSING & CANNING (Mango Pulp)

MANGO PULP MANUFACTURING

The fruits of semi solid texture is taken and sorted by either manually or by automatic sorting machine. Then the fruits are washed either by detergent solution or clean water thoroughly to remove dirt, soils and other impurities sticking on the surfaces offruits. This washing or cleaning operation is followed by automatic washing machine or manually washed. The fruits are now ready for steaming operation. By steaming operation the fruits become soft. These are now passed through a pulper machine which is power driven and comprising of a perforated cylindrical sieve and revolving wooden or metallic paddles. The pulp passing through the sieve is collected in stainless steel or wooden barrels. The pulp is then Deacrated under vacuum of 27-28 ind. mercury pressure and heated in an vacuum pan evaporator at temperature 84-88°C. Then suitable preservative such as potassium metabisulfite (sulphur dioxide) or sodium benzoate at amount 350 PPM is added and mixed homogeniously. Then it is filled in sterilized cans, and the cans are passed through exhaust box heated with hot air. The cans are then sealed by double seaming machine. The sealed cans are pasteurized in boiling water for 15-35 minutes. After pasteurization process is complete the cans are taken out, cooled and stored in cool dry place. Then packed in cartons or cardboard boxes.

CHEMICAL PRESERVATIVES

The most common preservatives used in fruit juices are the potassium and sodium salts of sorbic, benzoin and sulfurous acids. The amount of sodium benzoate should not be greater then 0.1 wt% in any case and a common rate of addition of 0.08% may import an objectionable odour. Potassium metabisulfite, and potassium Sorbate can also be used as preservatives. Instead of a sulfite salt, So_2 can also be added as a gas (350-600 ppm) but So_2 must be removed before canning as it can be reduced by tin creating an H_2S odour and darkening the interior of the container.

The preservative used should be dissolved in a minimum amount of water before addition to juice to prevent the immediate precipitation resulting from its direct addition to juice it should be added after pasteurization.

LABELLING & CASING

Where production is small, labels are ordinarily applied to containers manually. Where labour costs are high, or where volume is large, the use of automatic labelling machine is necessary.

The containers are usually cased manually after labelling, the exception being in operations which produces large volume of a single container sizes. Automatic casers are not adjustable and therefore, usually confined to large volume operations. Glass containers are hard cased normally to prevent breakages.

STORAGE

All caned and glass packed mango juice are subject to a loss of flavour, colour and vitamins during storage.

The most acceptable storage is that in which the temperature remains nearly constant at about 70°F. These conditions should be maintained within commercial practibility.

QUALITY CONTROL

Consumers of food products are "brand" conscious and owners of established brands attempt to pack merchandise of uniform quality for this and other reasons.

In juice production where product is homogeneous less difficulty is achieving uniformity is encountered in many products. However in case of mango juice it is a bit difficult due to the numerous available variety of mangoes in market.

The flavour of juice is generally greatly dependent upon the acid and ugar present. Tests for these constituents are relatively easy to perform.

PLANT ECONOMICS

Rated Plant Capacity	=		2.00 Tons/Day

LAND & BUILDING

Total Land Area 1000 Sq.mt.	=	Rs.	18,40,000.00

PLANT & MACHINERY

1. S.S. Tank for washing for mango
2. Pulp Extractor
3. Stainless Steel pulp collection tank
4. Dearator
5. Semi Automatic filling machine for can filling.
6. Boiler
7. Water Chiller
8. Can double seamer
9. Exhaust Box
10. Carton sealing machine
11. Conveyor Belt & elevators

FIXED CAPITAL

1.	Land & Building	Rs.	18,40,000.00
2.	Plant & Machinery	Rs.	23,60,000.00
3.	Other Fixed Assets	Rs.	6,50,000.00
	Total	Rs.	48,50,000.00

RAW MATERIALS

1. Ripe mangoes
2. Preservatives like sodium benzoate
3. Other like sugar, salt, flavours etc.
4. Cartons

TOTAL WORKING CAPITAL/MONTH

1.	Raw Material	Rs.	10,55,250.00
2.	Salary & Wages	Rs.	60,250.00
3.	Utilities & Overheads	Rs.	1,22,000.00
	Total	Rs.	12,37,500.00

TOTAL CAPITAL INVESTMENT

Total Fixed Capital	Rs.	48,50,000.00
Total Working Capital for 3 Months	Rs.	37,12,500.00
Total	Rs.	85,62,500.00

TURN OVER/ANNUM

By sale of 12,00,000 Nos. Cans of Mango Pulp (500 gms) Rs. 2,40,00,000.00

PROFIT SALES RATIO = Profit/Sales x 100 = 27.71%

RATE OF RETURN = Operating profit/T.C.I x 100 = 78.38%

BREAK EVEN POINT (B.E.P) = 33.65%

Chapter 33

MINI FLOUR MILL (ATTA)

Mini Flour mill serve the purpose of processing wheat to convert it into Atta. Wheat grains are the seeds of the wheat plant which is able to grow in kinds of soil and under widely differing climatic conditions. The principle wheats of commerce belong to the botanical groups Triticum vulgane, Triticum drum and triticum compactum. A grain of wheat is avoid in shape fine hains.

The grains of what consists of three main parts, the enveloping skins, the embroyo and the endosperm. The relative proportions of these parts vary with the plumpness of the grain but average composition of wheat is 85% endosperm, 2.4% embroyo and 14.5% enveloping skins.

The enveloping skins are pericarp which consists of the eipdorumis, epicarp and endocarp. The percarp represent about 6% of the grain. The seed cost consisting of the tests the byaline layer which comprises about 2% of the grain. The aleuorone layer representing about 6.5% of the grain wheat show a wide range of analytical data which is not unexpected in view of the many varieties which are grown and the very different conditions under which they are cultivated. The range of data normally encountered is as follows :

PERCENTAGE

Moisture	10.0	-	17.0
Protein	8.5	-	14.0
Fat	2.0	-	2.50
Fibre	2.0	-	2.50
Mineral matter	1.5	-	2.0
Sugars	2.0	-	3.0
Starch	63.0	-	71.0

MANUFACTURING PROCESS

The milling process breaks open the wheat kernel and reduces the particles formed as to separate the outer and inner portions of the kernel. Bran and gram are almost completely separated from the white interior portions in the milling of refined flour.

When the entire kernel is ground and no separations are made, the product is whole white flour. The following steps are involved in milling wheat, Wheat selection blending sieving, purifying reducing classifying and some combination of maturing bleaching and diastric or enriching treatment of the flour. It is not necessary that all these operations be performed is every flour mill. But either these operations are performed as such as or combination of these operations to serve the some purpose are performed in the flour mills.

1 Wheat selection and Blending
2. Cleaning
3. Conditioning or Tempering
4. Milling

PLANT ECONOMICS OF MINI FLOUR MILL (ATTA AND CHOKER)

Rated Plant Capacity =		22.40 MT./Day
LAND & BUILDING (Land area 350 sq.mts.) =	Rs.	13,48,500.00

PLANT & MACHINERY

1. Reel Machine for wheat cleaning.
2. Elevator Conveyor
3. Emery Rula
4. Worm Conveyor
5. Chakki
6. Pneumatic Conveyor
7. Centrifugal Machine
8. Fan Low Pressure.
9. Piple
10. Pulley/Belting/Shafts etc.
11. Motor
12. Water Dampner
13. Storage Bins
14. Plat Form
15. Tube-well with storage tank

FIXED CAPITAL

1.	Land & Building	Rs.	13,48,500.00
2.	Plant & Machinery	Rs.	6,12,000.00
3.	Other Fixed Assets	Rs.	1,75,000.00
	TOTAL	Rs.	21,35,500.00

RAW MATERIALS

1. Wheat
2. Gunny bags

TOTAL WORKING CAPITAL/MONTH

1.	Raw Material	Rs.	31,40,600.00
2.	Salary & Wages	Rs.	69,000.00
3.	Utilities & Overheads	Rs.	1,24,600.00
	TOTAL	Rs.	33,34,200.00

TOTAL CAPITAL INVESTMENT

Total Fixed Assets	Rs.	21,35,500.00
Total Working Capital	Rs.	66,68,400.00
TOTAL	Rs.	88,03,900.00

TURN OVER/ANNUM

1. By selling of Atta 6586 MT
2. By selling of Chokar 146 MTS.

Rs. 4,66,30,520.00

PROFIT SALES RATIO = Profit / Sales x 100 = 10.71 %

RATE OF RETURN = Operating profit / T.C.I x 100 = 56.75 %

BREAK EVEN POINT (B.E.P) = 33.82 %

Chapter 34

MILK POWDER & GHEE

Milk Powder is the milk that has been dried or desiccated. This is usually done by heating the milk. The final product contains less than three percent water. Milk powder can be prepared from whole milk. Milk from which fat has been partially removed, or from skim milk.

There are a number of advantages in converting milk into milk powder. Milk contains eighty-seven percent water and because of this it gets spoilt quickly. It also needs special and bulky containers for transport. On the other hand, milk-powder takes up only one-eight of the space of the original milk. Besides, milk in powder form can keep for a long period as much as six to eight months under tropical conditions.

There are three main types of plant for producing milk powder or dried milk.

i) Roller driers
ii) Spray driers
iii) Vacuum roller driers.

PROPERTY OF MILK POWDER

The most of important practical property of milk powder is its "solubility", which is measured by the proportion which can be reconstituted into solution or colidal suspension in water. Spray powder usually gives figures of about 99 percent, while roller powders give figures of about 90 percent. It should be noted, however, that the solubility of a powder may be increased considerably neutralization of the milk, since the excess sodium irons bring more protein and phosphate into solution.

Milk for spray powder is not commonly neutralized, but for roller powder milk is frequently neutralized down to a lactic and acidity of 0.12 percent or even less. When considering solubility figures of powders, therefore, consideration must be given to

i) The method of testing

ii) The degree of neutralization

Unfortunately there is no official method of measuring solubility, and slight differences in technique can easily lead to considerable differences in results.

It is often difficult to get agreement between laboratories for this reason.

The amount and nature of the sediment when the two types of powder are reconstituted are highly characteristic and together with the odour and taste usually enable the reconstituted milk to to readily identified.

In concentrates of 50 percent, total solids ageing and crystallisation of the lactose may result in from 10 to 90 percent. If fat becoming free on foam drying (extractable) by carbon tetrachloride). This excess can be prevented by heating the concentrate immediately before drying, a free fat value of less than 10 percent, being possible. Free fat can be decreased by increasing homogenisation pressure, and it increases with decreased powder particle size. Dispersibility is slightly decrease by increasing free fat.

The properties of the dry milk are due largely to the constituents of the milk from which it is made.

COMPOSITION OF MILK-POWDER

The average composition of milk powders:-

	Whole Milk powder percent	**Skim Milk powder percent**
Water	3.5	3.5
Fat	26.5	1.0
Protein	25.5	52.0
Ash	6.0	8.0

PROCESS OF MANUFACTURE OF MILK POWDER

There are mainly two process:

i) Roller drying

ii) Spray drying

Although Roller drying is widely preferred:-

ROLLER DRYING:-

The basic type is the just-Hatmaker, and consists of two steam heated rollers about 5 feet long by 2- 1/2 feet in diameter. They have a clearance of about 0.02 inch. Which may vary according to the conditions of processing.

ii) Spray Drying:

This method consists essentially in directing a spray of hot, precondensed milk into a current of hot air. There are three main types:-

i) Simple spray

ii) Revolving sprinklers
iii) Revolving disc.

Spray drying plant much bulkier than roller drying for given output, and spray powder costs more to produce. The product is, however, so much better, that it can only be a matter of time before nearly all milk powder is produced by the spray process. The confectionery and other industries will doubtless continue to accept roller powder.

The stages in spray drying are essentially the following :

i) Reception

ii) Clarification or filtration

iii) Cooling

iv) Storage

v) Preheating (160° to 190°F)

vi) Precondensing at about 110°F to about 42 percent total sides.

vii) Atomising in chamber, hot air entering at about 330° and leaning at about 200°F.

viii) Separation of powder

ix) Packing

MANUFACTURING PROCESS OF GHEE

Butter (unsalted) is dumped in the butter melter, which is a vertical jacketed stainless steel cylindrical tank fitted with an agitator (provided with reduction gear to work on variable speeds). If the butter is very cold and hard, it should be cut into small pieces before heating. Then a steam inlet to the jacket is opened and the agitator run at low speed.

The tipping tank, which is jacketed at the bottom, is filled with clean water and heated to 77-79°C (170 - 174°F) by opening the steam inlet of the jacket. The centrifugal oil separator is then started and when it has attained full speed, the hot water from the tipping tank is run into it. When the water has completely run out, the discharge valve of the butter melter is gradually opened to allow the melt to enter into the oil separator. The rate of the flow of the melt is so regulated as to avoid overflow. The melt is now separated into oil and serum.

The oil flows into the float-controlled balance tank and thence into the vacuum pan due to suction. Here it is dehydrated at 56-63°C (133-145°F) under a vacuum of 57-62 cm. of mercury. At the end of the operation, the vaccum is broken and butteroil allowed to flow by gravity into the receiving kettle for subsequent cooling, packaging and storage at room temperature.

PLANT ECONOMICS

Rated Plant capacity =125000.00 KGS./Day
LAND & BUILDING (Land Area 4 Acre) Rs. 1,26,25,000.00

PLANT & MACHINERY

1. Storage Tanks
2. Feed Pump with motor
3. Preheater, Jacketted Type with all accessories
4. Plate heat exchanger with all accessories
5. Spray Drier with atomizer & complete accessories
6. Cream Separator
7. Boiler
8. Chilling Plant
9. Milk Powder filling/Sealing unit (Automatic)
10. Cream Heating tank with jacket System
11. Pouch weighing filling sealing Machine for Ghee packing
12. Pumps, Valves, Pipe Lines & other tanks, water pumps etc.
13. Laboratory Testing Equipment
14. D.G. Set

FIXED CAPITAL

1.	Land & Building	Rs. 1,26,25,000.00
2.	Plant & Machinery	Rs. 1,37,80,000.00
3.	Other Fixed Assets	Rs. 47,75,000.00
	TOTAL	Rs. 3,11,80,000.00

RAW MATERIALS

1. Milk
2. Citric Acid
3. Magnesium Oxide
4. Misc. Chemicals, NaCl, $CaCo_3$ etc.
5. Tin Containers
6. Pouches for Ghee & Milk

TOTAL WORKING CAPITAL/MONTH

1. Raw Material	Rs.	4,56,45,375.00
2. Salary & Wages	Rs.	7,13,900.00
3. Utilities & Overheads	Rs.	4,65,000.00
TOTAL	Rs.	4,68,24,275.00

TOTAL CAPITAL INVESTMENT

Total Fixed Assets	Rs.	3,11,80,000.00
Total Working Capital for 1 Month	Rs.	4,68,24,275.00
TOTAL	Rs.	7,80,04,275.00

TURN OVER/ANNUM

1. By Sale of 1500000 Kgs. of Skimmed Milk Powder
2. By Sale of Ghee 2250000 Kgs.
3. By Sale of Milk 8125000 Lts.

TOTAL Rs. 61,37,50,000.00

PROFIT SALES RATIO = Profit / Sales x 100 = 6.15 %

RATE OF RETURN = Operating profit / T.C.I x 100 = 48.41 %

BREAK EVEN POINT (B.E.P) = 34.34 %

Chapter 35

PAPAD AND BARIYAN PLANT

The Word "PAPPAD" is quite familiar with Indians. Pappad is a common Indian food normally taken with meals. Some time before, pappads were made at home by the ladies and most of them know the process of making them. At present also some of the housewives are making these, but their number has decreased considerably.

Pappad's are of different types i.e. made from urad dal, potatoes, rice etc. However, process of making all of them is very simple and absolutely identifical except the formulations which may change according to one's taste. Pappad's may be made by using red or black pappers and their quantities may also be altered to make the product strong or light in chilly.

Base for all types of pappad in is Urad's pulse. Good quality pappads are made by urad only whereas in cheap quality pappads beson is also mixed.

Bariyan are traditional have name made item. It is generally consumed by either making Lussy or by adding in curry as per required charge of taste. The bariyan are manufactured from different cecal variety edible product. The bariyan are generally prepared in all Indian houses from Urad dal, Moong dal, Soyabean and others. These are tasty things and add taste to the lunch and dinners.

PROCESS OF MANUFACTURE OF PAPPAD

Pappad may be manufactured by a single type of pulse flour or combination of various pulse flour. The rice flour is also added to reduce the cost of the pappad. However, following formulation is suggested for the pappad making.

Urad Pulse Flour	1000 Parts
Black Pepper	25 Parts
Sodium Bi Carbonaye	10 Parts
Zeera	15 Parts
Hing Water	10 Parts
Salt	25 Parts

All the ingredients are first taken according to their weighted quantities and then pre mixed. Now, the premixed mass is taken into a dough kneading machine. Required quantity of water is added and the whole content is kneaded at minimum speed to get homogenous lump of the dough. After 30 minutes resting it is divided into balls of about 6-8 kg mass. Now, this ball is placed on the conveyor belt of the automatic dough sheeting machine. The belt is moved to and thickness is gradually decreased using the lever handle till the final thickness of about 2.5 to 2 mm sheet is obtained. The conveyor belt takes the sheet to the sheet cutting machine.

The sheet is now cut into round shaped and tailing materials are then again mixed fed to the sheeting machine. After round cut of the pappad, the pappad is sent for sun drying or a drying chamber in which hot air at 27-30°% of moisture content.

The pappad are then packed into the printed plastic packs. This plastic back may contain about 100 pappads or as per market requirements.

MANUFACTURING PROCESS OF BARIYAN

Urad Dal/Moong Dal	-	100 kgs.
Red chillies powder	-	1/2 kgs.
Salt	-	2 kgs.
Hing	-	100 gms.
Other spices	-	100 gms.

First of all soak the Urad dal or Moong dal for a night in a vessel with 1.5 times the clear water. The dals are first thoroughly washed and left off all the night for soaking. In the morning stain out the dals from that vessel and pass through grinding machine. Then add the previously mixed ground spices and salts and again homogeneously mix it. The pasty mass is now ready for extension. As the quantity of mass is extruded from the machine, it is placed on PP or PE flim to dry either in sun or using special drying chamber. The dryed bariyan are now ready for packing in polyethylene. Packets with suitable brand name. Then sold in the market.

PACKAGING OF PAPPAD

Papad should be packed either by count (25, 50 or 100 to a pack) or by weight (250 g 500 g 1kg) or in any other suitable manner. The material used for packaging of Papad should be moisture-proof and non-toxic, such as, pouches made from PET/LDPE and BOPP/LDPE.

AUTOMATIC PAPPAD PLANT & MACHINERY

Complete new line of Pappad Plant of 250 kgs./8 hour Shift complete with Dryer.

Dough Mixing Machine Stainless Steel SS 304 Lined capacity 20 kg. with 2 HP Electric Motor & Gear Box.

Dough Sheet Extruder Unit : With independent 1 HP Drive and Reduction Gearing.

Inter Table : SS 18 Swg Line for Sheet transport between Extruder and Gauge Rollers.

3 Pairs of Gauge Rollers : Three pairs of precision gauge rollers heavy duty duly hard chromed with independent adjustment of sheet thickness between gauge rollers.

Two sets of Dough sheet transport rollers with Drives.

Two sets of Stainless Steel Knives to Gauge rollers.

One set rotary cutting rollers.

One set rubber rollers to cutting rollers.

One food grade conveyor system for conveying Pappads to Dryer.

One combined Pappad & Wadi Dryer.
Size 6' x 4' x 6.5' High capacity 150 Kg. Wt. 1200 Kg. gross including 4" insulation.
Oil consumption 17 ltr. in 12 Hrs. *(Summer)* 24 ltr. in 15 Hrs. *(Winter)*
Insulation Mineral Wool
Electric Motor 1 HP 3 Phase 1400 RMP
Tray Size 1 Meter x 1 Meter
Side Sheeting Covering : 18 Gauge Galvanised or S.S as per order (Optional)

The dryer can be heated Electrically or with LPG. The electrical heating load is 6 kw. The electrical load of Drive Motors is 6.5 HP i.e. Mixer 2 HP, Extruder 1 HP, Sheeter 2 HP, Air Blower .5 HP. Oven Drive 1 HP. Total 6.5 HP.

Note : Above stated dryer is suitable for drying of Pappads as well as for drying of Wadi's

The estimated price of above complete automatic pappad making plant complete with dryer for an output of 250 kg. Pappads of Lizzat (5.5) size per 8 hours shift would be approx. Rs. 5 Lacs. Automatic Pappad Packing Machine Pouch Type would be around 3 lacs.

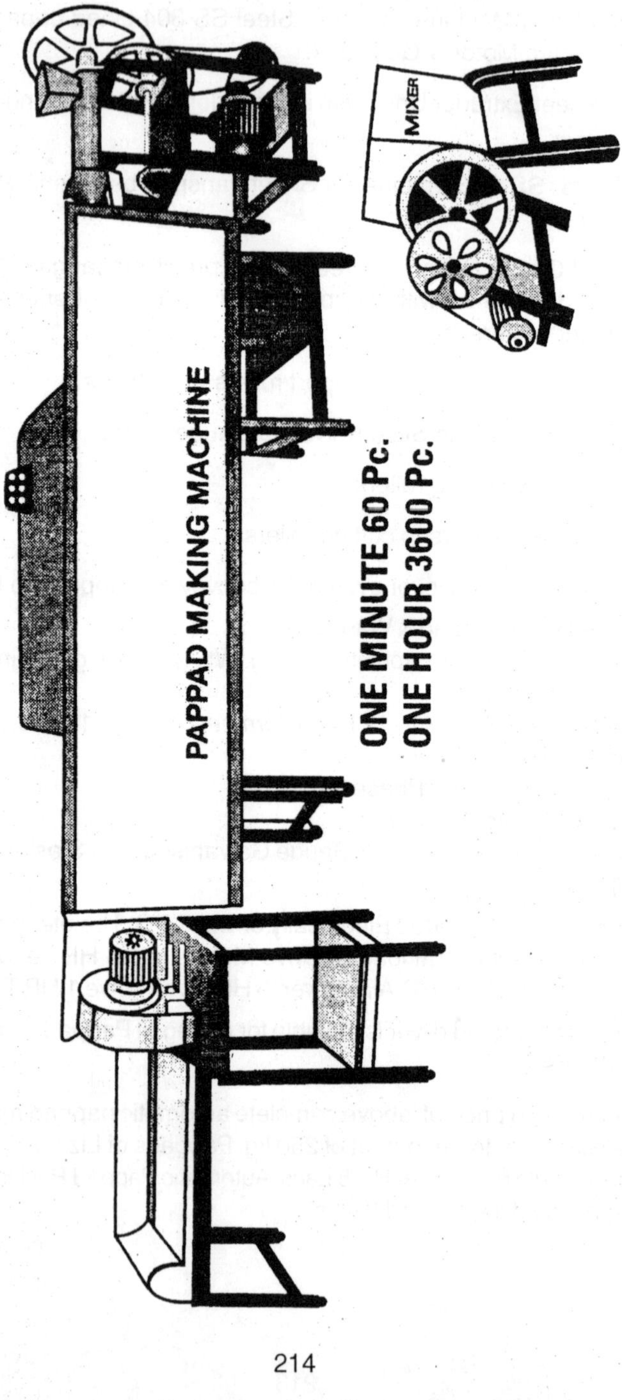
PAPPAD MAKING MACHINE
MIXER
ONE MINUTE 60 Pc.
ONE HOUR 3600 Pc.

PLANT ECONOMICS

Rated Plant Capacity = 1.10 Mt./Day

LAND & BUILDING

Land Area 1000 Sq. = Rs. 9,50,000.00

PLANT & MACHINERY

1. Sifter
2. Dough mixer
3. Automatic dough sheeting machine
4. Automatic sheet cutting machine
5. Air drying chamber
6. Pack sealing machine
7. Weighing balance/machine
8. Wet grinding machine
9. Automatic extruder for making bariyan
10. Miscellaneous Equipments

Wet Grinder

FIXED CAPITAL

1.	Land & Building	Rs.	9,50,000.00
2.	Plant & Machinery	Rs.	13,60,000.00
3.	Other Fixed Assets	Rs.	2,10,000.00
	TOTAL	Rs.	25,20,000.00

RAW MATERIALS

1. Black urad, dal, flour
2. Black pepper
3. Sodium bicarbonate
4. Zeera
5. Hing water
6. Salts
7. Urad dal
8. Moong dal
9. Red chillies power
10. Other spices
11. Hing
12. Packing materials

TOTAL WORKING CAPITAL/MONTH

1. Raw Material	Rs.	3,16,138.00
2. Salary & Wages	Rs.	35,624.00
3. Utilities & Overheads	Rs.	39,000.00
TOTAL	Rs.	3,90,762.00

TOTAL CAPITAL INVESTMENT

Total Fixed Capital	Rs.	25,20,000.00
Total Working Capital for 3 Months	Rs.	11,72,286.00
TOTAL	Rs.	36,92,286.00

TURN OVER/ANNUM

Sale of 180 ton of Pappad &
150 ton Bariyan — Rs. 81,60,000.00

PROFIT SALES RATIO = Profit/Sales x 100 = 28.66%

RATE OF RETURN = Operating profit / T.C.I x 100 = 63.35%

BREAK EVEN POINT (B.E.P) = 38.92%

Chapter 36

PERFUME FOR SOAP, DETERGENT AND AGARBATTI etc. YARA YARA

Yara Yara, chemical formula CIO H_7OC H_3 is white having crystalline flakes. Chemically it is known as beta - naphthyl methyl ether or Z- methoxynaphthalene or methyl naphthyl ether.

It is useful in the preparation of perfumery. It does not occur in nature but it is available as synthetic product being widely used in manufacture of soap and Agarbattis. Perfumery today is based mainly on synthetics as against natural products in the past. Because of the non-availability of natural ingredients in the quantities that the world needs as well as at prices which are commercially not viable, so that whole perfumery has changed and viewing situation existing at 1980's it may be concluded that perfumery is totally a perfumery of aroma chemicals today. The perfumery industry as such in India, we always keep on saying that we are atleast fifty years behind the Western countries. May be some 100 or 200 years back when we were in this line we were exporting gums and spices and all that, and we were extracting attars especially in UP and Kanpur and if not mistaken we were the first to extract the absolute from the jasmine flowers. Of course the process is completely outdated today but had been very interesting at that time. In a by-gone era when systematic scientific investigations of essential oils were unfamiliar and synthetic organic chemistry was at its infancy, India had a pre-eminent position in fragrance business. It is estimated that over 2000 synthetic materials and about 200 essential oils are used by the perfumery and flavour industry coming to aroma chemical it may be noted that many aroma chemicals have become commodity items over the years and presently the scope of this turn hence includes speciality chemicals and these commodity chemicals as well. Hardly there exists any home who does not use soaps and agarbattis using perfumery synthetic chemical. Yara Yara is fast being consumed as perfumery chemical by various industries particularly soap and the agarbattis industry.

PROCESS OF MANUFACTURE

Yarayara (beta-naphthol methyl ether) is manufactured by two processes. Firstly by heating beta-naphthol and methyl alcohol in presence of sulfuric acid secondly by methylating beta-naphthol with dimethyl sulfate.

For production of 10 Kg. yarayara the raw materials required are as follows:

Yarayara	100 Kg.
B.Naphthol	91 Kg.
Methanol	20 Kg.
Sulphuric acid	5 Kg.

PLANT ECONOMICS

Rated Plant Capacity = 100.00 Kgs./Day Yara Yara

LAND & BUILDING (Land 300 sq.mt) Rs. 2,67,000.00

PLANT & MACHINERY

1. Reaction kettle with stirring heating arrangements
2. Filtration Unit
3. Pan dryer
4. PVC lines storage vessels
5. Packing equipment
6. Weighing scales
7. Lab testing equipment
8. Depolluting equipment

FIXED CAPITAL

1. Land & Building	Rs.	2,67,000.00
2. Plant & Machinery	Rs.	5,80,000.00
3. Other Fixed Assets	Rs.	1,40,000.00
TOTAL	Rs.	9,87,000.00

RAW MATERIALS

1. Beta-naphthol
2. Methanol
3. Sulphuric acid

TOTAL WORKING CAPITAL/MONTH

1. Raw Material		Rs.	1,40,312.00
2. Salary & Wages		Rs.	22,320.00
3. Utilities & Overheads		Rs.	26,000.00
	TOTAL	Rs.	1,88,632.50

TOTAL CAPITAL INVESTMENT

Total Fixed Capital		Rs.	9,87,000.00
Total Working Capital for 2 Months		Rs.	3,77,265.00
	TOTAL	Rs.	13,64,265.00

TURN OVER/ANNUM

Return by sale of 30000 kgs of yara yara flakes	Rs.	39,00,000.00

PROFIT SALES RATIO = Profit / Sales x 100 = 30.03 %

RATE OF RETURN = Operating profit / T.C.I x 100 = 85.84 %

BREAK EVEN POINT (B.E.P) = 37.32 %

Chapter 37

POTATO CHIPS / WAFFERS

Potato chip is a snack-food item very popular for picnics, cinema halls, journeys, evening tea and may be served at any time. These are much consumed by all age group children. This profile provides a small scale plant which requires few capital investment. The whole plant and machinery are fluently available in India and almost in every state of India. Few addresses have also been added in this book to enable the entrepreneur for buying these machines.

Snack food like potato chips in recent years have made impressive trends in food industry. The approximate composition of chips is as follows:-

Moisture	-	2%
Protein	-	6.7%
Fat	-	37.1%
Carbohydrate	-	51.1%
Minerals	-	3.00%

For chips manufacture sugar contents of potatoes should be over S.G (Specific Gravity) 1.080 i.e (minimum 20% solids content).

STEPS IN THE PROCESS OF MANUFACTURE EMPLOYED AS FOLLOWS:

1. Inspection of feed stocks and manual removal of obviously trash on a conveyor belt.

2. Mechanical washing and stoning of potatoes using brushes with gravity separation of stones in a vertical fume.

3. Steam or water peeling of potatoes usually by steam jet surface loosing of the skin followed by a dry abrasive skin removal treatment and then the use of brushes and water sprays thus minimize water usage and concentrating the skin residues.

4. Inspection and triming by hand in a conveyor belt.

5. To maintain continuity of production a buffer tank is usually provided at this point containing a weak solution of SO_2 or sodium meta bisulfate to avoid enzymic blackening during the holding period.

6. Slicing of potatoes to the desired thickness using multiple knives.

7. Washing slices free of starch and use chemical separation of slivers and nubbins concominatantly with dewating the slices.

8. Blanching of the slices in steam or hot water (160°- 200°F) (71-93°C) which amounts to a partial pre cooking. blanching times will depend on slice thickness and the blanch temperature and can be from 3 or 4 times upwards.

9. Drying the slices by shaking and by air blast to avoid a water carry over and to start the dehydration continued in the next stage.

10. Frying or cooking on a conveyor in a thermostaticaly controlled bath of oil, the oil subjected to continuous re-circulation and filtration and indirectly heated by a mineral oil caloriefier with strictly controlled cooking time to ensure consistent product quality and colour.

11. Defaulting of crisp by shaker and by hot air blast.

12. Flavouring and salting of chips by dusting on the seasoning whilst the defaulted chips are being timber conveyed.

13. Cooling of the finished chips.

14. Packing of the chips as soon as possible in small sophisticated laminate package designed to prevent. The ingress of both oxygen and moisture.

During the processing of the potatoes to chips, the moisture contents of the potato has been reduced from 79% (Approx.)to 5% (Approx.) and of the 95% of dry malts in the chips 35-40% will be fat.

Taking into account peeling trimming and other small losses in the plant and the up take of fat the conversion ratio of potatoes the chips is around 4:1.

PROCESS OF MANUFACTURE

Potatoes received from fields are first checked for quality on conveyor belt. The spoiled ones are removed from the lot. The good potatoes are then washed well and with jet of water to remove mud and other materials. Then the clean potatoes are moved into the peeling section.

The peeled potatoes are sliced in a conscious slicing machine. The peeled potatoes are feed to the hopper of the slicing machine and are discharged out to dual potato slicing machine. The dual slicer are used to handle more potatoes continuously. Each slicer are separately powered by a variable speed gear head motor. The feed to the dual slicer are arranged in such a way that slice cutting rotor in either slice may be changed during operation. Rotary type slicer are used in most chips plants. Slice thickness varies from (1/15 to 1/30mm). Potato slices are washed in rotating reels in the additional jet of water under high pressure to remove starch from the potato slices.

The washed potato slices are dried in a dryer to remove moisture content.

The dried potato slices are treated chemically with sodium bisulfate alone or with phosphoric acid, sodium citrate or citric acid to prevent the formation of dark chips during trying. In this chemical treatment water or solution is heated up to 200°F and after rinsing slices are placed in the above hot solution for one or two minute and then sent into frying kettles.

For frying two types of process are in general use.

1. Batch frying
2. Continuous frying.

The simplest method for frying in batch frying provides for a slicer to be mounted on a batch directly above the frying vessel. This vessel may be either rectangular or flat bottom. Flat bottom tank with burner beneath or the tank may be of the immersion tube type.

After frying the chips are hand salted and packed. A uniform application 1.5 to 2 lbs of salt is applied to 100 lbs of chips. Mono sodium glutonate is used for flavour. One part of mono sodium glutonate to 10 parts of salt provides a good mixture.

Then the chips are packed to protect the content against development of rancidily.

Details of Machinery

This comprehensive machine (Picture is given) has been specially designed and constructed, keeping in mind the small tiny wafer manufacturing unit. Since it is low cost, individuals with limited funds can also invest in it and make a decent margin from the proceeds.

This machine combines three operation viz. peeling, Slicing and dehydration on a common base and drive, thus effecting a considerable saving in space and energy requirements.

The machine is sturdy and very easy to operate thus no extra skill or efforts are required.

Operation

Potatoes are fed into the peeling drum which has a special internal lining that peels off the potato skin which ratation. After this process is over, the peeled potatoes are fed from the hopper into the slicing section where the

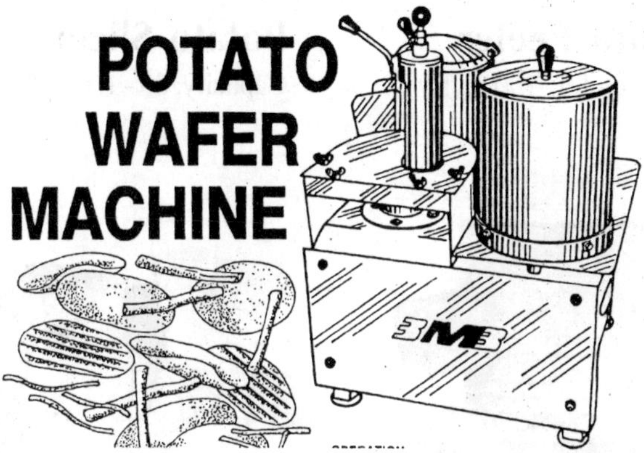

potatoes are sliced even by and quickly. These are then thoroughly washed and fed into the dehydrating stainless steel drum. On rotation the moisture from the potatoes is practically removed and they are ready for frying.

Technical Specifications : Single Phase
Motor : 1/2 HP
Capacity : 200 Kgs. of Potato per 8 Hours
Dimension : 23" x 23" Height 36"
Sali Blade Chips : Medium & Thick

Potato Peeler
Capacity: 80 - 100 kg/hr

Potato Slicer
Capacity: 80 - 100 kg/hr

Nitrogen Flushing Machine

Pillow packing of Potato Wafer pouches

Optional vacuumising system

PLANT ECONOMICS

Rated Plant Capacity	=		0.50 MT/Day

LAND & BUILDING

Land Area 500 sq.mt	=	Rs.	6,75,000.00

PLANT & MACHINERY

1. Potato peeler
2. Power operated slicing machine
3. Blancher
4. Electrical Heater
5. Weighing machines
6. Hydro extractor
7. Deep Fat Fryer
8. Automatic packing cum sealing machine

FIXED CAPITAL

1. Land & Building	Rs.	6,75,000.00
2. Plant & Machinery	Rs.	1,50,000.00
3. Other Fixed Assets	Rs.	1,10,000.00
TOTAL	Rs.	9,35,000.00

RAW MATERIALS

1. Hand Picked Potatoes
2. Edible oil
3. Other chemicals
4. Packing materials

TOTAL WORKING CAPITAL/MONTH

1. Raw Material	Rs.	1,90,000.00
2. Salary & Wages	Rs.	54,000.00
3. Utilities & Overheads	Rs.	18,000.00
TOTAL	Rs.	2,62,000.00

TOTAL CAPITAL INVESTMENT

Total Fixed Capital	Rs.	9,35,000.00
Total Working Capital for 3 Months	Rs.	7,86,000.00
TOTAL	Rs.	17,21,000.00

TURN OVER/ANNUM

Sale of 150 MT Potato Chips	Rs.	45,00,000.00

PROFIT SALES RATIO = Profit/Sales x 100 = 20.86%

RATE OF RETURN = Operating profit/T.C.I x 100 = 54.03%

BREAK EVEN POINT (B.E.P) = 45.39%

Chapter 38

PICKLES

Formulations & Preservatives for some important type of pickles

1. Apple Pickle:-

Recipe

A.	1.	Sour apples	1.8 Kgs.
	2.	Spritor cider vinegar	0.84 Litres.
	3.	Sugar	0.90 Kgs.
	4.	Cinnamon Stick	7.5 qm.
	5.	All Spices	1 Teaspoonful
	6.	Cloves whole	20 (in numbers)

Procedure : Peel, core and slice the apple place the slice in water to prevent their browning. Boil the vinegar, sugar and spices, for 5 minutes. Then add the slice and simmer the mass till the pieces become soft take out the fruit and pack into Jars. Reboil the vinegar and sugar to a syrupy consistency, pour it not on the slices and seal the Jars. It desired, spices may be added to the Jars.

2. Green Chilli Pickle

Recipe

1.	Green Chillies	500 grms.
2.	Tamarind	100 grms.
3.	Jaggery	100 grms.
4.	Corriander Leaves Salt, powdered red Chillies, mustard seeds.	Each two tea spoons
5.	Black gram dal	4 Tablespoon
6.	Turmeric Powder	0.25 Teaspoon
7.	Gingerlly Oil	0.25 Pint

Where 1 Pint - $4.732 \times 10^{-4} m^3$.

Procedure : Slice a hole in chillies taking core not to split them . Soak the tamarind in one pint of water for about half an hour. Finally strain the Juice.

Heat the oil and mustard seeds black gram and coriander leaves.

Add green chillies and fry till chillies are dry. Add tamarind turmeric, chilli powder, salt and Jaggery. Simmer stirring constantly til liquid dries cool and preserve in air right Jar.

3. Mixed Vegetable Pickle :

Recipe :

1.	Turnips	4 lbs.
2.	Carrots	2 lbs.
3.	Cauliflower	1 lb.
4.	Garlic	4 lb.
5.	Green Ginger	100 grms.
6.	Onion	0.25 lb.
7.	Chilli Powder	2 table spoon.
8.	Garam Masala	1 table spoon.
9.	Jaggery	2 lb.
10.	Vinegar	0.75 Pint
11.	Mustard Oil	1 Pint
12.	Turmeric Powder	1 Tea spoon
13.	Ground mustard Seeds	1 Tea spoon
14.	Salt to taste	as per requirements.

Slice turnips into 0.25 inch. dises. Quarter corrots length wise and cut cauliflower into 2 inch. pieces. Boil water in a large sauce pan, add a the vegetable and cook for 5 minutes to soften. Drain of the water and spread on a clear towel to dry wipe off excess water.

Grind ginger onions and garlic together to a paste Heat oil and fry the paste add remaining spices and salt and fry till the oil floats to the pp. cool and add vegetables shake vessel to mix well put in a large jar and keelo in the sun for 2-3 days till vegetable turn a little sour shake the bottle well each day.

Heat vinegar will Jaggery and boil. Cool and add to the vegetables, place Jar in the sun for another two days till well blended and tender. Preserve in air tight Jars.

4. Mutton Pickle :

1.	Muttons	5 lbs.
2.	Ginger	1 lb.
3.	Onions	1 lb.
4.	Garlic	2 lbs.
5.	Mustard Oil	1.5 Pint

6.	Vinegar	1.5 Pint
7.	Cloves	15
8.	Cardamoms	12
9.	Nutmeg	0.75 tea spoon
10.	Salt	4 table spoon
11.	Chilli Powder	2 table spoon
12.	Ground Mace	1 table spoon
13.	Mango Powder	2 table spoon

Preparation :

Cut the meet into 1-5 inches cubes. Put in a large sauce pan to simmer without adding any water, till all liquid from the meat dries up keep on one side. Grind the onions, Garlic and ginger to paste. Heat oil and fry the paste till brown.

Add meat pieces, mix well and fry. Add 0.5 pint vinegar, all the remaining spices and cool for 5 minute stirring continuously remove from heat. Pour in remaining vinegar and cool. Put in air tight jars and keep for a week before use.

5. Mango Pickles

1.	Mango Slices	10 Kgs.
2.	Salt powders	2.5 Kgs.
3.	Methi Ground	1.25 Kgs.
4.	Kalaunji ground coarsely	
5.	Turmeric Powder	300 grms.
6.	Red Chilli Powder	300 grms.
7.	Aniseed	300 grms.

Preparation :

Mix the mango slices with the common salt powder place the mixture in a glazed Jar. Keep it in the sun for 4-5 days till the slices turn pale yellow. Then mix other ingredients with the slices and smear them with a little sarson (rape seed) oil. Then pack the pickle in a glass or glazed jar and cover with a thin layer of sarson oil the pickle will be ready in 2-3 weeks.

6. Turnip Pickle :

Sweet turnip pickle in oil are highly popular in India select sound turnips, preferably with a pink skin wash them thoroughly. Peel and slice them into pieces of convenient size. preferably 1/2 to 1/2 inch. thickness.

1.	Prepared Turnip	10 kgs.
2.	Red Chillies	8 oz.
3.	Black Pepper	4 oz.
4.	Mustard	1/2 Kg.
5.	Spices (Caraway & Cinnamon)	2 oz.
6.	Dried dates	8 oz.
7.	Tamarind	8 oz.
8.	Ginger fresh chopped	8 oz.
9.	Onion fresh chopped	1 oz.
10.	Garlic chopped	4 oz.
11.	Salt	1 Kg.
12.	Vinegar	26 oz.
13.	Jaggery	1/2 Kg.
14.	Rape Seed Oil	1/2 Kg.

Blanch the turnip pieces for 5-6 minutes in boiling water chop the ginger, onions and garlic and fry then in a little oil soak tamarind and dates in water overnight. Prepare a thick extract of the tamarind by maceration and pass it through thin mustin cloth to remove. Seeds Removes the stones from the dates and slice them into small pieces. Grind black pepper, red chillies and all the other spices. Mix all these ingredients except gur and rap seed oil with the prepared turnip pieces. Fill the mass into the Jars and keep the letter in the sun for 5-6 days. Then add the gur in the form of a thick syrup and again place the Jar in the Sun for 3-4 days. Add the rape seed oil and pack the pickle in store Jars.

7. Cauliflower Pickle

1.	Prepared Cauliflower	20 kgs.
2.	Salt	1.25 kgs.
3.	Chilli Powder	0.75 kgs.
4.	Cumin	2 oz.
5.	Cloves	2 oz.
6.	Cardamom	1 oz.
7.	Cinnamon	2 oz.
8.	Ginger Green	2 oz.
9.	Onions chopped	0.75 kg.
10.	Mustard seeds	0.75 kg.
11.	Pape Oil Seed	2.25 kgs.

Take fully developed and compact heads of cauliflower. Remove the outer leaves and the central stalk cut the flowers into pieces, wash, drain and place them in the sun for 2-3 hours to remove surface moisture.

Take all spices except mustard and grind them into a fine powder fry them in the oil, when the spices turn brown add the cauliflower pieces and mix the whole mass thoroughly. When the cauliflower pieces turn slightly soft allow them to cool when the mass has cooled down to room temperature, add mustard and mix it thoroughly. Place the mixture in the sun for 5-7 days then add 2.5 kgs of vinegar and again place it in the sun for 3 more days.

8. Jack Fruit Pickle

1. Brined Jack Fruit slices	9.07 kgs.
2. Salt	0.56 kgs.
3. Chilli Powder	170 grms.
4. Cumin	28 grms.
5. Clove	28 grms.
6. Cardamom	14 grms.
7. Cinnamon	28 grms.
8. Dry Ginger	14 grms.
9. Onion chopped	283 grms.
10. Mustard Seed	28 grms.
11. Ginger Oil	1.12 grms.
12. Garlic	28 grms.
13. Vinegar	1.12 kg.
14. Sugar	1.12 kg.

Fry chopped ginger onion, garlic and mustard seeds in a little oil til they turn brown. Add these and the rest of spices to the Jack fruit slices and fill the mass into glazed Jars. Mix well and place the Jars in the sun for 3 to 4 days, stirring the mass occasionally. Add sugar and vinegar, again mix well and keep the Jar in the sun. The pickle will be ready in another into glass or glazed corthen Jars and pour sufficient oil an top to cover the pieces well.

MANUFACTURING DETAIL I.E. PICKLING PROCESS

Pickling Process

Pickling is done is two stages:- (i) By curing or fermentation with dry salting or fermentation in brine, or salting without fermentation; and (ii) by finishing and packing.

Dry Salting

In this method, the vegetable is treated with dry salt. The salt extracts the juice from the vegetable and forms the brine, which is fermented by lactic acid-forming bacteria. The method of dry-salting in general, is as follows.

The vegetable is prepared, washed thoroughly in running cold water, drained and weighed. For every 100 kg of the prepared vegetable, 3 kg of salt is used. The vegetable is placed about 2.5 cm. deep in the keg or barrel and is sprinkled with a small quantity of salt from the weighed amount. Another layer of the vegetable is added and again sprinkled with salt. The salt is added, layer by layer, in this manner till the keg is three-quarters full. Then one or two-folds of cheese cloth are spread over the salted vegetable, tucking in the cloth at the sides, and then placing a wooden board on the top of it. A clean stone, which is not acted upon by salt and organic acids, is placed on the board to press the vegetable so as to form a brine. Generally, a stone weighing about 4.54 kg will be sufficient in the case of a 22.10 litres keg. If necessary, additional weight may be placed, in case brine does not form after the material has stood for sometime. Generally, brine is formed in about 24 hours.

After packing the vegetable, the keg is placed in a warm and dry place and fermentation is allowed to proceed. In a short time, due to osmosis, juice from the vegetable forms the brine covering the whole mass. The weighted board helps to keep the vegetable submerged in the brine.

As soon as the brine is formed, fermed, fermentation starts and bubbles of carbon dioxide begin to rise from the liquid. Fermentation is usually completed in 8 to 10 days under favourable conditions which are attained in the temperature range of 27° to 32°C. In cold weather, however, it may take 2 to 4 weeks for the fermentation to be complete. When the fermentation is over, gas bubbles cease to form and rise. This may be confirmed by tapping the keg gently.

The product may now be preserved and kept by excluding air. If this is not done, 'pickle scum' a kind of wild yeast, appears on the surface. It soon destroys the lactic acid formed by fermentation with the result that the pickle is ultimately spoilt.

According to Round and Lang, air can be exhausted or expelled in the following manner:-

Method I. An air-seal on the surface of the brine can be made by pouring on top of it an edible oil-like rape seed oil or cotton seed oil. The oil, being lighter than the brine, floats on the surface and thereby prevents the access of air to the pickle below. A layer of oil about a 0.6 cm. thick is generally sufficient to keep the pickle indefinitely. The only drawback in this otherwise simple method is that the vegetable cannot be taken out from the container without getting covered with the oil. To overcome this, the oil may be removed from the surface by decanting, sysphoning or skimming, or by making it overflow by adding more brine to the deg.

Method II. After dry salting and fermentation, the barrel or keg is filled with the vegetable to its maximum capacity, and the cover replaced. A 1.25 cm hole is bored in the head. Then the barrel is filled to the brim with the brine so that very little air is left inside. It is allowed to stand for about 48 hours, or till such time that bubbles of gas cease to rise. If necessary, more brine is added at intervals to keep the barrel full. When the bubbling has stopped, the vent-hole is closed tightly and the barrel kept in a cool and dry place. The product packed in this manner will keep indefinitely.

Fermentation in Brine

Steeping of the vegetable in a salt solution of pre-determined concentration for a certain length of time is called brining. This type of treatment is adopted in the case of cucumbers and similar vegetables, which do not contain sufficient juice to form brine with dry salt.

Brine Preparation

Brine can be prepared by dissolving common salt in water and filtering it through jelly bags to remove insoluble impurities. The amount of brine necessary to cover the vegetable is usually equal to about half the volume of the material to be fermented. To be more precise, if a keg of 45.4 litres capacity is to be packed, the amount of brine required would be 22.7 litres. It is preferable to make the whole quantity of brine needed for the day in one lot.

Brining is the most important step in pickling. Although no set of conditions, ordinarily practicable in pickle-making will destroy or retard the growth of every kind of bacteria, yet the growth of a majority of them is checked in a brine containing 15 percent salt. Lactic acid bacterial, which are salt-tolerant, can flourish in a brine of 8 to 10 percent strength only.

Fermentation takes place fairly well in a brine containing approximately 5 percent salt (20° Salometer). In a brine containing appromixately 10 percent salt, fermentation proceeds somewnat slowly. To some extent fermentation takes place up to 15 percent also, but at 20 percent strength, all fermentation stops. It is, therefore, customary to place the vegetables in 10 percent salt solution to allow lactic acid fermentation to take place and then to increase the proportion of salt gradually, so that by the time the pickle is ready, salt concentration would have reached 15 percent level. It is to be borne in mind that vegetables contain a certain amount of moisture, which exudes from them in the presence of salt and lowers the strength of the brine. The brine strength can, however, be maintained by adding dry salt. The time required for proper fermentation is determined by experience.

Keeping Quality

Properly brined vegetables will keep well in vinegar for a long time. The duration of brining is of importance. If the vegetables are soaked for a short time of about 12 hours only, the curing of the vegetable tissues will be incomplete with the result that the pickle will not have proper textures and taste. Brining has, therefore, to be controlled properly. On curing, the vegetables become semi-translucent, and their colour changes from green to dark olive green or yellowish green. This is an indication of correct curing. This usually takes 4 to 5 weeks. By this method, the vegetables can be kept more or less for an indefinite period, provided the right storage conditions are maintained. If the vegetables is to be kept in brine of 10 percent or less, all air should be excluded from the containers. During curing, the vegetables lose their 'raw' flavour and become firm and crisp.

With salt. In this method, vegetables are packed with a large quantity of salt to inhibit fermentation. In practice, generally 25 kg of salt is mixed with every 100 kg of the prepared vegetables.

The cured vegetables are drained, and excess salt is removed by soaking them in cold or warm water, as may be necessary. After removing the salt, the vegetable are stored for several weeks in plain vinegar of 10 percent (100 grain) strength. This treatment reduces the tendency of the vegetable to shrivel when packed in sweetened and spiced vinegar and also helps absorption of vinegar by the vegetable tissues.

Spiced Vinegar. Spiced vinegar should always be kept ready so that it is available at the time of pickling. It is made as follows:-

Method I. The ground spices are soaked in vinegar and set aside for 2 to 3 months, stirring occasionally. The spices are then squeezed out, and the vinegar allowed to stand. When it has become clear, it is decanted or syphoned from the sediment.

Method II. The spices are boiled with the vinegar till the flavours are extracted fully. The extract is then filtered.

Method III. Essential oils of spices are used. This, however, does not always impart to the product the original aroma of the spices.

The kind and quantity of spices required depend upon the piquancy desired in the pickle. There are numerous recipes, each having its own adherants. A few of these are given here to serve as guidelines.

According to Poultney, sweet spiced vinegar is made as:

RECIPE

Sugar	213.1 kg
Clove, hole	4.9 kg
Coriander seed	5.8 kg
Mustard seed	7.2 kg
Cardamom seed	0.67 kg
Celery seed	0.56 kg
Ginger, whole	1.69 kg
Caraway seed	0.22 kg
Vinegar	227.3 litr.

The sugar is dissolved in vinegar by heating. The spices placed in linen bags, are suspended in the vinegar. The batch is simmered gently for 6 hours and is then allowed to cool. The bags are removed and the vinegar filled into casks for storage.

According to him, spiced vinegar with essential oils is made as follows:

RECIPE

Oil of ginger	42 g
Oil of cloves	39 g
Oil of mace	8 g
Oil of coriander	85 g
Oil of mustard	49 g
Oil of cardamom	226 g
Oil of bay	28 g
Vinegar	908 litres.

The essential oils are stirred with the vinegar. For proper emulsification a little gum may be added. The oils may also be mixed with sugar and then dissolved in the vinegar.

According to Campbell, the following recipe gives a good spiced vinegar.

RECIPE

White vinegar (100 grains)	90.9 litres
Water	77.2 litres
Garlic	311g
Cayenne, finely ground	680 g
Cloves, headless, finely ground	1360 g
Mace, finely ground	226 g
Coriander, finely ground	1360 g
Mustard, finely ground	1360 g
Cardamom, finely ground	226 g
Bay leaves, finely ground	680 g
Caraway, finely ground	92 g
Ginger, finely ground	907 g

The spices should be leached in the vinegar for about a week.

Packing Methods

Pickled onions and mixed pickles should be packed finally into bottles or jars loosely so as not the damage the shape and appearance of the pieces. Fresh vinegar is then added to fill up the spaces between the pieces. The bottles or jars are then allowed to stand for a while, with the lids loosely on, covered again with more vinegar, if necessary and then closed air-tight. They are stored for a few days, the storage period depending upon the vegetable, etc., so as to ensure thorough absorption of the vinegar before the pickles are sent to the market.

Causes of Spoilage

Different kinds of spoilage occur in pickles. They are dealt with briefly in the following paragraphs.

Shrivelling

Shrivelling occurs when vegetables like cucumber are placed directly in a very strong solution of salt or sugar and even in very strong vinegar. To avoid this, weak solutions should be used to start with, increasing their strength gradually.

Bitter Taste

This results from the use of strong vinegar. It can also be caused by cooking the pieces for a long time and also by oversicing.

Blackening

This is caused by iron, which enters through the brine or from the equipment. Sometimes, specific organisms also cause blackening.

Dull and Faded Products

Pickles become dull and faded due to either insufficient curing or use of material of inferior quality.

Softness and Slipperiness

This is owning to the action of bacteria and is the most common form of spoilage. It is invariably owing to inadequate covering with brine or owing to the use of a weak brine. By using a brine of proper strength and by keeping the pickle well below the surface of the brine, this kind of spoilage can be eliminated.

PROCESS FLOW SHEET

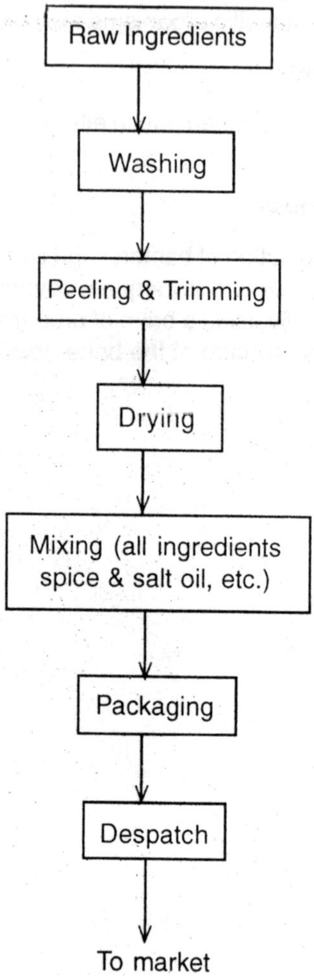

PLANT ECONOMICS

Rated Plant Capacity = 800.00 Kgs./Day

LAND & BUILDING

Total Land Area 500 Sq. Mt. = Rs. 8,25,000.00

PLANT & MACHINERY

1. Fruit & Vegetables Washing tanks
2. Knives
3. Preparations Tables
4. Weighing balance
5. Chopping Machine
6. Grinder
7. Peeling & Cutting equipments.
8. Steam Jacked Vessels

FIXED CAPITAL

1.	Land & Building	Rs.	8,25,000.00
2.	Plant & Machinery	Rs.	2,85,000.00
3.	Other Fixed Assets	Rs.	1,13,500.00
	Total	Rs.	12,23,500.00

RAW MATERIALS

1. Mango
2. Mix Vegetables
3. Turnips
4. Jack Fruit
5. Apple
6. Green Chilli
7. Cauliflower
8. Muttan
9. Salt
10. Vegetable oil

TOTAL WORKING CAPITAL/MONTH

1.	Raw Material	Rs.	4,46,000.00
2.	Salary & Wages	Rs.	51,875.00
3.	Utilities & Overheads	Rs.	42,000.00
	Total	Rs.	5,39,875.00

TOTAL CAPITAL INVESTMENT

Total Fixed Capital	Rs.	12,23,500.00
Total Working Capital for 3 Months	Rs.	16,19,625.00
Total	Rs.	28,43,125.00

TURN OVER/ANNUM

By Sales of 800 X 300 = 2,40,000 Kgs. per Annum Rs. 96,00,000.00

PROFIT SALES RATIO = Profit/Sales x 100 = 25.96%

RATE OF RETURN = Operating profit/T.C.I x 100 = 87.66%

BREAK EVEN POINT (B.E.P) = 30.23%

Chapter 39

PROCESSED FOOD

MANUFACTURING PROCESS FOR FRUIT JUICES

1. CLEANING:

Any species of fruit like those under the mandrin orange group from which juice is to be extracted after peeling can be simply cleansed by means of a rotary washer. Those citrus fruits from which juice is extracted by reamer without peeling are cleansed more scruplously, i.e. in two stage, by rotary brusher.

2. WARMING TREATMENT :

The second rotary washer is used as warm water tank, because fruits are easily peeled if they are warmed. In this case, temperature and warming time should be properly adjusted so that the temperature of warming treatment is so soften the peel only.

3. PEELING :

Warmed fruits with peels are received on a trimming table, on which they are peeled by female workers.

4. JUICE EXTRACTION :

Peeled fruits are cut into two or four pieces. Then the juice is extracted out of them by popular and finisher, with extraction yielding 40-50 per cent.

When they are put under extraction by reamer, fruits with peel are cut into two pieces of about the equal size, and the manually done so by applying them to the reamer head.

5. PRE HEATING:

Extracted juice is heated to about 90°C for the purpose of making inactivate enzyme and bacteria contained in it, and then is cooled down to about 40°C.

6. CENTRIFUGALIZATION :

Extracted fruit juice which contains a considerable amount of pulp is applied to the centrifuge for the purpose of re-separation of pulp. it is to be noted, however, that juice containing some amount of pulp has a better demand in which case pulp is of course left without being re-separated.

7. DEAERATION :

Fruit juice when applied to the pulper, finisher and centrifuge, is mixed up with a considerable amount of air. Therefore, it needs be dearrated to prevent the juice from bad effect to be caused after wards by the air. The suitable vacuum in the dearator is 60-100 mm Hgabs.

8. SEASONING :

Bottled soft drinks on the market are usually comprised of pure juice properly diluted and seasoned with essence colours, activators, citric acid, sweetenings, etc. in the proper degree.

9. STERILIZATION :

Fruit juice is before being canned or bottled, sterilized at a temperature of 90°C-95°C for 30 seconds, and then it is canned or bottled while it is hot.

10. FILLING INTO CANS :

Sterilized hot juice is delivered to the juice filler, whereby it is canned in No.2 cans or No.3 cans.

11. SEAMING OF CANS :

Cans filled with juice are delivered to the seamer, vacuum seamer in this case, by which they are seamed.

12. COOLING :

Seamed cans are cooled next for 3-5 minutes by the rotary cooler and are taken out of it. If the cans are excessively cooled, water drops are sometimes formed on the surface when they are exposed to the open air. Therefore, they need be taken out at the most appropriate degree of temperature.

The temperature is to be determined properly according to the atmospheric temperature, humidity etc.

13. MARKING ON CAN LIDS :

Can lids are to be impressed with marks by can maker beforhend.

14. LABELLING AND BOXING :

When printed cans are not used lables are affixed to the cans on their side, and 2 dox of No. 2 cans are packed in a box storage and delivery to the market.

SQUASHES :

Squashes are juices which are sweetened and have more fruit pulps. The squashes are prepared from all varieties of fruit by mixing strained juices with filtered heavy sugar syrup to contain about 35-40% sugar in the finished products.

MANUFACTURING PROCESS FOR SAUCES & KETCHUP

Sauce of any fruit can be prepared but the most popular sauce. It is also used as chutney. Manufacturing process of all varieties of fruits sauces is almost similar.

First, the fruits are peeled, sliced, and ground. The spices, and other additives are added. Thickening agents also are added to prevent or retard sedimentation of the solid particles in suspension. In India, apple pulp is often used for this purpose. Sometimes, the fruit, which is used for making sauce, is boiled pulped as a filler. The starches of maize potato, arrowroot, sago and rye also are used as thickening agents. The use of Indian gum locust, kernel gum tragacanth, karaya gum, gelatin, irish moss, pectin and other similar substances is also advised. These are however, as good as the starches.

Formula for Tomato Sauce:

Tomato pulp (6% soluble solids)	29.250 Kgs.
Cardamom, pepper and cumin in equal quantities	8.5 gms.
Cinnamon, broken	10 gms.
Cloves, headless	8.5 gms.
Mace	5.7 gms.
Salt	5.7 gms.
Onions, chopped	154 gms.
Garlic ground	18 gms.
Sugar	2.140 Kgs.
White vinegar 100 grain	580 c.c.
Red Chilli powder	15 gms.

It is cooked to about half its volume i.e. about 28% solids, Eng point is determined by refractometer. It is filled into plain cans and processed for 45 min in boiling water.

CHILLI SAUCE

To 22.4 kgs. of peeled tomatoes, add 1 kg. of sugar 10 gm. of red chillies 0.9 Kg. of washed, peeled finely chopped onions, and the following spices tied loosely in a cloth bag.

Mace	7 gms.
Cinnamon broken	18 gms.
Cumin cardamom and black paper in equal quantities	22.5 gms.
Ground white paper	10 gms.
Ground ginger	10 gms.

Cook the whole mass in steam :- jacketed kettle to about 25.2 Kgs. crushing tomatoes with a ladle, if necessary. Add 2.14 Kgs. of kgs. of sugar and 0.675 Kg of salt and 1.57 Kgs (100 grain) vinegar. Continue the cooking of the mass further for about 5-10 minutes after which pack immediately in plain a cans seal and sterilize for half an hour in boiling water.

TOMATO KETCHUP

Ketchup is a product obtained from properly prepared strained tomatoes with spices, salt, sugar and vinegar. The ketchup is made directly from the raw tomato pulp but it can be prepared from tomato paste, as the raw material, prepared elsewhere. In many case only clean wholesome tomatoes of intense red colour and of meaty not watery textury should be used for the purpose. High acidity and rich tomato flavour are the additional desirable qualities. Tomatoes are washed sorted, trimmed, cut and pulped.

The juice is then in some cases concentrated to 1.06 sp gravity, IN some plans, the juice is directly mixed with ingredients and then cooked. In majority of plants the partially concentrated pulp of 1.06 sp gravity is heated to boiling in open stainless steel or glass lined kettles, and cooked a short time final desired solid content with the required quantities of salt, vinegar, onion powder or chopped raw onions and a mixture of certain spices.

PLANT ECONOMICS

Rated Plant capacity = 10000.00 Bottle/Day

LAND & BUILDING

Total Land Area 2000 Sq. Mt. = Rs. 30,08,000.00

PLANT & MACHINERY

1. Hammer Mill
2. Neutralising vessel, equipped with jacket, agitator etc.
3. Filtration press
4. S.S. Lining mixers equipped
5. Pressure storage tanks & Sealing
6. Automatic bottling machine
7. Cooling/Conditioning Units
8. Clarification Vessels
9. Centrifuges
10. Evaporators
11. Deaerator
12. Pasteurisation units
13. Spray Drier
14. Motor pipes
15. Boilers
16. Generator

FIXED CAPITAL

1.	Land & Building	Rs.	30,08,000.00
2.	Plant & Machinery	Rs.	25,31,000.00
3.	Other Fixed Assets	Rs.	5,50,000.00
	Total	Rs.	60,89,000.00

RAW MATERIALS

1. Fruits
2. Sugar
3. Citric Acid
4. Glass Bottles & Other Packing Materials

TOTAL WORKING CAPITAL/MONTH

1.	Raw Material	Rs. 12,21,750.00
2.	Salary & Wages	Rs. 1,42,500.00
3.	Utilities & Overheads	Rs. 1,66,000.00
	Total	Rs. 15,30,250.00

TOTAL CAPITAL INVESTMENT

Total Fixed Capital	Rs. 60,89,000.00
Total Working Capital for 3 Months	Rs. 45,90,750.00
Total	Rs. 1,06,79,750.00

TURN OVER/ANNUM

By Sale of 30,00,000 Bottles of Squash/Year	Rs. 3,00,00,000.00

PROFIT SALES RATIO = Profit/Sales x 100 = 28.28%

RATE OF RETURN = Operating profit/T.C.I x 100 = 79.45%

BREAK EVEN POINT (B.E.P) = 35.32%

Chapter 40

POUCH FILLING FOR SAUNF, SUPARI, ILAICHI etc.

POUCH FILLING FOR SAUNF, SUPARI, ILAICHI ETC.

The ingredients used for making non-line, non-cutch type pan masala are as saunf, mishri, Ilaichi, chikni supari (Scented supari) or sweetened scented supari & scented chhuara in different composition.

FORMULATION	ONE POUCH (6 GMS WT.)
1. MISHRI	1 GM
2. CHIKNI OR SWEETENED SUPARI	1.5 GM
3. SWEETENED & SCENTED	1 GM
4. SAUNF	2.0 GM
5. ILAICHI	1 PC OR 0.5 GMS.

The information subscribed on the packing is as below :-

1. Name & place of manufacture
2. Trade name of product, if any.
3. Net contents, when packed
4. Date and batch no. of production
5. Price excluding local taxes.
6. I.S.I. Mark,if any
7. Speciality of the product,if any

PROCESS

Mix the above ingredients in the ratio as given in the formulation using a ribbon blend mixer. After mixing all the ingredients it is filled in pouches directly - by automatic weighing, automatic pouch filling and pouch sealing machine.

The process flow diagram show the process wise operation.

POUCH FILLING

Pouches are plastic coated paper packs used for packaging of various items such as sauces, ready-made vegetable & pan masala.

In pouches, the basic things are LDPE coated paper and polypropylene. The first is the printing on the coated paper. The coated papers are easily available in the market.

Extrusion laminating is a process where the layer of film are joined at the extrusion die-using the heat of the extrusion process to weld the different films together.

After this goes to the pouch filling machine where it is filled with pan masala according to the capacity. Finally it is pressed and packed.

In India, now we have multi-coloured printed laminates and stand up pouches available with complete system for automatic and semi automatic filling of the same.

The different synthetic films and combination for the manufacture of pouches are :-

1. 200 gauge high density polyethylene (HDPE).

2. Laminate of 12 micron metallised polyester/150 gauge low density polyethylene (LDPE)

3. Laminate of 60 gms maplitho paper/0.04 mm foil /150 gauge low density polyethylene.

4. 250 gauge polypropylene (PP)

5. 250 gauge polypropylene and further sealed in a pouch made from a laminate of 12 micron metallised polyester/150 gauge low density polyethylene.

6. Laminate of 12 micron polyester/0/012 mm Aluminium foil/40 micron high molecular weight high density polyethylene (HMHDPE).

POUCH FILLING FOR SAUNF, SUPARI, ILAICHI etc.

PROCESS FLOW CHART

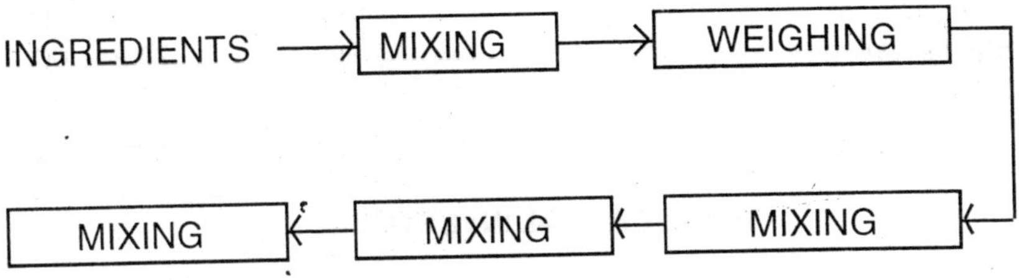

PLANT ECONOMICS

Rated Plant Capacity = 300.00 Kgs/Day

PLANT & MACHINERY

1. Feeding and self sealing Machine,
2. Betel Nut Cutter
3. Ribbon Blend mixer
4. Automatic Weigh balance

FIXED CAPITAL

1. Plant & Machinery		Rs	2,28,000.00
2. Other Fixed Assets		Rs	76,000.00
	TOTAL	Rs	3,04,000.00

RAW MATERIALS

1. Mishri
2. Chikni Supari
3. Sweetened & Scented Chhuara
4. Saunf
5. Ilaichi
6. Pouches for packaging

TOTAL WORKING CAPITAL/MONTH

1. Raw Material	Rs	6,70,000.00
2. Salary & Wages	Rs	20,248.00
3. Utilities & Overheads	Rs	11,912.00
TOTAL	Rs	7,02,160.00

TOTAL CAPITAL INVESTMENT

Total Fixed Capital	Rs	3,04,000.00
Total Working Capital for 3 Months	Rs	21,06,481.00
TOTAL	Rs	24,10,481.00

TURN OVER/ANNUM

By selling of 15000000 pouches of Pan Masala	Rs	1,12,50,000.00

PROFIT SALES RATIO = Profit / Sales x 100 = 20.84 %

RATE OF RETURN = Operating profit / T.C.I x 100 = 97.26 %

BREAK EVEN POINT (B.E.P) = 21.27 %

Chapter 41

PROCESSED CHEESE

Cheese is the product made from the curd obtained from whole or skimmed milk, with or without added cream, by coagulating the casein and further treatment, of the separated curd by ripening ferments, special molds or seasoning. Cheese has not been the popular item of food in India mainly because animal rennet is used in the its preparation. Preparation such as surti paneer, bandal and Ducca Cheese, which are popular in certain parts are allied to cheese.

Composition of Cheese

The composition of cheese depends upon the variety. All cheese contain the same constituents of milk but in varying proportions. The most variable constituents are fat and water.

MANUFACTURING PROCESS

Cheese is a often made from milk which has been subjected some heat treatment but not enough to qualify pasteurised milk as measured by the phosphate test. Temperatures from 145-150°C and an exposure time of a about 15 seconds may be used. This heat exposure destrous many bacterial capable of causing difficulty in cheese making and ripening. The treatment is not enough to destroy all the enzymes of milk and some bacterial of value in cheese ripening probably sourning. Cheese made from milk heated in this fashion develops more flavour than does cheese made from pasteurized milk such cheese must be egged for 60 days before sale unless it is to be used for manufacturing purposes, when it will be given an additional heat treatment. Cheese made from pasteurised milk may be solid at any time after its manufacture.

Curd Formation

A characteristic of all cheese making is the formation of a cured or the coagulation of the milk coagulation is brought about by means of the action of lactic acid produced by fermentation, by the action of rennet or pepsin or by a combination of lactic acid and rennet.

In either case, it is the casein of milk which is congealed to form the cured. Casein is coagulated readily by acids, and by enzymes, such as rennet and pepsins. The chemical changes involved in the case of acids coagulation of and enzymes coagulations and distinctly different. When milk is coagulated by lactic acid, the calcium of calcium casenate probably units with the lactic acid to form calcium lactate. The casein is bet free and from a firm"gel" or cured. This change in milk is brought about by other acids.

The rate of rennet coagulation is influenced by several factors, such as the temperature and the acidity of the milk. In the case of the hard variety of cheese, sufficient rennet in added to the milk to bring about a complete coagulation is 15 to 20 minutes. After adding and mixing, rennet to milk the fist signs of coagulation may be observes in 8 to 10 minutes. It will be observed that there is slight thickening of the milk, flocculant cured particles will become visible to the age, and finally, the casein will form a firm gel.

When the coagulation is dependent upon the action of lactic acid produced by the bacterial fermentation of lactose, form 5 to 16 hours, may be required before sufficient acid is produced to bring about coagulation. After comlete coagulation when is separated by passing coagulated milk through press when cheese being formed a rectangular block. Now these cheese will pass through fitting machine and packing machine. Then Packaged cheese is kept at 10°C for 6 months for ripening Then it is marketed.

PLANT ECONOMICS

Rated Plant capacity = 290.00 Kgs./Day

PROCESSED CHEESE 220 Kgs./DAY

CREAM 70 Kgs./DAY

LAND & BUILDING (Land 500 sq. mtrs.) Rs. 10,30,000.00

PLANT & MACHINERY

1. Cheese Vat (Jacketed)
3. Cream Separator
4. Milk Cans
5. Cheese cutting table
6. Cheese knives
7. Cheese Hoops
8. Cheese Press
9. Cheese Grinder
10. Ghee kettle
11. Weighing balance platform type
12. Weighing balance,
13. Deep freezer large vertical, multidoor
14. S.S. Pump
15. Bulk Cooler
16. Plastic Vats

17. Centrifuge for fat test (both electrically/manually tested)
18. Boiler
19. Cheese filling and packaging Machine automatic type.
20. Processed cheese kettle
21. Pipe fittings, Pumps, valves and other

FIXED CAPITAL

1.	Land & Building	Rs.	10,30,000.00
2.	Plant & Machinery	Rs.	10,21,500.00
3.	Other Fixed Assets	Rs.	2,00,000.00
	TOTAL	Rs.	22,51,500.00

RAW MATERIALS

1. Milk
2. Starter
3. Colour, salt etc.
4. Packaging material with labels

TOTAL WORKING CAPITAL/MONTH

1.	Raw Material	Rs.	5,06,250.00
2.	Salary & Wages	Rs.	47,125.00
3.	Utilities & Overheads	Rs.	22,750.00
	TOTAL	Rs.	5,76,125.00

TOTAL CAPITAL INVESTMENT

Total Fixed Capital	Rs.	22,51,500.00
Total Working Capital for 2 Months	Rs.	11,52,250.00
TOTAL	Rs.	34,03,750.00

TURN OVER/ANNUM

1. By sale of 90000 Packs of 400 gms each Processed cheese
2. By sale of 1,50,000 Packs of 200 gms each of processed cheese
3. By sale of 21000 kgs of cream

TOTAL Rs. 1,05,00,000.00

PROFIT SALES RATIO = Profit / Sales x 100 = 24.67 %

RATE OF RETURN = Operating profit / T.C.I x 100 = 76.11 %

BREAK EVEN POINT (B.E.P) = 33.95 %

Chapter 42

RICE PUFF

Rice puff being one of the most nutritious food and is consumed as breakfast food not only in India but elsewhere in the world. Protein-calorie malnutrition (PCM) amongst children is prevalent in some parts of the country. Many efforts have been undertaken to ameliorate this socio-economic problem. One of these is the formulation of high protein foods. Rice puff is becoming increasingly popular in many states Rice contains high amounts of fat and proteins, although there are some difference in varieties popularizing Rice in the diet will help in combating protein-calorie malnutrition in children to a certain extent.

RAW MATERIALS

Rice is the chief raw material for a Rice Mill. Rice is a khariff crop like jawar, bajra, maize groundnut & cotton etc.

MANUFACTURING PROCESS

Usually rice is used as the raw material for the puffed rice. It is cleaned before puffing to reduce the amount of bran present on the finished product.

PUFFED RICE

General Considerations

Puffing process may be conveniently divided into two types (i) atmospheric pressure procedures which rely upon the sudden application of heat to obtain the necessary rapid vaporization of water and (ii) pressure - drop processes which involve suddenly transferring super-heated, moist particles into a space at lower pressure. In the latter case the pressure drop may be achieved by releasing the seal on a vessel containing a product which has been equilibrated with high temperature steam or it may be secured by transferring the hot material from the atmosphere into an evacuated chamber.

The puffing phenomenon results from the sudden expansion of water vapour (steam) in the interstice of the granule. The particle is fixed in its expanded state by the dehydration resulting from the rapid diffusion of the water vapour out of it. Gun puffing may result in an increase of apparent volume (bulk density decrease) of sixfold to eightfold for rice.

Puffed products must be maintained at about three percent moisture (or less) in order to have the desired crispness. Even at five percent moisture a definite toughness becomes evident. These levels are more critical and harder to maintain in foods which have been gun puffed.

DETAILS OF PROCESS

Generally, Rice puff can be manufactured by following two process.

1. Oven-puffed process, and
2. Gun-puffed process.

Oven-puffed process is most widely used for manufacturing of rice puff.

OVEN PUFFED PROCESS

Rice are used as the raw material for rice puff. After cleaning and classifying according to size, the rice is tempered with added moisture in steel bins of small diameter at approximately 85°F of 24 hours. The rice (tempered) is weight in requisite (say 1400 lbs.) quantity and fed to the toasted croker.

To secure the puffed effect, the cooled and tempered Rice is passed through toasting ovens at 500° to 600°F. Transit time is about 45 to 60 seconds. The material is then visually inspected for colour and agglomeration and sent to the packing line.

PLANT ECONOMICS

Rated Plant Capacity = 1.00 Ton/Day

LAND & BUILDING

Land Area 1000 sq.ft. = Rental Based

PLANT & MACHINERY

1. Automatic Puffed Rice Making Machine
2. Bag stiching machine
3. Hot pouch sealing machine
4. Weighing balance

FIXED CAPITAL

1. Land & Building		Rs.	Rental
2. Plant & Machinery		Rs.	1,26,200.00
3. Other Fixed Assets		Rs.	25,000.00
	TOTAL	Rs.	1,51,200.00

RAW MATERIALS

1. Rice
2. Salt
3. Jute bags
4. Polythene bags
5. Polypack

TOTAL WORKING CAPITAL/MONTH

1. Raw Material		Rs.	3,72,250.00
2. Salary & Wages		Rs.	25,935.00
3. Utilities & Overheads		Rs.	24,125.00
	TOTAL	Rs.	4,22,310.00

TOTAL CAPITAL INVESTMENT

Total Fixed Capital		Rs.	1,51,200.00
Total Working Capital for 3 Months		Rs.	12,66,930.00
	TOTAL	Rs.	14,18,130.00

TURN OVER/ANNUM

By sale of Puffed Rice 300 tons Rs. 55,50,000.00

PROFIT SALES RATIO = Profit/Sales x 100 = 4.61%

RATE OF RETURN = Operating profit/T.C.I x 100 = 18.05%

BREAK EVEN POINT (B.E.P) = 64.58%

Chapter 43

SNACK FOOD

Today, a whole new generation of food products floods the market, catering to entirely new breed of consumers. Rapid industrialization and rising standards of living have not only pushed the boundings of the market but have also brought about general changes in the profile of Indian consumer. Snack foods have got tremendous demand in throughout India and also having bright future demand.

The average composition of a properly fired rice snack is as follows:-

Moisture	-	3 %
Protein	-	6.7 %
Fat	-	37.1 %
Carbohydrates	-	51.2 %
Minerals	-	3.0 %

MANUFACTURING PROCESS

Cereal grits are used as raw material for making snacks. Initially, it is ground into a paste and after the treatment of steaming, this is kneaded to produce dough containing about 15% moisture. The remaining process is un-operational sequence, as follows:-

Humidification

While corn grits or rice grits, which form the raw material, contain generally between 13% to 15% moisture, the appropriate moisture content of the raw material for the manufacture of snack ranges between 14% to 16%. Humidifier consists of tumbler which uniformly and appropriately applies moisture to the grits. The meshes of the grits range between 14 to 16, and after being humidified are inserted into a container or receptacle where they are left quietly for a period of about twenty minutes to enable the moisture to penetrate and saturate the grits uniformly.

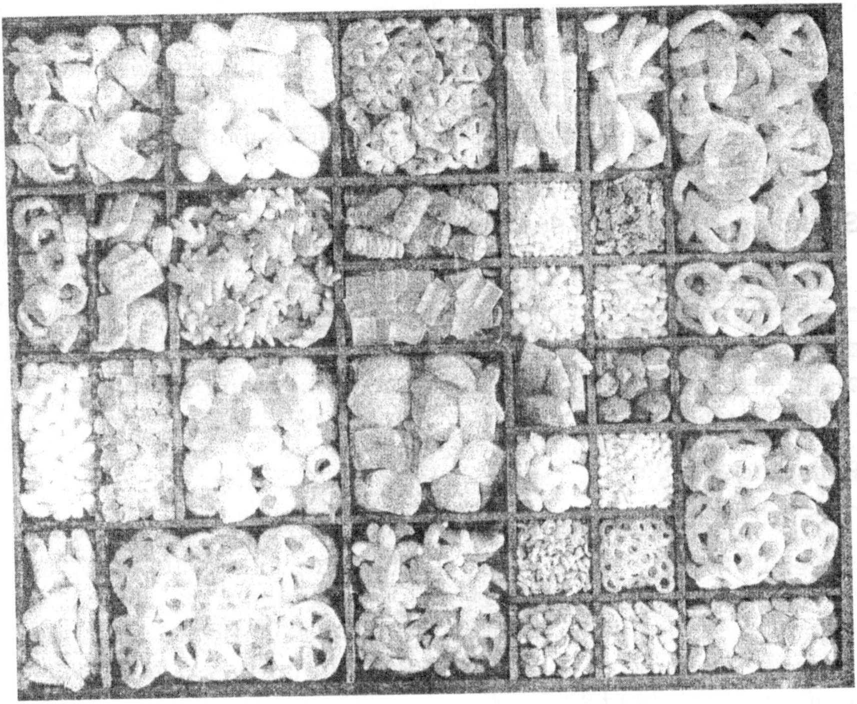

Puffing

After humidification, the grits are fed into the cylinder of puff machine by means of a screw, carried in a forward direction, and as the cereal grits move ahead, the space between the cylinder and the screw is narrowed. High pressure is generated and, at the same time, because of friction heat, the temperature of the raw-material reaches as high as 180°C more or less.

The raw material, which is sufficiently gelated by the generation of this high temperature and pressure, is forced out into the atmosphere through tiny holes in the die where upon, as a result of the large pressure difference, moisture is instantaneously evaporated and, including bubbles, is inflated to form and produce expanded material (puffed product).

Cutting

The inflated material, which has been extruded, is cut into requisite length by a rotary cutter.

Roasting

As moisture still remains in the expanded material which has been cut up into requisite lengths, it is slightly roasted in a rotary oven, and simultaneously with drying, the flavouring of the cereals are drawn out.

Seasoning (By rotary seasoning machine)

The surface of the expanded material (puffed product) which comes out of the rotary oven is flavoured and seasoned by a spraying of vegetable oil and seasoning. By the rotation of a slightly slanted drum, the expanded material is uniformly flavored and seasoned as it moves forward.

Finishing & Drying

The puff snack, which has been flavoured and seasoned with oil and seasoning powder, possess little moisture, and therefore needs no finishing and drying. However, in the event that the seasoning, juices are watery, the puff snack is dried by a finishing and drying machine. Drying is adequately performed by the passage of air at a temperature of about 80°C.

Packaging

Snack foods deteriorate due to moisture and oxygen, a film is utilized which prevents permeation of moisture and gases. Packing and packaging are both performed by an automatic bag making, filling and packaging machine. Before packing and packaging weighing is undertaken either manually or automatically as the case may be.

Protein Snack

Ingredients		*(Kgs)*
Cracker Meal	-	125
Bread Flour	-	85
Sunflower Meal	-	85
Promine D	-	15
Gum Arabic	-	3
Onion Salt	-	2

Celery Salt	-	1
Water	-	80

Process

Mix all dry ingredients and add sufficient water to make a paste that will just flow. Extrude into desired shape into deep fat at 375°F and fry until light brown. Drain dry. Add salt as desired.

Protein Crackers

Promine - D	-	40 gms
Wheat Flour (General purpose)	-	360 gms
Salt	-	20 gms
Ammonium Bicarbonate	-	15 gms
Hydrogenated Vegetable shortening	-	100 gms
Water	-	240 gms

Process

Mix dry ingredients, add water, and knead. Then pass through extruder and puffing machine then pack into desired packaging materials.

PROCESS DETAILS

The manufacture of a composite cereal by the gun puffing method is described as follow.

Corn cones, oat flour, and a flavour pre-mix consisting of salt coloring substances, flavoring compounds, etc. are combined in a screw conveyor with interrupted flights. The homogenous mixture is dumped through a rotary valve into a continuous steam-jacketed cooker. Water is added by a metering device so that the product going to the extruder is at 38 to 40 percent moisture content.

Auger-induced pressure extrudes strands of cooked dough around the periphery of a circular die. A knife travelling over the die surface cuts the strands into short pellets. The pellets may be solid or have a hollow center. The pellets go to a tumbling cooker which reduces the surface moisture and prevents the occurrence of agglomeration. The product is piled about three inches deep on the metal belt of a proctor and sehwarz oven.

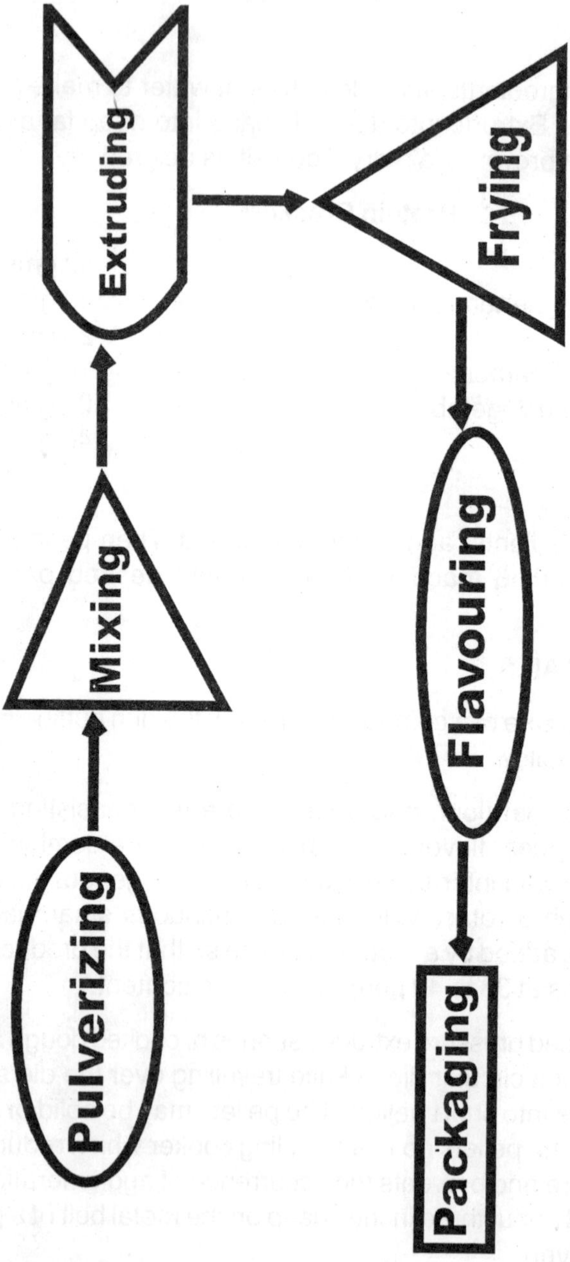

PROCESS FLOW CHART FOR NAMKEEN SNACKS

Solid pellets at 15 to 16 percent moisture content may be bumped between rolls to make a disc-shaped particle with serrated edges.

The guns, so-called, are pressure vessels about six inches in diameter and 30 inches long. They are provided with a steam inlet, a bleed-off valve, and a means for heating the gun-usually by a gas flame. A charge of pellets at 11 to 12 percent moisture content is dropped into the open end of the gun from a gravity chute leading from the storage bins on the floor above. The end of the gun is sealed by a trip-valve. All valves are closed, sealing the gun. If the gun is heated by gas flames, it is slowly rotated while the temperature, and consequently the pressure, is slowly built up. The temperature may reach 500° to 800°F, and the pressure at the end point may be 100 to 200 lb. per sq. in. This process may take 5 to 7 minutes.

When the pressure reaches the necessary level, the end of the gun is suddenly opened by a trigger mechanism. The contents explode into a cage or bin provided with a floor opening leading to a conveyor belt. The material is then visually inspected for color and agglomeration and sent to the packing line.

There can be almost endless variations on the preceding method. Cocoa can be added to the dough to make a chocolate flavoured confection. Products may be made of any colour for which there is a suitable edible dye. Shapes canbe varied within a wide range. Raw materials may be almost any combination of cereals.

Some composite-dough, gun-puffed cereals are the trade-marked Mix, Coco-Puffs, Jets, Trix, Cheerious etc.

Details of Snacks Food Plant

The solid design of all parts, precision & extremely accurate manufacturing methods ensure in combination of minimum maintenance requirements & trouble free operation. The machine is precisely designed to ensure minimum power consumption. The extruder is so versable that by just replacing sets of nozzles the user has the advantage of changing the shape of the final product.

The versability of the extruder can be gauged from the fact that the user can make use of either of the following raw materials. Corn grit rice grit, wheat samolina, sabudana etc.

SNACKS FOOD PLANT

TECHNICAL SPECIFICATIONS

	CAPACITY (in KG/hr.)	BARREL LENGTH (in mm)	SCREW DIA (in mm)	MAIN MOTOR DRIVE (H.P.)	CUTTER MOTOR DRIVE (H.P.)	FEEDER MOTOR DRIVE (H.P.)	COOLING SYSTEM	MIXER MOTOR DRIVE (H.P.)	CONVORISED OVEN DRIER TOTAL ELECTRIC (H.P.)
SNACKS FOOD PLANT	80 TO 100	458	70	25	1/2 D.C.	1/2 D.C.	1.2 H.P. A.C. BLOWER	3 A.C.	

DETAILS OF PLANT & MACHINES

Cap: 150 kgs/hour Puff Snack Making Plant.

Sl.No.	Machine or Equipment	Unit	Power Rating
1.	Humidifier made of S.S.-320	2 No.	1.2 KW
2.	Screw Conveyor	1 No.	1.5 KW
3.	Grain puff machine	3 No.	52 KW
4.	Conveyor	1 No.	0.4 KW
5.	Conveyor	1 No.	0.4 KW
6.	Rotary oven, gas fired, L.P.G. gas consumption 8 kgs/hour	1 No.	0.75 KW
7.	Conveyor	1 No.	0.4 KW
8.	Seasoning service tank, gas fired, L.P.G. Gas consumption 2 kgs/hour	1 No.	0.4 KW
9.	Rotary seasoning machine	1 Nos.	0.4 KW
10.	Powder spraying system	1 Nos	1.6 KW
11.	Conveyor	1 No.	0.4 KW
12.	Bucket Type Conveyor	1 No.	1.5 KW
13.	Automatic weighing machine	3 No.	
14.	Automatic packing machine	1 No.	0.4 KW
15.	Conveyor	1 No.	0.2 KW
16.	Compressor	3 No.	17.1 KW

PLANT ECONOMICS

Rated Plant Capacity = 1300.00 Kgs./Day

LAND & BUILDING

Land Area 2000 sq.mt. = Rs. 21,50,000.00

FIXED CAPITAL

1. Land & Building	Rs.	21,50,000.00
2. Plant & Machinery	Rs.	26,50,000.00
3. Other Fixed Assets	Rs.	5,00,000.00
TOTAL	Rs.	53,00,000.00

RAW MATERIALS

1. Proamine D
2. Wheat Flour
3. Salt
4. Ammonium Bicarbonate
5. Hydrogenated Vegetable shortening
6. Packaging materials

TOTAL WORKING CAPITAL/MONTH

1. Raw Material	Rs.	10,76,500.00
2. Salary & Wages	Rs.	1,22,360.00
3. Utilities & Overheads	Rs.	1,85,000.00
TOTAL	Rs.	13,83,860.00

TOTAL CAPITAL INVESTMENT

Total Fixed Capital	Rs.	53,00,000.00
Total Working Capital for 3 Months	Rs.	41,51,580.00
TOTAL	Rs.	94,51,580.00

TURN OVER/ANNUM

By sale of 390000 kgs. Rs. 2,34,00,000.00

PROFIT SALES RATIO = Profit/Sales x 100 = 18.98%
RATE OF RETURN = Operating profit/T.C.I x 100 = 46.99%
BREAK EVEN POINT (B.E.P) = 46.29%

Chapter 44

SOYA MILK & PANEER

Soyabeans are very much popular as food crop in most of the countries all over the world where a large number of food products are prepared from soyabean seeds. As edible oil milk and milk products giving sources crop the soyabeans are getting wide acceptance. In India too since last few decades. Soyabean seeds have a high nutritional composition; and can be converted in to various states, tastes, colours, flavours and other quality substances.

As far as the use of soyabean is concerned it has taken a place from soap industry to food industries like. The soya milk, in particular has been developed like a boon for human beings as large. The speciality lies in the fact that in the reasons when traditional cow milk buffalo milk is not available in sufficient quantity, this milk serves the purpose almost equitably to other animal milk type.

PROCESS OF MANUFACTURE

Soyamilk has a good storage stability. Pasteurized soyamilk could be stored for about one week at 5°C. The milk could be stored in bottles, plastic sachets or in bulk containers.

Basic raw material for processing of soyamilk is soyabean.

From 1 Kilogram of good quality soyabean about 10 litres of soyamilk is produced.

Soyabean is air dried and spread on floor for picking up stove pieces, debars, and other unwanted material. The prepared soyabean is then fed to Dalralaing, Machine. The shell mixed Dal is separated for Dal & husk. The Dal is further removed of contaminated shell be air blanching method. The soyabean Dal is now put to a blancher for steam heating where the dal is sufficiently cooked for 2-3 hours. It should not be overcooked. The cooked Dal is removed from the blancher and fed to a nut grinder and ground very fin. The ground soyabean is diluted to desired milk consistency. The milk is stirred & mixed in a storage can. It in this diverted to homogenizer. After it is homogenised it is diverted to be pasteurized where it is subjected to steam heating as will as ice cooling in succession. After it is pastwrind the material is stored in milk tanks. Flavour & sweating agents are also mixed as required & suitably homogenised.

The soyamilk is paced in suitable containers & sent to cold room for storage.

PREPARATION OF PANEER

Attempts have been made to prepare paneer from blended soya milk with mixed milk. Soyamilk is prepared form 'Hardea' variety of soya seeds by the illinois process. The milk standardized to 3.5% fat blended with soy milk and modified milk at 10% 15% and 35% soyasolid levels is used.

Citric acid is used as a coagulatic. Paneer prepared from modified milk having 20% milk soya it found acceptable. In the form of raw paneer, the product is soft compared to lower levels of soy solids.

MOISTURE:-

The ordinary moisture determination, by drying to constant weight at 10°C really measure all volatile matters as well as water. Aldehyde, Ketones acids alcohols etc. are the volatile matters which are not measured separately in paneer but as moisture content. Production of soyamilk paneer consists of the following steps:-

Milk Preparations:-

The milk intended to be converted in to paneer is strained through a muslim cloth in a vat. Thoroughly mixed/blended with morning evening collects. The temperature of the milk is raised to 85% by circulating hot water in the vat jacket.

Ripening:-

Milk is then ripened with a suitable starter. The required quantity of a good lacto stirred is strained through a muslin cloth in to the milk and mixed thoroughly.

Renneting:-

The required sennet quantity is diluted in water and mixed thoroughly with the milk.

Setting Time:-

The coagulation time is altered without any more of stirring still the curd is properly precipitated and set.

Whey extraction:-

After whey removed the curd is make at one and of the vat and cut into lumps of convenient and uniform sizes and turned over to facilitate removal of remaining whey as well as imprethe compactness of body and texture. The lumps are placed one above the other till the desired acidity body and texture is obtained.

Milling:-

When the acidity has reached 0.8 to 0.9% and the texture is like the chicken meat, the paneer is ready formilling. Hot iron test should give 3/4 to 1 1/4 length of threads Aeration, salting (if required) and hooping is done hereafter pressing:-

Pressing:-

So prepared paneer is placed under press platens kept horizontal in pain & parallel to each other (Face wise) the pressure is increased gradually. This lot is altered to remain under pressure for a few hours.

Hot bath after taking form the press it is given hot bath at about 140°CF for a few seconds.

There after the paneer is dressed and kept in the churning room at 55°F to 60°F. Here after the paneer can be kept in refrigerator for damp together before it is finally sold to the retailers.

PLANT ECONOMICS

Rated Plant Capacity	=	1000 Ton/Year
LAND & BUILDING (Land Area 2000 sq.mts.)		Rs. 23,95,000.00

PLANT & MACHINERY

1. SOYA MACHINERY:-
   Wet Grinder
2. Dry Roller Grinder
3. Husk Separator
4. Air blower fan
5. Blancher
6. Homogeniser
7. Pasteuriser
8. 10 M-que Tanks
9. Ice Plant
10. Packing Plant
11. Circulator
12. Lab. equipments & fittings
13. Water softener
14. PANEER:- Storage tank
15. Transfer/transportation cans
16. Cans
17. Double jacketed vat
18. Blending/mixing vessel
19. Coal fired small industrial Boiler
20. Hydraulically operated press

21. Centrifnge
22. Strainers, Hair sieve knives dry & wet bulb thermometer Thermometers, Lactomet. Pans, para. weight Machine

FIXED CAPITAL

1.	Land & Building	Rs.	23,95,000.00
2.	Plant & Machinery	Rs.	21,43,500.00
3.	Other Fixed Assets	Rs.	2,25,000.00
	TOTAL	Rs.	47,63,500.00

RAW MATERIALS

1. Soyabean
2. Lactic Acid
3. Salt, Acid and Sugar
4. Coal
5. Lubricating oil, & packaging etc.

TOTAL WORKING CAPITAL/MONTH

1.	RAW MATERIAL	Rs.	7,45,000.00
2.	SALARY & WAGES	Rs.	52,250.00
3.	UTILITIES & OVERHEADS	Rs.	29,750.00
	TOTAL	Rs.	8,27,000.00

TOTAL CAPITAL INVESTMENT

Total Fixed Capital	Rs.	47,63,500.00
Total Working Capital for 2 Months	Rs.	16,54,000.00
TOTAL	Rs.	64,17,500.00

TURN OVER/ANNUM

1. By sale of 600 tons of soyamilk
2. By sale of 400 MT of soyapaneer

TOTAL Rs. 1,50,00,000.00

PROFIT SALES RATIO = Profit / Sales x 100 = 20.21 %

RATE OF RETURN = Operating profit / T.C.I x 100 = 47.24 %

BREAK EVEN POINT (B.E.P) = 44.57 %

Chapter 45

SCENTS AND PERFUMES

The perfumery Industry can be considered to have developed along many channels. A rich variety of odoriferous materials occurs naturally as products of plants and animal metabolism. A few decades ago perfumes were composed primarily from natural material. Later isolates obtained form them were also used for compounding perfumes for example terpene alcohol and geraniol which have a lose odour, have been obtained from citronella oil.

Today, the variety of available natural perfume and flavouring materials is small compared to several thousands of synthetic materials. However the importance of natural perfume materials have not been lost.

Natural perfumes are mostly products of plant metabolism and they occur generally in the form of volatile oils. The fragrance of flowers is due to the presence in the petals of minute traces of essential oils which may be in the free state as in rose and lavender or in the form of glycosides, under favourable conditions are decomposed by appropriate enzymes with the formation of volatile oils. Fragrant materials frequently exists in leaves, steams, barks, roots, heart woods etc. of various species in the plant. Natural exudations from some plants also contain odoriferous compounds these includes gums balsams and oleoresins which form valuable raw materials for perfumes because of their soft and tanacions odour. Animal perfumes like musk, ambergris and civet are important in formulations of finished perfumes.

The separation of fragrant principles from plant is by no means an easy matter the process commonly employed are distillations, enfleurage, maceration, expression and solvent extraction.

PROCESS OF MANUFACTURE

Distillation:-Distilled oils may lack some component which is not volatile enough or which is lost during distillation. Three types of distillation are in use:-

1. Water distillation.
2. Water & Steam distillation
3. Live Steam Distillation

The plant material containing the odoriferous principles may need cominution before treatment.

Flowers & Leaves do not need cominution as the cell walls are sufficiently thin to permit the removal of oil.

The water distillation method in which the plant materials is brought into direct contact with boiling water in a closed apparatus with the condenser attached at the top is the oldest and is still in use in some places as in case of rose petals & orange blossoms.

In the water steam distillation method direct contact of plant material with the still is avoided b y supporting the material on a perforated grid or screen inserted at some distance above the bottom of the still.

The lower part of the still is filled with water to a level some what below the grid and the charge is subjected to distillation by passing low pressure steam. The water beneath the perforated grid is discard after the completion of distillation and replaced with fresh water .

Steam distillation method differ from the water & steam distillation method in that no water is kept in the bottom of the still. Live steam at 40-100 lv/eg. m in injected through steam coils below the change. The pressure within the vessel may be controlled according to the nature of the material handled.

The oils separated by distillation are sometimes rectified or fractioned by hydro distillation at reduced pressure for improving their colour & odour objectionable impurities are removed in the foreruns & late runs during rectification.

The principal odoriferous constituents of most of the essential oils are oxygenated compounds (alcohols, esters, ethers, aldehydes, ketones, lactones, phenols, phelols ethers etc.) They are usually accompanied by terpenses and esquiterpenses which can be separated by fractional distillation in vacuum or by solvent extraction. The usual practice is to separate the terpenses by vacuum distillation and then extract to terpene less oil with dilute alcohol or other solvent to remove in bringing the oil in to contact with solvent partially soluble in each other e.g. pentance and di methyl alcohol, in a tower. The oil flowing counter current to the solvent mixture. One of the solvent (pentane) dissolves the terpens while the other (methyl alcohol), the oxygenated compounds.

For water distillation or water-steam distillation the still consists of a tin lined copper vessel fitted with a mashroori shaped lid of the same material, a bent bamboo wrapped with rope and coated with a clay mixture sieve as a condenser.

The shorter end of the bamboo passes through a hole in the lid and the larger end is led to a tin lined copper receiver which is kept cool by immersion in a cold water reservoir or in a flowing stream.

The distillate is transferred to a coper decante and left over night the floating oil is removed and the water transferred to the still with a fresh change of material.

Extraction Process:-

Enfleurage or extraction of perfume by contact with cold fat is the method used for certain flowers, particularly jasmine and tube rose which continue to elaborates. Their characteristic odoriferous principle even after packing. In such cases extraction with solvents results in loss of perfume.

In the "Enflourage Process" batch of fresh flowers are lightly layerd over a specially prepared fat base (refined lard or beef suet) known as corps. The fat is spread in a thin layer on both sides of a glass plate supported on a rectangular wooden frame or chases. Several chasis are placed one above the other so that the flowers get sandwiched between two layers of fats which absorbs the perfume as it is given off. Spent flowers are removed and replaced by fresh blooms. The glass slab is reversed (patage) several times that both surface absorb the perfume. Also the absorption surface is increased by cutting furrows by means of a comb. Removal of state flowers and changing of fresh flowers is continued until then fat is saturated with the perfume.

The pomade is scraped from the plates, extruded with 95% Alcohol and the extract cooled to -15°C and filtered. The clear solution, known as, extracts may be marketed as such or the solvent may be removed by vacuum distillation to yield the essential oil. The oil retained by flowers after defleurae is extracted with a volatile solvent to yield the absolute of chasis. In the "Maceration Process" the flowers are immersed in hot (60-70°) fat when the oil cells get ruptured and the contents pass into the fat. The fat is separated from spent material and used for the treatment of further batches of flowers. The fat retained by flowers is recovered by hydraulic pressing. The pomade thus obtained is marketed as such or it may be extracted with strong alcohol to yield extracts.

Extraction Volatile Solvent

It yield concretes and alcohol soluble absolutes with a true to nature odour the process has superseded maceration and is now largely used for the extraction of aromatic substances from flowers, leaves & mosses. In this process, fresh flowers are extracted at room temperature with a specially purified solvent e.g. petroleum ether of low boiling point (75°) or benzene. Both stationary and rotary extractors are in use. The former i.e. stationary on consists of vertical cylinders provided with perforated metal grids arranged horizontally around a central vertical shaft. The flowers are changed on grids. Extraction is affected by successive washing whereby each batch of flowers is brought into contact with the solvent three times. The final extract is distilled to recover the solvent.

The rotary extractor consists of a tinned iron drum rotating on a horizontal axis, the interior is divided into four compartments for holding flowers by means of perforated metal partitions. The solvent remains at the lowest part of the extractor and when one compartment is lifted in the course of the movement of the drum, the liquid seeps through the perforations and drips back to the bottom. Each batch of flowers receives three washing. The extract is pumped to a vacuum still and the solvent distilled off at a temperature about 60°, 90-9.5% of the solvent is recovered. The concentrate is cooled, filtered and further concentrated in vacuum. The floral concrete thus obtained considerable amount of plant waxes and pigments.

For preparing the absolute the concentrate is exhausted with warm alcohol and insoluble wax separated. The clear solution is cooled to -20 to -25°C when more wax separate out. The filtered clear solution can be used as such in perfumes.

N. The yield of perfume per kg of flowers is 4-8 gms generally by distillation cum Rectification process.

PLANT ECONOMICS

Rated Plant Capacity = 10.00 Kgs/Day Jasmine and Lily Flower Oil

Land & Building (Land 1000 Sq. mt.) Rs. 9,30,000.00

PLANT & MACHINERY

1. Feeding Hopper with Bucket elevator
2. Rotary Extractor
3. S.S. Jacketed evaporation tank
4. Condenser
5. Vacuum still (SS)
6. Solvent Storage tank (SS)
7. Baby Boiler
8. Pipes, fittings, vacuum pumps, valves, motor and other miscellaneous
9. Solvent Recycling Unit.
10. Laboratory testing Equipments and Instruments

FIXED CAPITAL

1. Land & Building	Rs.	9,30,000.00
2. Plant & Machinery	Rs.	6,50,000.00
3. Other Fixed Assets	Rs.	1,35,000.00
TOTAL	Rs.	17,15,000.00

RAW MATERIALS

1. Flower Fresh (Jasmine, Lily)
2. Solvent Petroleum ether
3. Glass bottles & Lables
4. Carton made of Cardboard

TOTAL WORKING CAPITAL/MONTH

1. Raw Material		Rs.	13,03,250.00
2. Salary & Wages		Rs.	63,780.00
3. Utilities & Overheads		Rs.	48,700.00
	TOTAL	Rs.	14,15,730.00

TOTAL CAPITAL INVESTMENT

Total Fixed Capital		Rs.	17,15,000.00
Total Working Capital for 2 Months		Rs.	28,31,460.00
	TOTAL	Rs.	45,46,460.00

TURN OVER/ANNUM

By Sale of 3000 Kg. flower oil Rs. 2,40,00,000.00

PROFIT SALES RATIO = Profit / Sales x 100 = 25.19 %

RATE OF RETURN = Operating profit / T.C.I x 100 = 132.96 %

BREAK EVEN POINT (B.E.P) = 19.94 %

Chapter 46

SPRAY (PERFUME)

"Attar" the indigenous fragrance held away over India till the arrival of the westernized, alcohol-based scents and sprays.

Attar may no longer hold the pride of place in the elite Indian homes now, but it still reigns supreme in traditional households and the countryside. while the speciality of attar is that its ingredients are entirely natural and, therefore, totally harmless. With the advent of extravagantly packaged spray perfumes, attar has lost its competitiveness. This being the case, imaginative packaging could perhaps not only revive attar's old glory but also make it the rage of the west.

The early Egyptian used perfume in their daily lives for cosmetic purposes, burning incense, in their temples and for embalming the bodies of their Pharaohs with aromatic substances. The Greeks and Romans learned the use of perfume from the Eastern races they conquered and it was only in the mid-10th century that France established her supremacy over the perfume trade.

MANUFACTURING PROCESS

Essence and Perfumery

General Procedure :- The essence and perfumery are generally prepared by the following ways.

1. These can be extracted from flowers leaves and woods. After extraction recovered by vacuum distillation water in cool conditions.

2. Essence and perfumery are prepared generally by blending of pure essence with alcohol blending and mixing is the process of easiest way to be preparation of essence and perfumery.
For the preparation of essence and perfumery it is required to confirm of the formula of which blending operations can be done to give the exact product.

3. Essence and perfumes can be produced by chemical synthetic way.

Present case I am dealing with the formulation and blending cross for the production of essence and perfumery.

The basic formula of perfumes and essence are given.

Synthetic Rose otto No 1056

		Parts
Citronellol	-	200
Phenylethyl Alcohol	-	100
Geraniol Palmarosa	-	200
Rhodinol	-	200
Guaiace wood	-	50
Eugenol	-	
Innone Alpha		5
Cinnamic Alcohol	-	50
Phenyl Acetic Acid	-	40
Phenyl acetic Aldehyde	-	3
Trichloro Phenyl Methyl Carbinyl Acetate	-	80
Un decylenic Aldehyde	-	2

Red Roses, No-1057

		Parts
Phenyl Ethyl Alcohol	-	150
Rhodinol	-	200
Ionone	-	300
Cinnamic Alcohol	-	150
Rhodinyl Acetate	-	100
Trichloro Phenyl Methyl Carbinyl Acetate	-	50
Jasmine Compound	-	50

A finished perfume may be prepared as follows :

Violet, No. 1068

Parma violet compound	100
Victoria violet compound	40
Cassie absolute	5
Rose otto	1
Civet absolute	1
Musk ketone	1
Santal	2
Ambergris tincture, 3 per cent	30
Musk tincture, 3 per cent	20
Alcohol	800
	1000

PLANT ECONOMICS

Rated Plant Capacity	=	2400.00 Bottles/Day Aerosol Spray
Land & Building (Land 200 Sq.Mts.)	Rs.	5,30,000.00

PLANT & MACHINERY

1. Different Storage Tanks
2. Mixing vessel
3. Refrigeration unit
4. Distillation unit.
5. Liquid filling Machine.
6. Labelling Machine.
7. Heater Unit.
8. Miscellaneous.

FIXED CAPITAL

1. Land & Building	Rs.	5,30,000.00
2. Plant & Machinery	Rs.	2,52,000.00
3. Other Fixed Assets	Rs.	50,000.00
TOTAL	Rs.	8,32,000.00

RAW MATERIALS

1. Essence Compounds
2. Ethyl Alcohol
3. Glass Bottles and Packaging Materials

TOTAL WORKING CAPITAL/MONTH

1. Raw Material		Rs.	7,27,500.00
2. Salary & Wages		Rs.	26,093.00
3. Utilities & Overheads		Rs.	85,500.00
	TOTAL	Rs.	8,39,093.00

TOTAL CAPITAL INVESTMENT

Total Fixed Capital		Rs.	8,32,000.00
Total Working Capital for 3 Months		Rs.	25,17,279.00
	TOTAL	Rs.	33,49,279.00

TURN OVER/ANNUM

1. 25 Ml. capacity bottles 360000 Nos.
2. 50 Ml. capacity bottles 240000 Nos.
3. 100 Ml. capacity bottles 120000 Nos

TOTAL Rs. 1,27,20,000.00

PROFIT SALES RATIO = Profit/Sales x 100 = 14.78 %

RATE OF RETURN = Operating profit / T.C.I x 100 = 56.10 %

BREAK EVEN POINT (B.E.P) = 41.21 %

Chapter 47

SUPARI (BETEL NUT)

FORMULATIONS

Formulation - 1 (Sweet Scented Supari)

Betel-nut flakes	-	5 kgs.
Fresh milk	-	3 ltrs.
Sugar	-	1 kg.
Water	-	500 ml.
Menthol Crystal	-	5 gms.
Yellow colour/Caramel colour	-	10 gms.
Musk essence	-	15 ml.
Rose essence	-	25 ml.

Process of Manufacturing:-

1. First of all mix the musk essence and rose essence in a glass bottle and left for some days after capping the glass bottle air tight.

2. Heat the milk in a stainless steel vessel till boiling.

3. Add the supari flakes in milk with stirring.

4. Continue heating the milk with supari till all the milk get evaporated. After this it is kept aside for cooling.

5. Prepare the sugar syrup by heating water and sugar mixed together.

6. Add colour in desired quantity to the sugar syrup.

7. Then this sugar syrup is mixed with the prepared supari with uniformity.

8. The above supari is now put on a stainless steel screen/stainer to ooze out excess syrup from it.

9. Then the above finished supari is sprayed with the previously mixed essences from glass bottle, and again mixed homogeneously.

10. The product is now packed in polythene pouches or plastic bottles as per customers requirement.

Formulation - 2

(Scented sweet chikni Supari)

Chikni Supari	-	2 kgs.
Pure Desi Ghee	-	150 gms.
Elaichi Dana	-	50 gms.
Jayatri	-	20 gms.
Jaiphal	-	15 gms.
Clove	-	25 gms.
Menthol flakes	-	4 gms.
Saccharine	-	5 gms.
Rose essence	-	10 ml.
Rose water	-	100 ml.

Process of Manufacturing :-

1. Cut the chikni supari in small pieces or flakes.
2. Add Ghee in the supari flakes and mix uniformly so that ghee will be coated on the surface.
3. In another stainless steel vessel prepare a liquid of saccharine and rose water homogeneously.
4. In another vessel, crush the Elaichi Dana, Jaiphal, Jayatri, Clove etc. into a mix form along with menthol flake powder.
5. Now mix the supari flakes (as prepared in the first step) with this elaichi, jaiphal, Jayatri, Clove and menthol mix uniformly.
6. Then spray the Rose water and rose essence, saccharin mix on the above mix.
7. Then pack this supari mix in polythene pouches and plastic bottle as per customers requirement.

PROCESS DESCRIPTION

First, the small pieces of betelnut are wetted in presence of water, then kept in sun for 1-2 hrs. to reduce the moisture. Edible colour are mixed on as per requirements.

Now rubbed these pieces with ghee to make them greasy. After greezing of nuts, it is pulverized in pulveriser, now dry in sun for 1-2 hrs. only. Then they are baked in a iron cauldron for a few minutes to develop a pleasant aroma, care is taken that it is not overbaked. Now perfumes are added i.e. Rose Isuase, Casia Oil, Orange Oil, elaichi..... etc., as required. Other additives are also added as Kesar, Sugar, Sucrose....etc, to make it in favouring flavour, during this mixing they are rubbed well with both hands.

Towards the end 1-2 kg coconut chips are added and mixed thoroughly. Mainly we mix scent to our "Supari" are as follows.

1. Oil Rose/Geranium/Menthol
2. Musk Perfume
3. Propylene glycol.

After this the "SCENTED SUPARI" is ready for sale.

FORMULATION OF SCENTED SUPARI

1.	Betelnut (Pieces)	90.00 %
2.	Propylene Glycol	3.50 %
3.	Oil Rose Geranium	2.00 %
4.	Menthol	2.50 %
5.	Musk perfume	1.50 %
6.	Peppermint	.50 %
		100.00 %

FOR SCENTED COLOURED SUPARI

1.	Glycerin (To Make it wet)	3 %
2.	Edible Rosy Colours	1/2 %
3.	Menthol	1/2 %
4.	Eucalyptus Oil	1/2 %
5.	Sugar	1 %
6.	Saccharine	2 %
7.	Supari	92.5%

FLOW SHEET DIAGRAM

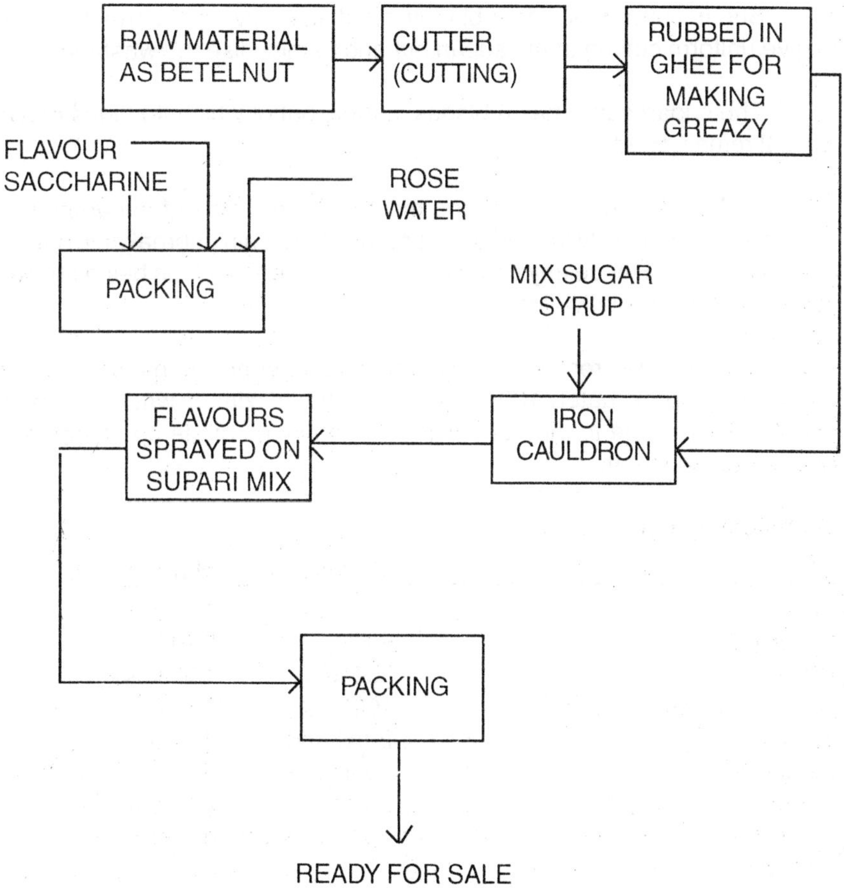

FLOW SHEET DIAGRAM OF SCENTED SUPARI

PLANT AND MACHINERY DETAILS

Supari Cutter (Model No. SC-02):-

Supari cutter has longer blades, fixed and moving at perfect angles to give uniform cutting of the supari nut and to minimise the wastage.

The supari cutter has 6 blades in total, out of which 4 blades move while 2 remain fixed.

Blades, as such, remain the most treasured part of supari cutter, since they are specially treated and hardened to remain unbreakable during cutting process. Hence any chance of iron. Splinters or chips being thrown into the output is totally eliminated.

Supari cutter renders a high quality cutting and enhanced output capacity of approximately 100 kg per hour at the maximum wastage rate of just 7%. This is due to the right alignment of blades made up of superior quality cutting metal.

Technical Specifications:-

		Machine - I	Machine - II
Size of machine	:	10 inches	5 inches
Motor capacity	:	5 HP	3 HP
Weight	:	300 kgs.	150 kgs.
Cutting capacity per hour	:	100 kgs	5 kgs.
Number of Blades	:	2 fix, and	4 rotating
Length of Blades	:	10 inches	5 inches
Occupying space	:	25 sq.ft.	25 sq.ft.
Covering arrangement for workman safety and	:	special covering protection dust.	

Sieving Machine (Model No: SMS - 05):-

After cutting, supari nuts are placed into the sifter to separate the useful stock of any kind of supari dust and wastage.

The sifter has a tilted sieve operated by motor and when switched on moves in a zig-zag electric fashion throwing aside the perfectly cut pieces of supari not from the dust which automatically filters down the sieve into the tray just beneath.

Motor, mounted on the base of machines, shakes the sieve via a V-Belt which is designed to do quick and efficient sieving operation.

Sieving net is made up of stainless steel to avoid any rusting by the moisture of stock.

Technical Specification:-

Size of machine	:	24" width X 52" length
Motor	:	1 HP (3 phase)
Weight	:	150 kgs.
Occupying space	:	24 sq.ft.
Sifting capacity	:	100 kgs/hr.
Body Built by	:	Mild steel
Wiremesh	:	Stainless steel.

Mixer - II

Mixer - II has a rotating drum which is operated by electric motor. While stationery, the lid of the drum is positioned upwards and can be opened by loosening two long wheel odscrew nuts to fill in the stock. Afterwards, the lid is closed and machine switched on.

The electric motor keeps the drum rotating. The stock inside goes up and down and in circles, and all the ingredients therein are perfectly mixed, given the proper time.

Technical Specifications:-

Motor	:	1 HP /220 Volt AC
Drum Capacity	:	5 $ft.^3$
Drum rotation	:	40 RPM
Occupying space	:	24 sq.ft.

PLANT ECONOMICS

Rated Plant Capacity	=	300.00 Kgs. /Day
LAND & BUILDING		
Land required 500 sq.mts.	=	Rs. 10,25,000.00

PLANT & MACHINERY

1. Supari Cutter
2. Sieving Machine
3. Mixing machine
4. Automatic weighing, filling, pouch sealing machine.
5. S. S. Tank & other tools etc.
6. Miscellaneous equipments

FIXED CAPITAL

1. Land & Building	Rs.	10,25,000.00
2. Plant & Machinery	Rs.	2,95,000.00
3. Other Fixed Assets	Rs.	3,20,000.00
TOTAL	Rs.	16,40,000.00

RAW MATERIALS

1. Betel nut
2. Milk
3. Sugar
4. Menthol Crystal
5. Food Colour, Saccharine
6. Musk essence
7. Rose essence
8. Packaging Materials

TOTAL WORKING CAPITAL/MONTH

1. Raw Material	Rs.	6,23,125.00
2. Salary & Wages	Rs.	40,750.00
3. Utilities & Overheads	Rs.	52,250.00
TOTAL	Rs.	7,16,125.00

TOTAL CAPITAL INVESTMENT

Total Fixed Capital	Rs.	16,40,000.00
Total Working Capital for 3 Months	Rs.	21,48,375.00
TOTAL	Rs.	37,88,375.00

TURN OVER/ANNUM

By sale of 90,000 kgs of sweet - scented supari	Rs.	1,17,00,000.00

PROFIT SALES RATIO = Profit / Sales x 100 = 19.25 %

RATE OF RETURN = Operating profit / T.C.I x 100 = 59.46 %

BREAK EVEN POINT (B.E.P) = 36.60 %

Chapter 48

TOMATO PRODUCTS MANUFACTURING (Tomato Sauce, Ketchup, Tomato Puree & Tomato Powder)

MANUFACTURING PROCESSES

TOMATO PRODUCTS

Tomato Juice, Ketchup, sauce and soup, and chilli sauce are some of the important products made from tomatoes. The method of preparing these are described below :

TOMATO JUICE

For this product, only plant-ripened tomatoes should be used. All green, blemished and over-ripe fruits should be rejected as they adversely affect the quality of the pack. Juice made from over-ripe tomatoes is usually thin and unpleasant in taste and aroma.

The Yield, colour and flavour of the juice depend on the ripeness of tomatoes, the variety used and the place where grown. The following points should be kept in view to ensure good quality of the juice :

1. The juice should be of deep red colour. As the red colour in tomatoes is contained in the fibres, as much of the fibrous portion as possible should be incorporated in the juice.

2. The juice should have the characteristic flavour of tomatoes.

3. The acidity of the juice should be about 0.4 percent.

4. The vitamins present in fresh tomatoes should go into the juice. Their retention depends on the method of extraction employed. It has been found that while carotene is fairly resistant to heat and oxidation in the various processes of preparation. Vitamin C is lost appreciably, particularly during the screening of the juice, due to oxidation.

5. For uniformity in quality, either the tomatoes used should be from one stock and place or the juice should be suitably blended.

WASHINGTHETRIMMING

More rinsing of tomatoes in water in not enough, because mould filaments and other micro-organisms, found in their cracks, wrinkles, folds and otem cavities, are not easily dislodged. For through cleaning, they should be washed in running water. For work on a large scale, rotary washers are used.

Great care should be taken in trimming. The loss on account of trimming etc. as worked out In India, various from 4.0 to 17.0 percent. With an average of about 8.0 percent. This heavy wastage is largely due to the absence of standard varieties and defects in picking, transport and marketing of the produce.

CRUSHING

After trimming, tomatoes are out into small pieces before boiling. Alternately, they may be crushed by means of wooden roller-crushers.

PULPING

Tomatoes can be pulped by the hot or cold process described below :

HOT PULPINGs

The crushed tomatoes are boiled in their own juice in steam jacketed kettles or aluminium pans for 3-5 minutes to facilitate pulping. The process has the following advantages;

1. The tendency of the juice to separate into liquid and pulp can be overcome if the natural pectin present in the seeds and the skin can be incorporated. During boiling, the pectin is released, and this thickens the pulp. The ectase enzymes, which would otherwise hydrolyse the natural pectins present in tomatoes and make the juice thin, are also destroyed during boiling.

2. Heating sterilizes the juice partly thereby checking to some extent the growth of living organisms which cause fermentation, etc. It also inactivates the oxidatie enzymes which destroy Vitamin C.

3. A light cooking release the colour present in the skin.

4. The yield of juice is higher than in cold to satisfy the market demand. The flavour of the cold-pulped juice is much sharper and more acidic. This is due to the pressure applied in this process whereby the juice surrounding the seeds which is richer in acid and poorer in sugar than the other portions of the tomato is extracted first. On account of this, the cold-break juice is also of lighter consistency than that obtained from hot

pulping. It has, however, a good fresh flavour.

EXTRACTION OF JUICE

There are two types of extractors in use, the continuous spiral press and the cyclone.

CONTINUOUS SPIRAL PRESS

This consists of a long spiral screw which presses the tomatoes against a tapered screen of fine mesh having 25 holes per linear inch, each hole with a diameter of 20/1000 of an inch. The juice passes through the screen while the skin and seeds are expelled at the other end of the machine. When these machines are open.

COLD PULPING

The tomatoes are crushed and passed as such through a pulper. This process has the following defects:

1. As compared to the hot process, the extraction of juice is somewhat difficult. The yield also is smaller.

2. Air gets incorporated in the juice in the process of extraction and oxidizes Vitamin C there are, however, machines available now-a-days which considerably eliminate the mixing-up of air.

3. The juice extracted by this process in somewhat light in colour.

4. The process has to be finished quickly to avoid spoilage, especially during the initial stages of preparation.

Recently, Penfold has pointed out that pulping gives a juice whose flavour and consistency are different from those of the hot-break juice. The manufacturers have, therefore, to decide about the type most likely operated at a speed of about 250 revolutions per minute, there is little or no incorporation of air in the juice. The tomatoes passing through the hopper should have a jet of steam playing on them to prevent oxidation and destruction of the vitamins.

TOMATO PUREE

Concentrated tomato pulp without skin or seeds, with or without added salt and containing not less than 8.37 per cent. of salt-free tomato solids, is called 'Medium tomato puree'. If it is further concentrated so that it contains not less than 12 per cent, solids, it is called 'Heavy tomato puree'.

PREPARATION

The first step is the preparation of tomato pulp. This is made from plant ripened tomatoes in the same manner as tomato juice.

PULP CONCENTRATION

Concentration of the pulp is done in two types of vessels, namely, (i) open cookers and (ii) vacuum pans.

OPEN COOKERS

For work on a small scale, aluminium patilas will do. For large-scale production, glass-lined tanks or made of stainless steel, monel metal or nickel and fitted with flash coils are used. The open pan method although employed generally, has obvious disadvantages. During boiling, the juice comes into contact with the he oxygen of the air. which not only destroys the Vitamin C in it, but also makes the juice brown. Lal Singh and Girdhari Lal have pointed out that unless special equipment is used to prevent the incorporation of air during the entire manufacturing process, a considerable loss of vitamin C takes place. Buytter or an edible oil is added to the juice during boiling to prevent it from foaming. boiling-over, sticking or burning. Incidentally it also helps in lessening oxidation. This method has now, however, been superseded by the vacuum pan method which gives a product of superior quality.

VACUUM PAN

The installation of a vacuum pans is rather expensive. Its main advantage is that the juice can be boiled at a much lower temperature, i.e. at about 160°F., thus helping in the retention of the original colour and flavour of the tomatoes to a marked degree. As air also is removed during boiling, there is very little likelihood of oxidation or Vitamin C losses. In order to sterilize the product, the vacuum is broken towards the end and the temperature raised to 212°F. for about 10 minutes.

PULP CONSISTENCY

The processes used for concentration of tomato pulp are as follows :

METHOD 1

The pulp is poured into the boiling pan till the heating coils are covered. Heating is then commenced more juice is added and the heating continued6 till the pan is full of pulp. Heaving is then stopped and the total solid content of the pulp is determined. If the solid content is higher than the required percentage, more juice is added to lower it : if it is lower, concentration is continued till the desired consistency is reached. Manufacturers find this method easy to follows.

METHOD II

In this case, a known volume of the juice is concentrated to a known volume of the finished pulp. The juice is let into the boiling tank and, when the coils have been covered, heating is started and the tank is filled to capacity. Heating is continued till the pulp begins to boil vigorously. Steam is then shut off momentarily and the volume of hot pulp is measured with a measuring rod. Then a small sample is drawn for determining the tomato solids by the specific gravity method. While the determination of the solids is being done, boiling of the pulp in the pan is continued. By making use of standard Tables the pulp is boiled to the desired specific gravity. Since both the original and final measurements of volume are taken at the boiling point, temperature correction is not necessary or the reading.

THE END POINT

The total solids in the juice, at the start, during cooking and at the finishing point can be determined either with a specific gravity hydrometer or with an vacuum at 70°C. In practice, the first two methods are used as they are simple.

PACKING

Puree can be packed in plain as well as in enamelled cans. The cans are usually filled with scalding-hot puree at 180°F - 185°F and sealed without exhausting. Sixteen-ounce cans are processed at 212°F for 20 minutes. Larger cans are not generally processed, the temperature of the hot puree itself being sufficient for sterilization.

TOMATO PASTE

A concentrated tomato juice or pulp, without seeds and skins and containing not less than 25 percent of solids, is known as tomato paste. If the pulp is further concentrated so as to contain 33 percent. or more of tomato solids, it is called concentrated tomato paste. Common salt, basil leaf or sweat oil of basil leaf also may be added. Part of its acidity may be neutralised with sodium bicarbonate or carbonate. Ordinarily tomato juice can be concentrated to about 14-15 per cent. Tomato solids in open pans, but for higher concentration, vacuum pans are necessary. The initial concentration is generally carried out in open pans and the product is finished in vacuum pans.

Since the product is very thick, the total solids are determined by an Abbe refractometer.

TOMATO COCKTAIL

Tomato cocktail is gaining popularity in may high class hotels and restaurants. It is prepared just before serving and is also served from stock. In the latter case, the cocktail is preserved by pasteurizing it in bottles. Recipes may differ, but the main constituent is tomato juice to which common salt, vinegar, Worcestershirs sauce, lemon or lime juice, tabasco sauce, etc. are added in different proportions to suit the palate. Two typical formulas are given below :

FORMULA 1

Tomato Juice (Sp. Gr. 1.020)	10 lb.
Cloves (headless), whole	1.5 gm
Cumin, Black peeper and cardamom in equal quantities	4.5 gm.
Cinnamon, broken	1.5 gm.
Coriander seeds	1.5 gm.
Red chillies, Kashmiri (finely ground)	0.25 gm.
Vinegar (10 percent acetic acid)	10 oz.
Common Salt	45 gm.

Simmer the tomato juice with the spices loosely tied in a cloth bag for about 20 minutes in a covered vessel and then add lime juice, vinegar and common salt.

FORMULA II

Tomato juice (sp. Gr. 1.010)	10 lb.
Cloves (headless), whole	1.5 gm
Cumin	1 gm.
Black Pepper	1 gm.
Cardamon	1 gm.
Red Chillies, Kasmiri (finaly ground)	0.25 gm.
Ginger	1.5 gm.
Lime Juice	1.5 oz.
Vinegar (10 percent. acetic acid)	7.5 gm.
Common salt)	45 gm.

TOMATO KETCHUP

Tomato ketchup is made by concentrating tomato juice or pulp without seeds and pieces of skin. Spices, salt sugar, vinegar, onions garlic etc, are added to the extent that it contains not less than 12 percent tomato solids and 28 percent. total solids.

RAW MATERIAL

Select only sound ripe tomatoes of deep red colour. Cut off all green and yellowish portion. Green fruit should not be used as it will made the ketchup inferior in colour and flavour.

JUICE EXTRACTION

The juice is extracted in the same manner as in tomato juice or puree.

JUICE STANDARDIZATION

The raw juice is a thin water fluid and its specific gravity varies with the kind of fruit and the duration of boiling. It follows, therefore, that spices have to be added each time in varying proportions. This would, therefore, hot yield a standard product. Standardization can be achieved by using a recipe for juice of 1.0220 specific gravity (filtrate of pulp of 5.66° Brix). Keeping the other ingredients constant, and equivalent amount of juice of any other specific gravity can be coveniently added.

RECIPES

There are several recipes which give good ketchup. Recipe I given by Lal Singh and Girdhari Lal, with slight variation has become popular with the manufacturers in this country. the remaining three recipes are popular in other countries.

RECIPE I

Tomato Juice (Sp. Gr. 1.022 - 1.027)	6 gal.
Onions, chopped	375 gm.
Garlic, chopped	25 gm.
Cloves, whole, headless	10 gm.
Cardamom	4 gm.
Black pepper	4 gm.
Zira	4 gm.
Macc (Jalvatri), not ground	2.5 gm.
Cinnamon (broken)	17.5 gm.
Vinegar, 6% acetic acid	2.5 lb.
Sugar	2.0 gm.
Salt	312 gm.
Red Chillies	12.5 gm.

TOMATO SOUP

In preparing tomato soup, the first step is to make tomato pulp, in the same way as for tomato juice. The main constituents of this soup are : tomato juice, butter or cream, spices, arrowroot (a thickening agent) etc. These are added in various proportions to suit the taste.

The following typical formula yields a good soup :

Tomato juice (Sp. Gr. 1.0220)	7 gal.
Onions, finely chopped	13 oz.
Cinnamon, broken	5 gm.
Cloves whole, headless	5 gm.
Ground white pepper	7 gm.
Red chillies, ground (Kashmiri)	0.7 gm.
Cumin (Zira) cardamom and black pepper in equal quantities	5.3 gm.
Ginger dry ground	4.2 gm.
Cream (30 percent) or butter butter	1 1/4 lb or
Arrowroot starch	4 1/2 oz.
Sugar	17 oz.
Common Salt	1 1/2 oz.

PREPARATION OF TOMATO SAUCE

For the preparation of tomato sauce following recipe should be used.

TOMATO PULP

PREPARATION

Neutralize about 1/6 acidity of the juice by adding a thin paste of sodium bicarbonate made with water. Place 6 gallons of the juice in a boiling pan and heat it. While it is being concentrated, add spices tied loosely in a muslin bag as is done in the case of tomato ketchup. In the meantime, mix arrowroot and butter (or cream) with the remaining one gallon of juice to form a smooth paste. When the juice in the pan gets concentrated, add this mixture. Again boil to the desired consistency, stirring it continuously to prevent clotting of the starch, etc. At the end, add sugar and boil the mixture for about about two minutes to dissolve them. Fill the soup into cans.

STERILISATION

Sterilize at 240°F for 45 minutes in the case of A 2 cans and for 40 minutes in the case of 1 lb. milk or jam-size cans. Cool quickly after processing.

TOMATO SAUCE

PREPARATION OF TOMATO SAUCE

For the preparation of tomato sauce following recipe should be used.

Tomato pulp (6% Soluble Solids)	29484 gm.
Cardamon, Pepper and Cumin (Zir) in equal quantities	8.5 gm.
Cinnamon, broken	10 gm.
Cloves (head less)	8.5 gn.
Mace (not ground)	5.7 gm.
Common Salt	700 gm.
Onions (chopped)	200 gm.
Garlic ground	18 gm.
Sugar	2500 gm.
White Vinegar (100 grain)	580 c.c.
Red Chilli powder	15 gm.

Took the above ingredients in a kettle, heat it by steam to make a paste like product until it contains total soluble solids around 25% by refractometer.

When the product contains soluble solids around 25%., then stop steaming put the recipe in the packaging system for packing, then store and sale in the market.

PROCESS FLOW SHEET FOR SAUCES

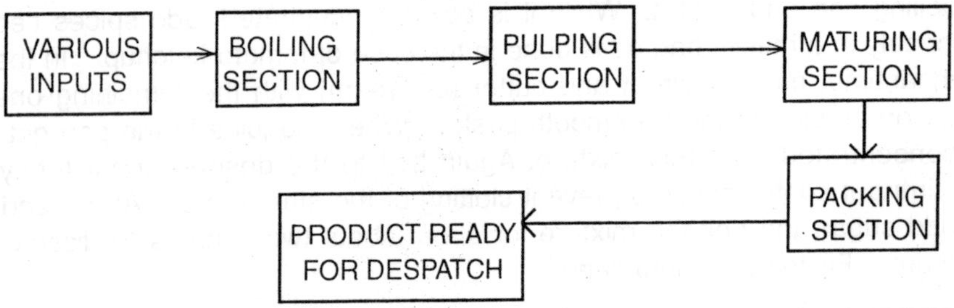

PLANT ECONOMICS

Rated Plant Capacity = 1100.00 PAC/Day

LAND & BUILDING

Total Land Area 195 Sq. Mt. = Rs. 5,32,000.00

PLANT & MACHINERY

1. Vertical Boiler
2. Hydraulic Juice Press,
3. Pulper
4. Juice Presturizer
5. Steam Jacketted Kettle
6. Sterilization Tank
7. Super Crown Corking Machine
8. Rotary Fruit &Vegetable Washing Machine
9. Aluminium Trays
10. Storage And Mixing Tanks (S.S.)
11. Platform type weighing scale
12. Automatic Pouch filling machine
13. Automatic Pouch and Ketchup filling
14. Bottle Washing Machine
15. Vacuum filling machine
16. Portable stirrer
17. Preparation Tables
18. Testing equipments & Instruments
19. Blanching Equipment
20. Stainless steel peeling
21. Fruit and Vegetables Slicer
22. Fruit Crater,

FIXED CAPITAL

1.	Land & Building	Rs.	5,32,000.00
2.	Plant & Machinery	Rs.	9,17,500.00
3.	Other Fixed Assets	Rs.	1,60,000.00
	Total	Rs.	16,09,500.00

RAW MATERIALS

1. Tomatoes
2. Sugar
3. Chemicals/Salts spices
4. O.T.S. Flattened
5. Empty glass bottles
7. Crown Corks
8. Plastic Caps
9. Labels
10. Cardboard Boxes
11. Pouches

TOTAL WORKING CAPITAL/ANNUM

1.	Raw Material	Rs. 12,10,384.00
2.	Salary & Wages	Rs. 6,21,000.00
3.	Utilities & Overheads	Rs. 3,18,400.00
	Total	Rs. 21,49,784.00

TOTAL CAPITAL INVESTMENT

Total Fixed Capital	Rs. 16,09,500.00
Total Working Capital for 3 Months	Rs. 5,37,446.00
Total	Rs. 21,46,946.00

TURN OVER/ANNUM

By sale of Tomato Juice in 1,30,000 of 200 ml pouch pack
Tomato pure in 1,00,000 Pack 200 gms/pack
Tomato ketchup 1,00,000 pack 500 gms pack

Total Rs. 37,15,000.00

PROFIT SALES RATIO = Profit/Sales x 100 = 22.46%

RATE OF RETURN = Operating profit/T.C.I x 100 = 38.87%

BREAK EVEN POINT (B.E.P) = 57.00%

Chapter 49

TONED MILK

There are different kinds of milk obtained from different animals, like cows, buffalow, goat, camel and many others. But generally we use goat milk cow milk, and buffalow milk. The following gives analysists of milk from goat and cow.

INGREDIENTS	COW MILK	GOAT MILK
WATER	87.40	87.54
SOLIDS	0.75	0.85
CASEIN	3.00	3.00
ALBUMEN	0.4	01.00
FATS	3.	754.50
SUGARS	4.	704.50

People with very low vitality to live on milk products for some time, with fruit to supplement it. In some foreign countries, milk obtained from animals like vama salue Hippopotamies, Gluens pig and Blue whole etc. is used.

Buffalo milk contains more sugar and more casein. it's analysis is as under.

Water	-	82.2%
Protein	-	4.75%
Minerals	-	0.80%
Casein	-	4.45%
Calcium	-	0.203%
Vitamin A	-	0.162%
Fats	-	7.10%
Phosphorus	-	0.125%
	Total	99.890%

India posses an enormous cattle (180 million) and buffaloes (61 million) population but the annual milk production has reached only about 30 million tonnes. The low milk production is primarily due to the low-potential of animals and lack of adequate nutrition.

MANUFACTURING PROCESS OF TONED MILK

Frist of all skimmed milk powder is procured from the market. For the Production of 100 kgs of tonned milk, 9 kgs of skimmed milk powder is taken in a stainless steel vessel fitted with agitator and motor.

Now in this stainless steel vessel calculated quantity of Butter oil (2 kgs) is added.

Calculated quantity of Hot water (89 liters) is added at 60^{0}C for the preparation of toned milk and the entire mass is homogenised.

The toned milk thus formed is sent for pasteurization to kill the germ. It is further tested and packed in pouches and sent for marketing.

STANDARDISATION

Milk is standardised according to ISI (now B.I.S.) specification or according to requirements by wholesaler.

HOMOGENISATION

Fioteted milk is fed into homogenizer. Homogenization is the process by which the milk is emulsified and are further divided to produce a more stable emulsion that will not separate on standing. The fat is emulsified with liquid part of milk that are at water mostly. Hence to prevent sedimentation of fat in milk that homogenization process is done. But this way high quality homogenized milk is produced.

After feeding the milk into homogenizer, the pressure of the homogenizer is increased about 2500 psi. However, of this pressure does not produce milk that meets the standard, it may be necessary to use a pressure high as 3000 to 3500 LB.

A uniform, steady pressure is necessary to secure satisfactory homogenization. The milk should have a slight, positive pressure. Otherwise air may be drawn into the pistons which causes the needles of the pressure gauge to vibrate. Such a result indicates irregular presssure.

Sediment may appear in the operation which is undesirable. To reduce sediment, clarification is done.

CLARIFICATION

The milk is passed through a clarifier is it leaves the homogenizer.

Cold milk clarification is preferred to hot milk. This clarification operation can be perform before homogenization but the complete clarification can be achieved at this stage clarifier can be replaced by cream separator but since the separator bowl is not designed to hold a large amount of sediment and consequently is not efficient for clarifying a large volume of milk. However, this operation can be omitted to get high quality milk.

PASTEURISATION

The milk after clarification is passed through a plate heat exchanger for pasteurisation. In plate heat exchanger (P.H.E.) the milk is pasteurized by UHT method. It is modern method of pasteurisation of milk and used where large volumes of milk are handled. The UHT pasteuriser gives a continuous flow of milk which is fully pasteurised and free from pathogens.

After complete processing, milk is stored in cold upto chilling conditions so that unwanted micro organisms/pathogenic micro organism can not be developed in the processed milk. It is sacred until delivered for distribution to wholesalers.

Testing

The testing of milk is an essential for the quality control purposes however may be done prior to storage under freezing condition.

Distribution

After Complete processing, the toned milk is checked for proper pasteurisation by quality controller. Then the milk at 1 or 2°C is supplied to the wholesalers present at distant places by the tanker or by filling in the big stainless steel cans. Under chilling conditions Temp may rise to 7 to 8°C during transportation.

PLANT ECONOMICS

Rated Plant Capacity	= 50000.00 LTS/Day
LAND & BUILDING (Land 20000 sq.mts.)	Rs. 1,21,00,000.00

PLANT & MACHINERY

1. Complete Plat & Machineries with erection & commissioning
2. Laboratory equipments

FIXED CAPITAL

1.	Land & Building	Rs.	1,21,00,000.00
2.	Plant & Machinery	Rs.	2,45,00,000.00
3.	Other Fixed Assets	Rs.	54,00,000.00
	TOTAL	Rs.	4,20,00,000.00

RAW MATERIALS

1. Skimmed Milk Powder
2. Butter oil
3. Chemicals for laboratory & process
4. Pouches

TOTAL WORKING CAPITAL/MONTH

1.	Raw Material	Rs.	80,54,500.00
2.	Salary & Wages	Rs.	3,19,200.00
3.	Utilities & Overheads	Rs.	21,70,000.00
	TOTAL	Rs.	1,05,43,700.00

TOTAL CAPITAL INVESTMENT

Total Fixed Capital	Rs.	4,20,00,000.00
Total Working Capital	Rs.	2,10,87,400.00
TOTAL	Rs.	6,30,87,400.00

TURN OVER/ANNUM

By sale of pouch of milk (500 ml) Rs. 19,80,00,000.00

PROFIT SALES RATIO = Profit / Sales x 100 = 27.39 %

RATE OF RETURN = Operating profit / T.C.I x 100 = 85.96 %

BREAK EVEN POINT (B.E.P) = 34.99 %

Chapter - 50

Suppliers of Plant & Machineries

PAPPAD M/C

Continental Equipment India Pvt. Ltd.
B-66, Phase-I
Okhla Industrial Area
New Delhi - 110020
Ph:. 26816297, 26816298
Fax: 26815297
E-Mail :
continental@ceipldel.xeedel.xeemail.com

Guru Nanak Engineering Works
D-107, Sector-7
Noida - 201301
Gautam Budh Nagar
Ph:. 0188-91-24542530, 24519360
Fax: 0118-91-24535160
E-Mail :
meera@del3.vsnl.net.in

Inventure India bv.
24, Gold Fields Plaza
45, Sassoon Road
Pune - 411 001
Tel : 91-212-2620237
Fax : 91-212-2621534

Jaswanttray Damodardas Bhuta
kansara Bazar
Kandoliya Sheri
Sihor - 364 240
(Dist. Bhavnagar), Gujarat
Ph:. 02846- 223040

Om Engineering Works
1514, Sector 34D Chandigarh - 160017
Ph:. 0172-2607920
Fact: Industrial Area
Rajpura - 140401
Dist. Patiala
Ph:. 01762-224710

Parbhat M.T. Mfrs Co.
B-23/4, Wazirpur Industrial Area, Delhi -1110052

Raj Products & Equip.
P.B. No. 8075
397 S.V. Road
Vile Parle (W),
Mumbai - 400056
Ph:. 28192250, 28192750
Fax: 91-22-28192750
Fact: 8, Amar Industrial Estate, Navghar Road
Bhayander (E) - 401105

RadeMaker B.V.
Plantijnweg
23, P.O. Box : 416,
4100 AK
Culemborg,Holland

Reliance Engineering Works
4065, Sector-46D
Chandigarh - 160047
Ph:. 2605682, 2653927
Fax: 91-172-2662330

CORN FLAKES PLANT

Aifso Enterprises
A-1, Veena Beena App.
Sewri (W), Mumbai - 15
Ph:. 24130926, 24168838
Fax:. 91-22-24137339
E-Mail :
aifso@bom3.vsnl.net.in
Website : www.aifso.com

PASTA MAKING MACHINE

Agaram Industries
126, Nelson Road
Aminjikarai
Chennai - 600029
Ph:. 091-44-23741413/09844
Fax:. 91-44-23741529
E-Mail : agaram@vsnl.com
Website :
www.agaramindia.com

SNACKS FOOD M/C

G.L. Extrusion System Pvt. Ltd.
Khasra No.172/12, GaliNo.4
Gurga Park, Main Road
Nasirpur Dabri Village
New Delhi - 110045
Ph:. 25557242

Guru Nanak Engineering Works
D-107, Sector-7, Noida.
Gautam Budh Nagar
Ph:. 0188-91-24542530, 24519360
Fax: 0118-91-24535160
E-Mail :
meera@del3.vsnl.net.in

Heat & Control Pvt. Ltd.
3, Anurag G-131
First Main Road,
Anna Nagar East
Chennai - 600102
Ph:. 91-44-26441455, 26451814
Fax: 91-44-26441466
E-Mail :
heatandcontrol@vsnl.net.in

Website :
www.heatandcontrol.com

Kanchan Metals Pvt. Ltd.
38, Strand Road
Kolkatta - 700001
Ph:. 91-33-22109092/93/217
Fax: 91-33-22433808
E-Mail : kanchan@vsnl.com
Website :
www.kanchan.com
Chennai
No31, First Floor
Wallajah Road
Chennai - 600002
Ph:. 91-44-28415213/5347
Fax: 91-44-28415214
E-Mail :
kmplmad@md4.vsnl.net.in

M. Son Industries
D-33, Sector-2
Noida - 201301 (U.P)
Telefax: 011-8-24552177, 24538397
E-Mail :
mson@nda.vsnl.net.in
mson2002@yahoo.com
Website :
www.food-machines.com

Param Consultancy Services Pvt. Ltd.
5, Victoria Building,
27, S.A. Brelvi Road
Fort, Mumbai - 400001
Ph:. 22661332, 22642920/21
Fax: 22660125

PRS Technologies Pvt. Ltd.
D-26, 2nd Floor, NDSE
Part-II, New Delhi - 110049
Ph:. 91-11-26252176/77
Fax: 91-11-26252178
E-Mail :
info@prs-technologies.com
Regd. Off.
63, Bombay Samachar Marg
Mumbai - 400001
Ph:. 91-22-22358111
Fax: 91-22-22358181
Switzerland Off.
Baarerstrasse-57
63007, Zug
Ph:. 041-27295271
Fax: 041-27295270
Bangalore Off.
3rd Floor, Silver Jubilee Block, 3 Cross, Mission Road, Bangalore - 560027
Ph:. 080-22299555
Fax: 080-22299550
E-Mail :
info_bnglr@prs-technologies.com

S.R.F. International
C-8, Commercial Complex
Safdarjung Development Area
New Delhi - 110016
Ph:.0091-11-26858993 to 97
Fax: 0091-11-26863603, 26961494

Sangram Engineering Ltd.
B-5, Supercon, Aundh
Pune - 411007
Ph:.0121-2366935, 2342302
Fax: 0212-2349673

S.S. Engineering Works
B-25, Khanpur Extn.
Devili Road
New Delhi - 110062
Ph:. 26081475

Sakav Food Machines
133 Dewan Industrial Estate
No. 6
Navghar Vasai Road (E)
Dist. Thane - 401210
Ph:. 91-250-2338946
Fax: 912-2340793
E-Mail :
sakav@technologist.com

S.D. Engineering Pvt. Ltd.
E-53, Sector-7
Noida - 201301
Ph:. 0118-24529703, 24549729
Fax: 0118-2452970
E-Mail :
sp_engg@hotmail.com

CONFECTIONERY M/C

Autopack Machines Pvt. Ltd.
101-C, Poonam Chambers
Dr. A.B. Road, Worli, Mumbai - 400018
Ph:. 24934406, 24974800, 24924806
Fax: 91-22-24964926
E-Mail :
autopack@bom3.vsnl.net.in

Advance Packaging
P.O.Box 9209, Gala No. 17
Jai Mata Ji Society
Perubaug Compound,
Asalpha Link Road
Ghatkopar (W), Mumbai - 400084
Ph:. 25101665
Fax: 25099284
E-Mail :
adpackage@yahoo.com

Apaar Packaging Pvt. Ltd.
C-143, Greater Kailash-I
New Delhi - 110048
Ph:. 26464683, 26413094, 26464028
Fax: 91-11-26461250
E-Mail : encore@pragin.com

Bhartiya Printers
T-4/27, Mangol Puri Industrial Area
Ph-I, New Delhi - 110083
Ph:. 27923284, 27923772, 25255787
Fax: 27910675
E-Mail :
bhartiya@ndf.vsnl.net.in

Best Packaging Machineries
16/5, Plot A-38, Karkhana Bagh
Mathura Road,
Faridabad - 121002
Ph:. 0129-2291384

Bombay Engineering Industry
R.No. 6, (Extn.) Sevanthibai Bhavan
Chimatpada, Marol Naka
Andheri (E), Mumbai - 400059
Ph:. 28369368, 28215795
Fax: 28369368
E-Mail : bommars@bom7.vsnl.net.in
Website : http://bej.jump.business.com

Dhiman Industries
Head Office & Works
Dhakni Gate, Nakodar - 144040
Dist. Jalandhar, Punjab
Ph:. 91-1821-220018, 220118, 222118
Fax: 91-1821-221118
E-Mail : info@dhimangroup.com
New Delhi Office:
53/19, Old Rajinder Nagar
New Delhi - 110060
Ph:. 91-11-25783731, 25842114
Fax: 91-11-25744865
E-Mail : delhi@dhimangroup.com
Ahmedabad Office:
G-1, Sulabh Apartment
Near Gurudwara Gobind Dham
Behind Westernd Park,
Thaltej, Ahmedabad
Ph:. 079-26843724, 26756119 (R)
Mobile : 29825006724
E-Mail : ahd@dhimangroup.com
Website : www.dhimangroup.com

Friends Packaging
Parvesh Marg, Railway Road
Gali No.2
Near Rajiv Gandhi Chowk,
Old Faridabad (Haryana)
Ph:. 0129-2297519

Gurdeep Packaging Machines
Hari Chand Mill Compound
LBS Marg, Vikhroli
Mumbai - 400079
Ph:. 25783521, 25772846, 5795982
Fax: 91-22-25772846

Indian Packaging Machinery
I-15, DLF Industrial Estate
Phase-I, Faridabad (Haryana)
Ph: 91-2276112, 2274518, 2217044,2295734, 2278737
Fax: 91-129-2274518

Jet Pack Machines
C-18, Nand Jyot Industrial Estate
Safed Pool, Kurla - Andheri Road
Sakinaka, Mumbai - 400072
Ph:. 28516489, 28515561
Fax: 28516489
E-Mail : jetpack@vsnl.com

Multi Pack Systems Pvt. Ltd.
2nd Floor, Patriot Complex
Ellora Park, Vadodara - 390007
Ph:.0265-2339128,2351799
Fax: 0265-2330701
E-Mail : mktg@multiwrap.com

New Indo International
135-A, Begumpur, Malviya Nagar
New Delhi - 110017
Ph:. 011-26213289, 26217476, 26445315
Fax: 011-26228290

Pac Wel Equipments
233, Gobind Udyog Bhavan
Bal Rajeshwar Road,
Mulund (W)
Mumbai - 400080
Ph.022-25603491, 25904110
Fax: 91-22-24149362
E-Mail : pacwel@bom7.vsnl.net.in
Website : www.pacwelpackaging.com

Qasco Engineers & Industries
Village Badkhal, NIT
Faridabad - 121001
Ph:. 0129-25419252, 25414963
Fax: 25414963

Raksha Packaging
1447, Sector-15, Faridabad - 121007
Ph:. 0129-2284484
Fax: 91-129-2260558

Rado Packaging Machines Pvt. Ltd.
39, Mausam Vihar
Delhi - 110051
Ph:. 22240673/89-255190

Rieco Industries Ltd.
1162/2, Shivaji Nagar
Pune - 411005
Ph:. 2325384, 2325215
Fax: 0212-2323229

Rollon Packaging Pvt. Ltd.
Plont No. 329, Sector 24
Faridabad - 121005
Ph:. 0.129-2232603, 2234939, 2230059
Fax: 91-0129-2233255

S.B. Packaging Ltd.
Vardhman Plaza, Inder Enclave
Paschim Vihar, New Delhi - 110087
Ph:. 25673052/9193
Fax: 25672501
E-Mail : info@sbpackagings.com
Website : www.sbpackagings.com

Santu Foods Pvt. Ltd.
G.No. 131-A & B, Behind
Rine Tiles Old Buder
Bhavnagar - 364001
Ph:. 0278-2424211

Samarpan Fabricators Ltd.
Plot A-182/A-183, Road 16/Z
Wagle Industrial Estate
Thane - 400604
Ph:. 25821842, 25820373,
25820029
Fax: 91-22-25820033
E-Mail :
samarpan1@vsnl.com
Wbsite :
www.samarpanindia.com

Wraptech Machines Pvt. Ltd.
Dharamchand Industrial
Estate
Deonar Village Road
Mumbai - 400088
Ph:. 25512138, 25583596
Fax: 91-22-25570726
E-Mail :
abm@wrapmachine.com
Website :
www.wrapmachine.comAkar

PERFUME M/C

REFRIGERATION UNIT

Rinac India Ltd.
No. 5, "Saraswathi Nivas"
Main Channel Rd.
Saraswathipuram
Ulsoor
Bangalore, Karnataka-
560008
India
TEL : +91 (0) 80 25542929
FAX : +91 (0) 80 25511750
E-mail: rinac@vsnl.com

Hill Thermal Teknics
C-2, Navgeeta
Saint Antony's Rd.
Chembur
Mumbai, Maharashtra-
400071
India
TEL : +91 (0) 22 25556227
FAX : +91 (0) 22 25556227

New Refrigeration Engineers
RZ-B-36, Tatiala Extn.,
B/h Primary School, Part-I
Uttam Ngr.
New Delhi, NCT of Delhi-
110059
India
TEL : +91 (0) 11 25646624
FAX : +91 (0) 11 25635908

Shefa Engineers Pvt. Ltd.
D-162
Phase-I
Okhla Indl. Area
New Delhi, NCT of Delhi-
110020
India
TEL : +91 (0) 11 26811883
FAX : +91 (0) 11 26810986
E-mail:
shefa@del3.vsnl.net.in

Ventaire Inc.
304, Ashwamegh Avenue,
Nr. Mithakhali, Six Roads
Navrangpura
Ahmedabad, Gujarat-
380009
India
TEL : +91 (0) 79 26400944
FAX : +91 (0) 79 26400944

Hill Thermal Teknics
C-2, Navgeeta
Saint Antony's Rd.
Chembur
Mumbai, Maharashtra-
400071
India
TEL : +91 (0) 22 25556227
FAX : +91 (0) 22 25556227

Cooling People (Pune) Pvt. Ltd.
No. 9, 2nd Flr.,
Swaroop Cmplx.
Karve Rd.
Pune, Maharashtra-411004
India
TEL : +91 (0) 20 2333092
FAX : +91 (0) 20 2360270

DISTILLING MACHINE

Praj Industries Ltd.
"Praj House", Bavdhan
Pune, Maharashtra-411021
India
TEL : +91 (0) 2139 51511
FAX : +91 (0) 2139 51718
E-mail: info@praj.net

Dipesh Engg. Works
3, Sheroo Villa
87, J P Rd.
Andheri (W)
Mumbai, Maharashtra-
400053
India
TEL : +91 (0) 22 26336729
FAX : +91 (0) 22 26315507
E-mail:
kjpatel_71@hotmail.com

Dhopeshwar Chem-Tech Group
A-16, Co-op. Indl. Est.
Balanagar, Hyderabad,
Andhra Pradesh-500037
India
TEL : +91 (0) 40 23771579
FAX : +91 (0) 40 23772450
E-mail:
dhopesh@hd2.dot.net.in

Dhopeshwar Engg. Pvt. Ltd.
A-16, CIE, Balanagar
Hyderabad,
Andhra Pradesh-500037
India
TEL : +91 (0) 40 23771579
FAX : +91 (0) 40 23772450
E-mail:
dhopesh@hd2.dot.net.in

Eskeyar Pvt. Ltd.
B-126, 1st Stage
Peenya Indl. Est.
Bangalore, Karnataka-560058
India
TEL : +91 (0) 80 28394596

Kothari Pharma
C-11
M K Brothers Indl. Est.,
Jarimari
Andheri-Kurla Rd.
Andheri (E)
Mumbai, Maharashtra-400072
India
TEL : +91 (0) 22 28510837
FAX : +91 (0) 22 28513584
E-mail:
chandrakant@kothariapharma.com

Metal Plants
17, Anupam Indl. Est. No. 2
Off Pt. M M Malviya Marg
Mulund (W) Mumbai,
Maharashtra-400080
India
TEL : +91 (0) 22 5654607
India
TEL : +91 (0) 11 25183085
FAX : +91 (0) 11 25183085

Flare Combustion Systems
A-18, Hauz Khas
New Delhi,
NCT of Delhi-110016
India
TEL : +91 (0) 11 26868382
FAX : +91 (0) 11 26868382
E-mail:
flarecombustion@id.eth.net

Indcon Boilers Ltd.
D-170, Phase-I
Okhla Indl. Area
New Delhi,
NCT of Delhi-110020
India
FAX : +91 (0) 22 25610628
E-mail: koppa@bol.net.in

Mojj Engg. Systems Ltd.
81-B/15, MIDC
Bhosari, Pune,
Maharashtra-411026
India
TEL : +91 (0) 20 27120360
FAX : +91 (0) 20 27122836
E-mail: mojjpune@ip.eth.net

Rashma Fabricators & Engineers
S-190, MIDC, Bhosari
Pune, Maharashtra-411026
India
TEL : +91 (0) 20 27122648
FAX : +91 (0) 20 27122648

Sharpenn Technologies Pvt. Ltd.
D-56, Shanmugananda,
MIDC Nerul, Navi Mumbai,
Maharashtra-400706
India
TEL : +91 (0) 22 27907202
FAX : +91 (0) 22 27907205
E-mail:
subra@bom3.vsnl.net.in

Anand Dis-Brew Engg. Works
5, Rajinder Ngr. Indl. Area
Mohan Ngr.
Ghaziabad, Uttar Pradesh-201007
India
TEL: +91 (0) 120 24627318
FAX: +91 (0) 120 24721508

Steel Crafts Fabrications
45-D, Dhawalgiri Apts.
Sect. 11 Noida, Uttar
Pradesh-201301
India
TEL : +91 (0) 120 2554241

BOILERS INDUSTRIAL

Bharat Heavy Electricals Ltd.
Jeevan Tara Bldg.
5, Sansad Marg
New Delhi,
NCT of Delhi-110001
India
TEL : +91 (0) 11 23347331
FAX : +91 (0) 11 23342769

Crupp Metals
Kh. No. 56/1, Mundka
Rohtak Rd. New Delhi,
NCT of Delhi-110041
TEL : +91 (0) 11 26811440
FAX : +91 (0) 11 26812425
E-mail: indcon@vsnl.com

Kemtech International Ltd.
A-125, Shivalik
Malviya Ngr. P.O.
New Delhi, NCT of Delhi-110017
India
TEL : +91 (0) 11 26682346
FAX : +91 (0) 11 26684589
E-mail: kemtech@vsnl.com

Lal Sons & Co.
A-45, Phase-I
Mayapuri Indl. Area
New Delhi, NCT of Delhi-110064
India
TEL : +91 (0) 11 25138121
FAX : +91 (0) 11 25147483

Lalsons Machines Pvt. Ltd.
A-45, Phase-I
Mayapuri Indl. Area
New Delhi, NCT of Delhi-110064
India
TEL : +91 (0) 11 5143223
FAX : +91 (0) 11 5147483

Alfa Entech (Guj.) Pvt. Ltd.
504, Suyojan
Hotel President Lane
Off C G Rd.,Navrangpura
Ahmedabad, Gujarat-380009
India
TEL : +91 (0) 79 26426555
FAX : +91 (0) 79 26566106
E-mail: parikh@icenet.net

Energy Process Equipments
29, GIDC Indl. Est.
National Highway No. 8
Por Ramangamdi
Vadodara, Gujarat-391243
India
TEL : +91 (0) 265 2830375
FAX : +91 (0) 265 2830975

Fluidtech Boilers Pvt. Ltd.
2703, Phase-IV, GIDC
Vatva, Gujarat-382445
India
TEL : +91 (0) 79 25830105
FAX : +91 (0) 79 25830041
E-mail: info@fluidltd.com

Isotex Corp.
3rd Flr., Laxmi Chmbrs.
Navjivan Rd.
Ahmedabad, Gujarat-380014
India
TEL : +91 (0) 79 27544321
FAX : +91 (0) 79 27541224
E-mail: isotex@icenet.net

Thermotech Systems Ltd.
Plot No. 2608
Phase IV, GIDC
Vatva, Gujarat-382445
India
TEL : +91 (0) 79 25842387
FAX : +91 (0) 79 25841634
E-mail:
thermotech@icenet.net

Global Engg. & Marketing Co.
913, J B Towers
Opp. Doordarshan Tower
Drive-In Rd.
Ahmedabad, Gujarat-380054
India
TEL : +91 (0) 79 26857299
FAX : +91 (0) 79 26857266
E-mail:
enggchem@kvrkgems.com

Par Techno-Heat Pvt. Ltd.
304,Shreyas Cmplx.,
B/h Dinesh Hall
Income Tax, Ashram Rd.
Ahmedabad,
Gujarat-380009
India
TEL : +91 (0) 79 26588258
FAX : +91 (0) 79 26585497
E-mail:
parboiler@cilmail.com

Pyron Engineers Pvt. Ltd.
Riddhi Siddhi Apt.
Satellite Rd.
Ahmedabad, Gujarat-380015
India
TEL : +91 (0) 79 26747945

C T Boiler Pvt. Ltd.
7/1B
Motilal Nehru Rd.
Kolkata,
West Bengal-700029
India
TEL : +91 (0) 33 24641005

Heiza Boilers (I) Pvt. Ltd.
P-7, Grahams Land
Kolkata,
West Bengal-700040
India
TEL : +91 (0) 33 24711526
FAX : +91 (0) 33 24711526

Texmaco Ltd.
Birla Bldg., 9/1
R N Mukherjee Rd.
Kolkata,
West Bengal-700001
India
TEL : +91 (0) 33 22204379
FAX : +91 (0) 33 22205833
E-mail:
texmaco@cal.vsnl.net.in

BLENDERS

Dhopeshwar Chem-Tech Group
A-16, Co-op. Indl. Est.
Balanagar, Hyderabad,
Andhra Pradesh-500037
India
TEL : +91 (0) 40 23771579
FAX : +91 (0) 40 23772450
E-mail:
dhopesh@hd2.dot.net.in

Dhopeshwar Engg. Pvt. Ltd.
A-16, CIE, Balanagar
Hyderabad,
Andhra Pradesh-500037
India
TEL : +91 (0) 40 23771579
FAX : +91 (0) 40 23772450
E-mail:
dhopesh@hd2.dot.net.in

Sreenex Machines Pvt. Ltd.
2-1-460/1, Nallakunta
Hyderabad,
Andhra Pradesh-500001
India
TEL : +91 (0) 40 27662606
FAX : +91 (0) 40 27619475
E-mail:
sreenex@hd2.dot.net.in

Surya Industrial Equipments
D-109, Phase-I
IDA, Jeedimetla
Hyderabad,
Andhra Pradesh-500055
India
TEL : +91 (0) 40 23096355
FAX : +91 (0) 40 23098163

Vascon Engg. Equipments
C-31/1
Indl. Est.
Sanathnagar
Hyderabad,
Andhra Pradesh-500018
India
TEL : +91 (0) 40 23708586
FAX : +91 (0) 40 23706433
E-mail:
vasconengg@yahoo.com

A G Industries
A-108, Lok Vihar
Pitampura New Delhi,

NCT of Delhi-110034
India
TEL : +91 (0) 11 27103194
FAX : +91 (0) 11 22113355

Jogindra Engg. Works
70, Rama Rd.
New Delhi, NCT of Delhi-110015
India
TEL : +91 (0) 11 25442112
FAX : +91 (0) 11 25453836
E-mail:
jogindra@ndf.vsnl.net.in

Kemtech International Ltd.
A-125, Shivalik
Malviya Ngr. P.O.
New Delhi, NCT of Delhi-110017
India
TEL : +91 (0) 11 26682346
FAX : +91 (0) 11 26684589
E-mail: kemtech@vsnl.com

Ahmedabad Industrial Engineers
402, `Shantam' Cmplx.
Gurukul Rd., Memnagar
Ahmedabad, Gujarat-380052
India
TEL : +91 (0) 79 27433061
FAX : +91 (0) 79 27420131

Cosywo Engg. Co.
15, Laxmi Co-op. Indl. Est.
Nr. Nagarvel Hanuman Mandir
Amraiwadi Rd.
Ahmedabad, Gujarat-380026
India
TEL : +91 (0) 79 22748168
FAX : +91 (0) 79 22748001
E-mail: cosywo@usa.net

Hovert Impex Pvt. Ltd.
Plot No. 3704
GIDC, Est., Phase-IV
B/h Nirma, Vatva
Ahmedabad, Gujarat-382445
India
TEL : +91 (0) 79 25830127
FAX : +91 (0) 79 25833127
E-mail:
hovert@ad1.vsnl.net.in

Navyug Industries
C-1/363, GIDC Est.
Odhav, Gujarat-382415
India
TEL : +91 (0) 79 22871945
FAX : +91 (0) 79 22871959
E-mail:
navyug@wilnetonline.net

Skylab Engineers & Fabricators
3/1, Revabhai Indl. Est. 1
Opp. Bhimnath Hotel
CTM Cross Rd.
Ahmedabad, Gujarat-380026
India
TEL : +91 (0) 79 25857829
FAX : +91 (0) 79 25850005
E-mail:
skylabeng_fab@yahoo.com

AEROSOL FILLING MACHINE

Automatic Devices
105 A, Hind Saurashtra Indl. Est.,
Marol, Andheri-Kurla Rd.
Andheri (E)
Mumbai, Maharashtra-400059
India
TEL : +91 (0) 22 28501376
FAX : +91 (0) 22 28593042
E-mail:
autodevices@vsnl.com

Samarpan Fabricators Ltd.
Plot A-182/A-183
Lane Z, Rd. 16
Wagle Indl. Est.
Thane, Maharashtra-400604
India
TEL : +91 (0) 22 25320373
FAX : +91 (0) 22 25820033
E-mail: samarpan@vsnl.com

Swami Samarth Consultants
303, Sujata Indl. Est.
Thane, Maharashtra-400601
India
TEL : +91 (0) 22 25345506
FAX : +91 (0) 22 25365061
E-mail:
swami_samarth@yahoo.com

STORAGE TANKS

Air Flow Pvt. Ltd.
13/1090, Naiwalan
Karol Bagh, New Delhi,
NCT of Delhi-110005
India
TEL : +91 (0) 11 25721236
FAX : +91 (0) 11 25752267
E-mail:
airflow@del3.vsnl.net.in

Alpha Process Vessels Pvt. Ltd.
A-90, 1st Flr., Amar Cly.
New Delhi, NCT of Delhi-110024
India
TEL : +91 (0) 11 26427087
FAX : +91 (0) 11 26467084

Ark Industrial Products Pvt. Ltd.
S-255,, Greater Kailash-II
New Delhi, NCT of Delhi-110048
India
TEL : +91 (0) 11 26236892
FAX : +91 (0) 11 26236898
E-mail:
akashyap@ndb.vsnl.net.in

Asm-Technoxi Air System Inc.
P.O. Box 4317
New Delhi, NCT of Delhi-110018
India
TEL : +91 (0) 11 26489275

Bays India
1767, Nai Basti
S P Mukherjee Marg
Delhi, NCT of Delhi-110006
India
TEL : +91 (0) 11 25588796
FAX : +91 (0) 11 25588807
E-mail:
bays@del3.vsnl.net.in

Bhiwadi Chemical Pvt. Ltd.
184, New Okhla Indl. Cmplx.,
Phase-I, Okhla Indl. Area
New Delhi, NCT of Delhi-110020
India
TEL : +91 (0) 11 26813624
FAX : +91 (0) 11 26474340

Dynamic Engineers
C-12, Yadav Ngr.
New Delhi, NCT of Delhi-110042
India
TEL : +91 (0) 11 27214104

Engineers Syndicate
A-2, F. F., Ring Rd.
Rajouri Garden
New Delhi, NCT of Delhi-110027
India
TEL : +91 (0) 11 25122357
FAX : +91 (0) 11 5124396
E-mail:
engrsynd@ndb.vsnl.net.in

Garg Rototechnik
14A/8, WEA, Karol Bagh
New Delhi, NCT of Delhi-110005
India
TEL : +91 (0) 11 25746509
FAX : +91 (0) 11 25195721

Indcon Boilers Ltd.
D-170, Phase-I
Okhla Indl. Area
New Delhi, NCT of Delhi-110020
India
TEL : +91 (0) 11 26811440
FAX : +91 (0) 11 6812425
E-mail: indcon@vsnl.com

Indcon Projects Equipment Ltd.
F-2/10, Phase-I
Okhla Indl. Area
New Delhi, NCT of Delhi-110020
India
TEL : +91 (0) 11 26819052
FAX : +91 (0) 11 26812915
E-mail:
indcon@del3.vsnl.net.in

Industrial Construction Co.
A 115, Vikas Marg
Shakarpur
Delhi, NCT of Delhi-110092
India
TEL : +91 (0) 11 22231497
FAX : +91 (0) 11 22231497

International Engineers
PP-4, Lane No. 10
Anand Parbat Indl. Area
New Delhi, NCT of Delhi-110005
India
TEL : +91 (0) 11 25751194
FAX : +91 (0) 11 25730972

Mac Therm Engg. Enterprises
A-2/5, DDA Cmplx.
Paschim Vihar
New Delhi,
NCT of Delhi-110063
India
TEL : +91 (0) 11 25681779
FAX : +91 (0) 11 25581168
E-mail:
jaitinmohindra@hotmail.com

Malik Chemi Process Pvt. Ltd.
D-37, Kirti Ngr.
New Delhi,
NCT of Delhi-110015
India
TEL : +91 (0) 11 25195892
FAX : +91 (0) 11 5195892
E-mail:
mcppldd@nde.vsnl.net.in

Abhinav Polymers
A/2, 3909, GIDC, Phase-IV
Vatva, Ahmedabad,
Gujarat-382445
India
TEL : +91 (0) 79 25833959
FAX : +91 (0) 79 25890833

Aero Engineers
Plot No. 3419
Phase-IV, GIDC
Vatva, Gujarat-382445
India
TEL : +91 (0) 79 25831556
FAX : +91 (0) 79 25891041
E-mail: aero@icenet.net

Airtech Engineers
32, P D Corporation Est.
Nr. Revabhai Est., CTM
Ahmedabad, Gujarat-380026
India
TEL : +91 (0) 79 25854303

Annapurna Fabricators
312, Ananamangal-II
C G Rd.
Navrangpura
Ahmedabad, Gujarat-380009
India
TEL : +91 (0) 79 26566709
FAX : +91 (0) 79 26462268
E-mail:
atrivedi@ad1.vsnl.net.in

Anu Udyog
Plot No. 1420
Phase-III, GIDC, Vatva
Ahmedabad, Gujarat-382445
India
TEL : +91 (0) 79 25893389
FAX : +91 (0) 79 25833388
E-mail: anu@as1.vsnl.net.in

Baroda Polyform Pvt. Ltd.
7, 1st Flr., Panorama Bldg.
Alkapuri, Vadodara,
Gujarat-390005
India

TEL : +91 (0) 265 2333719
FAX : +91 (0) 265 2340172

Cadam Enterprise
A Zydus Group Co.
3708/B, Phase-IV, GIDC
Vatva, Ahmedabad,
Gujarat-382445
India
TEL : +91 (0) 79 25891824
FAX : +91 (0) 79 25834923

Cosywo Engg. Co.
15, Laxmi Co-op. Indl. Est.
Nr. Nagarvel Hanuman
Mandir
Amraiwadi Rd.
Ahmedabad, Gujarat-380026
India
TEL : +91 (0) 79 22748168
FAX : +91 (0) 79 22748001
E-mail: cosywo@usa.net

Dipesh Engg. Works
3, Sheroo Villa
87, J P Rd.
Andheri (W)
Mumbai, Maharashtra-
400053
India
TEL : +91 (0) 22 26336729
FAX : +91 (0) 22 26315507
E-mail:
kjpatel_71@hotmail.com

Steelite Engg. Ltd.
103/5, Blackie House
Opp. GPO, V T
Walchand Hirachand Marg
Mumbai, Maharashtra-
400001
India
TEL : +91 (0) 22 22324093
FAX : +91 (0) 22 22610803
E-mail:
samir@steelitegroup.com

Abros Enterprises
12/8, D-1
MIDC, Chinchwad
Pune, Maharashtra-411019
India
TEL : +91 (0) 20 27475687
FAX : +91 (0) 20 27470678

Albaj Engg. Corp.
340, Clover Centre
Moledina Rd.
Pune, Maharashtra-411001
India
TEL : +91 (0) 20 2631511
FAX : +91 (0) 20 26137255
E-mail: albaj@vsnl.com

Alpha Beta Engg. Construction Pvt. Ltd.
222, Swastik Chmbrs.
CST Rd., Chembur
Mumbai, Maharashtra-
400071
India
TEL : +91 (0) 22 25224527
FAX : +91 (0) 22 25224237
E-mail:
alpha.beta@lwbbs.net

Amalgamated Industrial Composites Pvt. Ltd.
Unit No. 111/112
Ashok Service Indl. Est.
L B S Marg, Bhandup (W)
Mumbai, Maharashtra-
400078
India
TEL : +91 (0) 22 25904565
FAX : +91 (0) 22 25913611
E-mail:
maheshwary@amalgamated.
wiprobt.ems.vsnl.net.in

Amsons Steels Pvt. Ltd.
Opp. MIDC Office
Rd. No. 8, Thane,
Maharashtra-400604
India
TEL : +91 (0) 22 25821443
E-mail: polyplast@vsnl.com

Ashish Cans & Containers Pvt. Ltd.
S. No. 114/1/2
Urse Rd., Vadgaon
Talegaon Dabhade,
Maharashtra-410506
India
TEL : +91 (0) 2114 222615
FAX : +91 (0) 2114 222898

BOC India Ltd.
Oxygen House, P-43
Taratala Rd.
Kolkata, West Bengal-700088
India
TEL : +91 (0) 33 24014708
FAX : +91 (0) 33 24014410

Electronmetal Ltd.
7th Flr., 3C, Camac St.
Kolkata, West Bengal-700016
India
TEL : +91 (0) 33 22294369
FAX : +91 (0) 33 22172189

Forge & Fabrications (Calcutta) Pvt. Ltd.
Room No. 78, 3rd Flr., 5
Clive Row
Kolkata, West Bengal-700001
India
TEL : +91 (0) 33 22207882
FAX : +91 (0) 33 22207889
E-mail: forge@onlysmart.com

S K Oil Company
A Member Of SPA Group
1, A J C Bose Rd.
Kolkata, West Bengal-700020
India
TEL : +91 (0) 33 22827581
FAX : +91 (0) 33 22828584
E-mail:
spa.agrocal@gems.vsnl.net.in

Yantrique Construction Pvt. Ltd.
23A, 6th Flr., Room No. 18
Netaji Subhas Rd.
Kolkata, West Bengal-700001
India
TEL : +91 (0) 33 22209437
FAX : +91 (0) 33 22203528

LAB EQUIPMENTS

Accumax India
C-5A/184, Janak Puri
New Delhi, NCT of Delhi-110058
India
TEL : +91 (0) 11 25501092

Avante Global Services
225, Prakash Mohalla
East Of Kailash
New Delhi, NCT of Delhi-110065
India
TEL : +91 (0) 11 26233259
FAX : +91 (0) 11 26443097
E-mail: avante@vsnl.com

J Mitra & Company Ltd.
A-180, Phase-I
Okhla Indl. Area
New Delhi, NCT of Delhi-110020
India
TEL : +91 (0) 11 26818971
FAX : +91 (0) 11 26818970
E-mail: jml@del2.vsnl.net.in

Mittal Enterprises
2151, T-7C, New Patel Ngr.
New Delhi, NCT of Delhi-110008
India
TEL : +91 (0) 11 25702784
FAX : +91 (0) 11 2 5408375
E-mail:
mittalenterprises@vsnl.com

Sai Scientific Systems
67B, Main Mkt. Garhi
East Of Kailash
New Delhi, NCT of Delhi-110065
India
TEL : +91 (0) 11 26236097
FAX : +91 (0) 11 26479356

Standard Scientific Instruments Company (Regd.)
C-122, Phase-I, Ashok Vihar
Delhi, NCT of Delhi-110052
India
TEL : +91 (0) 11 27125213

Techniques Scientific Systems
100-A, Himayunpur
Safdarjung Enclave
New Delhi, NCT of Delhi-110029
India
TEL : +91 (0) 11 26162714
FAX : +91 (0) 11 26167249

Globe Scientific Glass Industries
B/h Amar Ice Factory
Nr. Chhani Jakat Naka
BEI Compound
Vadodara, Gujarat-390002
India
TEL : +91 (0) 265 2773131
FAX : +91 (0) 265 2773625

Inox India Ltd.
4th Flr., ABS Towers
Old Padra Rd.
Vadodara, Gujarat-390007
India
TEL : +91 (0) 265 2343125
FAX : +91 (0) 265 2333398
E-mail: inox@inoxindia.com

Thermolab Scientific Equipments Pvt. Ltd.
218, Sterling Chmbrs., 56
Mogra Village, Andheri (E)
Mumbai, Maharashtra-400059
India
TEL : +91 (0) 22 28353017
FAX : +91 (0) 22 28394562
E-mail:
madhav@bom3.vsnl.net.in

Equiptronics
409, Retiwala Indl. Est.
H A Palav Marg, Byculla
Mumbai, Maharashtra-400027
India
TEL : +91 (0) 22 23724260
FAX : +91 (0) 22 23739789
Email:equiptronics@maharashtradirectory.com

Hemraj Enterprises
227, Sonal Link Est.
Bldg. No. 2, Link Rd.
Malad (W)
Mumbai, Maharashtra-400064
India
TEL : +91 (0) 22 28628727
FAX : +91 (0) 22 28628727
E-mail:
sales@hemrajindia.com

Kulkarni & Sons
Madhavashram Ngr., Bldg. A
Mahajan Wadi, Shiv Mandir Rd.
Dombivili (E), Maharashtra-421201
India
TEL : +91 (0) 251 2472322
E-mail:
kulkarni&s@maharashtradirectory.com

Pathak Electrical Works
208 & 214
Bhola Bhagwan Indl. Est.
I B Patel Rd., Goregaon (E)
Mumbai, Maharashtra-400063
India
TEL : +91 (0) 22 28733209
FAX : +91 (0) 22 28749162
E-mail: pthk@vsnl.com

Vibsons Scientifics (I)
4/56 Ashok Wadi,
Prof. V S Agase Path
Off Bhawani Shankar Rd.
Dadar (W)
Mumbai,
Maharashtra-400028
India
TEL : +91 (0) 22 24375312
FAX : +91 (0) 22 28226632
E-mail:
vibsons@maharashtradirectory.com

Singhla Scientific Industries
5309/27, Punjabi Mohalla
Ambala Cantt.,
Haryana-133001
India
TEL : +91 (0) 171 2642878
FAX : +91 (0) 171 2642209
E-mail:
singhla@nde.vsnl.net.in

Triode Electronics
Nr. Nigar Cinema, Grain Mkt.
Ambala, Haryana-130001
India
TEL : +91 (0) 171 2631291
FAX : +91 (0) 171 2643324
E-mail:
charan_triode@yahoo.com

Hemraj Enterprises
227, Sonal Link Est., Bldg.
No. 2, Link Rd., Malad (W)
Mumbai,
Maharashtra-400064
India
TEL : +91 (0) 22 28628727
FAX : +91 (0) 22 28628727
E-mail:
sales@hemrajindia.com

Omega Electronics
36, Hathi Babu Ka Bagh
Jaipur, Rajasthan-302006
India
TEL : +91 (0) 141 2203694
FAX : +91 (0) 141 2204481
E-mail:
omega@sancharnet.in

Technico Laboratory Products
34, Poomagal
St.,Ekkattuthangal
Chennai, Tamil Nadu-600097
India
TEL : +91 (0) 44 22344965
FAX : +91 (0) 44 22344965
E-mail:
technico@md3.vsnl.net.in

Mahendra Scientific Instruments Manufacturing Co.
84/6, Factory Area
Fazalganj
Kanpur,
Uttar Pradesh-208012
India
TEL : +91 (0) 512 2231048
FAX : +91 (0) 512 2547431

Eastern Instruments
Mercantile Bldg., 3rd Flr.
C-Block, 9/12, Lal Bazar St.
Kolkata,
West Bengal-700001
India
TEL : +91 (0) 33 22435219
FAX : +91 (0) 33 22481653
E-mail:
easterninstruments@yahoo.com

Hardson S D & Co.
106B, Raja Dinendra St.
Kolkata,
West Bengal-700004
India
TEL : +91 (0) 33 25545366
FAX : +91 (0) 33 25545366
E-mail:
sdhardson@hotmail.com

Indian Instruments Manufacturing Co.
208, Bipin Behari Ganguly
St. (Bowbazar St.)
Kolkata,
West Bengal-700012
India
TEL : +91 (0) 33 22411848
FAX : +91 (0) 33 22415970
E-mail: iimc@cal.vsnl.net.in

BLENDERS

Dipesh Engg. Works
3, Sheroo Villa
87, J P Rd.
Andheri (W) Mumbai,
Maharashtra-400053
India
TEL : +91 (0) 22 26336729
FAX : +91 (0) 22 26315507
E-mail:
kjpatel_71@hotmail.com

Sreenex Machines Pvt. Ltd.
2-1-460/1, Nallakunta
Hyderabad,
Andhra Pradesh-500001
India
TEL : +91 (0) 40 27662606
FAX : +91 (0) 40 27619475
E-mail:
sreenex@hd2.dot.net.in

A G Industries
A-108, Lok Vihar
Pitampura, New Delhi,
NCT of Delhi-110034
India
TEL : +91 (0) 11 27103194
FAX : +91 (0) 11 22113355

Cosywo Engg. Co.
15, Laxmi Co-op. Indl. Est.
Nr. Nagarvel
Hanuman Mandir
Amraiwadi Rd.
Ahmedabad, Gujarat-380026
India
TEL : +91 (0) 79 22748168
FAX : +91 (0) 79 22748001
E-mail: cosywo@usa.net

Mecon Engg.
Opp. IIMB
Bannerghatta Rd.
Bangalore,
Karnataka-560070
India
TEL: +91(0) 80 26631217
FAX : +91(0)80 26646125

Arihant Engg. Works
124, Guru Nanak
Timber Mkt., Dhar Rd.
Indore,
Madhya Pradesh-452002
India
TEL : +91 (0) 7312380535
FAX : +91 (0) 7312380537

E-mail:
arihantengineering@epatra.com

Machinkraft Equipment
337, 3rd Rd.,
Sindh Hsg. Soc.
Aundh, Pune,
Maharashtra-411007
India
TEL: +91 (0) 20 25880353

BOILERS

Fluidtech Boilers Pvt. Ltd.
2703, Phase-IV
GIDC, Vatva
Ahmedabad,
Gujarat-382445
India
TEL: +91 (0) 79 25840105
FAX: +91 (0) 79 25840041
E-mail: info@fluidltd.com

Shri Indtex Boiler Pvt. Ltd.
Plot No. 1601
GIDC Est.,
Phase-I, Naroda
Ahmedabad,
Gujarat-382330
India
TEL : +91 (0) 79 22823057
FAX : +91 (0) 79 22820047
E-mail:
shiyug@wilnetonline.net

MJ Patel (India) Ltd.
118, P D'Mello Rd.
Nr. Carnac Bridge
Mumbai,
Maharashtra-400009
India
TEL : +91 (0) 22 23422114
FAX : +91 (0) 22 23427410
E-mail: mjpil@vsnl.net.in

Kemtech International Ltd.
A-125, Shivalik
Malviya Ngr. P.O.
New Delhi,
NCT of Delhi-110017
India
TEL : +91 (0) 11 26688343
FAX : +91 (0) 11 26680899
E-mail:
info@kemtechinternational.com

Bharat Heavy Plate & Vessels Ltd.
A Unit Of Bharat Yantra Nigam Ltd.
PO BHPV
Visakhapatnam, Andhra Pradesh-530012
India
TEL : +91 (0) 891 2517381
FAX : +91 (0) 891 2517626
E-mail:
bhpv.ec@rmj.sprintrpg.ems.vsnl.net.in

Nitasha Envirotech Pvt. Ltd.
1062-63, Phase-II
Indl. Area, Chandigarh,
Chandigarh (UT)-160002
India
TEL : +91 (0) 172 2656700
FAX : +91 (0) 172 2652998
E-mail:
nitasha1@glide.net.in

Indcon Boilers Ltd.
D-170, Phase-I
Okhla Indl. Area
New Delhi,
NCT of Delhi-110020
India
TEL : +91 (0) 11 26811440
FAX : +91 (0) 11 26812425
E-mail: indcon@vsnl.com

Thermotech Systems Ltd.
Plot No. 2608
Phase IV, GIDC
Vatva, Ahmedabad,
Gujarat-382445
India
TEL : +91 (0) 79 25842387
FAX : +91 (0) 79 25841634
E-mail:
thermotech@icenet.net

Ambica Engg. Works
16/A, 1st Main,
Modi Hospital Rd.,
W.O.C Road, 2nd Stage.
Bangalore,
Karnataka-560086
India
TEL : +91 (0) 80 23495370
FAX : +91 (0) 80 23496120
E-mail:
ambica_e_w@vsnl.com

Asian Boiler Engineers Pvt. Ltd.
130-A
Golanji Hill Rd.
Sewree, Mumbai,
Maharashtra-400015
India
TEL : +91 (0) 22 24131630
FAX : +91 (0) 22 24139624
E-mail:
abengg@bom3.vsnl.net.in

Bottling Machinery

Orbit Equipments Pvt. Ltd.
H.No. 8-2-82/11
Old Bowenpally
Secunderabad,
Andhra Pradesh-500011
TEL : +91 (0) 40 27750111
FAX : +91 (0) 40 27751199
E-mail:
orbiteqp@hd2.dot.net.in

Hymech Engineers Pvt. Ltd.
Plot No. 14
Rd. No. 10, MIDC
Marol, Andheri (E)
Mumbai,
Maharashtra-400093
India
TEL : +91 (0) 22 28300479
FAX : +91 (0) 22 28354620

Ramalakshmi Industries
38, Block-2,
SIDCO Electronic Cmplx.
Guindy, Chennai,
Tamil Nadu-600032
India
TEL : +91 (0) 44 24844663
E-mail:
adsite@giasmd01.vsnl.net.in

Anand Dis-Brew Engg. Works
5, Rajinder Ngr. Indl. Area
Mohan Ngr.
Ghaziabad,
Uttar Pradesh-201007
India
TEL: +91 (0) 120 24627318
FAX: +91 (0) 120 24721508

Sharp Engg. Corp.
A-17, B/h Shiva Scooter
Agency, Meerut Indl. Area
New Arya Ngr., Ghaziabad,
Uttar Pradesh-201003
India
TEL : +91 (0) 120 24720290
E-mail:
sharpengcorp@satyam.net.in

Cans Aluminium

Apex Cans & Containers
214, GIDC Est.
Makarpura, Vadodara,
Gujarat-390010
India
TEL : +91 (0) 265 2643210
FAX : +91 (0) 265 2643391

Drawcans Pvt. Ltd.
16, 8.5 KM
Bannerghatta Rd.
Bangalore,
Karnataka-560076
India
TEL : +91 (0) 80 26581203
FAX : +91 (0) 80 23461204
E-mail:
drawcans@satyam.net.in

Baldota Metal Udyog Pvt. Ltd.
Bldg. No. 13, Flat No. 1
Navjivan Soc.
Lamington Rd.
Mumbai,
Maharashtra-400008
India
TEL : +91 (0) 22 23083528
FAX : +91 (0) 22 23083528
E-mail:
aasish@bom5.vsnl.net.in

Meta Plast (I)
173, Gopalaswamy Koil St.
Ganapathy
Coimbatore,
Tamil Nadu-641006
India
TEL : +91 (0) 422 2531331
FAX : +91 (0) 422 2531115

Pukhrayan Industries
2A/333, Azad Ngr.
Kanpur,
Uttar Pradesh-208002
India
TEL : +91 (0) 512 2560488
FAX : +91 (0) 512 2357655

DAIRY MACHINERY

Mellcon Engineers Pvt. Ltd.
B-297, Phase-I
Okhla Indl. Area
New Delhi,
NCT of Delhi-110020
India
TEL : +91 (0) 11 26816530
FAX : +91 (0) 11 26816573
E-mail: mellcon@vsnl.net

Ved Engg.
B-38, Sect. 60
Noida,
Uttar Pradesh-201301
India
TEL : +91 (0) 118 24580507
FAX : +91 (0) 118 24580815
E-mail:
vaidant@del3.vsnl.net.in

Dipesh Engineering Works
3, Sheroo Villa
87, J P Rd.
Andheri (W)
Mumbai,
Maharashtra-400053
India
TEL : +91 (0) 22 26336729
FAX : +91 (0) 22 26315507
E-mail:
kjpatel_71@hotmail.com

Pragati Engineering Works
Plot No. 114
New Chikhloli, MIDC
Ambernath,
Maharashtra-421505
India
TEL : +91 (0) 251 2687407
FAX : +91 (0) 251 2685054
E-mail:
shantaflaker@vsnl.com

Shachi Engineering Pvt. Ltd.
5, Asmita Apt., 60
Mayur Cly., Kothrud
Pune,
Maharashtra-411029
India
TEL : +91 (0) 20 25453766
FAX : +91 (0) 20 25433786
E-mail:
shachi_engineering@@vsnl.com

Chengalva Engineers Ltd.
405, Shashank Residency,
St. No. 11, Tarnaka
Hyderabad,
Andhra Pradesh-500017

India
TEL : +91 (0) 40 27017397
FAX : +91 (0) 40 27018517
E-mail:
chenga@hd1.vsnl.net.in

Bholla Refrigeration & Engg. Co.
B-68/1, Phase-II
Naraina Indl. Area
New Delhi,
NCT of Delhi-110028
India
TEL : +91 (0) 11 25705406

Maxcare Marketing & Technical Services
J-188, Saket New Delhi,
NCT of Delhi-110017
TEL : +91 (0) 11 26967273
FAX : +91 (0) 11 26866464
E-mail:
maxcare188@hotmail.com

Harikrushna Techno-pride Engineering
52, Shanakr Indl. Est.
Nr. Revabhai Est., CTM
Amraiwadi
Ahmedabad,
Gujarat-380026
India
TEL : +91 (0) 79 25861526
FAX : +91 (0) 79 25860186
E-mail: hte@satyam.net.in

Synergy Agro-Tech Pvt. Ltd.
209, Ashoka Chmbrs.,
2nd Flr., Rasala Marg
Mithakhali, Ahmedabad,
Gujarat-380006
India
TEL : +91 (0) 79 26467219
FAX : +91 (0) 79 26402704
E-mail:
dsardaad1@sancharnet.in

Mellcon Engineers Pvt. Ltd.
B-297, Phase-I
Okhla Indl. Area
New Delhi,
NCT of Delhi-110020
India
TEL : +91 (0) 11 26816530
FAX : +91 (0) 11 26816573
E-mail: mellcon@vsnl.net

Mellcon Engineers Pvt. Ltd.
B-297, Phase-I
Okhla Indl. Area
New Delhi,
NCT of Delhi-110020
India
TEL : +91 (0) 11 26816530
FAX : +91 (0) 11 26816573
E-mail: mellcon@vsnl.net

DAIRY TANKS

Dipesh Engineering Works
3, Sheroo Villa
87, J P Rd., Andheri (W)
Mumbai,
Maharashtra-400053
TEL : +91 (0) 22 26336729
FAX : +91 (0) 22 26315507
E-mail:
kjpatel_71@hotmail.com

Pragati Engineering Works
Plot No. 114,
New Chikhloli
MIDC, Ambernath,
Maharashtra-421505
India
TEL : +91 (0) 251 2687407
FAX : +91 (0) 251 2685054
E-mail:
shantaflaker@vsnl.com

Aero Engineers
Plot No. 3419
GIDC, Phase-IV
Vatva, Ahmedabad,
Gujarat-382445
India
TEL : +91 (0) 79 25840720
FAX : +91 (0) 79 25841041
E-mail:
aero@aeroengg.com

Dhopeshwar Engineering Pvt. Ltd.
A-16, CIE, Balanagar
Hyderabad,
Andhra Pradesh-500037
India
TEL : +91 (0) 40 23771579
FAX : +91 (0) 40 23772450
E-mail:
dhopesh@hd2.dot.net.in

Febchem Engineering Works
Plot No. A/2
Sect. A, Indl. Area
Sanwer Rd., Indore,
Madhya Pradesh-452003
India
TEL : +91 (0) 731 2720467
FAX : +91 (0) 731 2723087
E-mail:
febchem@yahoo.com

Larsen & Toubro Ltd.
Heavy Engineering Divn.
Powai Works
Saki Vihar Rd.
Powai, Mumbai,
Maharashtra-400072
India
TEL : +91 (0) 22 28581401
FAX : +91 (0) 22 28581594
E-mail: 3870-sra@vedak.ltindia.com

Hilltake Industries
Palan Indl. Est.
P.O. Raypur,
P.S. Maheshtala
24 Parganas, West Bengal-743352
India
TEL : +91 (0) 33 24922668

DEHYDRATING OVEN

The Wesman Engg. Company Pvt. Ltd.
"Wesman Center", 8
Mayfair Rd., Kolkata,
West Bengal-700019
India

TEL : +91 (0) 33 22405320
FAX : +91 (0) 33 22478050
E-mail:
mailbox@wesman.com

A R Engg.
L-77, Additional MIDC
Satara,
Maharashtra-415004
India
TEL : +91 (0) 2162 244385
FAX : +91 (0) 2162 247569
E-mail:
arengineering@vsnl.com

AMI Industries
8, Surve Indl. Est.
1st Sonawala Cross Rd.
Goregaon (E)
Mumbai,
Maharashtra-400063
India
TEL : +91 (0) 22 28727120
FAX : +91 (0) 22 28734753
E-mail:
oven@bom5.vsnl.net.in

Grovers International
3, F4, Shankardham
Sundervan Cmplx.
Off Lokhandwala
Cmplx. Rd.
Andheri (W), Mumbai,
Maharashtra-400059
India
TEL : +91 (0) 22 6313092
FAX : +91 (0) 22 6313014
E-mail:
vivek@groversequip.com

Shirsat Electronics
133, Dewan Indl.
Est. No. 6, Navghar
Vasai Rd.(E), Thane,
Maharashtra-401210
India
TEL : +91 (0) 22 338946
FAX : +91 (0) 22 340793
E-mail:
sakav@technologist.com

FILTER PRESSES

Shivam Filterpress Pvt. Ltd.
78, 7th Flr.
City Centre, Nr. Swastik
Char Rasta
C G Rd., Navrangpura
Ahmedabad,
Gujarat-380009
India
TEL : +91 (0) 79 6563539
FAX : +91 (0) 79 6560627
E-mail:
sivamfil@ad1.vsnl.net.in

Fluidtech Boilers Pvt. Ltd.
2703m Phase-IV
GIDC, Vatva,
Gujarat-382445
India
TEL : +91 (0) 79 5830105
FAX : +91 (0) 79 5830041
E-mail: info@fluidltd.com

Shivam Filterpress Pvt. Ltd.
78, 7th Flr., City Centre,
Nr. Swastik Char Rasta
C G Rd., Navrangpura
Ahmedabad,
Gujarat-380009
India
TEL : +91 (0) 79 6563539
FAX : +91 (0) 79 6560627
E-mail:
sivamfil@ad1.vsnl.net.in

Gayatri Machine Products
12/2, Opp. Petrol Pump
CTM Char Rasta
Amraiwad
Ahmedabad,
Gujarat-380026
India
TEL : +91 (0) 79 5853128
E-mail:
jayshil@wilnetonline.net

Sachin Industries
77/8, Phase-I, GIDC
Vatva, Ahmedabad, Gujarat-382445
India
TEL : +91 (0) 79 5832204
FAX : +91 (0) 79 5832205

Guru Teg Engg. Co.
Nr. Fire Brigade
G T Rd., Miller Ganj
Ludhiana, Punjab-141003
India
TEL : +91 (0) 161 533976
FAX : +91 (0) 161 536804
E-mail:
gurutegexpeller@yahoo.com

Filtration Systems

AOF Filtration Systems Pvt. Ltd.
Plot No. 282, Phase-II
Kamalapuri Cly.
Hyderabad, Andhra
Pradesh-500073
India
TEL : +91 (0) 40 3545993
FAX : +91 (0) 40 3547627
E-mail: aof@sify.com

Kemtech International Ltd.
A-125, Shivalik
Malviya Ngr. P.O.
New Delhi,
NCT of Delhi-110017
India
TEL : +91 (0) 11 6682346
FAX : +91 (0) 11 6684589
E-mail: kemtech@vsnl.com

Fluid Air Filter Systems
G/3
Dev Darshan Cmplx.
Nr. G B Shah College
Vasna, Ahmedabad,
Gujarat-380007
India
TEL : +91 (0) 79 6633216
FAX : +91 (0) 79 6633216
E-mail: fafs@sify.com

Gopani Product Systems
6, Basement, "Sahyog"
Opp. Dinbai Towers
Lal Darwaja
Ahmedabad,
Gujarat-380001
India
TEL : +91 (0) 79 5501990
FAX : +91 (0) 79 5504236
E-mail:
gopani@wilnetonline.net

Powertech Pollution
Controls Pvt. Ltd.
1133-1134, 1st Flr.
1st Main Rd.
Yeshwanthpur
Bangalore,
Karnataka-560022
India
TEL : +91 (0) 80 3470250
FAX : +91 (0) 80 3374825
E-mail:
philipthomas@powertechindia.com

Britomatics Engineers Pvt. Ltd.
C-9, Nand Dham Indl. Est.
Marol, Andheri (E)
Mumbai,
Maharashtra-400059
India
TEL : +91 (0) 22 28505834
FAX : +91 (0) 22 28504999
E-mail:
britomatics@vsnl.com

Heatex Comptools Pvt. Ltd.
4540
Dr. Radhakrishnan Marg
Shanti Mkt.
Bhatinda, Punjab-151005
India
TEL : +91 (0) 164 2250338
FAX : +91 (0) 164 2255561
E-mail: heatex@glide.net.in

V R Filter Systems
34, Teachers Cly.
Opp. Cheran Maanagar
Coimbatore,
Tamil Nadu-641035
India
TEL : +91 (0) 422 2866629
FAX : +91 (0) 422 2866639

Dipesh Engg. Works
3, Sheroo Villa
87, J P Rd.
Andheri (W)
Mumbai,
Maharashtra-400053
India
TEL : +91 (0) 22 26336729
FAX : +91 (0) 22 26315507
E-mail:
kjpatel_71@hotmail.com

AOF Filtration Systems Pvt. Ltd.
Plot No. 282, Phase-II
Kamalapuri Cly.
Hyderabad, Andhra Pradesh-500073
TEL : +91 (0) 40 23545993
FAX : +91 (0) 40 23547627
E-mail: aof@sify.com

Chloromax
O-11A, Jangpura Extn.
New Delhi,
NCT of Delhi-110014
India
TEL : +91 (0) 11 24311667
FAX : +91 (0) 11 24321677
E-mail:
chloromaxindia@usa.net

K B Aqua Pure Pvt. Ltd.
7, Shopping Centre
Karam Pura
New Delhi,
NCT of Delhi-110015
India
TEL : +91 (0) 11 25169952
FAX : +91 (0) 11 25464157
E-mail:
kb_aqua@yahoo.com

S C Mohan & Co.
303, Sai Bhawan
Ranjit Ngr. Comml. Cmplx.
New Delhi,
NCT of Delhi-110008
India
TEL : +91 (0) 11 25706591
FAX : +91 (0) 11 25707162

Gopani Product Systems
6, Basement, "Sahyog"
Opp. Dinbai Towers
Lal Darwaja
Ahmedabad,
Gujarat-380001
India
TEL : +91 (0) 79 25501990
FAX : +91 (0) 79 25504236
E-mail:
gopani@wilnetonline.net

D I Filter Systems Pvt. Ltd.
C-94, 1st Flr.
Shivalik
Gurgaon, Haryana-122001
India
TEL : +91 (0) 124 26219575
FAX : +91 (0) 124 26226920
E-mail: difsp@ndl.vsnl.net.in

Powertech Pollution Controls Pvt. Ltd.
1133-1134, 1st Flr.
1st Main Rd.
Yeshwanthpur
Bangalore,
Karnataka-560022
India
TEL : +91 (0) 80 23470250
FAX : +91 (0) 80 23374825
E-mail:
philipthomas@powertechindia.com

FOOD PACKAGING

E C Packaging Pvt. Ltd.
14/7, Mile Stone
Mathura Rd.
Faridabad,
Haryana-121003
India
TEL:+91(0) 129 25277796
FAX:+91(0) 129 25255602
E-mail:
ecppl@del3.vsnl.net.in

Mamata Machinery Pvt. Ltd.
5/1/1A, Phase-I
GIDC, Ahmedabad, Gujarat-382445
India
TEL : +91 (0) 79 25832023
FAX : +91 (0) 79 25832026
E-mail:
mmpl@ad1.vsnl.net.in
www.mamata.com

Orbit Equipments Pvt. Ltd.
H.No. 8-2-82/11
Old Bowenpally
Secunderabad, Andhra Pradesh-500011
India
TEL : +91 (0) 40 27750111
FAX : +91 (0) 40 27751199
E-mail:
orbiteqp@hd2.dot.net.in

Kavacha Engg.
Plot No. D-45
Electronic Cmplx.
Kushaiguda
Hyderabad, Andhra Pradesh-500062
India
TEL : +91 (0) 40 27123665
FAX : +91 (0) 40 27120892

New Indo International
135-A, Begum Pur
Malviya Ngr.
New Delhi,
NCT of Delhi-110017
India
TEL : +91 (0) 11 26217476
E-mail: nii@ndf.vsnl.net.in

Mamata Machinery Pvt. Ltd.
5/1/1A, Phase-I
GIDC
Ahmedabad,
Gujarat-382445
India
TEL : +91 (0) 79 25832023
FAX : +91 (0) 79 25832026
E-mail:
mmpl@ad1.vsnl.net.in
www.mamata.com

E C Packaging Pvt. Ltd.
14/7, Mile Stone
Mathura Rd., Faridabad,
Haryana-121003
India
TEL: +91 (0) 129 25277796
FAX: +91 (0) 129 25255602
E-mail:
ecppl@del3.vsnl.net.in

Wintech Taparia Ltd.
3rd Flr., Shreesh Chmbrs.,
25/1, Y N Rd.
Indore,
Madhya Pradesh-452003
India
TEL : +91 (0) 731 2433950
FAX : +91 (0) 731 2430527
E-mail:
sales@wintechtaparia.com

H B Engg.
118, Gobind Udyog Bhawan
Bal Rajeshwar Rd.
Mulund (W)
Mumbai,
Maharashtra-400080
India
TEL : +91 (0) 22 25603491
FAX : +91 (0) 22 25688916
E-mail:
pacwel@bom7.vsnl.net.in

FREEZE DRYERS

Vacuum Instruments Company Ltd.
81, Regharpura
New Delhi,
NCT of Delhi-110005
India
TEL : +91 (0) 11 25764332
FAX : +91 (0) 11 25764986
E-mail:
vico@del2.vsnl.net.in

Infra Control Systems
B-7, Sahyog Soc.
Refinery Rd., Gorwa
Vadodara,
Gujarat-390016
India
TEL : +91 (0) 265 2387826
FAX : +91 (0) 265 2387723
E-mail: infra@bnpl.com

SS Stainless Equipments & Systems Pvt. Ltd.
R-366, Indl. Area
Rabale
Navi Mumbai,
Maharashtra-400701
India
TEL : +91 (0) 22 27602238
FAX : +91 (0) 22 27692377
E-mail:
ssstainless@vsnl.com

Enfab Industries Pvt. Ltd.
C-2, Shanthi Niwas
Mettuguda
Secunderabad,
Andhra Pradesh-500017
India
TEL : +91 (0) 40 27824343
FAX : +91 (0) 40 27830010
E-mail:
enfabs@hd1.vsnl.net.in

FROZEN FOOD MACHINERY

G-Tek Corp.
3, Mahavir Indl. Est.
Opp. Karelibaug
Telephone Exch.
Bahucharaji Rd.Karelibaug
Vadodara, Gujarat-390018
India
TEL : +91 (0) 265 2416211
FAX : +91 (0) 265 2424912
E-mail: info@gtek-india.com

Stadler Corp.
A-3/3
Surjit Singh Compound,
Shivaji Ngr.
Off Vakola Bridge
Santacruz (E)
Mumbai,

Maharashtra-400055
India
TEL : +91 (0) 22 26105212
FAX : +91 (0) 22 26105093
E-mail:
stadler44@hotmail.com

R & D Engineers
A-41, IDA, Phase-IV
Rd. No. 4
Kumatpally
Hyderabad,
Andhra Pradesh-500037
India
TEL : +91 (0) 40 23079121
FAX : +91 (0) 40 23078668
E-mail:
randengg@hd1.vsnl.net.in

FRUIT SLICERS

Kamal (E) Industries
Datta Bhavan
Kashinath Dhuru Rd.
Dadar (W), Mumbai,
Maharashtra-400028
India
TEL : +91 (0) 22 24221555
FAX : +91 (0) 22 24373474
E-mail: kei@vsnl.com

HAMMER MILL

Dipesh Engg. Works
3, Sheroo Villa
87, J P Rd.
Andheri (W)
Mumbai,
Maharashtra-400053
India
TEL : +91 (0) 22 26336729
FAX : +91 (0) 22 26315507
E-mail:
kjpatel_71@hotmail.com

Bevcon Wayors Pvt. Ltd.
Ground Flr.,
Kavya Delux Apts.
Madhuranagar
Hyderabad, Andhra
Pradesh-500038
India
TEL : +91 (0) 40 23732628
FAX : +91 (0) 40 23733626
E-mail:
bevconwayors@hotmail.com

Advance Dynamics Pvt. Ltd.
F-36, Central Mkt.
Kirti Ngr., New Delhi,
NCT of Delhi-110015
India
TEL : +91 (0) 11 25100716
FAX : +91 (0) 11 25449597

Alfa Engineers
862/7/B, GIDC
Makarpura
Vadodara, Gujarat-390010
India
TEL : +91 (0) 265 2652245
FAX : +91 (0) 265 2652245
E-mail:
alfaengineers@rediffmail.com

Chhatrapati Engg. Ltd.
Chatrapati House, 128/1B
Paud Rd.
Pune, Maharashtra-411029
India
TEL : +91 (0) 20 2339388
FAX : +91 (0) 20 2331939

HOMOGENISERS

Alfa Engineers
862/7/B
GIDC, Makarpura
Vadodara, Gujarat-390010
India
TEL : +91 (0) 265 2652245
FAX : +91 (0) 265 2652245
E-mail:
alfaengineers@rediffmail.com

Septu (I) Pvt. Ltd.
"Septu House", 12/7
P.O. Box 4, Urban Est.
Gurgaon, Haryana-122001
India
TEL: +91 (0) 124 26373010
FAX: +91 (0) 124 26322997
E-mail:
septu@del3.vsnl.net.in

Chemitherm Plants & Systems Pvt. Ltd.
No. 30
Anandha St., Alwarpet
Chennai,
Tamil Nadu-600018
India
TEL : +91 (0) 44 24996248
FAX : +91 (0) 44 24991778
E-mail:
chemthrm@md2.vsnl.net.in

Pasteur Engg. Company Pvt. Ltd.
15/8/A
The Mall, Dum Dum
Kolkata,
West Bengal-700080
India
TEL : +91 (0) 33 2593015
FAX : +91 (0) 33 25593015

LABORATORY EQUIPMENTS & SUPPLIERS

Jainsons (I) Regd.
International Export
Department
Jain Temple Bldg.
P.O. Box 17, Dal Mandi
Ambala Cantt.,
Haryana-133001
India
TEL : +91 (0) 171 2644198
FAX : +91 (0) 171 2643485
E-mail:
jainsird@sancharnet.in

Thermolab Scientific Equipments Pvt. Ltd.
218, Sterling Chmbrs.,
56, Mogra Village
Andheri (E), Mumbai,
Maharashtra-400059
India
TEL : +91 (0) 22 28353017
FAX : +91 (0) 22 28394562
E-mail:
madhav@bom3.vsnl.net.in

Intel Systems
5-234/2, H P Rd.
Moosapet
Hyderabad, Andhra Pradesh-500018
India
TEL : +91 (0) 40 23711379
FAX : +91 (0) 40 23713567
E-mail:
intelarch@mantraonline.com

Avante Global Services
225, Prakash Mohalla
East Of Kailash
New Delhi,
NCT of Delhi-110065
India
TEL : +91 (0) 11 26233259
FAX : +91 (0) 11 26443097
E-mail: avante@vsnl.com

Jainsons (I) Regd.
International Export Department
Jain Temple Bldg.
P.O. Box 17, Dal Mandi
Ambala Cantt.,
Haryana-133001
India
TEL : +91 (0) 171 2644198
FAX : +91 (0) 171 2643485
E-mail:
jainsird@sancharnet.in

Abhay Instruments & Controls
1307, 11, Thmn. Rd.
Vijay Ngr., Bangalore,
Karnataka-560040
India
TEL : +91 (0) 80 23302184

Equiptronics
409, Retiwala Indl. Est.
H A Palav Marg
Byculla, Mumbai,
Maharashtra-400027
India
TEL : +91 (0) 22 23724260
FAX : +91 (0) 22 23739789
E-mail:
equiptronics@maharashtradirectory.com

Mahendra Scientific Instruments Manufacturing Co.
84/6, Factory Area
Fazalganj Kanpur,
Uttar Pradesh-208012
India
TEL : +91 (0) 512 2231048
FAX : +91 (0) 512 2547431

MEAT PROCESSING MACHINERY

Superfreeze India Ltd.
WZ-92-A
Raja Garden, Ring Rd.
New Delhi,
NCT of Delhi-110015
India
TEL : +91 (0) 11 25122667
FAX : +91 (0) 11 25101061
E-mail:
corporate@superfreezeindia.com

Wintech Taparia Ltd.
3rd Flr., Shreesh Chmbrs.,
25/1
Y N Rd.
Indore,
Madhya Pradesh-452003
India
TEL : +91 (0) 731 2433950
FAX : +91 (0) 731 2430527
E-mail:
sales@wintechtaparia.com

Chengalva Engineers Ltd.
405
Shashank Residency, St. No. 11
Tarnaka
Hyderabad, Andhra Pradesh-500017
India
TEL : +91 (0) 40 27017397
FAX : +91 (0) 40 27018517
E-mail:
chenga@hd1.vsnl.net.in

POTATO CRISP MACHINERY

Wintech Taparia Ltd.
3rd Flr., Shreesh Chmbrs.,
25/1, Y N Rd., Indore,
Madhya Pradesh-452003
India
TEL : +91 (0) 731 2433950
FAX : +91 (0) 731 2430527
E-mail:
sales@wintechtaparia.com

Stadler Corp.
A-3/3
Surjit Singh Compound,
Shivaji Ngr.
Off Vakola Bridge
Santacruz (E)
Mumbai,
Maharashtra-400055
India
TEL : +91 (0) 22 26105212
FAX : +91 (0) 22 26105093
E-mail:
stadler44@hotmail.com

S P Engg.
E-53, Sect. 7
Noida,
Uttar Pradesh-201301
India
TEL:+91 (0) 120 24529703
E-mail:
sp_engg@hotmail.com

Rathod Machine Tools
"Ashok", 2, Mandi Plot
Rajkot, Gujarat-360004
India
TEL : +91 (0) 281 2388089

POUCH PACKAGING SERVICES

Labh Group Of Cos.
309
Chitrarath Cmplx.
Nr. Hotel President,
C G Rd.

Navrangpura
Ahmedabad,
Gujarat-380009
India
TEL : +91 (0) 79 26569261
FAX : +91 (0) 79 26467821
E-mail: labhgroup@vsnl.com

Meridian Market Resources
397, 1st `B' Main,
1st Stage
Phase-III
West Of Chord Rd.
Manjunathnagar
Bangalore,
Karnataka-560010
India
TEL : +91 (0) 80 23206315
FAX : +91 (0) 80 23206315
E-mail:
meripack@satyam.net.in

Atlas Packers & Movers
Gala 3, Singh Est.
Nr. Samta Ngr.
Rd. 3
Kandivli (E)
Mumbai, Maharashtra-400101
India
TEL : +91 (0) 22 28875648
FAX : +91 (0) 22 28867304
E-mail:
atlaspack@maharashtradirectory.com

Newman Press
268
Royapettah High Rd.
Royapettah
Chennai, Tamil Nadu-600014
India
TEL : +91 (0) 44 28267357
FAX : +91 (0) 44 28241252

Holoflex Ltd.
CN/2/1
Sect. 5
Salt Lake City
Kolkata,
West Bengal-700091
India
TEL : +91 (0) 33 23673300
FAX : +91 (0) 33 22426156
E-mail: info@holoflex.com

AKS Packaging Company Pvt. Ltd.
H-2, Suneja Chmbrs.
Alaknanda Shopping Centre
Kalkaji
New Delhi,
NCT of Delhi-110019
India
TEL : +91 (0) 11 26415374
FAX : +91 (0) 11 26474406

REFRIGERATION PLANTS

Skansen Engg. & Consultancy Co. Ltd.
Associated Company of
Alfa Laval
Dapodi
Pune, Maharashtra-411012
India
TEL : +91 (0) 20 2776321
FAX : +91 (0) 20 2779479

Ladhar Enterprises
Opp. Chattar Singh Park,
1096
Model Town Rd.
Ludhiana, Punjab-141002
India
TEL : +91 (0) 161 2400899
FAX : +91 (0) 161 2562475

Metro
D-35
Meerut Rd. Indl. Area
Ghaziabad,
Uttar Pradesh-201003
India
TEL : +91 (0) 120
24757568
FAX : +91 (0) 120
24713759
E-mail:
metro@mantraonline.com

Bharat Refrigeration Works
99, Paschim Vihar
New Delhi,
NCT of Delhi-110063
India
TEL : +91 (0) 11 25155450

Hindustan Refrigeration Stores
2, 4 & 5
Netaji Subhash Marg
Daryaganj, New Delhi,
NCT of Delhi-110002
India
TEL : +91 (0) 11 23271898
FAX : +91 (0) 11 23271152
E-mail:
higrop@ndb.vsnl.net.in

SPRAY DRYERS

Mojj Engg. Systems Ltd.
81-B/15
MIDC, Bhosari
Pune,
Maharashtra-411026
India
TEL : +91 (0) 20 27120360
FAX : +91 (0) 20 27122836
E-mail: mojjpune@ip.eth.net

Industrial Machinery Manufacturing Pvt. Ltd.
Plot No. 3607/9
GIDC Est., Vatva
Ahmedabad,
Gujarat-382445
India
TEL : +91 (0) 79 25831152
FAX : +91 (0) 79 25832216

SSP Ltd.
19, DLF Indl. Area,
Phase-II, 13/4,
Mathura Rd., Faridabad,
Haryana-121003
India
TEL:+91(0) 129 25275441
FAX:+91(0) 129 25277441
E-mail:
sspgroup@del2.vsnl.net.in

Febchem Engg. Works
A/2, Sect. A, Indl. Area
Sanwer Rd., Indore,
Madhya Pradesh-452015
India
TEL : +91 (0) 731 2720467
FAX : +91 (0) 731 2723087

Advance Equipment
B-18, Sect.7
Noida,
Uttar Pradesh-201301
India
TEL: +91(0) 120 24545560
FAX: +91(0) 120 24535160
E-mail:
meera@del3.vsnl.net.in

STORAGE TANKS

Dipesh Engg. Works
3, Sheroo Villa
87, J P Rd.
Andheri (W) Mumbai,
Maharashtra-400053
India
TEL : +91 (0) 22 26336729
FAX : +91 (0) 22 26315507
E-mail:
kjpatel_71@hotmail.com

Steelite Engg. Ltd.
103/5, Blackie House
Opp. GPO, V T
Walchand Hirachand Marg
Mumbai,
Maharashtra-400001
India
TEL : +91 (0) 22 22324093
FAX : +91 (0) 22 22610803
E-mail:
samir@steelitegroup.com

Anukul Industries
Shed No. 9B
Type III, APIIC
Kukatpally
Hyderabad, Andhra
Pradesh-500072
India
TEL : +91 (0) 40 23075844

Alpha Process Vessels Pvt. Ltd.
A-90, 1st Flr., Amar Cly.
New Delhi,
NCT of Delhi-110024
India
TEL : +91 (0) 11 26427087
FAX : +91 (0) 11 26467084

Asm-Technoxi Air System Inc
P.O. Box 4317
New Delhi,
NCT of Delhi-110018
India
TEL : +91 (0) 11 26489275

Bhiwadi Chemical Pvt. Ltd.
184
New Okhla Indl. Cmplx.,
Phase-I
Okhla Indl. Area
New Delhi,
NCT of Delhi-110020
India
TEL : +91 (0) 11 26813624
FAX : +91 (0) 11 26474340

Sudev Industries Ltd.
Opp. Best Western Surya
Hotel, 150
Jullena Comml. Cmplx.
Okhla Rd.
New Delhi,
NCT of Delhi-110025
India
TEL : +91 (0) 11 26829621
FAX : +91 (0) 11 26829621
E-mail: sudev@bol.net.in

Mass Kinematics Pvt. Ltd.
Alleluia Menezes Bldg.,
3rd Flr.,Opp. MES Inspection Bunglow, Altinho
Panaji
Goa, Goa-403001
India
TEL : +91 (0) 832 2437864
FAX : +91 (0) 832 2228091
E-mail:
kinemat@goatelecom.com

Aero Engineers
Plot No. 3419
Phase-IV, GIDC
Vatva, Gujarat-382445
India
TEL : +91 (0) 79 25831556
FAX : +91 (0) 79 25891041
E-mail: aero@icenet.net

Baroda Polyform Pvt. Ltd.
7, 1st Flr., Panorama Bldg.
Alkapuri
Vadodara, Gujarat-390005
India
TEL : +91 (0) 265 2333719
FAX : +91 (0) 265 2340172

WEIGHING MACHINERY

Weighman Industries
6-1-91/7-8
Nr. Telephone Bhavan
Saifabad
Hyderabad, Andhra
Pradesh-500004
India
TEL : +91 (0) 40 23235915
FAX : +91 (0) 40 23212239
E-mail:
weighman@altech_ipc.com

Narne Tulaman Manufacturers Pvt. Ltd.
S. No. 30
Balanagar
Hyderabad, Andhra
Pradesh-500037
India
TEL : +91 (0) 40 2279459

Airy Scales Co.
A-3, Chander Ngr.
Delhi, NCT of Delhi-110051
India
TEL : +91 (0) 11 22213242

Ashoka Metal Works & Co.
B-17, St. No. 9
Anand Parbat Indl. Area
New Delhi,
NCT of Delhi-110005
India
TEL : +91 (0) 11 25820307
FAX : +91 (0) 11 25820309

Deluxe Merchandise Ltd.
101
Alkapuri Shopping Centre,
Vishwas Cly., Alkapuri
Vadodara, Gujarat-390005
India
TEL : +91 (0) 265 2357934
FAX : +91 (0) 265 2332094
E-mail:
sales@delmerindia.com

POTATO CHIPS / WAFFERS

Avo Industries
14/9, Vithal Nagar, Solapur
Road, Hadapur
Pune - 411028
Ph:. 670932

Continental Equipment India Pvt. Ltd.
B-66, Phase-I, Okhla
Industrial Area
New Delhi - 110020
Ph:. 26816297, 26816298
Fax: 26815297
E-Mail : continental@ceipldel.
xeedel.xeemail.com

Dhiman Udyog
Plot No. 6026
Near Dakhni Gate
Nakodar - 144040
(Jalandar) Punjab
Ph:. 01821-220891,
222891, 222991
Fax: 01821-220919, 222891
Website : dhimanudyog.com

Dr. T. K. Food Consultants Pvt. Ltd.
2A, 4th Floor
Lentin Chambers,
Dalal Street
Mumbai - 400023
Tel : 22657206, 22651864
Fax : 22657206

Gardners Corp.
6, Doctors Lane
New Delhi - 110001
Ph:. 23344287, 23343640
Fax: 23717179

Greenfield Agencies
Shp No.6 Anuradha
Rest House, Tidke Colony
Nasik - 422002
Ph:. 2572587
Fax: 0253-2570087

Hariom Industries
Dhebar Road (South)
Atika Industrial Area
Rajkot - 360002 (Guj)
Ph:. 2363620, 2371438
Fax: 2371745
E-Mail :
hariomind@epatra.com

Heat & Control Pvt. Ltd.
3, Anurag G-131
First Main Road,
Anna Nagar East
Chennai - 600102
Ph:. 91-44-26441455,
26451814
Fax: 91-44-26441466
E-Mail :
heatandcontrol@vsnl.net.in
Website :
www.heatandcontrol.com

Jaswanttray Damodardas Bhuta
Kansara Bazar
Kandoliya Sheri,
Sihor - 364 240
(Dist. Bhavnagar), Gujarat
Ph : 02846- 223040

Jwala Engineering Co.
12, Surve Industrial Estate
Sonawala Cross Road
No.1, Groregaon (E)
Mumbai - 400063
Ph:. 26903038, 28740279
Fax:022-28768768,
28414443

M.M.M. Buxabhoy & Co.
140, Sarang Street
1st Floor, Mumbai - 3
Ph : 23442902 / 23452532
Fax : 91-22-3425230
Email :
yusufs@giasbm01.vsnl.net.in

N.K. Engineering Works
6967/11, Multani Dhanda
Pahar Ganj
New Delhi - 110055
Ph:. 23522232, 27777804
Fax: 91-11-23512178

PRS Technologies Pvt. Ltd.
D-26, 2nd Floor, NDSE
Part-II, New Delhi - 110049
Ph:. 91-11-26252176/77
Fax: 91-11-26252178
E-Mail :
info@prs-technologies.com
Regd. Off.
63, Bombay Samachar
Marg
Mumbai - 400001
Ph:. 91-22-22358111
Fax: 91-22-22358181
Switzerland Off.
Baarerstrasse-57
63007, Zug
Ph:. 041-27295271
Fax: 041-27295270
Bangalore Off.
3rd Floor, Silver Jubilee
Block, 3 Cross, Mission
Road, Bangalore - 560027
Ph:. 080-22299555
Fax: 080-22299550
E-Mail :
info_bnglr@prs-
technologies.com

Ravi Steel Industries
G.T. Road,
Goraya - 144409
Ph:. 01826-262347
E-Mail :
ravi007@hclinfinet.com

S.D. Engineering Pvt. Ltd.
E-53, Sector-7, Noida
Ph:.0118-24529703, 24549729
Fax: 0118-2452970
E-Mail : sp_engg@hotmail.com

Sara Udyog
C-167, Sec- 10, Noida (U.P)
Ph : 9124521878

Sri Rajalaxmi Commercial
Kitchen Equip. Pvt. Ltd.
57 (Upstairs), Silver Jubilee Park Road,
Bangalore - 560 002
Tel : 22221054 / 22239738
Fax : 080-22222047

POTATO PEELING MACHINE

Ardeshir Jamshedji & Sons
Tata Mills Co-op.
Hsg. Soc. Ltd.
1/B-36-8th Floor
Elphinstone Road, Parel
Mumbai - 400012
Ph:. 24150327

Avo Industries
14/9, Vithal Nagar
Solapur Road
Hadapur, Pune - 411028
Ph:. 2670932

Gardners Corp.
6, Doctors Lane
P.B. No. 299
New Delhi - 110001
Ph:. 23344287, 23343640
Fax: 23717179

Gopal Brothers
75, G.B. Road
Delhi - 110006
Ph:. 22941441, 22526024
Br. GF-10/11, Mohan Tower
Wazirpur Industrial Area
Delhi - 110052
Also at: B-27, M.P. Enclave
Pritam Pura, Delhi

Hariom Industries
Dhebar Road (South)
Atika Industrial Area
Rajkot - 360002 (Guj)
Ph:. 2363620, 2371438
Fax: 2371745
E-Mail : hariomind@epatra.com

Mudhal Industries
J-11/84, Sanjay Market
Wazirpur, J.J. Colony
Delhi - 110052
Ph:. 27254704

N.K. Engineering Works
6967/11, Multani Dhanda
Pahar Ganj
New Delhi - 110055
Ph:. 23522232, 27777804
Fax: 91-11-23512178

Vipul Engineering Equipment
13th Girish Kunj
Road No. 3, Juhu Scheme
Vile Parle (W)
Mumbai - 400056
Ph:. 26145100, 28080692
Fax: 022-24943409

G.L. Extrusion System Pvt. Ltd.
Khasra No.172/12, GaliNo.4
Gurga Park, Main Road
Nasirpur Dabri Village
New Delhi - 110045
Ph:. 25557242

Guru Nanak Engineering Works
D-107, Sector-7, Noida
Gautam Budh Nagar
Ph:. 0188-91-24542530, 24519360
Fax: 0118-91-24535160
E-Mail : meera@del3.vsnl.net.in

Heat & Control Pvt. Ltd.
3, Anurag G-131
First Main Road,
Anna Nagar East
Chennai - 600102
Ph:. 91-44-26441455, 26451814
Fax: 91-44-26441466
E-Mail : heatandcontrol@vsnl.net.in
Website : www.heatandcontrol.com

Kanchan Metals Pvt. Ltd.
38, Strand Road
Kolkatta - 700001
Ph:. 91-33-22109092/93/217
Fax: 91-33-22433808
E-Mail : kanchan@vsnl.com
Website : www.kanchan.com
Chennai
No31, First Floor
Wallajah Road
Chennai - 600002
Ph:. 91-44-28415213/5347
Fax: 91-44-28415214
E-Mail : kmplmad@md4.vsnl.net.in

M. Son Industries
D-33, Sector-2
Noida - 201301 (U.P)
Telefax: 011-8-24552177, 24538397
E-Mail : mson@nda.vsnl.net.in
mson2002@yahoo.com
Website : www.food-machines.com

Param Consultancy
Services Pvt. Ltd.
5, Victoria Building,
27, S.A. Brelvi Road
Fort, Mumbai - 400001
Ph:. 22661332, 22642920/21
Fax: 22660125

PRS Technologies Pvt. Ltd.
D-26, 2nd Floor, NDSE
Part-II, New Delhi - 110049
Ph:. 91-11-26252176/77
Fax: 91-11-26252178
E-Mail : info@prs-technologies.com

Regd. Off.
63, Bombay Samachar Marg
Mumbai - 400001
Ph:. 91-22-22358111
Fax: 91-22-22358181

Switzerland Off.
Baarerstrasse-57
63007, Zug
Ph:. 041-27295271
Fax: 041-27295270

Bangalore Off.
3rd Floor, Silver Jubilee Block, 3 Cross, Mission Road, Bangalore - 560027
Ph:. 080-22299555
Fax: 080-22299550
E-Mail :
info_bnglr@prs-technologies.com

S.R.F. International
C-8, Commercial Complex
Safdarjung Development Area
New Delhi - 110016
Ph:. 0091-11-26858993 to 97
Fax: 0091-11-26863603, 6961494

Sangram Engineering Ltd.
B-5, Supercon, Aundh
Pune - 411007
Ph: 0121-2366935, 2342302
Fax: 0212-2349673

S.S. Engineering Works
B-25, Khanpur Extn.
Devili Road
New Delhi - 110062
Ph:. 26081475

Sakav Food Machines
133 Dewan Industrial Estate No. 6
Navghar Vasai Road (E)
Dist. Thane - 401210
Ph:. 91-250-2338946
Fax: 912-2340793
E-Mail :
sakav@technologist.com

S.D. Engineering Pvt. Ltd.
E-53, Sector-7
Noida - 201301
Ph:. 0118-24529703, 24549729
Fax: 0118-2452970
E-Mail :
sp_engg@hotmail.com

Continental Equipment India Pvt. Ltd.
B-66, Phase-I
Okhla Industrial Area
New Delhi - 110020
Ph:. 26816297, 26816298
Fax: 26815297
E-Mail :
continental@ceipldel.xeedel.xeemail.com

Guru Nanak Engineering Works
D-107, Sector-7
Noida - 201301
Gautam Budh Nagar
Ph:. 0188-91-24542530, 4519360
Fax: 0118-91-24535160
E-Mail :
meera@del3.vsnl.net.in

Inventure India bv.
24, Gold Fields Plaza
45, Sassoon Road
Pune - 411 001
Tel : 91-212-2620237
Fax : 91-212-2621534

Jaswanttray Damodardas Bhuta
kansara Bazar
Kandoliya Sheri
Sihor - 364 240
(Dist. Bhavnagar), Gujarat
Ph:. 02846- 223040

Om Engineering Works
1514, Sector 34D
Chandigarh - 160017
Ph:. 0172-607920
Fact: Industrial Area
Rajpura - 140401
Dist. Patiala
Ph:. 01762-224710

Parbhat M.T. Mfrs Co.
B-23/4, Wazirpur Industrial Area, Delhi -1110052

Raj Products & Equip.
P.B. No. 8075
397 S.V. Road
Vile Parle (W),
Mumbai - 400056
Ph:. 28192250, 28192750
Fax: 91-22-28192750
Fact: 8, Amar Industrial Estate, Navghar Road
Bhayander (E) - 401105

RadeMaker B.V.
Plantijnweg
23, P.O. Box : 416,
4100 AK Culemborg,Holland

Reliance Engineering Works
4065, Sector-46D
Chandigarh - 160047
Ph:. 2605682, 2653927
Fax: 91-172-2662330

Heat & Control Pvt. Ltd.
3, Anurag G-131
First Main Road Anna Nagar East
Chennai - 600102
Ph:. 91-44-26441455, 26451814
Fax: 91-44-26441466
E-Mail :
heatandcontrol@vsnl.net.in
Website :
www.heatandcontrol.com

Jaswanttray Damodardas Bhuta
kansara Bazar, Kandoliya Sheri, Sihor - 364 240
(Dist. Bhavnagar), Gujarat
Ph : 02846- 223040

Ravi Steel Industries
G.T. Road, Goraya - 144409
Ph:. 01826-262347
E-Mail :
ravi007@hclinfinet.com

Sara Udyog
C-167, Sec- 10,
Noida (U.P)
Ph : 9124521878

PULVERISER

N.K. Engineering Works
6967/11, Multani Dhanda
Pahar Ganj
New Delhi - 110055
Ph:. 23522232, 27777804
Fax: 91-11-23512178

Rieco Industries Ltd.
1162/2, Shivajinagar
Pune - 411005
Ph:. 020-25535384, 25535215
Fax: 020-25533229
E-Mail : rieco@vsnl.com
s_pune@rieco.com
Website : www.rieco.com

M/s. Advance Quality
Controls
Ph:. 0129-25263017, 5291556
E-Mail :
aqc1@rediffmail.com

Ambika Vijay Works
1H, Laxmi East Link Road
West, Mumbai - 53
Ph:. 26366894

Chandra Orgo-chem Combines
306, Belscot Tower, Link Road, Lokhand Wala Complex, Andheri
Mumbai - 53
Ph:. 23430789

Dhiman Udyog
6026, Kapurthala Road
Nakodar - 144040
(Dist. Jalandhar), Punjab
Ph:. 01821-220891, 222891
Fax: 0091-1821-220891
Website:www.dhimanudyog.com

Dolphin Engineering Works
6, Baburam Ghosh Lane
P.O. Hatkhola, Kolkatta - 5
Ph:. 22399378

D.P. Pulveriser Works
76, Nagindas Master Road
Fort, Mumbai - 23
Ph:. 22675724, 22670976
Fax: 022-22676435

FlourTech Engineers P Ltd.
16/5, Mathura Road
Faridabad - 121002 (Har.)
Ph:.0129-25291556, 25263017
E-Mail :
flourtech@rediffmail.com

Frigmaires Engineers
Post Box:16353
Janta Industrial Estate
No.8L, Parel, Mumbai - 13
Ph: 24941694

Hind Pulverizer Works
B-3/2, Ambica East
Near Sukhram Nagar
Ahemdabad - 23
Ph:. 22747451, 22744018
Fax : 079-22747451

JDP Enterprises
13, Kharwa Lane, Samad Building
Mumbai - 400004
Ph:. 23810054

Jikosha Engineering Corp.
2, Ratna Jyoti Industrial Estate, Vile Parle - West
Mumbai - 56
Ph:. 26711312

K.B. Engineering
B-58, Kiran Industrial Estate
M.G Road, Goregaon (West)
Mumbai - 62
Ph:. 28720616

Kaps Engineers
831, GIDC, Makarpura
Baroda - 10 (Gujarat)
Ph:. 25781933, 25756760
Website : www.vmkaps.com
E-Mail :
kapsvm@ad1.vsnl.net.in

Kabir Engineers Works
Niramay, B/H Suvidha Centre
Paldi, Ahemdabad - 7
Ph:. 26620270
Fax: 26576497

Kaps Engineers
Samrat Silk Mills Compound
L.B.S. Marg, Vikhroli (West)
Mumbai - 400079 (M.S)
Ph:. 91-22-25781933
Fax: 25785741
E-Mail :
vmsrehls@bom4.vsnl.net.in

Litho Tech Engineers
Sector-10/B25/Sh-13
Shanti Nagar, Mira Road
East, Mumbai - 7
Ph:. 28110182

Micro Pulverizer
Manufacturing Work
Universal Compound,
Old Nagar Das Road,
Andheri (East),
Mumbai - 69
Ph:. 28209725

Modern Fabricators
25/4, Industrial Area
Anand Parbat,
New Delhi - 110005
Ph:. 25722888

Precious Fab-Cast Pvt. Ltd.
4809, Ph-4, GIDC, Vatva,
Ahmedabad - 445 (Gujarat)
Ph:. 25832237
Fax : 25830026

Premier Engineering Works
7/23, Gali No. 7
Anand Parbat
Industrial Area
New Delhi - 110005
Ph:.25730730

Ruby Engineering Work
Memnee Building
1750, Imtimkar Road
Nagpada, Mumbai - 8
Ph:. 23088552

Sreema Engineering Works Pvt. Ltd.
148/1A, Ultadanga
Main Road
Kolkatta - 67
Ph:. 23561639

S.S. Industries
Netaji Palkar Road
Asalpe Ghatkopar
West, Mumbai - 84
Ph:.25110336

Saxena Indusrtries
W-300, TTC, MIDC Rabale
New Bombay - 400701
Ph:.27692445

Techmac Engineering Works
310, Usha Kiran Building,
Commercial Complex
Azadpur, Delhi - 33
Ph:. 27137027

Trover Pharmamach
6214, Kapurthala Road
Opp. Suraj Palace
Nakodar - 144040
(Distt. Jalandhar)
Ph:. 1821-220318
Fax:91-1821-223599
E-Mail :
sanjeev@troverindia.com

Vimal Enterprises
40, Than Ranchhod
Chawl Rabari Colony
Amwadi
Ahemdabad - 26
Ph:. 22168420

Vohra & Co.
523, Rishi Nagar
Rani Bagh, New Delhi - 34
Ph:. 27104651

DISINTEGRATER

Dolphin Engineering Works
6, Baburam Ghosh Lane
P.O. Hatkhola
Kolkatta - 5
Ph:. 22399378

A-One Packaging Machines
D-312, Sector-10, Noida
Ph:. 914443437
Fax: 0118-24526188

B.R. Pouch Packing Machines Pvt. Ltd.
C-22/15, Sector-57
Noida-201301
Ph:. 9124582871
Fax: 0118-24584930
E-Mail :
mailinfo@bropouchpkngmchs.com
Websit :
www.brpouchpkngmchs.com

Baba Packaging
14, Krishna Palace
Neelam Flyover
Faridabad - 121007
Ph:. 0129-25291107
Fax: 0129-25240741
E-Mail :
baba@ndb.vsnl.net.in
Website :
www.babapackaging.com

Dear Packaging Pvt. Ltd.
B-2, Laghu Udyog Kendra
I.B. Patel Road
Goregaon(E)
Mumbai - 400063
Ph:. 91-22-28733894,
8764434/876
Fax: 91-22-8760237
E-Mail :
hira@bom5.vsnl.net.in

Heat & Control Pvt. Ltd.
3, Anurag G-131
First Main Road
Anna Nagar East
Chennai - 600102
Ph:. 91-44-26441455,
26451814
Fax: 91-44-26441466
E-Mail :
heatandcontrol@vsnl.net.in
Website :
www.heatandcontrol.com

Hassia Redatron Packaging Machinery Pvt. Ltd.
15/A, Kondhwa Budruk
Gidwani Compound
Pune - 411048
Ph:26930341, 24003041/43
Fax: 24003042
E-Mail :
redatron@pn2.vsnl.net.in

Kaizen Enterprises
A-5, Trupti, G.V. Scheme
Road # 4, Mulund (E)
Mumbai - 400081
Ph:. 25646873
E-Mail :
kaizen@zeenext.com

M-Tech Engineers
Plot No.33, Gali No.1,
Sewa Sadan Block
Fazal Pur, Mandawali
Delhi - 110092
Ph:. 22232356

N.K. Engineering Works
6967/11, Multani Dhanda
Pahar Ganj
New Delhi - 110055
Ph:. 23522232, 27777804
Fax: 91-11-23512178

Nichrome India Ltd.
Safire Park Galleria
2nd Floor Pune-Mumbai
Road, Wakadewadi
Shivajinagar, Pune-411005
Ph:. 24011001
Fax: 24011010

E-Mail :
corpoff@nichrome.com
punbrn@nichrome.com
Website : www.nichrome.com

N.S. Packaging Pvt. Ltd.
C-69, Sector-2, Noida
Ph:. 9124535119
Fax: 91-24514973
E-Mail :
nsindia@mantraonline.com

Packmech Engineers
23/4,
Kailash Industrial Estate
B/h.CMC, Odhav
Ahmedabad - 382415
Ph:. 079-22876181
Fax: 079-22876893
E-Mail :
powervac@satyam.net.in

Recon Machine Tools Pvt. Ltd.
37, Sarvodaya Industrial Estate
Mahakali Caves Road
Andheri (E)
Mumbai - 400093
Ph:28344973,28343931/1753
Fax: 28361074
E-Mail :
recon@bom3vsnl.net.in
Website :
www.reconmachine.com

Sara Udyog
C-167, Sec- 10,
Noida (U.P)
Ph : 9124521878

Saurabh Engineers
11, Upvan Co. Op. Housong Society Ltd.
132, Foot Road
Ahmedabad - 51
Ph:. 26765115, 26760292
Fax: 91-79-26765115, 22740288
E-Mail :
indvac@ad1.vsnl.net.in
Website : www.indvac.com

Unique Associates
5-C/18, B.P. NIT
Faridabad - 121001
Ph:. 91-129-2411450, 2413458, 2413617
Fax: 91-129-413458

WEIGHING SCALES/ MACHINES

Atcom Technologies Ltd.
6/A, Lalwani Industrial Estate
14, G.D. Ambedkar Road
Vadala (E),
Mumbai
Ph:022-24146343, 24165000
Fax: 022-24140250
E-Mail :atcom@vsnl.com
Website :
www.atcoweighing.com

Bombay Industrial Engineers
13, Crystal Apartments
Gulmohar Cross Road
11, JVPD, Mumbai - 400049
Ph:. 26232810
Fax: 26201914
E-Mail :
ijeshgal@bom5.vsnl.in

Jay Instruments & Systems Pvt. Ltd.
C-64, TTC Induistrial Area
Turbhe
Navi Mumbai - 400705
Ph:. 91-22-27672955/0092
Fax: 91-22-27670161
E-Mail :
jayinst@bom8.vsnl.net.in

NITROGEN FLUSHING & SEALING MACHINE, VACUUM

Packmech Engineers
23/4, Kailash Industrial Estate, Odhav
Ahmedabad - 382415
Ph:. 0091-79-22876181, 22876893
Fax: 0091-79-22872851

Pakona Engineers (I) Pvt. Ltd.
22-D, Wadia Charities Building
1st Floor
S.A. Brelvi Road Fort
Mumbai - 400023
Ph:. 22854138, 22826751
Fax: 22876171, 22870470

Saurabh Engineers
11, Upvan Co-op. Housing Soc. Ltd.
132, Ft. Ring Road
Ahmedabad - 380051
Gujarat
Ph:. 0091-79-26425115, 26448292
Fax: 0091-79-26425115

CRUSHIHG & GRINDING MACHINES (Disintegrators)

Adair Dutt & Co. (I) Pvt. Ltd.
5,B.B.D. Bagh East.
Kolkata-700001

Frederick Herbert,
10, Second Pasta Lane,
Colaba,
Mumbai-400005

Ganesh Engineering Works.
1507, Ganesh Pura,
Main Market, Tri Nagar,
Delhi-110035
Phones : 27117972

Industrial Scientific Corporation,
BA-148B, Janakpuri
New Delhi-110058.

Metrex Scientific Instruments Pvt. Ltd.
WH-20,
Mayapuri Industrial Area,
Phase-I,
New Delhi-110064
Ph.: 25130702,25138271

Monarch Engineering Works.
13, Kharwa Gali,
6th Kumbharwada,
Mumbai-400004

Raman & Well Pvt. Ltd.
Chateau MArine,
3rd Floor, 133, Netaji
Sabhash Road,
Mumbai-400020
Ph.: 22049164, 22049527,
22856397
Gram. RAMANWELL.
Fax 2: 2023042

Talson Industries (India)
Shed No. 128, Block B,
Sector II, Noida,
Ghaziabad-201207 (U.P)

Toshniwal Brothers Pvt. Ltd.
Industrial Estate, Makhupura,
Ajmer-305002 (Rajasthan).

MIXERS/BLENDERS
(Cone,Double,Cone, Drum, Mass, Paste, Planetary, Powder, Ribbon, Roto-cube, Sigma-blade)

Accumax Engineering
C-5A/184, Janakpuri,
New Delhi-110058,
Telex. 25501092

Alliance Engineering Co.
Trisandhya Building,
97, D. Phalke Road,
Dadar CR, Mumbai-400014,
Ph.: 24112461, 24156510
Gram. QUICKMIX.
Fax: (022) 24138307,
24137648,

Amit Trading Co.
21, Chewool Wadi,
Dr. M.B.Velkar Street
(Kolbhat Lane),
Kalbadevi Road,
Post Box No. 2691,
Mumbai-400002
Phone : 22056895

Bectochem Engineers,
B-202, Rising Sun
Apartment,
Juhu Tara Road,
Opp.Palmgrove
Hotal, Santa Cruz.
Mumbai-400009
Ph.: 28500300, 28500057,
28502400
Gram. BECENG
Fax: 022-28506785

Burman Plant & Machinery Co.(P) Ltd.
36, Sarkar Lane,
Kolkata-700007
Phone : 22411340
Fax : (91) (33) 2296077

Dalal Engineering Pvt. Ltd.
Post Box. No. 63,
Thane-400601
(Maharashtra)
Phones : 022-25343577,
25343528
Fax. 022-25345570,
E-Mail: dalalfac@vsnl.com.

Flora Engineering Corporation,
28-A, Phool Bag.
Rampura (Near Railway
Crossing)
Delhi-110035

Gem Pharma Machineries
Plot No. A/82, Road No.16,
Towards Kisan Nagar,
Wagle Estate, Thane-400604
(Maharashtra)
Phones : 022-25820257,
25814158
Telex : 91-022-25826387
E-Mail :
Gemmumbai@hotmail.com.

POWDER FILLING MACHINE

Amba Engineers
6, Laxmi Industrial Estate,
Navnit Prakashan
Compound,
Ajod Dairy Road, Rakhial,
Ahmedabad-380023
Phone : (079) 22743948,
Gram. AMBAFILL
Fax : (079) 22743048

EEE CEE & Co.
1, Anant Estate,
Opp. Comet Estate, Rakhial,
Ahmedabad-380023
(Gujarat)
Phone : 079-22743075
Fax : 079-22743075

Machino Medicinia Pvt. Ltd
WZ-12, Phool Bagh,
Rampur More, Delhi-110035
Phone: 91-11-25447399,
25430672
Gram. ASIAN SALE
Fax: 91-11-5156151

N.K.Engineering Co.
Plot No. 1808
Phase-III, GIDC,Vatva,
Ahmedabad-382445
Telefax. 91-79-25891746

Supar Seals Company
WZ-12, Phool Bagh,
Rampura More,
Delhi-110035
Phones : 91-11-25447399,
25430672
Gram. ASIAN SALE
Fax: 91-11-25156151

Virajka Machinery Mfg Co.
5, Shrine Industrial Estate,
Rakhial,
Ahmedabad-380023

BAKERY MACHINERY

Aifso Enterprises
A-1, Veena Beena Apts.
Sewree (W), Mumbai,
Maharashtra-400015
TEL : +91 (0) 22 24130926
FAX : +91 (0) 22 24137339
E-mail:
aifso@bom3.vsnl.net.in

Muez-Hest Process Technologies Pvt. Ltd.
231, Blue Rose Indl. Est.,
Nr. Cable Corp.,W E Highway
Borivali (E) Mumbai,
Maharashtra-400066
TEL : +91 (0) 22 28544826
FAX : +91 (0) 22 28541758
E-mail:
muezhest@bom5.vsnl.net.in

Sun Beam Machines (India) Pvt. Ltd.
Plot No. 141, IDA
Bollaram, Hyderabad,
Andhra Pradesh-502325
TEL : +91 (0) 8458 279723
FAX : +91 (0) 8458 279078
E-mail: smipl@satyam.net.in

Cannon Engineering Industries
P.O. Box No. 6984, 105/106
Retiwala Indl. Est.
H A Palav Marg
Byculla (E)
Mumbai,
Maharashtra-400027
TEL : +91 (0) 22 23727203
FAX : +91 (0) 22 23737413
E-mail: cannon@bol.net.in

NSW India Ltd.
Plot No. 43, Sect. 34
EHTP
Gurgaon, Haryana-122001
TEL: +91 (0) 124
26371106
FAX: +91 (0) 124
26372859
E-mail:
corporate@nswindia.com

Machinkraft Equipment
337, 3rd Rd.,
Sindh Hsg. Soc.
Aundh
Pune,
Maharashtra-411007
TEL : +91 (0) 20 25887464
FAX : +91 (0) 20 25880353
E-mail:
info@machinkraftequipment.com

New Era Machines Pvt. Ltd.
Campa Cola Lane
Dhandari Kalan
G T Rd.
Ludhiana,
Punjab-141010
TEL : +91 (0) 161 2510777
FAX : +91 (0) 161 2510776
E-mail:
sales@neweramachines.com

R&D Engineers
A-41, IDA, Phase-IV
Rd. No. 4
Kukatpally
Hyderabad,
Andhra Pradesh-500037
India
TEL : +91 (0) 40 23079121
FAX : +91 (0) 40 23078668

Anukamp Engineers Pvt. Ltd.
6-3-841/9/1
Opp. Sheeshmahal
Ameerpet
Hyderabad,
Andhra Pradesh-500016
TEL : +91 (0) 40 23323024

Gemini Engineers
12B, Shama Apts., 138/1
Prenderghast Rd.
Secunderabad,
Andhra Pradesh-500003
TEL : +91 (0) 40 23078519
FAX : +91 (0) 40 27810751
E-mail: info@gemni.com

Gemni Engineers
F-4, IDA, Kukatpally
Gandhi Ngr.
Hyderabad,
Andhra Pradesh-500037
TEL : +91 (0) 40 27810750
E-mail: info@gemni.com

Royal Oven Equipments
2-3-655/C/21
Durganagar,
Amberpet
Hyderabad,
Andhra Pradesh-500013
TEL : +91 (0) 40 27037712

Soubhagya Confectionery Pvt. Ltd.
307, Nirmal Towers
Punjagutta
Hyderabad,
Andhra Pradesh-500082
India
TEL : +91 (0) 40 23353855

Supra Cool & Hot Systems Pvt. Ltd.
Plot No. 193
Shed No. 67,
IDA, Phase-II
Cherlapally,
Hyderabad,
Andhra Pradesh-500051
TEL : +91 (0) 40 27266141
E-mail:
sunilmuppidi@yahoo.com

Reliance Engineering Works
Kothi No. 4065
Sect. 46-D
Chandigarh,
Chandigarh (UT)-160047
TEL : +91 (0) 172 2605682
FAX : +91 (0) 172 2652781

Sikander Engineering Works
Kothi No. 4065
Sect. 46-D
Chandigarh,
Chandigarh (UT)-160047
TEL : +91 (0) 172 2605682
FAX : +91 (0) 172 2652781

A1 Baker Enterprises
23, Bhera Enclave
New Delhi,
NCT of Delhi-110087
TEL : +91 (0) 11 25586150

AG Industries
A-108, Lok Vihar
Pitampura
New Delhi,
NCT of Delhi-110034
TEL : +91 (0) 11
227103194
FAX : +91 (0) 11
222113355

Bake Well Engineers
471-A
Jheel Khuranja
Delhi,
NCT of Delhi-110051
TEL : +91 (0) 11 22245767
FAX : +91 (0) 11 22219522

Baker Enterprises
23, Nr. Peera Garhi
Bhera Enclave,
New Delhi,
NCT of Delhi-110087
TEL : +91 (0) 11 25266238
FAX : +91 (0) 11 25266150
E-mail: bredo@vsnl.com

Flora Engg. Corp.
28-A, Phool Bagh
Rampura
Delhi,
NCT of Delhi-110035
TEL : +91 (0) 11
25415335

Harison Engineers
B-1673, Main Rd.
Shastri Ngr.Delhi,
NCT of Delhi-110052
TEL : +91 (0) 11
23645146

HCS Enterprises
Kaushak Rd. No. 2
Saroop Ngr.
Delhi,
NCT of Delhi-110042
India
TEL : +91 (0) 11
27290530
FAX : +91 (0) 11
27291305

Nagpal Brothers
C-127
Phase-II
Mayapuri Indl. Area
New Delhi,
NCT of Delhi-110064
India
TEL : +91 (0) 11
25400407
FAX : +91 (0) 11
25403884
E-mail:
nagpalbr@del3.vsnl.net.in

NBE Food Systems Pvt. Ltd.
B-97/1, Phase-I
Naraina Indl. Area
New Delhi,
NCT of Delhi-110028
India
TEL : +91 (0) 11
25797764
FAX : +91 (0) 11
25797525

New Bakery Machines
RZ, B-36
Matiala Extn., Part-I
Uttam Ngr.
New Delhi,
NCT of Delhi-110059
India
TEL : +91 (0) 11 25335115
FAX : +91 (0) 11 25336487

Prabhat M T Manufacturing Co.
B-23/4
Wazirpur Indl. Area
Delhi, NCT of Delhi-110052
TEL : +91 (0) 11 27457831

Premier Engineering Works
B-136, Phase-I
Okhla Indl. Area
New Delhi,
NCT of Delhi-110020
TEL : +91 (0) 11 26818210
FAX : +91 (0) 11 26816508
E-mail:
premierengineers@mantraonline.com

Relief Equipment Co.
A-23/1, (B)
Phase-I
Naraina Indl. Area
New Delhi,
NCT of Delhi-110028
TEL : +91 (0) 11 25792553
FAX : +91 (0) 11 25792553

Sifter Group Of Industries
Plot No. 227, Sect.24
Faridabad,
Haryana-121005
TEL : +91 (0) 129 25240150
FAX : +91 (0) 129 25230039
E-mail: sifter@tatanova.com

Sifter International
227, Sect. 24
Faridabad,
Haryana-121005
TEL : +91 (0) 129 5231154
FAX : +91 (0) 129 5230039
E-mail: sifter@tatanova.com

Bismac Manufacturers
35/3, R R Cmplx.
100 Ft. Rd.
Peenya, Bangalore,
Karnataka-560057
India
TEL : +91 (0) 80 28399616
FAX : +91 (0) 80 28393781
E-mail:
bismac2002in@yahoo.com.in

Dolar Equipments Pvt. Ltd.
83, 7th Main, Phase-III
Peenya Indl. Area
Bangalore,
Karnataka-560058
TEL : +91 (0) 80 28393000
FAX : +91 (0) 80 23511238
E-mail: dolar@sify.com

Mangal Metal Works
Plot No. 237/61-A
Nr. Basaveshwar Circle,
Goa VES, Khanapur Rd.
Belgaum,
Karnataka-590001
TEL : +91 (0) 831 2421877
FAX : +91 (0) 831 2434577
E-mail:
info@mangalmetals.com

Peenya Alloys Pvt. Ltd.
No. 248, 3rd Cross, 8th Main
Phase-III
Peenya Indl. Area
Bangalore,
Karnataka-560058
TEL : +91 (0) 80 28394259
FAX : +91 (0) 80 28396536
E-mail:
jominsol@satyamn.net.in

Arihant Engineering Works
124,
Guru Nanak Timber Mkt.
Dhar Rd., Indore,
Madhya Pradesh-452002
TEL : +91 (0) 731 2380535
FAX : +91 (0) 731 2380537
E-mail:
arihantengineering@epatra.com

Kaps Engineers
Samraat Silk Mills
Compound, LBS Marg
Vikhroli (W)
Mumbai,
Maharashtra-400079
TEL : +91 (0) 22 25781933
FAX : +91 (0) 22 25785741
E-mail:
vmsrehls@bom4.vsnl.net.in

Grovers Pvt. Ltd.
3F4, Shankardham
Sundervan Cmplx.
Off Lokhandwala Cmplx.
Andheri (W)
Mumbai,
Maharashtra-400053
TEL : +91 (0) 22 26314574
FAX : +91 (0) 22 26313014
E-mail:
vivek@groversequip.com

Mars Process Engineering Pvt. Ltd.
F-II, 22/2, MIDC
Pimpri
Pune,
Maharashtra-411018
TEL : +91 (0) 20 25675728

Aifso Industrial Equipment Co.
A-1, Veena Beena Apts.
Sewri (W)
Mumbai,
Maharashtra-400015
TEL : +91 (0) 22 24130926
FAX : +91 (0) 22 24137339
E-mail:
aifso@bom3.vsnl.net.in

Jayco Metal Crafts & Engineering
3, Pilot Indl. Est.
Navghar, Vasai (E)
Thane,
Maharashtra-410210
TEL : +91 (0) 22 26785620
FAX : +91 (0) 22 26796702
E-mail:
response@jaycocranes.com

Kamal Export Industries
Datta Bhavan
Kashinath Dhuru Rd.
Dadar (W), Mumbai,
Maharashtra-400028
TEL : +91 (0) 22 24221555
FAX : +91 (0) 22 24373474
E-mail: kei@vsnl.com

Prima Engineering Industries
Plot T-113, MIDC
Bhosari
Pune, Maharashtra-411026
TEL : +91 (0) 20 27120621
FAX : +91 (0) 20 27120294
E-mail:
primabek@pn2.vsnl.net.in

RM Engg. Works
No. 3, Jama Masjid Lane,
Kherani Rd.
Sakinaka, Mumbai,
Maharashtra-400072
TEL : +91 (0) 22 28520743
FAX : +91 (0) 22 28523484

Ultra International
502, Maganlal Chmbrs.
Iron Mkt., Mumbai,
Maharashtra-400009
TEL : +91 (0) 22 23427424
FAX : +91 (0) 22 23437417
E-mail:
daksh@bom3.vsnl.net.in

KS Engineering Works
Factory Area
Patiala, Punjab-147003
TEL : +91 (0) 175 2361535
FAX : +91 (0) 175 2305274
E-mail:
dhimanjasbir@usa.net

Mohan Lal & Sons
Abchal Ngr.
Factory Area
Patiala, Punjab-147001
TEL : +91 (0) 175 2364781
FAX : +91 (0) 175 2364781
E-mail: sonu-
sudhir@hotmail.com

New Era Industries
Campa Cola Lane
Dhandari Kalan
Ludhiana,
Punjab-141010
TEL : +91 (0) 161 2510777
FAX : +91 (0) 161 2510776
E-mail:
sales@neweramachine.com

Sunrise Industries
11-A
Opp. Gurudwara Sadh
Sangat Sahib
Factory Area
Patiala, Punjab-147001
TEL : +91 (0) 175 2223440
FAX : +91 (0) 175 2221504

Doris (India) Engineers Pvt. Ltd.
No. 389, 390
Arcot Rd., Kodambakkam
Chennai,
Tamil Nadu-600024
TEL : +91 (0) 44 24801098
FAX : +91 (0) 44 24815652
E-mail:
machines@dorisindia.com

Vikaash Packaging
120, Mugappair Rd.
Padi, Chennai,
Tamil Nadu-600050
India
TEL : +91 (0) 44 26521703
FAX : +91 (0) 44 26521703
E-mail: rvs@eth.net

Arun's Engineering Works
SF No. 213
Sitra Kalapatti Rd.,
Nr. LMW Unit VIII
Kalapatti (Post)
Coimbatore,
Tamil Nadu-641035
TEL : +91 (0) 422 2665622
FAX : +91 (0) 422 2665633
E-mail:
info@arunsengineering.com

Balakrishnan Motor & Iron Works
No. 67, Seevalaperi Rd.
Palayamkottai
Tirunelvelli,
Tamil Nadu-627002
TEL : +91 (0) 462 2574944
E-mail: scorpio@vsnl.com

Imayam Engineering Works
Near Eachanari Rly. Gate
Pollachi Main Rd.
Coimbatore,
Tamil Nadu-641021
TEL : +91 (0) 422 2875938
FAX : +91 (0) 422 2875938

Superheat Furnaces Pvt. Ltd.
E-23, 6th Phase
Sidco Indl. Est.
Hosur (TN),
Tamil Nadu-635126
TEL : +91 (0) 4344 2576882

Thermo Electric Furnaces
286, SIDCO Indl. Est.
Ambattur Chennai,
Tamil Nadu-600098
TEL : +91 (0) 44 26253389
FAX : +91 (0) 44 26253389

Techman Enterprises
A-82, Sect. 58
Noida,
Uttar Pradesh-201301
TEL : +91 (0) 120 24582680

Balilias Engineering Company Pvt. Ltd.
6th Flr., Commerce House,
Room No. 6A, 2
Ganesh Chandra Avenue
Kolkata,
West Bengal-700013
TEL : +91 (0) 33 22377877
FAX : +91 (0) 33 22482070

Mechtech Designers & Engineers Pvt. Ltd.
19-D, Dr. A K Paul Rd.
Behala, Kolkata,
West Bengal-700034
TEL : +91 (0) 33 24920053
FAX : +91 (0) 33 24581499
E-mail: laha@satyam.net.in

Oriental Machinery (1919) Pvt. Ltd.
25
Rajendra Nath Mukherjee Rd.
Kolkata, West Bengal-700001
TEL : +91 (0) 33 22484840

BAKERY OVEN

Mars Process Engineering Pvt. Ltd.
F-II, 22/2, MIDC, Pimpri
Pune,
Maharashtra-411018
TEL : +91 (0) 20 25675728

NSW India Ltd.
Plot No. 43, Sect. 34
EHTP
Gurgaon, Haryana-122001
TEL:+91(0) 124 26371106
FAX:+91(0) 124 26372859
E-mail:
corporate@nswindia.com

Aifso Enterprises
A-1, Veena Beena Apts.
Sewree (W), Mumbai,
Maharashtra-400015
TEL : +91 (0) 22 24130926
FAX : +91 (0) 22 24137339
E-mail:
aifso@bom3.vsnl.net.in

Sun Beam Machines
(India) Pvt. Ltd.
Plot No. 141, IDA
Bollaram, Hyderabad,
Andhra Pradesh-502325
TEL : +91 (0) 8458 279723
FAX : +91 (0) 8458 279078
E-mail: smipl@satyam.net.in

Reliance Engineering Works
Kothi No. 4065
Sect. 46-D
Chandigarh, Chandigarh
(UT)-160047
TEL : +91 (0) 172 2605682
FAX : +91 (0) 172 2652781

Associated Industrial Furnaces Pvt. Ltd.
2/5, Sarai Jullena
Okhla Rd., New Delhi,
NCT of Delhi-110025
TEL : +91 (0) 11 26842411
E-mail: aifdli@ndb.vsnl.net.in

Baker Enterprises
23, Nr. Peera Garhi
Bhera Enclave
New Delhi,
NCT of Delhi-110087
TEL : +91 (0) 11 25266238
FAX : +91 (0) 11 25266150
E-mail: bredo@vsnl.com

HCS Enterprises
Kaushak Rd. No. 2
Saroop Ngr.
Delhi, NCT of Delhi-110042
TEL : +91 (0) 11 27290530
FAX : +91 (0) 11 27291305

Metro Equipment Co.
WZ-75, Nr. Inderpur
Main Todapur Rd.
New Delhi,
NCT of Delhi-110012
TEL : +91 (0) 11 25729443
FAX : +91 (0) 11 25285780
E-mail:
hotelneeds@hotmail.com

Quality Equipment Co.
89, Mahavira St.
Haiderpur
Delhi, NCT of Delhi-110088
TEL : +91 (0) 11 27496536
FAX : +91 (0) 11 27659243
E-mail:
qualityequipco@hotmail.com

CS Medical Pvt. Ltd.
143H
Bommasandra Indl. Area
Hosur Rd., Bangalore,
Karnataka-562158
TEL : +91 (0) 80 27833792
FAX : +91 (0) 80 27834913
E-mail:
info@csaerotherm.com

Dolar Equipments Pvt. Ltd.
83, 7th Main, Phase-III
Peenya Indl. Area
Bangalore,
Karnataka-560058
TEL : +91 (0) 80 28393000
FAX : +91 (0) 80 3511238
E-mail: dolar@sify.com

Jomind Furnaces Pvt. Ltd.
248, Indl. Est., Phase-III
3rd Cross,
8th Main, Peenya
Bangalore,
Karnataka-560058
TEL : +91 (0) 80 28394259
FAX : +91 (0) 80 8396536
E-mail:
jominsol@satyam.net.in

Arihant Engineering Works
124
Guru Nanak Timber Mkt.
Dhar Rd., Indore,
Madhya Pradesh-452002
TEL : +91 (0) 731 2380535
FAX : +91 (0) 731 2380537
E-mail:
arihantengineering@epatra.com

Cannon Engineering Industries
P.O. Box No. 6984, 105/106
Retiwala Indl. Est.
H A Palav Marg
Byculla (E), Mumbai,
Maharashtra-400027
TEL : +91 (0) 22 23727203
FAX : +91 (0) 22 23737413
E-mail: cannon@bol.net.in

Admir Ovens
Plot No. 1/E/4
Shivaji Ngr., Govandi
Mumbai,
Maharashtra-400043
TEL : +91 (0) 22 25511718
FAX : +91 (0) 22 25568446
E-mail:
admir@bom5.vsnl.net.in

Aggni Heaterss
No. 6, Kasthuribai St.
(Old Sathy Rd.)
Ganapathy, Coimbatore,
Tamil Nadu - 641006
TEL : +91 (0) 422 2533070
E-mail:
aggniheaters@yahoo.com

Thermo Electric Furnaces
286, SIDCO Indl. Est.
Ambattur, Chennai,
Tamil Nadu-600098
TEL : +91 (0) 44 26253389
FAX : +91 (0) 44 26253389

Taurus Baker Machinery Pvt. Ltd.
B-82 & 83, Sect. 2
Noida,
Uttar Pradesh-201301
TEL:+91 (0) 120 24443028
FAX:+91 (0) 120 24443028

Mechtech Designers & Engineers Pvt. Ltd.
19-D, Dr. A K Paul Rd.
Behala, Kolkata,
West Bengal-700034
TEL : +91 (0) 33 24920053
FAX : +91 (0) 33 24581499
E-mail: laha@satyam.net.in

BAKERY DIES & MOULDS

Smith's Engineering Works
139-A, GIDC, Phase-II,
Vatva, Ahmedabad,
Gujarat-382445

TEL : +91 (0) 79 25831534
FAX : +91 (0) 79 25836512
E-mail:
smithsengg@yahoo.com

Pooja Engg.
J-118, Ansa Indl. Est.
Saki Vihar Rd.
Saki Naka, Mumbai,
Maharashtra-400072
TEL:+91 (0) 22 228523274

Mohan Lal & Sons
Abchal Ngr.
Factory Area
Patiala, Punjab-147001
TEL : +91 (0) 175 2364781
FAX : +91 (0) 175 2364781
E-mail: sonu-
sudhir@hotmail.com

Sunrise Industries
11-A, Opp. Gurudwara Sadh
Sangat Sahib
Factory Area
Patiala, Punjab-147001
TEL:+91 (0) 175 22223440
FAX :+91 (0)175 22221504

Electro Dies & Tools
Plot No. 5, Rd. No. 4
22, Godam Extn.
Indl. Est.
Jaipur, Rajasthan-302006
TEL : +91(0)141 22215239
FAX : +91(0)141 22212492
E-mail:
joharihari@satyam.net.in

Indo-Danish Tool Room
M-4 (Part), Phase-VI
Tata Kandra Rd.
Gamharia
Jamshedpur,
Jharkhand-832108
TEL : +91 (0) 657 2408061
FAX : +91 (0) 657 2407723
E-mail: idtr@dte.vsnl.net.in

AG Industries
A-108, Lok Vihar
Pitampura
New Delhi,
NCT of Delhi-110034
TEL : +91 (0) 11
27103194
FAX : +91 (0) 11
22113355

Dazzle Engineers
S-21B, St.12,
Anand Parbat Indl. Area
New Delhi,
NCT of Delhi-110005
TEL : +91 (0) 11
25726480
FAX : +91 (0) 11
25815120

Flowtech Air Pvt. Ltd.
B-86, Phase-II
Okhla Indl. Area
New Delhi,
NCT of Delhi-110020
TEL : +91 (0) 11
26821095
FAX : +91 (0) 11
26463856

Sara Engineering Works
D-15, Suvidha Apts.
Sect. 13, Rohini
New Delhi,
NCT of Delhi-110085
TEL : +91 (0) 11
27108316
FAX : +91 (0) 11
27245178
E-mail:
saraengg@del3.vsnl.net.in

SPICES

Alok Technical & Marketing Services Pvt Ltd.
P.B. No. 8, Chandra Building
Kalkaji Temple,
New Delhi - 110019
Ph:. 26439427, 26439318,
26469234
Fact: A-96, Bhiwandi
Industrial EstateDist. Alwar
Rajasthan
Tel 407
Exec. Dr. Vinod Chandra, Dr.
Ratan C. Paliwal
Pr. Food Processing
Machinery/Plants, Canning
Machinery, Bakery Plants,
Confectionery Machinery,
Mixers, Blenders, Reactors,
Separators

A.T.E. Enterprises Ltd.
A-19, CTS No. 689, Veera
Desai Road,
Andheri (W), Mumbai - 400
053
Tel. : 91-22-263466 10
Fax : 91-22-26346609
Email : pumps@ateel.com

B.R. Pouch Packing Machines Pvt. Ltd.
C-22/15, Sector-57
Noida-201301
Ph:. 9124582871
Fax: 0118-24584930
E-Mail :
mailinfo@bropouchpkngmchs.com
Websit :
www.brpouchpkngmchs.com

Bombay Engineering Industry
R.No. 6, (Extn.) Sevanthibai
Bhavan
Chimatpada, Marol Naka
Andheri (E),
Mumbai - 400059
Ph:. 28369368, 28215795
Fax: 28369368
E-Mail :
bommars@bom7.vsnl.net.in
Website : http://
bej.jump.business.com

Bombay Industrial Engineers
13, Crystal Apartments
Gulmohar Cross Road
11, JVPD, Mumbai - 400049
Ph:. 26232810
Fax: 26201914
E-Mail :
ijeshgal@bom5.vsnl.in

(Complete Plant Supplier for Toffee/Hardboiled Candy, Chewing Gum Plant)

Dhiman Industries
Head Office & Works
Dhakni Gate,
Nakodar - 144040
Dist. Jalandhar, Punjab
Ph:. 91-1821-220018, 220118, 222118
Fax: 91-1821-221118
E-Mail : info@dhimangroup.com

New Delhi Office:
53/19, Old Rajinder Nagar
New Delhi - 110060
Ph:. 91-11-25783731, 25842114
Fax: 91-11-25744865
E-Mail : delhi@dhimangroup.com

Ahmedabad Office:
G-1, Sulabh Apartment
Near Gurudwara Gobind Dham
Behind Westernd Park,
Thaltej, Ahmedabad
Ph:. 079-26843724, 26756119 (R)
Mobile : 9825006724
E-Mail : ahd@dhimangroup.com
Website : www.dhimangroup.com
Pr. Complete Plant Suppliers of Confectionery Unit, Toffee Plant, Candy Plant, Bubble Gum Plant

Dhiman Udyog
Plot No. 6026, Near Dakhni Gate
Nakodar - 144040 (Jalandar) Punjab
Ph:. 01821-220891, 222891, 222991
Fax: 01821-220919, 222891
Website : dhimanudyog.com
Pr. Confectionery Plant Machinery

Emersion Engineering Enterprises
Near Gate Station
Surendranagar - 363001
Ph:. 221940 & 3351
Pr. Confectionery Machine, Chewing Gum, Bubble Plant

Eskeryar Engineering Co. Pvt. Ltd.
10/5, Developed Plot
Ambattur Industrial Estate
Chennai - 600058
Ph:. 2654137, 2654851
Fax: 24991447, 2652369
Exec.:P.K.N. Panicker (MD)
Pr. Toffee Cookers, Fondant Machine, Express Sugar Dissolvers, Emulsifiers, Miscrofilm Cookers

Friends Packaging
Parvesh Marg, Railway Road
Gali No.2
Near Rajiv Gandhi Chowk,
Old Faridabad (Haryana)
Ph:. 0129-2297519
Pr. F.F.S. & Candy Pillow Wrapping Machine, Automatic Form-Fill-Seal Machine

General Engineering Works TheOld Post Office Road
Udupi - 575101 (Karnataka)
Ph:. 8495
Pr. Confectionery Machinery, Biscuit Plant, Bubble Gum/Chewing Gum Machinery, Canning Equipment

General Mechanical Industries
National Tankiwala Indutrial Estate
Steelmade Compound
Marol Maroshi Road
Andheri (E), Mumbai - 400059
Ph:. 28343751 / 28328362
Fax: 26340567
Pr. Confectionery Equipment

Hindustan Engineering Co.
Aban House, 25-31,
Ropewalk Street
Opp. K. Dubash Marg
Fort, Mumbai - 400023
Ph:. 2243068
Pr. Bread Macking Machinery, Bakery Machinery, Confectionery Machinery, Extruder, Vermicelli, Popcorn Machinery, Potato Wafer Plant

K.S.J. Foods & Services Pvt. Ltd.
C/o. 7-87, Visnu Prasad
Mahant Road
Vile Parle, Mumbai - 400057
Ph.: 2573294
Pr. Biscuit Macking Machine, Bakery Equipment, Confectionery Plant Flour Based, Homogenizer, Kitchen Equipment, Pasta Making Plant

Marshal Engineers
140, Anna Salai, Saidapet
Chennai - 600015
Ph.: 22352863, 22353805
Fax: 22351783
Fact:. 5, Leo Industrial Estate
Pallikkaranai, Chennai - 601302
Ph.: 22353182
Exec. S. Lakshmanan
Pr. Bottle Washing Machine, Vacuum/Volumetric Filling Machine, ROPP Sealing Machine, Labelling Machines, S.S. Slat/Belt Conveyors, Filter Presses, S.S. Tank, Vessels, Stirrers, Sigma Mixers, Ribbon/ Paddle/Cone Mixers, Ointment/Paste Filler, Jacketted Vessels with Stirrers

National Engineering Co.
No. 65, Street, John's
Church Road
Cleveland Town,
Bangalore - 560005
Ph:. 2577532, 23334623
Pr. Bubble/Chewing Gum
Plant

N.S. Packaging Pvt. Ltd.
C-69, Sector-2
Noida (U.P)
Ph:. 91-24535119
Fax: 91-24514973
E-Mail :
nsindia@mantraonline.com

Paresh Engineering Co.
74/B, Sanjay Building No. 5
Mittal Industrial Estate
M. Vasanji Road, Marol Naka
Andheri (E),
Mumbai - 400059
Ph:. 28501794
Fax: 28509193
Pr. Bubble/Chewing Gum
Plant

S.J. Roy
B-59, Defence Colony
New Delhi - 110024
Ph.: 24623224, 24694689
Fax: 24623224
Exec. S.J. Roy
Pr. Food Machinery for
Noodles, Vermicelli & other
Pasta Products, Dough
Sheeters, Bakery &
Confectionery Machine,
Chocolate, Chewing Gum
Machine etc.

Saffaire India
No. 51, Juhu Supreme
Shopping Centre
Cross Road No. 8, JVPD
Scheme
Mumbai - 400049
Ph.: 26203998
Exec. P. Mani
Pr. Turnkey Food Projects in
the field of Dairy, Fruit &
Vegetable Processing
Machinery, Bakery/
Confectionery Industries

Sangram Engineering Ltd.
B-5, Supercon, Aundh
Pune - 411007
Ph.: 0212-2366935,
2342302
Fax: 0212-2349673
Pr. Milk Products Processing Machinery, Chocolate &
Confectionery Plant, Amla/
Chyawanprash Making
Plant

Sharma Engineering Works
7, Bhagat Singh Road
Old Rohtak Road, New
Delhi - 110007
Ph.: 27771721
Pr. Automatic Confectionery
Machines, Diesel Bhatti,
Vacuum Pump, Rope Sizing
Machine, Toffee Sizing
Machine, Pouch Machine,
Toffee Cutters

Standard Machinery Sales Co.
546, Mount Road,
Teynampet
Chennai - 600018
Ph.: 24341496, 24349918
Fax: 24341463
Pr. Confectionery &
Packaging Machines

Trover Pharma Machine (Regd.)
Alongside Octroi Post
Kapurthala Road, Nakodar -
141310
Ph.: 01821-220318
Fax: 091-01821-220318
Br. M. Narayana Chetty,
Ganesh Traders
71, Govindappa Street,
Chennai - 600001
Ph.: 25228249, 25225932
Exec. S. Dhiman
Pr. Tablet Making Machine,
Pulverising Machine, Powder,
Mixing & Kneading Machine,
Sugar Coating Machine,
Toffee Wrap Machine,
Vacuum Pumps, Cooling
Plates, Candy Making Plants

Jetpac Sadguru Sai Packaging Industries
MIG-35, Apiic Colony, Kamal
Nagar
Hyderabad-500 062
Ph: 27127194,
Fax: 27120892

Indian Packaging Machinery
I-15,
DLF Industrial Estate
Phase-I, Faridabad
(Haryana)
Ph: 91-2276112, 2278737
Fax: 2274518

Chemac Eqpts. Pvt. Ltd.
M.J. D'Souza Compound
Safedpool,
Sakinaka
Mumbai- 400 072
Ph: 2851 0777 / 6986,
28592352
Fax: 28516986
E-Mail:
chemac@bom4.vsnl.net.in

PULVERISER/ GRINDER

M/s. Advance Quality Controls
Ph:. 0129-25263017,
25291556
E-Mail : aqc1@rediffmail.com

M/s. Ambika Vijay Works
1H, Laxmi East Link Road
West, Mumbai - 53
Ph:. 26366894

M/s. Babbar Engineering
688/335, Munshi Ram Bagh
Near Ranjit Nagar
New Delhi - 110 008
Ph:. 25705367, 25705363
Also at: 8007/11
Multani Dhanda,
Paharganj
New Delhi - 110 055
Ph:.23522232, 23677804
Fax: 23512178

M/s. Chandra Orgo-chem Combines
306, Belscot Tower, Link Road
Lokhand Wala Complex
Andheri, Mumbai - 53
Ph:. 23430789

M/s. Dhiman Udyog
6026, Kapurthala Road
Nakodar - 144040
(Dist. Jalandhar) Punjab
Ph: 01821-220891, 222891, 222991
Fax: 0091-1821-220891
Website:www.dhimanudyog.com

M/s. Dolphin Engineering Works
6, Baburam Ghosh Lane
P.O. Hatkhola
Kolkatta - 5
Ph:. 22399378

M/s. D.P. Pulveriser Works
76, Nagindas Master Road
Fort, Mumbai - 23
Ph:. 22675724, 22670976
Fax: 022-22676435

M/s. Flour Tech Engineers (P) Ltd.
16/5, Mathura Road
Faridabad - 121002
(Haryana)
Ph:.0129-25291556, 25263017
E-Mail:
flourtech@rediffmail.com

M/s. Frigmaires Engineers
Post Box:16353
Janta Industrial Estate No.8L
Parel, Mumbai - 13
Ph:. 24941694

M/s. Hind Pulverizer Works
B-3/2, Ambica East
Near Sukhram Nagar
Ahemdabad - 23
Ph:. 22747451, 22744018
Fax : 079-22747451

M/s. JDP Enterprises
13, Kharwa Lane,
Samad Building
Mumbai - 400004
Ph:. 23810054

M/s. Jikosha Engineering Corp.
2, Ratna Jyoti Ind. Estate,
Vile Parle West, Mumbai - 56
Ph:. 26711312

M/s. K.B. Engineering
B-58, Kiran Industrial Estate
M.G Road,
Goregaon (West)
Mumbai - 62
Ph:. 28720616

M/s. Kaps Engineers
831, GIDC, Makarpura
Baroda - 10 (Gujarat)
Ph:. 25781933, 011-25756760
Website : www.vmkaps.com
E-Mail:
kapsvm@ad1.vsnl.net.in

M/s. Kabir Engineers Works
Niramay,
B/H Suvidha Centre
Paldi,
Ahemdabad - 7
Gujarat
Ph:. 26620270
Fax: 26576497

M/s. Kaps Engineers
Samrat Silk Mills Compound
L.B.S. Marg,
Vikhroli (West),
Mumbai - 400079 (M.S)
Ph:. 91-22-25781933
Fax: 25785741
E-Mail:
vmsrehls@bom4.vsnl.net.in

M/s. Litho Tech Engineers
Sector-10/B25/Sh-13
Shanti Nagar
Mira Road - East
Mumbai - 7
Ph:. 28110182

M/s. Micro Pulverizer Manufacturing Work
Universal Compound,
Old Nagar Das Road,
Andheri (East),
Mumbai - 69
Ph:. 28209725

M/s. Modern Fabricators
25/4, Industrial Area
Anand Parbat,
New Delhi - 110005
Ph:. 25722888

M/s. Precious Fab-Cast Pvt. Ltd.
4809, Ph-4, GIDC, Vatva
Ahmedabad - 445
Gujarat
Ph:. 25832237
Fax : 25830026

Chapter - 51

Suppliers of Raw-Materials

Janak Dehydration Pvt. Ltd.
P.B. 58, Keri Bazar
Old Darbargadh
Mahuva - 364290
Ph:. 02844-227763, 227764, 227765
Fax: 022-28612735
E-Mail :
jkmehta@bom5.vsnl.net.in
Mumbai Office
B/305, Sunder Dham, Ram Bagh Lane, Off. S.V. Road
Borivli (W), Mumbai-400092
(Dehydrated Onions, Garlic in Various forms including free flowing powders of Onions & Garlic)

Kancor Flavour & Extracts Ltd.
24/2014, Willing Island
Indira Gandhi Road
Cochin - 682003
Ph:. 0484-2669879, 2669910
Fax:. 0484-2669878
E-Mail :
mktg.fid@kancorflavours.com
(Flavour for Snack Food, Namkken etc.)

Kamani Oil Industries
317-Pooran Asha Building
Narsi Natha Street
Mumbai - 400009
Ph:. 022-23435968
Fax: 022-23435964
E-Mail :
kamani@bom2.vsnl.net.in
(Refined Vegetable Oils, Speciality Frying Oil with Excellent shelf Life)

Potato Foods & Flavours
30, Hathi Khana
Azad Market, Delhi 110006
Ph:. 23539247, 23539879
Fax:. 91-11-27537062

E-Mail :
poddarfoods@yahoo.com
(Flavours Seasonings & Blended Spices for Ready to Eat Snacks, Pappad, Namkeens etc.)

BOTTLES

Touro Trades,
809, Katra Neel,
Chandni Chowk,
Delhi-110006
Phones: Off: 23975346
Resi. 22814781
Fax : 011-23924988
Deals in : Aluminium Bottles 5 ml. to 25 kg, Aluminium Fancy Caps (Golden) Aerosole & Refilable Spray mist devices, Glass Bottles for perfume & cosmetics
Contact Person :
Varun Seth

Apanjan Glass Industries
3-A, Chowranghee Place,
Room No. 17, (1st Floor)
Kolkata-700013

Bajaj Commercial Corporation
B-5/11, Mahesh Nagar,
S.V.Road,, Goregaon (W),
Mumbai-400062
Phone : 26723867

Barkha Bottle Bhandar
Sukhadiya Gram
Behind Sector-D,
Indore-452003 (M.P)
Phone : 2442241

Borosil Glass Works Ltd.
44, Khanna Construction House,
Dr. R.G. Thadani Marg,
Worli, Mumbai-400050
Phone : 24930362/0360 /0370
Gram. BOROSIL
Telex. 011-75351 BOROSIL
Fax : 24948161

East India Glass Industries
Jessore Road, P.O.
Ganganagar,
24-Parganas-743 250 (West Bengal)
Phone : 25522383

Flamingo Blow-Pack
57, Laxmanbhai Estate,
Near Revabhai Estate,
Near Shreeji Hotel,
Amraiwadi,
Ahmedabad-380026 (Gujarat)

Haldyn Glass Ltd.
Off Western Express Highway,
Goregaon (East)
Mumbai-400063
Phone : 28730311-14, 28742480-2,
Gram. PILFERPROOF
Telex : 011-70047 HGWL IN
Fax : 91-22-28735231,

E-Mail:
vintar@giashm0.1.vsnl.net.in.
Website: http://
ww.infoindia.com/haldyn.

Indian Scientific Glass Industries
4A, Luis Annexe, Pandurang Budhkar Marg,
Mumbai-400013
Phones :
24309556,24222870,
Gram. KHEMKAPLUS.
Telex : 011-73684 ISGI IN
Fax : 91-22-24304379,
24309556

CAPS
(Aluminium, etc)

Touro Trades,
809, Katra Neel,
Chandni Chowk,
Delhi-110006
Phones: Off: 23975346
Resi. 2814781
Fax : 011-23924988
Deals in : Aluminium Bottles 5 ml. to 25 kg, Aluminium Fancy Caps (Golden) Aerosole & Refilable Spray mist devices, Glass Bottles for perfume & cosmetics
Contact Person : Varun Seth

Aar Es Pharma
5, Lakhpat Rai Lane,
Bahadur Gunj,
Allahabad-211003 (U.P)

Bengal Metal Industries
10, Chaulpatty Road,
Beleghata,
Kolkata-700010
Phone : 2359448

Bombay Glass Blowing Industries
7, J.K.Industrial Estate,
Off. Mahakali Caves Road,
Andheri (East)
Mumbai-400093
Phone : 28329530
Fax : 28363208,
E-Mail :
bomglass@bom5.vsnl.net.in.

Bottle Closures,
16, Keytuo Industrial Estate,
Kondivita Road,
Andheri (E)
Mumbai-400059
Phone : 28387366

Central Tin Works
Chinchpokli Corner Lane,
Mumbai-400027
Gram. TINOBOXES

Container & Commodities Trading Co.
108, D. New Chinch Bunder,
Mumbai-400009

Datta Tin Works Pvt. Ltd.
Srikandath Road,
Ernakulam,
Cochin-682016 (Kerala)
Phone : 235199.

Everest Glass Emporium,
No.D-39, 2nd Floor,
P-36, India Exchange Place,
Kolkata-700001
Phone : 22429417
Gram. PRINTOGLASS.

Friend's & Co,
'Kailash', 320,
Sir Bhalchandra Road,
Matunga (C.Rly)
Mumbai-400019

Ghanshyam Das Somani & Co.
Somani Bhawan, 2060,
Ramlalaji Ka Rasta,
Jaipur-302003
Phones : 2568060, 2568061
Gram. GHANSHAM CO.
Fax : 91-141-565505

CAPSULE PRINTERS

Capsule Printers
KC-141, Old Kavi Nagar,
Ghaziabad-201001 (U.P)
Phone : 2853405

Gravure Art,
327, Pragati Industrial Estate,
N.M.Joshi Marg,
Mumbai-400011
Phones : 23091013,
23091982

Pharmaprints
Mehta Industrial Estate,
2nd Floor, Andheri-Kurla Road,
Chakala, Andheri (East)
Mumbai-400093
Phones : 28326575

CAPSULES
(Gelatin Hard)

Bharti Healthcare Ltd.
S-6, 2nd Floor,
Green Park Extn.
New Delhi-110016
Phones :26533603/04/05
/06
Fax : 91-11-26534205.

Capsugel India Ltd.
SCO No. 1134-35,
Ist Floor, Sector 22-B,
Chandigarh-160022
Phones : 0172-2706696,
2708115,
Fax : 0172-743734
E-Mail:
Capsugel.india@hotmail.com.

Es En Pharma
5, Lakhpat Rai Lane,
Bahadurganj.
Allahabad-211003 (U.P)

J.Raj & Co.
62/6, Nana Sunkerseet Smruti,
380382 J.Sunkersett Road, (Girgaum)
Mumbai-400002

Khanna Pharma
J.H.Building 2nd Floor,
1683, Bhagirath Palace,
Chandni Chowk,
Delhi-110006
Phones : 22962094, 22963554,
Fax: 23267258

Medi Caps Ltd
401, 4th Floor,
12/2, Chetak Centre.
R.N.T. Marg,
Indore-452001 (M.P)
Phones : 0731-25184345, 2514062
Fax : 0731-2528269

Pharma Caps Enterprises
B-B-12, Dilkhush Industrial Estate,
Azadpur Industrial Area,
G.T. Karnal Road,
Delhi-110033
Phones : 27118442

CLOSURES & SEALS
(Pilfer Proof)

Alpine Packers & Closurs
C-3/98, Ashok Vihar, Phase II,
Delhi-110052
Phone : 27226151

Bharati Engineers,
3727-28/29,Dariba Pan.
Opp. Shtiela Cinema,
New Delhi-110055
Phone : 27524749

Chempion Packaging Industries
29 RE/4, Street No. 4 ,
Anand Parbat Industrial Estate,
New Rohtak Road,
New Delhi-110005.

Goleria Rubber Products
3, Manisha Bldg.
Mathuradas Cross Road,
Irani Wadi,
Behind Asian Bakery,
Kandivli (W)
Mumbai-400067
Phone : 022-28616004, 28016720, 2807315
Fax : 022-28073151, 28616004

Harison & Co,
23/25, Paradise Lane,
L.J.Road,
Mahim
Mumbai-400016

Indian Glass Agency
39/1, Site No. IV.
Industrial Area,
Sahibabad (Ghaziabad) (U.P)
Phone : 2201385

Indopack
9/110, Anand Parbat Industrial Area,
(Opp. Anand Parbat Police Station),
New Delhi-110005,
Phones : 25729308,2 5742695
Fax : 25752330

Jeffrey & Basack Pvt. Ltd.
29, Madan Mitter Lane.
Kolkata-700006

Kiv Group Industries,
Sunmill Compound,
Lower Parel,
Mumbai-400003

Larsons & Toubro Ltd.
L & T House, Narotham Morarji Marg,
Ballard Estate,
Mumbai-400001
Phones : 022-2268121 (9 Lines)

Lion Engg. Polymer Products
D/3, Surjit Sangam,
Mathuradas Road,
Kandivili (W)
Mumbai-400067
Phone : 28078876

CONTAINERS
(Cardboard,Glass, Plastic,etc)

Agra Bottle Stores
17/37, Prayag Market,
Old Banaras Bank,
Phulatti Bazar,
Agar-282003 (U.P)
Phone : 2367158, 2368116

Alpha Containers
1, Jash Market,
Ring Road,
Surat-395002 (Gujarat)
Phone : 0261-2638100 (5 Lines)
Fax : 0261-2623545, 2623546, 2633217
E-Mail : alpha@alphage.com.
Website : http:// www.alphage.com.

Anand Timber Traders
170, Reay Road,
Mumbai-400010
Phones : 28725768, 28121224, 28514650, 28512098

Arora Metal Industry,
Ist Floor, 66,Ezra Street,
(G.P.O Box No. 2289),
Kolkata-700001
Phone : (033) 22254367, 22254170
Gram. Metal Seal.

Bajaj Glass Enterprises,
B-5/10, Mahesh Nagar,
Goregaon (w),
Mumbai-400062
Phones : 26723867

Bhagwandas Devshi Pvt. Ltd.
87, Shamaldas Gandhi Marg.
Mumbai-400002
Phones : 2311084
Gram. EMBOT

Bharat Associated Industries
P-5, B.R.B. Basu Road,
2nd Floor,
Kolkata-700001
Phones : 2317470

CORKS

Delhi Bottle Stores
142, Tilak Bazar,
Delhi-110006

Duttsinha & Co.
67, Ezra Street,
Kolkata-700001

Indian Agencies
Bari Road,
Bakerganj
Patna -800004

Injecto Pack (India)
G-49, City Centre, 570,
M.G. Road,
Indore-452001 (M.P)
Phones : 2531343, 2472802

J.H. Mehta & Brothers
Dev Ashish,
1st Floor, Near Klassic Gold Hotel,
Ellisbridge,
Ahmedabad-380006
Phones : 26564949, 2404824
Fax : 91-26446646
E-Mail :
jhmehta@ghahd.gbblobal
net.ems.vsnl.net.in

Mukherjee Bottle & Co.
105, Akhil Mistry Lane,
Kolkata-700009
Phones : 033-23508906

New Bottle & Pasti Stores,
Chhotelal's Chawl,
Outside Delhi Gate
Ahmedabad-380004

Nitco (Glassware) Pvt.Ltd
36, Brabourne Road,
Kolkata-700001

Peojee Bottling Co.
63, Bangur Avenue,
Block D. kolkata-700055

CONFECTIONERY

Pioneer Confectionery Works
The18, Bhattacharjee Para Lane
Kolkatta - 700036
Ph:. 52-27657

S.A. Chemicals
4/33, Malad Co-op. Housing Society
Poddar Park, Malad (E)
Mumbai - 400097
Ph:. 91-22-28839590
Fax: 91-22-28835341

Sun Dye Chem
B-4/3092, Vasant Kunj
Aruna Asaf Ali Marg
New Delhi - 110070
Ph:. 26122196, 26122197
Fax: 91-11-6122488

Sayaji Sethness Ltd.
17/18, GVMM, Odhav
Ahmedabad - 382410
Ph:. 079-22876000,
22875100
Fax: 079-22871338
E-Mail :
ssl@maizeproducts.com
Website :
www.maizeproducts.com

COCONUT CREAM

Fresh Coconut Products Ltd.
Kaduppissery P.O.,
Trichur Dist.
Kerala - 680 698
Tel : 0488- 2860871/904/304
Fax : 0488-2860304
Mumbai Off : 87-Q,
Jess Bonn Villa,
1st Floor, Old CST Road,
Kalina,
Santacruz (E), Mumbai - 400029
Tel : 6171343
Fax : 022-26183160

COCOA POWDER

Ace International
13/21, Laura Building
First Dhobi Talao Lane
Mumbai - 400002
Ph:. 22001413, 22008169
Fax: 91-22-22093240

A.L. Chaudhry & Co.
5994, Chaudhry Bhavan
Jawahar Nagar, Delhi - 110007
Ph.: 23918252, 23914778,
22933320

Blue Bird Food Products
441-42-43, Inside Crawford Market
Mumbai - 400001
Ph:. 23438419, 23430153,
23442568

Cadbury India Ltd.
Cadbury House, 19,
Bhulabhai Desai Road
Mumbai - 400026
Ph.: 24939558/59/60/61/
63/66
Fax: 24973181
Fact. 1st Pokharan Road
Thane
Ph.: 25330238/0240
Exec. J.M. Robertson

Delhi : 601/603, Tolstoy House, Tolstoy Marg
New Delhi - 110001
Ph:. 23320358
Fax: 23350266

Cocoa Products & Beverages Ltd.
Mount Poonamallee High Road
Manapakkam,
Chennai - 600089
Ph:. 2432978

Dr. Writer's Food Products Pvt. Ltd.
199, Airlines Building
J. Tata Road Churchgate Reclamation
Mumbai - 400020
Ph.: 22047291, 22047327, 2221863/65

Jai Bharat Products
Sham Wadi, Ranade Road
Dadar (W), Mumbai - 400028
Ph.: 24303624

P.M. Vora & Co.
Ramesh Chamber, First Floor
14, Garibdas Street, Vadgadi
Mumbai - 400003
Ph:. 23438487, 23445367, 23443573
Fax: 23446013
E-Mail : hopl@bom5.vsnl.net.in

CORN SYRUP

Anil Starch Products Ltd.
Anil Road, P.O.Box 10009
Ahmedabad - 380025
Ph:. 22123222
Fax: 22110731

Maize Products
P.O. Kathwada - Maize Products
Ahmedabad - 382430
Ph:. 2887581\85
Fax: 2872438

Riddhi Siddhi Starch Chemicals Ltd.
(GOKAK Div.)
Sri Raghavendra Krupa, No. 85
P.O.Box 8044, 9th Cross Road
Raj Mahal Vilas Extn.
Bangalore - 560080
Ph:. 23344634, 23344658
Fax: 23312004

DEXTRIN

Maize Products
P.O. Kathwada - Maize Products
Ahmedabad - 382430
Ph:. 2887581\85
Fax: 2872438

Rahmath Starch Products
P.O. Thekkumuri
St. Kerala - 679506
Ph:. 0493-2335312

Rajaram And Brothers
11/13, Botawala Bldg., 3rd Floor,
Homiman Circle,
Mumbai - 400 023
Tel : 22661916, 22621239
Fax : 22665868
Fac : at Mandsaur - 458001
Tel : 251135/36/43
Fax : 07422-253291

The Sukhjit Starch & Chemicals Ltd.
609-A, Ansal Chambers-II
Bhikaji Cama Place,
New Delhi - 110066
Ph:. 26171583
Fax: 011-26184322
Also at: Phagwara (Punjab) - 144401
Ph:. 260314, 261516, 262144
Fax: 01824-261669

DEXTROSE

Anil Starch Products Ltd.
Anil Road, P.O.Box 10009
Ahmedabad - 380025
Ph:. 22123222
Fax: 22110731

Maize Products
P.O. Kathwada - Maize Products
Ahmedabad - 382430
Ph:. 2887581\85
Fax: 2872438

Olin Chemicals
A-303, Padmavati Nagar
Gen. Arunkumar Vaidya Marg
Goregaon (E)
Mumbai - 400063
Ph:. 28406988, 28413111
Fax: 28734332

Riddhi Siddhi Starch Chemicals Ltd.
(GOKAK Div.)
Sri Raghavendra Krupa, No. 85
P.O.Box 8044, 9th Cross Road
Raj Mahal Vilas Extn.
Bangalore - 560080
Ph:. 23344634, 23344658
Fax: 23312004

Rajaram And Brothers
11/13, Botawala Bldg., 3rd Floor,
Homiman Circle, Mumbai - 400 023
Tel : 2661916, 2621239
Fax : 2665868
Fac : at Mandsaur - 458001
Tel : 251135/36/43
Fax : 07422-253291

The Sukhjit Starch & Chemicals Ltd.
609-A, Ansal Chambers-II
Bhikaji Cama Place, New Delhi - 110066

Ph:. 6171583
Fax: 011-6184322
Also at: Phagwara (Punjab) - 144401
Ph:. 260314, 261516, 262144
Fax: 01824-261669

S.A. Chemicals
4/33, Malad Co-op. Housing Society
Poddar Park, Malad (E)
Mumbai - 400097
Ph:. 91-22-28839590
Fax: 91-22-28835341

DIACETYL

Kushalchand Sons
Devkaran Mansion, Block No.1
Room No. 07/3, 2nd Floor
79, Princess Street
Mumbai - 400002
Ph:. 208-20937, 205-22190/ 209-20784
Fax: 91-22-208-24265

FAT (CHOCOLATE/ COATING/ CONFECTIONERY)

Kamani Oil Industries
317, Pooran Asha Building
Narsi Natha Street
Mumbai - 400009
Ph:. 23420241,42/43
Fax: 23435964
E-Mail : kamani@bom2.vsnl.net.in

FLAVOURS/ COLOURS/ PRESERVATIVES/ ESSENCE & EMULSIONS

M/s. Amit Fine Chem
A-32, Siddhi Apartment
Ashok Nagar, Kandivali (E)
Mumbai - 400101
Ph:. 28870920
Fax: 28871551
(Citric Acid, Sodium Benzoate, Flavours, Preservatives)

M/s. Bayer India Ltd.
Bayer House, Central Avenue
Hiranandani Gardens, Powai
Mumbai - 400076
Ph:. 25779300
Tele/Fax: 25777732
(Flavours)

M/s. FAB Flavours & Fragrances Pvt. Ltd.
B-16, Phase-II, S.A.S. Nagar
Mohali - 160055
Ph:. 0172-2672305, 2673521
Fax: 91-0172-2674469
Also at: 70-A, Rama Road, New Delhi - 110015
Ph:. 25431556
Fax: 25104412
(Food Colour, Preparations Fragrances & Food Additives etc.)

Fragrance Flavour & Perfumes
GH-13/53, Paschim Vihar
New Delhi - 110084
Ph:. 25259771

M/s. Fine Organics
(Food Chemicals Division)
15/2, Neelkanth Market, M.G. Road
Ghatkopar (East), Mumbai - 400077
Ph:. 25116900,02/ 25154384/ 5154380/ 25154495
Fax: 91-022-25153215, 25162276
(Finacon-Cac-Beverage Clouding Agent Concentrate, Food Emulsifiers, Glyceryl Mono Stearate, Sodium Stearoyl-2-Lactylate, Whipped Topping Concentrates etc.)

M/s. Haarmann & Reimer GmbH
P.O. Box 1253, D-37601, Holzminden
Germany
Ph:. +49-5531-900
Tele/Fax: +49-5531-2901649
(Flavours)

M/s. High Tech Flavors
Saraswati Niwas
V.S.Agashe Road, Dadar (W), Mumbai - 400028
Ph:. 24372164
(Flavours for Jam, Jellies, Processed Food etc.)

M/s. Integrated Trading Company
150/51, Reay Raod (W)
Mumbai - 400033
Ph:. 23727378, 23737092
Fax: 91-22-23738794
(Food Colours & Additives)

M/s. Jani Industries
291, Samuel Street
Mumbai - 400003
Ph:. 23444225
Fax: 91-22-23423026
(Food Colours)

M/s. Kushal Chand Sons
Devkaran Mansion, Block No. 1
2nd Floor, Room No. 07/ 3,79,
Princess Street,
Mumbai - 400002
Ph:. 22080937, 22052190, 22090784
Fax: 91-22-22084265
(All Kind of Food Additives such as Flavour Enhancers, Preservatives, Antioxidants, Proteins, Citric Acids & other Food Chemicals)

M/s. L. Liladhar & Company
257-259, Samuel Street
Vadgadi, Mumbai - 400003
Ph:. 23422988, 23447690
(Food Colour & Flavours)

M/s. Liberty Chemical Works
Mogra Road, Off. Nagardas Road
Andheri (E),
Mumbai - 400069
Ph:. 28326420, 28326480
Fax: 26121892
(Food Preservative Chemicals)

Nova Flavours & Fragrances Pvt. Ltd.
Lakhmids Bhuvan, Room No.4
First Floor, 88/92, V.V. Chandan Street
Vadgadi, Mumbai - 400003
Ph:. 23438487, 23445367, 23443573
Fax: 91-22-23446013
E-Mail : hopl@bom5.vsnl.net.in
(Flavours, Emulsions & Paste)

M/s. Narmada Food Colours Pvt. Lts.
Sanghrajka House, 4th Floor
431, Dr. Dadasahed Bhadkamkar Marg
Opera House,
Mumbai - 400004
Ph:. 23801315/16
Fax: 23801337
(ISI Marked Primary & Blended Food Colours)

M/s. Perfect Chemicals
1, New Navyug House
14, Dhirubhai Parikh Marg
Princess Street, Mumbai - 400002
Ph:. 22017623, 22062483, 22063378, 22006427
Fax: 22017623
(Food Chemicals Including Citric Acid, Orange Oil, Pectin, Sodium Bicarbonate etc.)

M/s. Roha Dyechem Ltd.
Suryodaya Mill Compound
M.P. Mill Road, Tardeo,
Mumbai - 400034
Ph:. 24939006, 24945924, 4920855, 4947847
Fax: 022-24939795, 24952631
(Food Colours & Lake Colours)

M/s. Radha Sales Corporation
304, AVG Bhavan, M-3,
Connaught Circus
New Delhi - 110001
Ph:. +91-11-23324100, 23352200
Fax: +91-11-23317776, 3712563
(Fruits Oils, Flavours, Food Grade)

M/s. Robin Chemicals Pvt. Ltd.
103, N.M.M. Road
Aminjikaraj, Chennai - 600029
Ph:. 24802806, 24837514
Fax: 044-24802220
(Flavouring Essences, Food Colours)

M/s. Royal Marketing
No. 11, 1 Cross Street
Loest C.I.T. Nagar, Chennai - 600035
Ph:. 2456023, 2455726
(Colours, Foodgrade)

M/s. S. Chandanmull Mutha
2, Nyniappa Niack Street
Chennai - 600003 (T.N)
Ph:. 25355609, 25350999
(Additves, Foodgrade, Chemicals Food Grade, Colours & Flavours Food Grade)

M/s. S. Flavours & Fragrances India
Nava Vivek Industrial Estate
Mogul Lane, Mahim, Mumbai - 400016
Ph:. 2466671, 2467983
(Food Grade Flavours)

Sun Dye Chem
B-4/3092, Vasant Kunj
Aruna Asaf Ali Marg
New Delhi - 110070
Ph:. 26122196, 26122197
Fax: 91-11-26122488

M/s. Sharda Trading Company
22, Commercial Chambers
First Floor, 179 Yusuf Meherali Road
Mumbai - 400003
Ph:. 23414401, 23427874
Fax: 3427865
(Citric Acid & other Food Chemicals)

M/s. Sesu International
Room No. 2, 4th Floor Sai Chambers, 367/69
N. Natha Street, Mumbai - 400009
Ph:. 23414444, 23426402
Fax: 022-23420832
(Citric Acid, Chemicals Food Grade)

M/s. Sibco Enterprises
10, Ezra Street
Kolkatta - 700001
Ph:. 2266239, 2265500
(Chemicals Food Grade)

M/s. Sterling Chemi Pharma
11/11 1st Floor, Mani Bhuvan-C
S.V. Road, Goregaon (W)
Mumbai - 400062
Ph:. 2872406, 28732061
(Citric Acid, Orange Oil, Acetic Acid)

M/s. Sun Dye Chem
B-4/3092, Vasant Kunj
Aruna Asaf Ali Marg
New Delhi - 110070
Ph:. 26122196, 26122197
Fax: 91-11-26122488
(Foodgrade, Additives, Food Colours, Food Chemicals)

M/s. Superchem Corporation
129/3, Suraj Villa, Bhaudaji Road
Matunga, Mumbai - 400019
Ph:. 24373210
(Foodgrade)

M/s. Synthite Industrial Chemicals Pvt. Ltd.
Synthite Valley, Kudayiruppu
Kolenchery - 682311
Ph:. 484-2760285, 2760316, 760652
Fax: 484-2760367
(Colours, Foodgrade)

M/s. Techno Process Consultants
D-26, Green Park (Main)
New Delhi - 110016
Ph:. 26518862
Fax: 011-26850045
(Processed Food Products Flavours)

M/s. The Aromatic Chemical & oil Co.
Ponpadi R.S. & P.O. 631213
Chengai Mgr. Distt., Tamil Nadu
Ph:. 041182-88322/04118-288344
Fax: 91-44-25341022
(Flavour, Foodgrade)

M/s. Venkatesh Chemicals
B-18, Vipul Apartments, Bhakti Marg
Mulund (W), Mumbai - 400080
Ph:. 23451021, 23451168
Fax: 23450331
(Food Colours)

Uma Brothers
C-110, Bhaveshwar Plaza
189, L.B.S. Marg,
Ghatkopar (W)
Mumbai - 400086
Ph:. 25004579, 25004510
Fax: 091-22-25000015
E-Mail :
umabroth@bom5.vsnl.net.in

M/s. Vital Neutraceuticals Pvt. Ltd.
5/6 B, Maruti Darshan CHS, Plot RX-4
MIDC Residential Area,
Dombivli (E) - 421203
Ph:. 2462774, 2455056
(Protein Hydrolysate (Soya & Caseine) for Food)

M/s. Vijay Industries
C/o. Eagle Trading Co., B/H Sadhna Talkies
Sultanpura, Vadodara - 390001
Ph:. 2460495, 2432439
(Flavouring Essences, Food Colours)

M/s. Vim Flavours
Viniketan, 1,
Krishna Society
Old Padra Road, Vadodara - 390015
Ph:. 2670488
(Flavours, Foodgrade)

M/s. Yash & Company
No. 157, B.V.K. Lyengar Road
Bangalore - 560053
Ph:. 228350
(Flavours, Foodgrade)

FOOD GUMS

Ace International
13/21, Laura Building
First Dhobi Talao Lane
Mumbai - 400002
Ph:. 22001413, 22008169
Fax: 91-22-2093240

Alok Chem Corp.
406, Garodia House
100/104, Kazi Sayed Street
Mumbai - 400003
Ph:. 23426390/ 5365/ 23415668
Fax: 91-22-23415668
E-Mail :
alokchem@bom2.vsnl.net.in

Indian Gum Industries Ltd.
401, Navbharat Estate
Zakaria Bunder Road,
Sewri (W)
Mumbai - 400015
Ph:. 091-022-24158059
Fax: 091-022-24158074/75
E-Mail :
kdesai@lucidgroup.com
E-Mail :
sbade@lucidgroup.com

Olin Chemicals
A-303, Padmavati Nagar
Gen. Arunkumar Vaidya Marg
Goregaon (E)
Mumbai - 400063
Ph:. 28406988, 28413111
Fax: 28734332

Kushalchand Sons
Devkaran Mansion, Block No.1
Room No. 07/3, 2nd Floor
79, Princess Street
Mumbai - 400002
Ph:. 208-20937, 205-22190/ 209-20784
Fax: 91-22-208-24265

Uma Brothers
C-110, Bhaveshwar Plaza
189, L.B.S. Marg, Ghatkopar (W)
Mumbai - 400086
Ph:. 25004579, 25004510
Fax: 091-22-25000015
E-Mail :
umabroth@bom5.vsnl.net.in

Kapadia Gumchem Industries
3, Mint Road, Room No. 30
2nd Floor, P.O.Box. No. 1160
Fort, Mumbai - 400001
Ph:. 22695073, 22659091, 22617217
Fax: 91-22-22619423

S.A. Chemicals
220, Udyog Bhavan, Sonawala Road
Goregaon (E),
Mumbai - 400063
Ph:. 28764700
Fax: 91-22-28769532
E-Mail : sac@sachemicals.com

GLUCOSE SYRUP

Anil Starch Products Ltd.
Anil Road, P.O.Box 10009
Ahmedabad - 380025
Ph:. 22123222
Fax: 22110731

Maize Products
P.O. Kathwada - Maize Products
Ahmedabad - 382430
Ph:. 2887581\85
Fax: 2872438

Rajaram And Brothers
11/13, Botawala Bldg., 3rd Floor,
Homiman Circle, Mumbai - 400 023
Tel : 22661916, 22621239
Fax : 22665868
Fac : at Mandsaur - 458001
Tel : 251135/36/43
Fax : 07422-253291

The Sukhjit Starch & Chemicals Ltd.
609-A, Ansal Chambers-II
Bhikaji Cama Place, New Delhi - 110066
Ph:. 26171583
Fax: 011-26184322
Also at: Phagwara (Punjab) - 144401
Ph:. 260314, 261516, 262144
Fax: 01824-261669

S.A. Chemicals
4/33, Malad Co-op. Housing Society
Poddar Park, Malad (E)
Mumbai - 400097
Ph:. 91-22-28839590
Fax: 91-22-28835341

GLUTEN

Rajaram And Brothers
11/13, Botawala Bldg.,
3rd Floor,
Homiman Circle,
Mumbai - 400 023
Tel : 22661916, 22621239
Fax : 22665868
Fac : at Mandsaur - 458001
Tel : 251135/36/43
Fax : 07422-253291

Riddhi Siddhi Starch Chemicals Ltd.
(GOKAK Div.)
Sri Raghavendra Krupa, No. 85
P.O.Box 8044, 9th Cross Road
Raj Mahal Vilas Extn.
Bangalore - 560080
Ph:. 23344634, 23344658
Fax: 23312004

The Sukhjit Starch & Chemicals Ltd.
609-A, Ansal Chambers-II
Bhikaji Cama Place, New Delhi - 110066
Ph:. 26171583
Fax: 011-26184322
Also at: Phagwara (Punjab) - 144401
Ph:. 260314, 261516, 262144
Fax: 01824-261669

G.M.S

Ace International
13/21, Laura Building
First Dhobi Talao Lane
Mumbai - 400002
Ph:. 22001413, 22008169
Fax: 91-22-22093240

Kushalchand Sons
Devkaran Mansion,
Block No.1
Room No. 07/3,
2nd Floor
79, Princess Street
Mumbai - 400002
Ph:. 208-20937, 205-22190/ 209-20784
Fax: 91-22-208-24265

P.M. Vora & Co.
Ramesh Chamber, First Floor
14, Garibdas Street, Vadgadi
Mumbai - 400003
Ph:. 23438487, 23445367, 23443573
Fax: 23446013
E-Mail : hopl@bom5.vsnl.net.in

GELATINE

Amrutlal Bhurabhai & Co.
Anand Bhawan, Princess Street
Mumbai - 400002
Ph:. 22011023, 22011024, 22068856, 22050235, 22019187
Exec. Hemant L. Pandaya

Blue Bird Food Products
441-42-43, Inside Crawford Market
Mumbai - 400001
Ph:. 23438419, 23430153, 23442568
Exec. Anantrai S. Shah

Bombay Sales Agency
93/5, Dr. Maheshwari Road
Marine House, Mumbai - 400009
Ph:. 23721670, 23735032
Fax: 23735032
Exec. A.N. Surani

Crown Foods Co.
55/57, Budhavihar Marg
Two Tank, Mumbai - 400008
Ph:. 23099579, 23078467
Fax: 23096057

Gobinram Chellaram & Co.
Gaumukh Bhavan, 2nd Floor
18, Masjid, Mumbai - 400009
Ph:. 23751673

Hindustan Drug House
867/8, Joshi Road, Karol Bagh
New Delhi - 110005
Ph:. 27525302, 27524566
Fax: 27524566

P.M. Vora & Co.
Ramesh Chamber, First Floor
14, Garibdas Street, Vadgadi
Mumbai - 400003
Ph:. 23438487, 23445367, 23443573
Fax: 23446013
E-Mail : hopl@bom5.vsnl.net.in

ICING SUGAR

Blue Bird Food Products
441-42-43, Inside Crawford Market, Mumbai - 400001
Ph:. 23438419, 23430153, 23442568

Milk Farm Fresh Foods
Milk Farm Nagar
Gupta Prayag Road
Delwada - 362510 (Guj)
Ph:. 02875-222562

Hindustan Drug House
867/8, Joshi Road, Karol Bagh
New Delhi - 110005
Ph:. 27525302, 27524566
Fax: 27524566

INVERT SYRUPS

S.A. Chemicals
220, Udyog Bhavan,
Sonawala Road
Goregaon (E),
M umbai - 400063
Ph:. 28764700
Fax: 91-22-28769532
E-Mail : sac@sachemicals.com

LECITHIN

Kushalchand Sons
Devkaran Mansion, Block No.1
Room No. 07/3, 2nd Floor
79, Princess Street
Mumbai - 400002
Ph:. 208-20937, 205-22190/ 209-20784
Fax: 91-22-208-24265

P.M. Vora & Co.
Ramesh Chamber, First Floor, 14, Garibdas Street, Vadgadi
Mumbai - 400003
Ph:. 23438487, 23445367, 23443573
Fax: 23446013
E-Mail : hopl@bom5.vsnl.net.in

MALTO DEXTRIN

Rajaram And Brothers
11/13, Botawala Bldg., 3rd Floor,
Homiman Circle, Mumbai - 400 023
Tel : 22661916, 22621239
Fax : 22665868
Fac : at Mandsaur - 458001
Tel : 251135/36/43
Fax : 07422-253291

Riddhi Siddhi Starch Chemicals Ltd.
(GOKAK Div.)
Sri Raghavendra Krupa, No. 85
P.O.Box 8044, 9th Cross Road
Raj Mahal Vilas Extn.
Bangalore - 560080
Ph:. 23344634, 23344658
Fax: 23312004

S.A. Chemicals
4/33, Malad Co-op. Housing Society
Poddar Park, Malad (E)
Mumbai - 400097
Ph:. 91-22-28839590
Fax: 91-22-28835341

MILK POWDER

P.M. Vora & Co.
Ramesh Chamber, First Floor
14, Garibdas Street, Vadgadi
Mumbai - 400003
Ph:. 23438487, 23445367, 23443573
Fax: 23446013
E-Mail : hopl@bom5.vsnl.net.in

S.A. Chemicals
4/33, Malad Co-op. Housing Society
Poddar Park, Malad (E)
Mumbai - 400097
Ph:. 91-22-28839590
Fax: 91-22-28835341

SUGAR PASTE

Indo Bakel Pvt. Ltd.,
43C, Mittal Tower,
Nariman Point,
Mumbai - 400 021
Tel : 22873636, 2288 1025
Fax : 22020065

STARCH

Anil Starch Products Ltd.
Anil Road, P.O.Box 10009
Ahmedabad - 380025
Ph:. 22123222
Fax: 22110731

Geeta Trading Company,
2105, Khari Baoli,
New Delhi - 110 006
Tel : 22513852

Ganga Bishan & Sons
142, Gadodia Market
Kari Baoli, Delhi - 110006
Ph:. 22943682

Md. Nasimuddin, I.A.S
Sagoserve, Salem - 636302
Ph:. 2447673, 2448046
Fax: 0427-2445028

National Starch & Chemical Co.
10, Finderne Avenue
P.O.Box 6500
Bridgewater,
New Jersey - 08807 90500
908 685 5000
Website :
www.nationalstarch.com

Punjab Maize Products Ltd.
Uppli Road,
Sangroor,
Punjab - 148 001
Tel : 234209
Fax : 230615

Punjab Maize Products Ltd.
A-8, DLF Indl. Area - 1,
Faridabad - 121 003 (Hr.)
Tel : 22765 50
Fax : 22768 84

Rajaram And Brothers
11/13, Botawala Bldg.,
3rd Floor,
Homiman Circle,
Mumbai - 400 023
Tel : 22661916, 22621239
Fax : 22665868
Fac : at Mandsaur - 458001
Tel : 251135/36/43
Fax : 07422-253291

Rahmath Starch Products
P.O. Thekkumuri
St. Kerala - 679506
Ph:. 0493-2335312

Riddhi Siddhi Starch Chemicals Ltd.
(GOKAK Div.)
Sri Raghavendra Krupa,
No. 85
P.O.Box 8044, 9th Cross Road
Raj Mahal Vilas Extn.
Bangalore - 560080
Ph:. 23344634, 23344658
Fax: 23312004

S.A. Chemicals
4/33, Malad Co-op. Housing Society
Poddar Park, Malad (E)
Mumbai - 400097
Ph:. 91-22-28839590
Fax: 91-22-28835341

S.A. Chemicals
220, Udyog Bhavan,
Sonawala Road
Goregaon (E),
Mumbai - 400063
Ph:. 8764700
Fax: 91-22-28769532
E-Mail :
sac@sachemicals.com

Hindustan Starch & Chemicals
2125, Tilak Bazar,
Khari Baoli,
New Delhi - 110 006
Tel : 23929329

The Sukhjit Starch & Chemicals Ltd.
609-A, Ansal Chambers-II
Bhikaji Cama Place, New Delhi - 110066
Ph:. 26171583
Fax: 011-26184322
Also at: Phagwara (Punjab) - 144401
Ph:. 260314, 261516, 262144
Fax: 01824-261669

117. MANUFACTURE OF TIN CONTAINERS
118. MANUFACTURE OF STORAGE TANKS, PRESSURE VESSELS, HEAT EXCHANGERS
119. MARK II HAND PUMPS
120. MARUTI WORKSHOP CUM - SERVICE STATION
121. MECHANICAL JACKS
122. METAL CUTTING DIE DESIGN
123. METAL CUTTING OF AND GRINDING WHEELS (ABBRASIVE CUTTING WHEELS)
124. METAL HOOKS & CLIPS
125. METAL SEPARATION (COPPER, TIN, LEAD) FROM SPENT WASH ACID
126. METALLIC RING JOINTS
127. METALLIC GASKET (SPIRAL WOUND)
128. MICROVEE & ABSOLUTE FILTER
129. MICROWAVE OVEN
130. MILD STEEL INGOTS
131. MINI STEEL PLANT
132. MODERN VEHICLE WORKSHOP
133. MOPED
134. M.S.HINGES
135. M.S.INGOT AND HR. STEEL STRUCTURALS
136. M.S.INGOT BY INDUCTION FURNACES
137. M.S.PIPES
138. M.S. WELDING ELECTRODE
139. MUFFLERS & SILENCERS FOR THREE WHEELERS
140. NAIL CUTTER WITH FILER & MANICURE
141. NICHROME WIRE
142. NICKEL LINED SCREENS
143. NON-FERROUS ALLOY ROLLING
144. NON-FERROUS FORGING
145. NON-FERROUS FOUNDRY
146. NON PRESSURE
147. INCANDESCENT LAMP
148. NUMBER COMBINATION LOCKS FOR LUGGAGES
149. NUTS & BOLTS
150. PAPER COATED ALUMINIUM AND COPPER WIRE
151. PETROMAX CONTAINER
152. PHOTO ETCHING OF STAINLESS STEEL PLATES
153. PIPE GALVANIZING PLANT
154. PISTON RING-AUTOMOBILE
155. PLANT PROTECTION EQUIPMENTS
156. PLATINUM LABORATORY APPARATUS
157. PRESSURE COOKER & ALUMINIUM UTENSILS
158. PRESSURE COOKER (ALUMINIUM)
159. PRESSURE DIE CASTING
160. PRINTED ALUMINIUM COLLAPSIBLE TUBES
161. PRINTED TIN CONTAINERS
162. PRINTING PRESS (CYLINDER MACHINE)
163. PUMPS FOR CHEMICAL INDUSTRY (SPECIAL)
164. RAILWAY SLEEPERS (M.S.)
165. RAZOR TWIN BLADE
166. R.C.C SPUN PIPES
167. RECONDITIONING OF M.S. DRUMS/BARRELS
168. RE-ROLLING COPPER AND BRASS SHEET AND RODS
169. RE-ROLLING MILLS
170. RESIN COATED SAND
171. RESIN CORED SOFT SOLDER WIRES
172. ROLLING MILL (BY INDUCTION FURNACE) & MANUFACTURE OF BARS, ANGLES, SQUARES, TUBES AND OTHERS
173. ROLLER BEARING & FORGING
174. ROLLING OF STAINLESS STEEL PATTA
175. RUBBER INSULATED PLIERS (HAND TOOLS)
176. RUBBING COMPOUND FOR AUTOMOBILES
177. SCIENTIFIC LABORATORY EQUIPMENTS
178. SCOOTER ASSEMBLING
179. SECONDARY LEAD EXTRAC -TION BY SCRAP BATTERY PLATES,PIPES & SHEET
180. SEAMLESS M.S. TUBES & PIPES
181. SELF TAPPING STEEL SCREW
182. SEWING NEEDLES
183. S.G. IRON & ALLOY STEEL
184. SHEET METAL PRODUCTS, (FERROUS/NON-FERROUS)
185. SHIP/MARINE CONTAINER
186. SHOCK ABSORBERS
187. SHOE EYELETS
188. SHOT AND GRITS BY AUTOMIZATION PROCESS
189. SHOVELS
190. SILICO MANGANESE ALLOYS
191. SILENCERS (MUFFLERS) EXHAUST & TAIL PIPE FOR ALL TYPES OF VEHICLES
192. SINTERED BEARING
193. SINTERED BUSHES
194. SINTERED METAL PRODUCTS
195. SOFT AND HARD FERRITES
196. SPANNERS
197. SPARK PLUGS
198. STEEL PLANT (ELECTRIC ARC FURNACE BASED- EAF)
199. SPHERIODAL GRAPHITE CAST IRON
200. SPRAY DRYER
201. STAINLESS STEEL HINGES
202. STAINLESS STEEL SHEET ROLLING TO PRODUCE STAINLESS STEEL UTENSILS
203. STAINLESS STEEL UTENSILS
204. STAPLE PINS,PAPER PIN, GEM CLIPS ETC.
205. STEEL CASTINGS
206. STEEL CHAIN
207. STEEL FOUNDRY
208. STEEL FURNITURES AND ELECTRICAL APPLIANCES
209. STEEL PLANT (MINI)
210. STEEL RODS AND COILS FROM SCRAPS
211. STEEL ROLLING MILL
212. STEEL STRIPS (COLD ROLLED) SILICON WITH GRAIN RIENTED FOR ELECTRIC USE
213. STEEL TRANSMISSION LINE TOWERS & ROLLING MILL TO PRODUCE STEEL SECTION
214. STEEL FURNITURES AND ELECTRICAL APPLIANCES
215. STEEL WIRE DRAWING AND GALVANIZING
216. STEEL WOOL
217. SUBMERGED ARC WELDED PIPES
218. SUBMERSIBLE PUMP MANUFACTURING
219. SUPER ENAMELLED COPPER WIRE
220. THREE WHEELERS
221. TIE-ROD ENDS
222. TIN CONTAINERS
223. TOOLROOM AND SHEET METAL PRODUCTS
224. TRACTOR TRAILERS
225. TRANSMISSION POWER FITTING
226. TUBULAR POLES
227. SUPER ENAMELLED COPPER WIRES
228. TUBULAR POLES FOR ELECTRICAL TRANSMISSION (BY FABRICATION PROCESS)
229. TUBULAR POLES OF M.S. & HIGH TENSILE STEEL
230. VACUUM CLEANERS
231. VACUUM FLASK (STAINLESS STEEL)
232. VALVES FOR REFRIGERA TION AND AIR-CONDITION
233. VEHICLE WELDING & PAINTING
234. VENETION BLIND
235. WASHING MACHINES (AUTOMATIC & COMPUTERISED)
236. WATER CONTROLLER (AUTOMATIC)
237. WATCH STRAPS/CHAINS/ BRACELETS/BELT BRASS & STAINLESS STEEL
238. WATER COOLERS
239. WELDED WIRE MESH
240. WELDING ELECTRODES
241. WICK STOVES
242. WIND MILL WINDOW FRAME (FERROUS & NON-FERROUS)
243. WRIST WATCH

359. DI ETHYL OXALATE
360. DI METHYL ORTHOPHTHALATE
361. DI-METHYL PHTHALATE
362. DICLOFENAC GEL
363. DIOCTYL PHTHALATE (DOP)
364. DI PHENYL GLYCERINE
365. DI PHENYL OXIDE
366. DINITRO-CHLORO BENZENE
367. DISTILLED WATER
368. DODECYL BENZENE SULPHONATE
369. DUSTLESS CHALK
370. EDTA & ITS SALTS
371. ELECTROLESS NICKEL PLATING ON PLASTICS
372. ENDOSULFAN
373. EPOXY RESIN BASED COMPOUND
374. ETHYL ACETATE
375. EHTYL ETHER
376. ETHYL ALCOHOL (POTABLE LIQUOR)
377. ETHYL HEXANOL
378. EXTRACTION OF ESSENTIAL OILS BY SUGAR CRITICAL FLUID (CARBON DIOXIDE) METHOD FROM FLOWERS, HERBAL & SPICES
379. FERRIC ALUM
380. FERRO CHROME LIGNO SULPHONATE
381. FERRO MANGANESE
382. FERRO SILICONE
383. FERRO VANADIUM FROM VANADIUM SLUDGE
384. FERROUS SILICATE
385. FERROUS SULPHATE
386. FERTILIZER FROM ANIMAL BLOOD & LEATHER WASTE
387. FLUORESCENT TUBE LIGHT POWDER
388. FOAMED PVC COMPOUNDING & ITS PRODUCTS
389. FORMALDEHYDE
390. FRACTIONAL DISTILLATION OF D.M.O (DEMENTHOLIZED OIL)
391. FRACTIONAL DISTILLATION OF ESSENTIAL OIL & MEDICINAL PLANT EXTRACT
392. FRICTION DUST (LIQUID & POWDER) FROM CNSL
393. FRUIT FLAVOURS
394. FURFURAL FROM RICE HUSK
395. GARLIC ACID
396. GASKET SHELLAC COMPOUND
397. GEAR OIL
398. GIBBERELLIC ACID
399. GLASS PUTTY
400. GLYCERINE
401. GOSSYPOL (POLY PHENOL) FROM COTTON SEED OIL
402. GUAR GUM POWDER
403. HAIR FIXER (HAIR GEL TYPE)
404. H - ACID
405. HENNA PASTE MAKING
406. HEPTAL DEHYDE
407. HIGH CARBON FERRO CHROME
408. HYDRATED CALCIUM SILICATE BRICK
409. HYDRATED LIME FROM SEA SHELL
410. HYDROCHLORIC ACID
411. HYDRO FLUORIC ACID
412. HYDROGEN PEROXIDE (BY AUTO-OXIDATION PROCESS)
413. ICE PACKS (SOLUTIONS TYPE, WHITE GEL TYPE, VIOLET SEMI SOLID POLYMER TYPE)
414. IMPROVING DROP POINT PARAFFIN WAX FROM 45-50°C TO 75-80°C
415. INDUSTRIAL ALCOHOL
416. INTEGERATED COMPLEX OF EASTER & ALLIED PRODUCTS (D.O.P, D.B.P, ETHYL ACETATE WIRE ENAMEL & CABLE JELLY)
417. IMFL (WHISKY) & COUNTRY LIQUOR
418. IRON OXIDE FOR MAKING FERITTE
419. IRON SULPHIDE
420. JUTE BATCHING OIL
421. KESH KALA TEL (HAIR DYE LOTION) (VASMOL 33, BLACK NITE TYPE)
422. L-LYSINE MONOHYDROCHLORIDE
423. LACTIC ACID FROM WHITE SUGAR BY FERMENTATION PROCESS
424. LDPE GRANULES FROM VIRGIN (LDPE RESIN)
425. LEAD EXTRACTION FROM BATTERY SCRAP
426. LEAD OXIDE (A) LEAD MONOXIDE (B) LEAD TETRA OXIDE (C) GREYLEAD OXIDE
427. LIQUID GLUCOSE & ITS BY PRODUCTS
428. LIQUID OXYGEN BOTTLING PLANT
429. LIQUID SHOE POLISH
430. LIQUID FLOOR POLISH
431. LUBE OIL VISCOSITY IMPROVED FOR P.P.G/P.E.G.
432. LUBRICANTS ASHLESS 100% COMBUSTION
433. MAGNESIUM CARBONATE AND MAGNESIUM BICARMONATE
434. MAGNESIUM HYDROXIDE POWDER
435. MAGNESIUM SILICATE
436. MAGNESIUM SULPHATE
437. MALACHITE GREEN
438. MALEIC ANHYDRIDE
439. MANGANESE SULPHATE
440. MANUFACTURING OF CARBON MONO-OXIDE WATER GAS
441. MENTHOL BOLD CRYSTALS FROM FLAKES
442. MENTHOL CRYSTAL & MENTHA OIL
443. MERCURIC OXIDE
444. METAL PRE-TREATMENT CHEMICALS
445. METHANE GAS BY SODIUM ACETATE & SODA LIME
446. METHYL ACETYL RICINOLATE
447. METOL
448. METOL FROM HYDROQUINONE & METHYLAMINE
449. MICANITE
450. MICRO NUTRIENT MIXTURE
451. MINERAL WATER
452. MINERAL WATER AND PET BOTTILNG PLANT
453. MINERAL WATER IN BOTTLES, GLASS AND POUCHES
454. MINI CEMENT PLANT (BY ROTARY KILN PROCESS)
455. MIXED FERTILIZER
456. MOSQUITO & FLIES REPELLENT AGARBATTI (INCENSE STICKS)
457. MONO CHLORO ACETIC ACID
458. MONOCROTOPHOS (TECHNICAL)
459. MOSQUITO COIL
460. MOSQUITO COIL & MAT
461. MOSQUITO MAT
462. MOTHER TINCTURE & BIO CHEMIC MEDICINES
463. NAPHTHALENE & PHENYL (INTEGRATED UNIT)
464. NATURAL MINERAL WATER BY REVERSE OSMOSIS PROCESS
465. NICKEL PLATING BRIGHTNER (PRIMARY OR CARRIER BRIGHTNER & SECONDARY BRIGHTNER)
466. NICKEL SULPHATE
467. NICOTINE FROM TOBACCO WASTE
468. NICOTINE SULPHATE FROM TOBACCO WASTE
469. NITRO BENZENE
470. NITRO CELLULOSE SANDING SEALER/LACQUER
471. NITRO MUSK
472. NITROGEN & OXYGEN GAS PLANT
473. NON-IONIC SURFACTANT (WETTING AGENT)
474. NO-CARB PASTE
475. OCTANOL
476. ORTHO NITRO PHENOL
477. OXALIC ACID FROM MOLASSES
478. OXALIC ACID FROMRICE HUSK
479. OXALIC ACID FROM TREE BARK
470. OXALIC ACID FROM WASTE VEGETABLES
471. OXYGEN GAS PLANT
472. OXYGEN GAS PLANT (AIR SEPERATION METHOD)
473. PARA-AMINO BENZOIC ACID
474. PARA-AMINO PHENOL
475. PARA TOLUENE SULPHONIC ACID
476. PECTIN FROM RAW PAPAYA
477. PERFUME (LEMON & OTHERS)

CRUDE NAPHTHA
570. TRIMETHYL AMMONIUM CHLORIDE
571. TRIPHENYL PHOSPHITE (T.P.P)
572. ULTRAMARINE BLUE (LIQUID)
573. UREA FORMALDEHYDE & MELAMINE FORMALDEHYDE POWDER
574. UNDECYLINIC ACID
575. VINYL ACETATE MONOMER
576. VITAMIN C
577. VITAMIN E
578. WASTE WATER TREATMENT PLANT FOR INDUSTRIAL SECTOR IN INDIA (ONLY MARKER SURVEY)
579. WIRE DRAWING LUBRICANT
580. WIRE ENAMEL
581. XANTHATES
582. YELLOW DEXTRIN
583. ZINC CHLORIDE
584. ZINC OXIDE
585. ZINC PHOSPHATING BY COLD PROCESS
586. ZINC SILICATE
587. ZINC STEARATE
588. ZINC SULPHATE
589. ZINC SULPHATE MONOHYDRATE
590. ACID BLACK
591. AURAMINE'O'
592. AZO DYES STUFF
593. DYE & DYE INTERMEDIATE
594. DYE INTERMEDIATES
595. MALACHITE GREEN
596. METHYLENE BLUE
597. PHTHALOCYANINE BLUE
598. PHTHALOCYANINE BLUE & GREEN
599. REACTIVE DYES
600. SULPHUR BLACK DYE
601. VAT DYES
602. WATER CHILLING PLANT
603. WADDING OIL (100%) FOR WADDING OF COTTON HOSIERY CLOTH IN THE DYEING PROCESS
604. WHITE OIL
605. WAX FLOOR POLISH

ELECTRICAL, ELECTONICS, COMPUTERS AND INFOTECH/IT PROJECTS

606. AIR CONDITIONING
607. ALUMINIUM ALLOY CONDUCTOR
608. ALUMINIUM CABLE
609. ALUMINIUM ELECTROYTIC CAPACITORS
610. AUDIO CASSETTE ASSEMBLING & RECORDING
611. AUDIO CASSETTES DUPLICATING RECORDING
612. AUDIO CASSETTES & AUDIO STUDIO
613. AUDIO CASSETTES PLANE & RECORDED
614. AUDIO MAGNETIC HEADS
615. AUDIO MAGNETIC TAPE
616. AUDIO/VIDEO CASSETTES
617. AUTO BULB/LAMPS
618. AUTOMATIC VOLTAGE STABILIZER
619. BATTERY PLATES
620. BACK OFFICE (Rs. 5000/-)
621. B/W TV & COMPUTER MONITOR PICTURE TUBE
622. BREAD BOARDS
623. CALL CENTRE
624. CAMERA (35 MM)
625. CAPACITORS
626. CARBON ELECTRODE USED FOR BATTERY CELL
627. CARBON POTETIOMETERS
628. CEILING FAN
629. CERAMIC INSULATOR
630. CHILDREN INFOTECH TRAINING INSTITUTE (Rs. 5000/-)
631. CHOKE AND PATTI
632. CHOKE AND STARTER
633. CHOKE USED FOR FLUORESCENT LAMPS
634. COLOUR TELEVISION
635. COLOUR AND BLACK & WHITE TELEVISION
636. COMPACT DISC
637. COMPACT DISC PLAYER (AUDIO/VIDEO)
638. COMPUTER EDUCATION INSTITUTE
639. COMPUTER ASSEMBLY
640. COMPUTER HARDWARE
641. COMPUTER KEYBOARD
642. COMPUTER PERIPHERALS
643. COMPUTER PRINTERS
644. COMPUTER RIBBON
645. COMPUTER RIBBON REINKING OR REFILLING
646. COMPUTER STATIONERY
647. COMPUTER STATIONERY &

IMPORTED HARDWARE PARTS
648. COMPUTER TERMINALS
649. COMPUTERISED WASHING MACHINE (AUTOMATIC)
650. COMPUTER SOFTWARE
651. CONDENSER FOR MOTOR USING MPP FILM
652. CONTENT DEVELOPMENT CENTRE (EOU) (Rs. 5000/-)
653. CONTROL PANEL BOARD
654. COOLING COIL FOR AIR CONDITIONERS
655. COPPER STRIP COIL FROM SCRAP
656. CORDLESS TELEPHONES
657. CYBER CAFE
658. CYBERKIOSK (Rs. 5000/-)
659. DATA PROCESSING CENTRE (Rs. 5000/-)
660. D.C. MICRO MOTORS
661. D.G.SETS
662. DISH ANTENNA AND CABLE T.V. NETWORK EQUIPMENT
663. DISTRIBUTION TRANSFORMERS & REPAIRS
664. DOMESTIC ELECTRICAL APPLIANCES- ROOM COOLER, WASHING MACHINE, WATER HEATER, ELECTRIC ROOM HEATER
665. E-SCHOOL
666. E-COMMERCE/BUSINESS
667. ELECTRIC ENERGY METER
668. ELECTRIC FANS
669. ELECTRIC HORN FOR AUTOMOBILE
670. ELECTRIC LAMP/GLS (INCANDESCENT LAMP)
671. ELECTRIC MIXER
672. ELECTRIC MOTORS UP TO 10 HP. REWINDING OF ALL TYPES OF MOTORS WATER PUMPS
673. ELECTRIC MOTOR WINDING (FOR FAN, MIXIES, ETC.)
674. ELECTRIC STEAM IRON
675. ELECTRICAL APPLIANCES
676. ELECTRICAL FIXTURES
677. ELECTRICAL STAMPING
678. ELECTROLYTIC CAPACITORS
679. ELECTROMAGNETIC RELAY
680. ELECTRONIC BALAST/CHOK
681. ELECTRICAL CHOKE
682. ELECTRONIC DIGITAL WATCHES
683. ELECTRONIC DIGITAL WEIGHING MACHINE
684. ELECTRONIC FIRE ALARM
685. ELECTRONIC GAS STOVE LIGHTERS
686. ELECTRONIC PRESSURE INDICATORS, ELECTRICALS, ELECTRONIC LIQUID LEVEL INDICATORS, ELECTRONIC TEMPERATURE INDICATOR, DIGITAL TACHOMETER
687. ELECTRONIC TELEPHONE INSTRUMENTS
688. ELECTRONIC TOYS
689. ELECTRONIC WATCHES & CLOCKS
690. FAX MACHINES
691. F.H.P MOTORS
692. FLOPPY DISKETTES
693. FLUORESCENT LAMP STARTER
694. FLUORESCENT TUBULAR

Above all the Detailed Project Report are available at *"ENGINEERS INDIA RESEARCH INSTITUTE"*. 4449, Nai Sarak (D), Main Road Delhi - 110 006

• Ph : 91-11-23918117, 2391 6431, 2392 0361, 31082370 • Fax : 91-11-2391 6431

• E-Mail : eirisidi@bol.net.in

LAMPS WITH INTRODUCTION TO MERCURY VAPOUR LAMP
695. FRANCHISEE COMPUTER EDUCATION CENTRE (Rs. 5000)
696. GAS DETECTOR (L.P.G)
697. GENERATOR SET & PUMP SETS
698. GENERATOR (BATTERY OPERATED)
699. GIS SERVICE CENTRE (GEOGRAPHICAL INFORMATION SYSTEMS)
700. HARDWARE FITTING FOR TRANSMISSION LINE (OVERHEAD LINE MATERIAL
701. HEADERS FOR TRANSISTOR ICS SEMI CONDUCTOR
702. H.T & L.T INSULATORS
703. H.T & M.V INDUSTRIAL CUBICAL SWITCH BOARD
704. INFORMATION MOVING DISPLAY (L.E.D TYPE)
705. INSURANCE CLAIM PROCESSING CENTRE (EOU) (Rs. 5000/-)
706. INTEGRATED CIRCUITS
707. INTERNET BASED STOCK TRADING (Rs. 5000/-)
708. INTERNET SERVICE PROVIDER (I.S.P.)
709. JELLY FILLED TELEPHONE CABLES
710. LAP TOP COMPUTERS
711. LEAD ACID BATTERIES
712. LEAD ACID BATTERY PLATES AND ASSEMBLING OF BATTERY
713. LEGAL TRANSCRIPTION & SECRETARIAL SERVICES CENTER (EOU)(Rs. 5000/-)
714. LIGHT EMITTING DIODES (L.E.D)
715. LINEAR ICS TRAINER KIT
716. LOUD SPEAKER
717. L.T TRANSFORMER REPAIRING
718. MEDICAL TRANSCRIPTION CENTRE
719. METAL FILM RESISTORS
720. METALLISED POLYPROPYLENE, POLYESTER FILM CAPACITOR
721. MICA BASE ELECTRONIC COMPONENTS
722. MICA PAPER WASTE PAPER FROM MICA WASTE
723. MICRO PROCESSORS TRAINER KITS BASED ON MICRO PROCESSORS
724. MINI COMPUTER (PERSONAL COMPUTER)
725. MINIATURE CIRCUIT BREAKER (M.C.B)
726. MINIATURE WATCH BATTERIES (BUTTON CELL)
727. MIXER/GRINDER (MIXI)
728. MONO CHROME COMPUTER MONITOR
729. MOTOR START ELECTROLYTIC CAPACITOR
730. MULTI LAYER P.C.B
731. MULTIPLE RELAY FOR LOW VOLTAGE
732. NEON INDICATOR
733. NEON SIGN MANUFACTURE
734. OPTICAL FIBRE CABLES
735. ON LINE SHOPPING MALL (Rs. 5000/-)
736. OPTO MECHANICAL & ELECTRICAL EQUIPMENTS
737. PHOTO COLOUR LAB
738. PICTURE TUBE (B/W)
739. PLAIN PAPER COPIER
740. PLASTIC FILM CAPACITORS
741. POLYESTER CAPACITORS
742. PORTABLE GENERATOR SET
743. PORTAL
744. PORTABLE TELEVISION(TV)
745. POWER CAPACITORS
746. POWER INVERTERS
747. POWER PLANT
748. POWER TRANSFORMERS UP TO 600 KVA
749. PRINTED CIRCUIT BOARD
750. PVC WIRES & CABLES
751. RE-CONDITIONING OF PICTURE TUBE
752. RESIN CAST CT & PT (1 KV)
753. SEMI CONDUCTOR DEVICE
754. SEMI CONDUCTORS FOR TRANSISTORS & DIODES
755. SETTING UP OF A VIDEO STUDIO
756. SMOKE DETECTORS
757. SOLAR CELLS
758. SOLAR MODULES
759. SOLAR PHOTO VOLTAIC SYSTEM
760. SOLDER FLUXES
761. SOLAR WATER HEATING PANELS
762. STEEL FURNITURE & ELECTRICAL APPLIANCES
763. STEREO AMPLIFIERS
764. STEREO CASSETTE RECORDERS/PLAYERS
765. STREET LIGHT FITTINGS SURGE SUPPRESSOR
766. TANTALUM CAPACITORS
767. TEFLON COATED ELECTRIC CABLE
768. TELEMEDICINE (DISTANCE HEALTH CARE) (Rs. 5000/-)
769. TELEPHONE CORD/CABLE
770. TELEPHONE (PUSH BUTTON TYPE)
771. TELEPHONE (PUSH BUTTON & CORDLESS)
772. TELEVISION (CTV & B/W)
773. TELEVISION (3-D)
774. TELEVISION DEFLECTION COMPONENTS
775. TELEVISION SIGNAL BOOSTERS
776. TELEVISION TUNERS
777. TRACTION BATTERIES
778. TRAINING INSTITUTE OF MEDICAL TRANSCRIPTION
779. TRANSFORMER FOR B/W TV
780. TRANSFORMER FOR VOLTAGE STABILIZER & E.H.T
781. TRANSMISSION POWER LINE FITTING
782. TRANSMISSION TOWER FITTING
783. TV AUDIO EQUIPMENT CABINETS & THEIR ASSEMBLING UNIT
784. UN-INTERRUPTED POWER SUPPLY (U.P.S)
785. VARIABLE FREQUENCY
786. VARIABLE VOLTAGE A.C. DRIVE
787. VIDEO CASSETTES (COMPLETE MANUFACTURING & ASSEMBLING)
788. VIDEO CASSETTES RECORDER (V.C.R)
789. VIDEO FILM STUDIO
790. VOLTAGE REGULATOR FOR AUTOMOBILES
791. VOLTAGE STABILIZERS
792. VOLTAGE STABLIZER & T.V. GAIN BOOSTER
793. WAX AND CHEMICAL COATED, BRAIDED TINSEL WIRE
794. WEBSITE DESIGN & E-MAIL REGISTERING
795. WELDING ELECTRODES
796. WIND ENERGY POWER PROJECT (10 MW)
796A WIRES (METAL)

FOOD, AGRO FOOD, PROCESSED FOOD, AGRO PLANTATION, CULTIVATION, FARMING, DAIRY/MILK, TOBACCO/PAN MASALA, BREWERY & DISTILLERY, EDIBLE OILS, EOU FOOD PRODUCTS AND ALLIED PRODUCTS

797. ALCOHOLIC BEVERAGES & VENEGAR FROM COCONUT WATER
798. ALCOHOL DRINKS FROM ETHYL ALCOHOL BY MIXING OF VARIOUS FLAVOURS
799. ANTI SCALE COMPOUND FOR ADDING INTO SUGAR JUICE BOILING
800. APPLE JUICE CONCENTRATED & DEHYDRATED FRUIT & VEGETABLES
801. ARTIFICIAL FISH MEAL FOR POULTRY FEED
802. AUTOMATIC BISCUIT PLANT
803. BABY CEREAL FOOD AND MILK POWDER
804. BACTERIA FOR CANE JUICE
805. BAKER'S YEAST
806. BAKERY INDUSTRY
807. BANANA PUREE
808. BEER & WINE
809. BEER PLANT (BREWERY)
810. BIDI
811. BIDI & CIGARETTE
812. BISCUIT PLANT

813. BREAD (AUTOMATIC PLANT)
814. BLACK PEPPER (SPICES)
815. BREAD AND BISCUITS
816. BREEDING FARM
817. BROILER CHICKEN
819. BUTTON MUSHROOM CULTIVATION & PROCESSING
820. CANNING OF RASAGULLAS IN METAL CANS
821. CAFFEIN FROM TEA WASTE
822. CANNING OF FRUITS & VEGETABLES
823. CASEIN AND BY-PRODUCTS
824. CASHEW FRUIT JUICE FROM CASHEW FRUIT APPLE
825. CASHEWNUT KERNEL EXTRACTION FROM CASHEWNUT FRUIT
826. CASHEWNUT SHELL LIQUID & KERNEL PROCESSING
827. CASHEW FENI
828. CATECHEU (BY CHEMICAL PROCESS)
829. CATTLE FEED FROM TAPIOCA
830. CHEWING & BUBBLE GUM
831. CHICKEN/SHEEP MEAT PROCESSING
832. CHOCOLATE (MILK)
833. CIGARETTE AND BEEDIES
834. COCOA BUTTER FROM COCOA MASS
835. COCONUT PRODUCTS & BY PRODUCTS PROCESS COMPLEX
836. COLD/SOFT DRINKS
837. COLLECTION OF MILK AND MILK MAKING POWDER
838. COLLECTION OF MILK AND PACKING IN POLYTHENE POUCH (1/2 KG.1 KG. & 2 KG.)
839. CONDENSED MILK (SWEETNED)
840. CONFECTIONERY INDUSTRY (TOFFEE & CANDY, SEMI-AUTOMATIC PLANT)
841. COUNTRY LIQUOR FROM MOLASSES
842. CIGARETTE
843. DAIRY FARM AND DAIRY (MILK) PRODUCTS (PASTEURISED MILK, BUTTER, GHEE, PANEER)
844. DAIRY FARM TO PRODUCE MILK & PACKING IN POUCHES (50%) & CAN(50%)
845. DAIRY FOR MILK PROCESSING
846. DAIRY FARM (BUFALO)
847. DAL (PULSE) MILL UNIT
848. DEHYDRATION OF CARROT & GARLIC
849. DEHYDRATION & CANNING OF FRUITS & VEGETABLES
850. DEHYDRATION OF FIGS
851. DEHYDRATION OF FRUITS AND VEGETABLES
852. DEHYDRATED ONIONS AND ONION POWDER
853. DRY ICE BY BREAKING OF AIR
854. DRYING OF RED CHILLIES, HALDI, DHANIA, AND GREEN PEAS
855. EGG POWDER (40,000 EGGS PROCESSING PER DAY)
856. EXPORT OF PROCESSED FOODS AND MARINE PRODUCTS
857. FISH CANNING & POUCHING
859. FISH FARMING (PRAWN & OTHER MARINE PRODUCTS)
860. FISH MEAL
861. FLOUR MILL AND MUSTARD OIL
862. FOOD COLOUR & ORASTED GROUNDNUT GRAM PEAS, ETC IN POUCHES
863. FROG LEGS PROCESSING
864. FROZEN MEATS PROCESSING
865. FOOD FLAVOURS (WHISKY) VODKA, GRAPE, BUTTER SCOTCH)
866. FOOD PRODUCTS COMPLEX (DEHYDRATED ONIONS, GARLIC POWDER & FLAKES, CATTLE FEED, TOMATO POWDER, TOMATO PRODUCTS, CANNED FRUITS & VEGETABLES, TOMATO PURE, GROUN NUT OIL, REFIND OIL, DEHYDRATED GRAPES, BANANA POWDER & WAFFERS)
867. FRUIT JUICE, JAM, JELLIES & ALLIED PRODUCTS
868. FRUIT JUICE, PICKLES PROCESSING AND CANNING
869. FRUIT JUICE MAKING & PACKING IN PLASTIC CONTAINER/POUCHES
870. FRUIT PROCESSING (JAM & JELLIES)
871. FRUIT PULP & JUICE CONCENTRATES
872. FRUIT & VEGETABLE DRYING (FREEZE DRYING METHOD)
873. GOAT & SHEEP FARMING
874. GRAM DALL/PULSE MILL
875. GRAPE DEHYDRATION
876. HARD BOILED CANDY (TOFFEE & CANDY)
877. HERBAL CIGARETTES
878. HONEY PROCESSING & PACKAGING
879. ICE CREAM OF DIFFERENT FLAVOURS
880. ICE CREAM STABILIZER
881. ICE MAKING PLANT
882. INDIAN MADE FOREIGN LIQUOR (I.M.F.L)
883. INSTANT FOOD (IDLI MIX, DOSA MIX, GULAB JAMUN MIX)
884. INSTANT FOOD (INSTANT FOOD & FAST FOOD PARLOUR)
885. INSTANT NOODLES
886. INSTANT TEA
887. INSTANT TEA FROM BLACK TEA
888. INTEGERATED STARCH BAKING POWDER/YEAST INDUSTRY
889. IODIZED SALT
890. IODIZED SALT (ORDINARY MOISTURE-LESS/FREE FLOWING IN PLASTIC BAGS AND CONTAINERS)
891. JAM, JELLIES, FRUIT JUICE & ALLIED PRODUCTS
892. KATHA AND CUTCH
893. KHANDSARI SUGAR
894. KHANDSARI SUGAR & IMFL
895. LACTIC ACID FROM WHITE SUGAR BY FERMENTATION PROCESS
896. LACTOSE & BY PRODUCTS PROCESSING FROM MILK
897. LIQUID GLUCOSE AND ITS BYE PRODUCTS
898. MACRONI AND VERMICILLI
899. MALT EXTRACTION FROM BARLEY
900. MANGO PROCESSING (MANGO PULP, JUICE & SLICES)
901. MAYUR BRAND TYPE CHEWING TOBACCO
902. MINERAL WATER
903. MILK PRESERVATION & MARKETING TO WHOLE SELLERS (INPOUCH PACKING BY UHT TECHNOLOGY)
904. MILK PROCESSING AND PACKAGING OF MILK PRODUCTS
905. MILK PRODUCTS (CASEIN, LACTOSE, GHEE & WHEY POWDER)
906. MILK TOFFEE
907. MINI FLOUR MILL
908. MINI SUGAR PLANT
909. MISRI (PEARL SUGAR CANDIES)
910. MODERN RICE MILL
911. MURABBA
912. MUSTARD OIL EXTRACTION & REFINING
913. MUTTON TALLOW
914. NAMKEEN INDUSTRY (BHUJIA, CHANA CHUR ETC.)
915. NAMKEEN & SWEETS
916. NON-BASMATI RICE FROM PADDY
917. OLEORESIN, ESSENTIAL OIL, DYES & POWDER OF SPICES
918. OLEORESIN EXTRACTION FROM DIPTERO-CARPUT TURMINATUS AND PINUS KHASYANA
919. OLEORESIN EXTRACTION FROM CHILLI
920. PAN MASALA AND POUCH

1059. BUFFALO HORN TIP, HOOF
1060. BANQUET HALL
1061. BUTTON
1062. CALCINED PETROLEUM (C.P) COKE
1063. CANVAS SHOES
1064. CANVAS SHOES, JUNGLE BOOTS
1065. CARBON BRUSH, BRUSH HOLDER & SLIP RING
1066. CEMENT SHEETS WITH COIR FIBRE & OTHER SEGMENTS
1067. CERAMIC TILES (GLAZED) BY DOUBLE FIRING/HEATING
1068. CHILDREN RECREATION CENTRE
1069. COAL BRIQUETTES
1070. COLD STORAGE & ICE
1071. COLD STORAGE FOR FRUITS AND VEGETABLES
1072. COMPRESSOR (HERMETIC) FOR AIR CONDITIONER
1073. COSTUME JEWELLERY/ IMITATION JEWELLERY
1074. DECORATIVE LAMINATED SHEET (SUNMICA)
1075. DIAMOND CUTTING & EXPORTS
1076. DRINKING STRAW FROM PROPYLENE
1077. ENGINEERING COLLEGE
1078. ENTERTAINMENT CLUB
1079. FASHION TECHNOLOGY INSTITUTE
1080. FAST FOOD PARLOUR
1081. FAST FOOD (INSTANT FOOD & FAST FOOD PARLOUR)
1082. FIRE EXTINGUISHERS (SODA ACID TYPE)
1083. FISH NET
1084. FLORICULTURE (CUT FLOWER ROSE) WITH GREEN HOUSE
1085. FLOOR COVERING SHEET
1086. FILM STUDIO (VIDEO)
1087. FLUSH DOOR, CHIP BOARD, WOOD WOOL & OTHER INSULATING BOARDS
1088. GAS DETECTORS OF L.P.G
1089. GEMS MANUFACTURING
1090. GLASS BOTTLE BY SCRAP
1092. GOAT & SHEEP FARMING
1093. GOLD ELECTROPLATING
1094. GOLD JEWELLERY (E.O.U)
1095. GOLD PLATED SILVER JEWELLERY & CUTLERY
1096. GRANITE SLAB AND TILES
1097. GREEN HOUSE
1098. HARD CHROMIUM PLATING
1099. HEALTH CLUB AND BEAUTY PARLOUR CUM HAIR SALOON WITH SONA BATH
1100. HEALTH CLUB CUM BEAUTY PARLOUR TRAININGINSTITUTE
1101. HORN TIP,HOOVE BUTTON
1102. HOSPITAL
1103. HOSPITAL (100 BEDS)
1104. HOSPITAL (200 BEDS)
1105. ICE MAKING PLANT
1106. IMITATION AND COSTUME
1107. JEWELLERY (NECKLACE, EARRINGS EAR TOP ETC.)
1108. INITMATE SCENT CHEMICALS FROM ALL TYPES OF FLAVOUR
1109. INVESTMENT CASTING
1110. JUTE, COIR, GLASS ROPE/ SUTLI
1111. JUTE TWINE
1112. L.P.G BOTTLING PLANT
1113. L.P.G REGULATOR (DOMESTIC PURPOSE)
1114. LAMINATED PARTICLE BOARD & HARD BOARD
1115. LAMINATED SAFETY AND TOUGHENED GLASS
1116. LEASING & HIRE PURCHASE
1117. LICHEN (CHARILA)
1118. MANILA ROPES
1119. MEDICAL COLLEGE
1120. MATCH UNIT FROM WAXED PAPER
1121. MEDIUM DENSITY FIBRE BOARD
1122. MELAMINE CROCKERY
1123. MINERAL WATER
1124. MINI CEMENT PLANT
1125. MIRROR SILVER, GOLDEN, PINK, BLACK & SMOKES
1126. MODERN ADVERTISING AGENCY WITH DTP & FILM STUDIO
1127. MOTEL/SMALL HOTEL
1128. MULTI COLOUR PRINTING
1129. MULTI STOREY COMMERCIAL COMPLEX ALONGWITH RESIDENTIALAND DELUX FLATS FOR FOREIGN TOURISTS & REVOLVING RESTAURENT AT THE TOP
1130. MULTIPLE LAMINATION INDUSTRY
1131. MUSHROOM GROWING AND PROCESSING (BY DEEP FREEZING METHOD)
1132. NEWS PAPER PRINTING
1133. NICKEL LINED INDUSTRIAL SCREEN
1134. OFFSET COLOUR PRINTING PRESS (SIX COLOUR)
1135. OFFSET PRINTING PRESS
1136. P.C.C ELECTRIC POLES
1137. PHOTOGRAPHIC DEVELOPER & FIXER
1138. PVC EXTRUSION PROFILE (DOOR & WINDOWS)
1139. POP-CORN
1140. PHOTO ETCHING OF S.S.
1141. PRE STRESSED CEMENT CONCRETE PIPES
1142. PILFER PROOF CAPS
1143. PILFER PROOF CAPS AND CROWN CAP
1144. POUCH MAKING & GRAVURE PRINTING (ROTO PRINTING)
1145. POULTRY & FISH FARMING (INTEGERATED UNIT)
1146. PRINTING OF TIN SHEETS
1147. READYMADE GARMENTS
1148. RESTAURANT
1149. ROSE PLANTATION AND ROSE OIL EXTRACTION
1150. ROTOGRAVURE PRINTING
1151. SAFETY BELTS
1152. SAFETY MATCHES
1153. SHOE LACES
1154. SILK COCOON CULTIVATION (GROWING OF SILK COCOON WARM)
1155. SILK SCREEN PRINTING FORMULATIONS FOR PLASTIC, PAPER & CLOTH
1156. SPIKENARD (JATAMANSI)
1157. STENCIL COATING SOLUTION
1158. SUGAR CANDY (MISRI)
1159. SUGAR CANE PLANTATION
1160. SUGAR CANE JUICE PRESERVATION
1161. SURAT ZARI
1162. SYNTHETIC SHOES & SOLES
1163. TEA PACKAGING INDUSTRY
1164. TENNIS BALLS
1165. THREE STAR HOTEL
1166. TRAVELLING AGENCY
1167. TRAYS, TROLLEYS FOR HOSPITAL WITH SCRATCHLESS COATING
1168. WAX EXTRACTS (TANNING POWDER)
1169. WIRE ROPE SLINGS
1170. WOOD WOOL SLAB
1171. WOODEN CANE FURNITURE WITH EXPORT POTENTIAL
1172. WOODEN FURNITURE
1173. WOODEN PANEL INCLUDING KILN SEASONING
1174. WOODEN FURNITURE
1175. WATCH CASE BUFFING
1176. WATCH DIAL
1177. WRIST WATCHES
1178. WATCHES (ELECTRONIC)
1179. ZEDOARY (KACHUR)

EDIBLE OILS, ESSENTIAL OILS LURICATIING OILS, GREASES, VEGETABLE OILS, WAXES, CAMPHOR, PERFUMES & PERFUMERY COMPOUNDS AND REFINED OILS ETC.

1180. AROMATIC PERFUMERY COMPOUND
1181. AEROSOL
1182. AGARBATTI PERFUMERY COMPOUND
1183. BEES WAX MANUFACTURE
1184. CAMPHOR
1185. CARDANOL FROM CASHEW NUT SHELL LIQUID
1186. CASTOR OIL
1187. CASTOR OIL DERIVATIVE OLEORESINS
1188. CHILLI OIL
1189. CITRONELLA OILS
1190. CLOVE OIL
1191. CONCENTRATE OF ROSE JASMINE & LILY ETC.
1192. COLOURED FLAME CANDLE

1193. CANDLES (SEMI-AUTOMATIC)
1194. CORN OIL (MAIZE OIL)
1195. DEHYDRATED CASTOR OIL
1196. EUGENOL FROM CINNAMON LEAF OIL
1197. EXTRACTION OF ESSENTIAL OIL (CARDAMON, JEERA, AJOWAN, GINGER OILS ETC. & PACKAGING OF GROUND SPICES)
1198. EXTRACTION OF JASMINE ESSENCE
1199. EXTRACTION OF ESSENTIAL OILS BY SUPER CRITICAL FLUID METHOD FROM FLOWERS, HERBS & SPICES
1200. EUCALYPTUS OIL
1201. EXTRACTION OF OIL FROM OIL SEED EXPANDEREXTRUSION TECHNOLOGY)
1202. FAT LIQUOR SULPHATED OIL
1203. FLAVOURS FOR FOOD
1204. GARLIC OIL & POWDER
1205. GINGER OIL, SANDALWOOD OIL AND NAGARMOTHA OIL
1206. GINGER OIL
1207. GINGER OIL & GINGER DUST
1208. INTEGERATED WAX COMPLEX
1209. IONONE FROM LEMON GRASS OIL
1210. JASMINE & LILLY FLOWER OIL
1211. LEMON GRASS OIL
1212. LIQUID PARAFFIN
1213. LUBE OIL & GREASE
1214. LUBRICATING OIL
1215. MENTHOL CRYSTALS
1216. MENTHOL OIL & CRYSTAL
1217. MICRO CRYSTALLINE WAX
1218. MUSTARD OIL (EDIBLE OIL)
1219. OIL FROM ARTEMISIA HERBS
1220. PALM OIL CRUSHING UNIT
1221. PAN MASALA
1222. PARAFFIN WAX
1223. PARAFFIN WAX FROM SLACK WAX
1224. REFINED OIL-SUN FLOWER OIL, GROUNDNUT OIL, STAFF FLOWER OIL & COTTON SEED OIL
1225. REFINED VEGETABLE OIL
1226. RECLAMATION OF USED ENGINE OIL
1227. RICE BRAN OIL (R.B.O)
1228. ROSE OIL EXTRACTION
1229. SMOKE LESS CANDLE
1230. SPICE OIL & OLEORESINS
1231. SOLVENT EXTRACTION PLANT (OIL CAKE BASED)
1232. SYNTHETIC ALMOND OIL
1233. SYNTHETIC TALLOW
1234. SYNTHETIC GHEE
1235. VEGETABLE OIL EXTRACTION & REFINING
1236. WADDING OIL (100%) FOR WADDING OF COTTON HOSIERY CLOTH IN DYEING PROCESS
1237. WAX EMULSION FOR TEXTILE
1238. WAX FLOOR POLISH

PAINT, ENAMEL, SOLVENTS, THINNERS, INKS & VARNISH

1239. ACRYLIC EMULSION PAINTS
1240. ALUMINIUM PAINT
1241. AUTOMOBILE PAINTS
1242. BALL POINT PEN REFILL INK
1243. BITUMINIOUS ROAD EMULSION
1244. BITUMEN
1245. BITUMINIOUS FELTS FOR WATER & DAMP PROOFING
1246. BITUMINIOUS ROAD EMULSION RAPID MEDIUM & SLOW SETTING
1247. BUFFING & POLISHING
1248. CEMENT PAINT FOR WHITE & GREY CEMENT

1249. DISPERSANT
1250. DRY DISTEMPER
1251. DRY DISTEMPER & CEMENT PAINT
1252. DUPLICATING INK BLACK FOR GESTNER DUPLICATOR
1255. EMULSION PAINTS (WATER BASED)
1256. HAMMERTONE PAINT
1257. INSULATING VARNISH & WIRE ENAMEL
1258. IRON OXIDE PIGMENTS
1259. INSULATING VARNISH (POLY VINYL BUTYRAL BASED, FFC GRADE)
1260. LIME COLOUR (CEMENT COLOUR)
1261. SYNTHETIC RED OXIDE FOR FLOORINGS
1262. SOLVENT & THINNERS
1263. MARKING INKS (WATER PROOF)
1264. METAL NAPHTHANATE (AS DRIER FOR PAINTS)
1265. N.C.PUTTY
1266. OFFSET PRINTING INK
1267. OIL BOUND DISTEMPER PAINT
1268. PAINT BRUSHES
1269. PAINT REMOVERS
1270. PAINT INDUSTRY
1271. PAINT & VARNISH
1272. PICTURE VARNISH
1273. POWDER COATING PAINT
1274. PRINTING INKS (OFFSET, FLEXO & ROTO GRAVURE)
1275. PRIMER PAINT & ENAMEL PAINT
1276. PUTTY & WATER PROOFING PAINT
1277. PRINTING INKS (FLEXO-GRAPHIC INK)
1278. PUTTY (METAL CASEMENT)
1279. RED OXIDE PRIMER (ANTI CORROSIVE)
1280. REFRECTORY PAINT (GRAPHITE BASED)
1281. SCREEN PRINTING INKS
1282. SILK SCREEN PRINTING INK FORMULATION FOR PLASTIC, PAPER, CLOTH
1283. STAMP & PAD INK
1284. STOVING PAINT
1285. SPIRIT SOLUBLE MALEIC RESIN
1286. TEXTURE PAINT
1287. THINNERS AND ITS ALLIED PRODUCTS
1288. TONER INK
1289. VARNISH THINNER (SOLVENT)
1290. VACUUM METALLIZING LACQUERS
1291. WOOD PRIMER

PHARMACEUTICAL, DRUGS, AYURVEDIC/HERBAL COSMETICS & MEDICINES, HOMOEOPATHIC MEDICINES, DISPOSABLE SYRINGE, DENTAL COLLEGE & FINE CHEMICALS ETC.

1292. AROMATIC PILLS
1293. ASPIRIN
1294. AYURVEDIC PAIN BALM OINTMENTS
1295. AYURVEDIC CHURAN AND TABLETS
1296. AYURVEDIC TABLETS (HAJMOLA TYPE)
1297. AYURVEDIC/HERBAL PHARMACY
1298. AYURVEDIC SHERBATS
1299. AYURVEDIC PRODUCTS
1300. BULK DRUGS (E.O.U)
1301. BLOOD BAGS
1302. CALCIUM GLUCONATE
1303. CAPSULE, TABLET & INJECTION WITH MODERN INSTRUMENTS
1304. CASHEW FENI
1305. CHLOROQUINONE PHOSPHATE (BULK DRUGS)
1306. CLINICAL THERMOMETER
1307. DENTAL CLINIC

Above all the Detailed Project Report are available at *"ENGINEERS INDIA RESEARCH INSTITUTE"*. 4449, Nai Sarak (D), Main Road Delhi - 110 006
● Ph : 91-11-23918117, 2391 6431, 2392 0361, 31082370 ● Fax : 91-11-2391 6431
● E-Mail : eirisidi@bol.net.in

1308. DENTAL COLLEGE
1309. DENTAL GRADE EUGENOL
1310. DEXTROSE MONOHYDRATE, LIQUID GLUCOSE
1311. DEHYDRATED ONION & ONION POWDER
1312. DEXTROSE POWDER (ANHYDROUS FROM STARCH)
1314. DEXTROSE SALINE SOLUTION
1315. DISTILLERY (I.M.F.L)
1316. DISPOSABLE NEEDLES FOR SYRINGES
1317. DISPRIN
1318. DISTILLED WATER
1319. EMPTY HARD GELATINE CAPSULES
1320. FILLING & PACKING OF CAPSULES
1321. GLUCOSE - D - POWDER
1322. GLYCERINE
1323. HERBAL COSMETICS
1324. HERBAL SHAMPOO
1325. HERBAL HAIR OILS (AYURVEDIC)
1326. HOMOE & BIO-MEDICINES WITH MOTHER TINCTURE
1327. HOMOEPATHIC MEDICINES
1328. HYPODERMIC NEEDLES
1329. I.V. FLUIDS
1330. IBUPROFEN
1331. INFUSION & TRANSFUSION SETS (I.V. SET)
1332. INJECTABLE FOR PHARMACEUTICALS
1333. INJECTION AMPOULES PACKAGING BOX
1334. INTEGERATED SURGICAL COTTON
1335. ICE MAKING PLANT
1336. ICE & COLD STORAGE
1337. LACTOSE & BY PRODUCTS PROCESSING FROM MILK
1338. LICHEN (JATAMANSI CHARILA)
1339. LIQUID GLUCOSE AND ITS BY-PRODUCTS
1340. L-LYSINE MONOHYDRO CHLORIDE
1341. LIQUID GLUCOSE FROM POTATOES
1342. MEDICAL COLLEGE
1343. NICOTINE FROM TOBACCO WASTE
1344. OINTMENT-AYURVEDIC (YELLOW & WHITE)
1345. PHARMACEUTICAL AND FOOD GRADE GELATINE
1346. PHARMACEUTICAL INDUSTRY (TABLETS, CAPSULES, LIQUID, GEL, OINTMENT POWDER INJECTABLE)
1347. PHARMACEUTICAL UNIT (EOU) WITH FORMULA TIONS, INJECTABLES, ETC. PYRIDINE & DERIVATIVES
1348. SALT (IODIZED SALT)
1349. SALINE & INJECTION WATER
1350. SALINE WATER & DEXTROSE SOLUTION (I.V.FLUID IN PLASTIC BOTTLES)
1351. SORBITOL
1352. STARCH (MAIZE)
1353. SURGICAL ADHESIVE PLASTER
1354. SURGICAL BANDAGES
1355 SURGICAL GLOVES
1357. SURGICAL COTTON
1358. SURGICAL COTTON AND BANDAGE
1359. SYNTHETIC CAMPHOR POWDER
1360. TABLETS & CAPSULES
1361. TISSUE CULTURE
1362. TINCTURE FROM RECTIFIED SPIRIT
1363. TRIMETHOPIME
1364. VETERENARY MEDICINES (ONLY FORMULATIONS)
1365. VITAMIN 'C', SORBITOL' ANHYDROUS DEXTROSE, STARCH

PULP, PAPER, STRAW/GREY BOARD, KRAFT PAPER, PACKAGING, PAPER CARRY BAGE, PAPER FROM AGRO WASTE & STATIONERY ETC.

1366. AMMONIA PAPER
1367. AUTOMATIC BOOK BINDING
1368. ADHESIVE (FEVICOL TYPE)
1369. ALL PIN & GEM CLIPS
1370. CARBON PAPER
1371. CARD BOARD
1372. CARBON LESS PAPER
1373. CELLPHANE PAPER
1374. COMPUTER FORMS & SECURITY PRINTING PRESS
1375. CORRUGATED BOARD & BOX (PRINTED & LAMINATED)
1376. CORRUGATED BOARD AND BOXES FROM FROM CARD BOARDS
1377. CORRUGATED CARTONS FROM PLAIN PAPERS
1378. CORRUGATRED PACKING & MATERIAL (BULB & TUBES PACKING)
1379. DESK TOP PUBLISHING
1380. DEFOAMING AGENT FOR PAPER PLANT
1381. DRINKING STRAW PAPER
1382. D.T.P CUM OFFSET PRESS
1383. EGG TRAYS
1384. EXERCISE NOTE BOOK, REGISTER AND PAD
1385. FLEXOGRAPHIC INK
1386. GREETING CARD BY OFFSET PRESS
1387. HAND MADE PAPER FILTER PAPER
1388. HARD BOARD
1389. INJECTION AMPOULES PACKAGING BOXES
1390. INSULATIING PAPER
1391. KRAFT PAPER
1392. KRAFT PAPER FROM BAGASSE
1393. LAMINATED PACKAGING PAPER WITH PRINTING
1394. LAMINATION & COATING ON PAPER
1395. M.G. PAPER FROM WASTE PAPER
1396. MILL PAPER FROM WASTE PAPER
1397. MILL BOARD FROM RICE & WHEAT STRAWS
1398. MILL BOARD FROM WASTE PAPER
1399. MINI PAPER PLANT FROM SISAL
1400. MINI PAPER PLANT
1401. MULTI WALL PAPER SACKS
1402. NEWS PAPER FOR CHILDREN
1403. NEWS PRINT PAPER FROM RICE STRAW BAGASSE
1404. NEWS PAPER CHILDRENS
1405. NEWS PRINT PAPER
1406. OFFSET AND TREADLE TYPE PRINTING PRESS
1407. MILL BOARD BASED ON RICE STRAW
1408. PAPER AND BOARD FROM STRAW
1409. PAPER & PAPER PRODUCTS
1410. PAPER ENVELOPES
1411. PAPER CARRY BAGS
1412. PAPER BOARD CARTON
1413. PAPER CONES FOR LOUD SPEAKERS
1414. PAPER FROM AKRA
1415. PAPER FROM BAGASSE WITH CORRUGATED BOARD & BOXES
1416. PAPER FROM BAMBOO
1417. PAPER GLASSES FOR BEVERAGES
1418. PAPER FROM RICE HUSK & WHEAT HUSK
1419. PAPER FROM TREE BARK, EUCALYPRUS WOOD
1420. PAPER PRODUCTS
1421. PAPER PLANT (WHITE WRITING & NEWS PAPER FOR PULP & WASTE PAPER)
1422. PAPER PLATES, PAPER GLASS
1423. PAPER CONES & TUBES
1425. PAPER PLANT WITH DTP & PRINTING & PUBLISHING UNIT
1426. PAPER BASED PHENOLIC SHEET
1427. PAPER CUP FOR ICE CREAM
1428. PAPER TUBES SPIRAL WINDING COMPOSIT CONTAINER
1429. PAPER LABLE FOR BEER BOTTLES
1430. PARTICLE BOARD & BLACK BOARD WITH SANDING & LAMINATION OF PARTICLE BOARD
1431. PARTICLE BOARD FROM RICE HUSK
1432. POUCH FILLING & MAKING FOR TOMATO SAUCE
1433. POUCH MAKING &

GRAVURE PRINTING
1434. PROCESSING OF PAPER FOR FEEDING IN COMPUTER
1435. PULP FROM BAMBOO & WOOD
1436. PAPER FILES
1437. PLAYING CARDS
1438. ROSIN SIZING AGENT (FOR PAPER PLANT)
1439. SAND PAPER
1440. SANITRY NAPKINS
1441. SILICON COATED PAPER
1442. STENCIL PAPER
1443. STRAW BOARD AND GREY BOARD
1444. STRAW BOARD & MILL BOARD
1445. STRAW BOARD AND PAPER BOARD
1446. TISSUE PAPER FACIAL
1447. TISSUE MOIST TOILETERY CLEANSING TISSUE AND RELATED PRODUCTS
1448. TISSUE PAPER ROLLS
1449. TETRA PACK FOR MILK PACKAGING, GHEE & OTHER LIQUIDS
1450. TOILET PAPER ROLLS
1451. TOILET PAPER & NAPKINS
1452. WAX COATED PRINTED PAPER
1453. WET FACE FRESHNER TISSUE
1454. WHITE WRITING & PRINTING PAPER
1455. WRITING & PRINTING PAPER (PAPER MILLS)

PLASTIC, B.O.P.P, ACRYLIC, DISPOSABLE PLASTIC PRODUCTS, PET PRODUCTS, P.V.C, H.D.P.E, P.P, L.D.P.E., P.U, A.B.S, THERMOFOARMING, MASTER BATCHES, & POLYMER AND RUBBER PRODUCTS, TYRE, TUBE, ADHESIVE, SHEET, COIR & MANY OTHERS

1456. ABS GRANULES FROM ABS SCRAPS FROM OLD T.V. CABINETS, WHITE GOODS ETC.
1457. ACRYLIC BEADS
1458. ACRYLIC COPOLYMER EMULSION
1459. ACRYLIC LATEX
1460. ACRYLIC SHEET
1461. ACRYLIC SHEET & MOULDED PRODUCTS
1462. ACRYLIC TEETH
1463. AUTO TUBES
1464. AUTO FLAPS FOR TRUCKS & BUSES
1465. AUTO TYRES & TUBES
1466. BABY BOTTLES (PLASTIC) WITH WHITESILICON RUBBER NIPPLES
1467. B.O.P.P. FILM
1468. B.O.P.P. PRESSURE SENSITIVE SELF ADHESIVE TAPE
1469. BABY NIPPLE (SILICON)
1470. BABY NIPPLE (BIG SIZE)
1471. BALLOON PLASTIC ADVERTISING
1472. BLISTER FILM PVC
1473. BLISTER PACKAGING & POUCH PAKAGING
1474. BLOW MOULDING PLASTIC CONTAINER
1475. COATING ON METALIZED POLYESTER FILM/METALISED PAPER/ ALIMINIUM FOIL
1476. COATING ON PLASTIC (ELECTROLYSIS) & GLASS
1477. COIR FOAM (RUBBERISED)
1478. COLOUR COATING ON PLASTICS
1479. COLOUR MASTER BATCHES FOR VARIOUS PLASTICS
1480. CYCLE TYRES AND TUBES
1481. DISPOSABLE PLASTIC CUPS GLASSES, ETC.
1482. DISPOSABLE PLASTIC SYRINGES & NEEDLES
1483. DISPOSABLE PLASTIC SYRINGES
1484. DOUGH MOULDING COMPOUND (D.M.C)
1485. EPOXY RESIN
1486. EXPANDED POLYESTRENE MOULDING (THERMOCOLE)
1487. F.R.P AUTO, SCOOTER ROOFS & CEILINGS
1488. F.R.P PRODUCTS (HELMET, WASHBASIN SHEETS, ROOFING SHEETS)
1489. FIBRE REINFORCED PLASTIC (HIGH PRESSURE MOULDING WITH SMC BMC AND DMC)
1490. FIELD RUBBER CONVERTED TO THE 60% LATEX RUBBER
1491. FLEXIBLE P.U. FOAM
1492. FORMALDEHYDE CROCKERY & OTHER ITEMS
1493. FORMALDEHYDE RESIN (UREA, PHENOL, MELEMINE)
1494. GASKET SHEET
1495. GUM BOTTLE (PVC)
1496. GLASS BEADS
1497. HDPE COATED PAPER SACK
1498. H.D.P.E. BAGS
1499. H.D.P.E. CONTAINERS (BLOW MOULDING)
1500. H.D.P.E. CONTAINER, POLY JARS BY INJECTION MOULDING (FOOD GRADE)
1501. H.D.P.E. JERRY CANS
1502. HDPE MANUFACTURING FROM ETHYLALCOHOL
1503. H.D.P.E PIPE AND FITTINGS
1504. H.D.P.E. PIPES
1505. H.D.P.E PRINTED BAGS
1506. H.D.P.E TWINES AND ROPES
1507. H.D.P.E. & L.D.P.E PIPES AND FITTINGS
1508. H.D.P.E/PP BOX STRAPPING
1509. H.D.P.E/PP WOVEN SACKS USING PLAIN LOOMS
1510. HOLOGRAM STICKERS-3D
1511. H.M BAG PLANT WITH PRINTING UNIT
1512. HAWAI CHAPPALS (RUBBER)
1513. I.V PLASTIC BOTTLE
1514. ICE CREAM CUP (PLASTIC)
1515. INJECTION MOULDED AUTO COMPONENTS
1516. INJECTION & BLOW MOULDED PLASTIC PRODUCTS
1517. INJECTION MOULDED PLASTIC PRODUCTS
1518. INTEGERATED COMPLEX ESTER'S & ALLIED PRODUCTS (D.O.P,D.B.P, & ETHYL ACETATE, BUYTL ACETATE, WIRE ENAMELS, JELLY CABLE COMPOUND)
1519. L.D.P.E. (LOW DENSITY POLY ETHYLENE) GRANULES FROM VIRGIN (L.D.P.E. RESIN)
1520. INTEGERATED SURGICAL RUBBER GOODS INDUSTRY
1521. INJECTION MOULDED PLASTIC BALLS
1522. L.D.P.E FROM ETHYL ALCOHOL
1523. LDPE MOULDED PRODUCTS
1524. LAMINATION OF COEXTRUSION MULTILAYER FILM IN ROLL FORM
1525. LATEX RUBBER
1526. LATEX RUBBER CONDOM
1527. MASTER BATCHES (COLOURED, P.V.C, L.D.P.E, H.D.P.E, ETC.)
1528. MELAMINE FORMALHYDE RESIN
1529. MOULDED LUGGAGE
1530. MULTI-LAYER (3 LAYER BAGS)
1531. MULTI-LAYER (3 LAYER) FILM WITH LAMINATION & PRINTING
1532. OIL SEAL
1533. PET BOTTLE/CONTAINERS
1534. PET BOTTLES FROM PRE FORM
1535. PET BOTTLE & MINERAL WATER
1536. PET PRE-FORM FROM PET RESIN
1537. PET PRE-FORM CUM PET BOTTLES
1538. PET PRE-FORM PET BOTTLES CUM MINERAL WATERS
1539. POLY CARBONATE RESIN
1540. PTFE COMPONENTS
1541. PU/PVC SOLE FOR SPORT SHOE BY IMPORTED M/C.
1542. PVC BATTERY SEPARATOR
1543. P.V.C COMPOUNDS (FRESH)
1544. P.V.C COMPOUNDS (SCRAP)
1545. P.V.C ELECTRICAL INSULATING TAPE
1546. P.V.C. EXTRUSION PROFILES
1547. P.V.C FITTINGS
1548. P.V.C FLEXIBLE FUSIBLE POWDER HEAT FUSIBLE POWDER
1549. P.V.C GRANULES (FOR

INSULATION & SHEETS GRADES)
1550. P.V.C GRANULES FROM PVC SCRAPS (WITH POLLUTION CONTROL)
1551. P.V.C HOSES
1552. P.V.C LEATHER CLOTH
1553. P.V.C FLEXIBLE PIPES
1554. P.V.C PIPES AND FITTINGS
1555. POLYTHENE BAGS (PRINTED)
1556. PVC PLASTICS FILM SHEET SOFT/RIGID
1557. PVC RESIN AND COMPOUND
1558. PVC RULAR
1559. PVC STABLIZERS (SINGLE PACK SYSTEM)
1560. PVC WIRE AND CABLES
1561. PAPER BASED PHENOLIC SHEET FOR ELECTRICAL
1562. PHENOL FORMALDEHYDE RESIN
1563. PHENOLIC RESIN
1564. PLASTIC BEADS FROM PLASTIC SCRAPS
1565. PLASTIC BUTTONS
1566. PLASTIC CANS
1567. PLASTIC COLLAPSIBLE TUBE
1568. PLASTIC CORRUGATED SHEET & BOXES
1569. PLASTIC FILM AND SHEETS WITH PRINTING FLEXO & ROTO/LDPE/HDPE/PP/HM/PVC
1570. PLASTIC FILTER MASTER BATCH & OTHER MASTER BATCHES FOR VARIOUS PLASTICS
1571. PLASTIC JERRY CANS
1572. PLASTIC GRANULES OR POWDER FROM PLASTIC SCRAP
1573. PLASTIC INJECTION MOULDED T.V. CABINETS
1574. PLASTIC ITEMS MANUFAC TURE FROM POWDER MELAMINE
1575. PLASTIC GOODS
1576. PLASTIC PIPES & TARPAULINES
1577. PLASTIC SHEET FROM SCRAP
1578. PLASTIC PLANT (BLOW MOULDING & INJECTION MOULDING)
1579. PLASTIC PRODUCTS (GOLD, SILVER, NICKEL)
1580. PLASTIC TOYS
1581. POLYESTER BEADING
1582. POLYESTER FILM
1583. POLYTHENE BAGS & AUTOMATIC PRINTING
1584. POLYTHENE PRINTED BAGS
1585. POLYURETHANE FOAM AND ITS PRODUCTS
1586. PROPYLENE FILM (PRINTED) & BAG MANUFACTURING
1587. PLASTIC MATS
1588. RAINBOW COLOUR ON PVC FILM & SHEET
1589. RED MUD PVC PIPES AND FITTINGS
1590. RE-RUBBERISED OF SOLID TYPE
1591. RESIN COATED SAND REXINE
1592. REXINE CLOTH & ALLIED PRODUCTS
1593. RUBBER ADHESIVE
1594. RUBBER AUTO PARTS
1595. RUBBER BELTING
1596. RUBBER MOULDING UNIT INCLUDING LINING RUBBER SHEETING
1597. RUBBER RECLAIMING
1598. RUBBER ROLLERS FOR TEXTILE MILLS & PAPER INDUSTRIES
1599. RUBBER & PLASTIC SHEETS, MATS & FLAPS
1600. RUBBER SHEET AND ALLIED HOSPITAL RUBBER GOODS
1601. RUBBERIZED PVC GASKET
1602. RUBBERISED COIR
1603. RUBBER COMPOUND FOR AUTOMOBILES
1604. SAFETY BELTS
1605. SILVER AND GOLD PLATING ON PVC AND NYLON-6
1606. SILICONE RUBBER NIPPLES/ TEATS
1607. SPECTACLE FRAMES (PLASTIC)
1608. SPUNGE RUBBER
1609. SURGICAL EXAMINATION GLOVES
1610. SYNTHETIC PEARL COATING ON POLYSTYRENE BEADS
1611. SYNTHETIC RUBBER ADHESIVE
1612. TEFLON MANUFACTURING
1613. TEFLON TAPE
1614. TEFLON TAPES & CABLES
1615. THERMOCOLE SHEET AND MOULDED PRODUCTS EXPANDED POLYESTERENE EXTRUSION PROFILES
1616. THERMOFORMED PACKAGING (BLISTER PACKAGING & POUCH PACKAGING)
1617. THERMOPLASTIC POLYURETHANE
1618. THERMOFORMED CUPS, PLATES & GLASS WITH HIPS SHEET
1619. THERMOCOLE
1620. THERMOCOLE BASED DISPOSABLE GLASS, CUPS & PLATES
1621. TOOTH BRUSHES
1622. TOY BALLOON, DECORA TIVE & INDUSTRIAL BALLOONS
1623. TREAD RUBBER
1624. TYRE RETREADING (HOT)
1625. TYRE RETREADING BY COLD PROCESS
1626. TYRE TUBES & FLAPS
1627. TYRE & TUBES
1628. UNSATURATED POLYESTER FOR REXINE
1629. V-BELT AND FAN BELT
1630. VINYL ASBESTOS AND PVC WALL PAPER
1631. VITON (FLUORO ELASTOMER)

SOAP, COSMETICS & PERFUMS

1632. ACID SLURRY, SYNTHETIC DETERGENT POWDER
1632. ACID SLURRY
1633. AGARBATTI SYNTHETIC, PERFUMERY COMPOUND
1634. AFTER SHAVE LOTION
1635. ANTISEPTIC CREAM
1636. BETA IONONE
1637. BLEACHING POWDER
1638. BLUE DETERGENT POWDER
1639. CLEANING POWDER (VIMTYPE)
1640. COLD CREAM
1641. COLOURED FLAME & PERFUMED CANDLES (RED, BLUE, GREEN FLAME)
1642. COSMETIC INDUSTRY (MODERN)
1643. COSMETIC INDUSTRY (SHAMPOO, SPRAY PERFUME, TALCUM POWDER
1644. DETERGENT POWDER (ARIEL TYPE)
1645. DETERGENT POWDER (NIRMA TYPE) FULLY AUTOMATIC PLANT
1646. DETERGENT WASHING POWDER
1647. FISH OIL SOAP
1648. GLYCERINE TRANSPARENT SOAP
1649. HAIR REMOVING CREAM
1650. HERBAL COSMETICS
1651. HERBAL SHAMPO & CREAM
1652. HERBAL/AYURVEDIC COSMETICS
1653. INCENSE POWDER, INCENSE STICKS & INCENSE CAKE
1654. OPTICAL WHITENERS
1655. ROSE OIL EXTRACTION
1656. SHAMPOOS (COCONUT OIL BASED COLD PROCESS)
1657. SHAVING CREAM
1658. SINDUR (KUMKUM)
1659. SOAP COATED PAPER
1660. SPRAY DRIED DETERGENT POWDER
1661. STAIN REMOVER
1662. TALCUM POWDER (FACE & TOILET POWDER)
1663. TOILET AND HERBAL SOAP
1664. TOOTH PASTE & POWDER
1665. WASHING DETERGENT POWDER AND WASHING SOAP
1666. WASHING POWDER LIQUID DETERGENTS, LOTION & SHAMPOO

ENTERTAINMENT CLUB WITH 4 STAR HOTEL
1779. HOSPITALS
1780. ICE CREAM PARLOUR
1781. INTERNET SERVICE PROVIDER (I.S.P.)
1782. MEDICAL COLLEGE
1783. MEDICAL COLLEGE, HOSPITAL & RESEARCH INSTITUTE
1784. MEDICAL TRANSCRIPTION CENTRE
1785. MENTAL RETARDATION HOSPITAL & CEREBRAL PALSY
1786. MOTEL/SMALL HOTEL
1787. MULTISTOREY COMMERCIAL COMPLEX
1788. MULTISTOREY RESIDENTIAL COMPLEX
1789. NURSERY SCHOOL
1790. NATURE CARE CENTRE
1791. NURSING HOME
1792. ONLINE SHOPPING MALL (RS. 5000/- REPORT)
1793. PORTAL
1794. REHABILITATION CENTRE FOR AGED & NEEDY PERSONS
1795. RESIDENTIAL CUM COMMERCIAL COMPLEX
1796. RESTAURANT
1797. RESTAURANT WITH PUB
1798. SCHOOL (PRIMARY)
1799. SCHOOL (HIGHER SECONDARY)
1800. THREE STAR HOTEL
1801. TOURIST CLUB
1802. TRAINING INSTITUTE FOR MEDICAL TRANSCRIPTION
1803. VIDEO FILM STUDIO
1804. WARE HOUSE
1805. WEBSITE DESIGN & E-MAIL REGISTERING

AGRO BASED INDUSTRIES

1806. COAL BRIQUETTES FROM AGROWASTE
1807. FURFURALFROM RICEHULL
1808. MUSHROOM CULTIVATION & PROCESSING (BUTTON)
1809. MUSHROOM GROWING & PROCESSING WITH AIR CONDITIONING
1810. MUSHROOM CULTIVATION & PROCESSING UNIT DEHYDRATION & PACKAGING OF OYSTER & PADDY STRAW MUSHROOMS
1811. ORGANIC MANURE
1812. PAPAYA CULTIVATION
1813. PAPAYA & TOMATO CULTIVATION
1814. PROCESSING & UTILISATION OF COCONUT
1815. PROCESSING OF SHEEP HAIR TO PRODUCE WOOL

BAKERY, CONFECTIONERY & FOOD PRODUCTS

1816. AGROLACTOR SOYA MILK
1817. APPLE FRUIT JUICE WITH CANNING BOTTLING
1818. AYURVEDIC SHARBAT
1819. BAKERY UNIT (PASTRIES, BREAD, BUNS, CAKE, TOFFEE ETC.)
1820. BAKING POWDER
1821. BANANA & ITS BY PRODUCTS
1822. BANANA POWDER
1823. BANANA WAFERS
1824. BANANA CULTIVATION
1825. BEER INDUSTRY
1826. DEHULLING OF JAUN FOR BEER
1827. BEER & WINE
1828. BEER, ALCOHOL, IMFL
1829. BESEN PLANT
1830. BISCUIT PLANT
1831. BREAD & BISCUIT PLANT
1832. BOTTLING PLANT COUNTRY LIQUOR FROM RECTIFIED SPIRIT
1833. BRANDY
1834. BREAD RUSKS
1835. CANNED FRUITS & VEGETABLES
1836. CANNING & PRESERVATION OF MEAT
1837. CANNING & PRESERVATION OF VEGETABLES
1838. CANNING OF MANGO PULP & MANGO SLICES
1839. CARBONATED BEVERAGS
1840. CASHEW FENI
1841. CASHEW NUT (DRIED & FRIED)
1842. CATTLE BREEDING
1843. CATTLE BREEDING & DAIRY FARM TO PRODUCE MILK
1844. CATTLE FEED FROM TAPIOCA
1845. CHEWING GINGER & AMLOKI
1846. CHEWING GUM
1847. CHILLI SAUCE
1848. CHILLI POWDER
1849. CHOCOLATE
1850. CIDER PLANT
1851. COCOA POWDER
1852. COCOA BUTTER & COCOA POWDER
1853. COCONUT SHELL POWDER
1854. COCONUT WATER
1855. COCONUT SWEET (WATERY)
1856. COCONUT MILK POWDER (DEHYDRATED)
1857. COCONUT PRODUCTS & BY PRODUCTS (INTEGRATED PLANT)
1858. COLD DRINK
1859. CURRY POWDER
1860. DAIRY FOR MILK PROCESSING (GHEE, BUTTER & PANEER)
1861. DAIRY PRODUCTS
1862. DAIRY PRODUCTS MILK PACKAGING IN POUCH (GHEE, BUTTER, ETC.
1863. DAIRY FARM TO PRDUCE MILK WITH PACKAGING (COW)
1864. DAIRY FARM TO PRDUCE MILK WITH PACKAGING (BUFALLOE)
1865. DAIRY FARM & MILK PRODUCTS
1866. DAL MOTH, CHANACHUR & BHUJIYA
1867. DEHYDRATION OF FRUITS & VEGETABLE
1868. DESICCATED COCONUT POWDER FROM COCONUTS
1869. DEHYDRATION & CANNING OF FRUITS & VEGETABLES
1870. DRY FRUIT ROASTING & PACKAGING
1871. DRYING OF RED CHILLIES, HALDI, DHANIYA, PEAS & GROUND NUT
1872. EGG POWDER
1873. FISH CANNING IN TIN & POUCHES
1874. FISH DEHYRATION (DRYING OF FISH)
1875. FISH MEAL
1876. FISH PROCESSING (BEAST FREEZING PROCESSES)
1877. FLAVOURS FOR FOOD INDUSTRIES
1878. FLOUR MILL (ROLLER)
1879. FROZEN MEAT
1880. FOOD DEHYDRATION (FRUITS & VEGETABLES)
1881. FRIED & ROASTED GROUND NUT, GRAMS, PEAR ETC.
1882. FRUIT JUICE MAKING & PACKAGING IN PLASTIC CONTAINER
1883. FRUIT JUICE IN TETRA PACK (DRINKS)
1884. FRUIT JUICE, SQUASHES, SAUCE & KETCHUP, JAM, JELLY, VINEGAR ETC.
1885. GARLIC FLAKES
1886. GARLIC POWDER
1887. GHEE & BUTTER
1888. GINGER (PULVERISED)
1889. GINGER GLAZING & PRESERVATION
1890. GINGER STORAGE
1891. GINGER PROCESSING
1892. GINGER OIL & GINGER DUST
1893. GINGER POWDER (DRY) & OLEORESIN
1894. GRAPE DEHYDRATION
1895. GRAPE CULTIVATION
1896. GRAPE JUICE
1897. HONEY PROCESSING & PACKAGING
1898. ICE CREAM & ICE CANDY
1899. ICE CUBE
1900. INVERT SUGAR
1901. IDLI MIX, DOSA MIX SAMBHAR MIX, VADA MIX, GULAB JAMUN MIX
1902. INSTANT COFFEE & INSTANT TEA

1903. INSTANT NOODLES
1904. INSTANT SOUPS
1905. IODIZED SALT FROM CRUDE SALT
1906. JAM CHUTNEY PICKLES & SQUASHES
1907. KATHA MANUFACTURING
1908. LECITHIN (SOYA BASED)
1909. LEMON & ITS PRODUCTS
1910. MACARONI MANUFACTURING
1911. MACARONI, SPAGHETTI, VERMICELLI & NOODLES
1912. MAIZE & ITS BY PRODUCTS MALTING PLANT
1913. MANGO PAPPAD (AAM PAPPAD)
1914. MANGO POWDER RIPE
1915. MANGO POWDER
1916. MANGO PROCESSING & CANNING (MANGO PULP)
1917. MEAT PROCESSING (CHICKEN MUTTON)
1918. MEAT PROCESSING (BUFFALO)
1919. MENTHOL BOLD FROM MENTHOL FLAKES
1020. MILK POWDER
1921. MILK POWDER & GHEE
1922. MILK POWDER, GHEE & SPICES
1923. MILK PRESERVATION & MARKETING TO WHOLE SELLERS
1924. MILK PRESERVATION & MARKETING TO WHOLE SELLERS (IN POUCHES)
1925. MILK TOFFEE MANUFACTURES
1926. MINERAL WATER
1927. MINERAL WATER IN POUCHES
1928. MINI FLOUR MILL ATTA MAIDA, SUJI & WHEAT BRAN
1929. MITHAI/HALWAI (SWEET & NAMKEEN)
1930. MUTTON PROCESSING
1931. PAN MASALA (MEETHA, SADA, ZARDA) MAKING & PACKING
1932. PAN MASALA AND POUCH MAKING
1933. PANEER (CHEESE)
1934. PAPAD & BARIYAN
1935. PAPAD PLANT
1936. PEPSICOLA IN POLYTUBES
1937. PETHA PACKAGING
1938. PICKLES
1939. PIGGERY/MEAT/CHICKEN PROCESSING
1940. PINE APPLE JUICE CANNING
1941. POTATO & ONION POWDER
1942. POTATO & ONION FLAKES
1943. POTATO CHIPS
1944. POTATO GRANULES
1945. POUCH FILLING FOR SAUNF SUPARI ILAICHI ETC.
1946. PRESERVATION OF RAWS MANGO JUICE
1947. PROCESSED CHEESE & MARINE PDTS.
1948. PULP FROM TARMARIND
1949. READYMATE PROCESSED FOOD
1950. RICE & CORN FLAKES
1951. RICE BASMATI (TRADING)
1952. RICE POLISHING & PACKAGING IN POUCH
1953. ROASTED/SALTED/MASALA/ CASHEW NUTS ALMONDS & PEA NUT
1954. ROLLER FLOUR MILL

INFOTECH/IT PROJECTS

1955 MEDICAL TRANSCRIPTION
1956. E-COMMERCE
1957. CYBERCAFE
1958. INTERNET SERVICE PROVIDER (ISP)
1959. COMPUTER EDUCATION CENTRE
1960. PORTAL (WEBSITE DESIGN)
1961. CALL CENTRE

TERMS AND CONDITIONS

FOR INDIA

1. Please ask for Quotations of Each *Market Survey Cum Detailed Techno Economic Feasibility Report.* Payable in advance through Draft/M.O./Cash in favour of 'ENGINEERS INDIA RESEARCH INSTITUTE', Delhi. Delivery by Regd.post within 2 Days. (Postage Free)

2. Ask for the Hi-Tech Projects Monthly magazine. Each Magazine covers many Project Profiles for selection of Industry.

FOR OVERSEAS

1. Please ask for Quotations in US $ of Each *Market Survey Cum Detailed Techno Economic Feasibility Report.* Payable in advance through Draft/M.O./Cash in favour of 'ENGINEERS INDIA RESEARCH INSTITUTE', Delhi. (Payable in India) Delivery by Regd.post within 4 Days.

2. Ask for the Hi-Tech Projects Monthly magazine. Each Magazine covers many Project Profiles for selection of Industry.

ENGINEERS INDIA RESEARCH INSTITUTE

4449, Nai Sarak (D), Main Road, Delhi - 110 006 (India)
Ph:. 91-11-23918117, 23916431, 23840361, 31082370
Fax: 91-11-23916431 E-Mail : eirisidi@bol.net.in
Website:www.startindustry.com
Also at : 4/27, Roop Nagar, Near Roop Nagar No. 1 School, Delhi - 110 007 (India) Ph:. 23840361